METHODS OF CRITICAL DISCOURSE STUDIES

EDITED BY
RUTH WODAK
MICHAEL MEYER

METHODS OF
CRITICAL
DISCOURSE
STUDIES 3RD EDITION

Los Angeles | London | New Delhi
Singapore | Washington DC

Los Angeles | London | New Delhi
Singapore | Washington DC

SAGE Publications Ltd
1 Oliver's Yard
55 City Road
London EC1Y 1SP

SAGE Publications Inc.
2455 Teller Road
Thousand Oaks, California 91320

SAGE Publications India Pvt Ltd
B 1/I 1 Mohan Cooperative Industrial Area
Mathura Road
New Delhi 110 044

SAGE Publications Asia-Pacific Pte Ltd
3 Church Street
#10-04 Samsung Hub
Singapore 049483

© Ruth Wodak, Michael Meyer and contributors 2016

First edition published 2001, reprinted 2004, 2005, 2006, 2007
Second edition published 2009, reprinted 2009, 2010, 2011, 2013, 2014
This third edition published 2016

Editor: Mila Steele
Assistant editor: James Piper
Production editor: Victoria Nicholas
Copyeditor: Elaine Leek
Proofreader: Emily Ayers
Indexer: Silvia Benvenuto
Marketing manager: Sally Ransom
Cover design: Shaun Mercier
Typeset by: C&M Digitals (P) Ltd, Chennai, India
Printed and bound in Great Britain by Ashford Colour Press Ltd

Library of Congress Control Number: 2015934957

British Library Cataloguing in Publication data

A catalogue record for this book is available from the British Library

ISBN 978-1-4462-8240-3
ISBN 978-1-4462-8241-0 (pbk)

At SAGE we take sustainability seriously. Most of our products are printed in the UK using FSC papers and boards. When we print overseas we ensure sustainable papers are used as measured by the Egmont grading system. We undertake an annual audit to monitor our sustainability.

CONTENTS

NOTES ON CONTRIBUTORS

Norman Fairclough is Professor Emeritus of Language in Social Life at Lancaster University in the UK. He has written extensively in the field of critical discourse analysis. His main publications include: *Language and Power* (1989), *Discourse and Social Change* (1992), *Media Discourse* (1995), *Critical Discourse Analysis* (1995), *Discourse in Late Modernity* (1990) (with Lilie Chaouliaraki) and *New Labour, New Language?* (2000). His main current interest is in language (discourse) as an element in the contemporary social changes that are referred to as 'globalization', 'neoliberalism', 'new capitalism', the 'knowledge company' and so forth.

Email: n.fairclough@lancaster.ac.uk

Markus Höllerer is Professor of Public Management and Governance at WU (Vienna University of Economics and Business) and Senior Scholar in Organization Theory at UNSW Australia Business School. His research interests are in organizational institutionalism, and his work spans a variety of empirical phenomena and settings. In more detail, academic interests include the dissemination and local adaptation of global ideas, in particular the heterogeneous theorizations and local variations in meaning, as well as the relationship between different bundles of managerial concepts and their underlying governance and business models in the public and private sectors. Recent work has been concerned with discursive framing as well as with visual and multimodal rhetoric. Markus' research has been published in scholarly outlets such as the *Academy of Management Annals*, *Academy of Management Journal*, *Journal of Management Studies*, *Public Administration* and *Research in the Sociology of Organizations*, as well as in books and edited volumes.

Email: markus.hoellerer@wu.ac.at

Siegfried Jäger has been a Professor for German Language at the University of Duisburg/Essen (Germany) since 1972, and since 1987 he has also been head of the Duisburg Institute of Linguistic and Social Research. His major research areas are discourse theory and critical discourse analysis based on Michel Foucault's theory. He has conducted several projects dealing with a broad range of topics, e.g. language barriers, right-wing extremism, immigration and racism in mass media and everyday talk, media coverage of crime, Jewish publications in the nineteenth century, Christian fundamentalism and anti-Semitism in the German and Polish mass media. For his publications, see diss-duisburg.de.

Email: s.jaeger@diss-duisburg.de

Dennis Jancsary is Post-doctoral Researcher at the Institute for Organization Studies, WU (Vienna University of Economics and Business), and at the Department of Organization, Copenhagen Business School. His research focuses on rhetoric and language use in the emergence, diffusion and change of institutions and knowledge. Recent work has been organized around qualitative and interpretative research strategies of analysing verbal and visual rhetoric in the production and (re-)construction of power, authority and legitimacy, specifically the use of argument and persuasion.

Email: dennis.jancsary@wu.ac.at

Majid KhosraviNik is a lecturer in Media and Discourse Studies at Newcastle University, UK. He is interested in theory, methods and application of critical discourse studies in a range of topics and media discourses including the intersection of discourse and (national/ethnic/group) identity. He has previously published on immigration identity discourses in mass media. Within the past few years, he has been working on theory and application of CDA on digital participatory environments, e.g. social media. He sits on the boards of a number of international journals, including *Critical Discourse Studies* and *Journal of Language and Politics* and is a co-founder of Newcastle Discourse Group. His co-edited book *Right-Wing Populism in Europe: Politics and Discourse* (with Ruth Wodak and Brigitte Mral), was published by Bloomsbury Academic in 2013. He is currently finalizing a manuscript on Iranian and British press discourses regarding Iran's nuclear programme for DAPSAC book series.

Email: majid.khosravinik@newcastle.ac.uk

Florentine Maier is assistant professor at WU (Vienna University of Economics and Business). She researches and teaches on non-profit management. Her research focuses on the spread of business-like ideas and methods to the non-profit sector, and on alternative – more democratic and egalitarian – forms of organizing. She often applies discourse analytic methods to investigate questions in this context.

Email: florentine.maier@wu.ac.at

Gerlinde Mautner is Professor of English Business Communication at WU (Vienna University of Economics and Business) and Honorary Visiting Professor at Cass Business School, City University London. She pursues research interests located at the interface of language, society and business. Her work also focuses on methodological questions, exploring the opportunities and challenges of interdisciplinary cooperation (e.g. between critical discourse analysis and critical management studies, and between CDA and corpus linguistics). In recent projects she has studied the influx of marketized language into a variety of lifeworlds, the treatment of language in management textbooks, and the interrelationships between discourse, space and the law.

Email: gerlinde.mautner@wu.ac.at

Michael Meyer works as a Professor for Business Administration at the Department for Management at WU (Vienna University of Economics and Business). He is head of the Institute for Non-profit Management. His research focuses on managerialism and the diffusion of management tools in non-profit organizations. His interests also include careers, non-profit governance, civic participation (volunteering, giving) and social entrepreneurship.

Email: michael.meyer@wu.ac.at

Renate Meyer is Professor of Organization Studies at WU (Vienna University of Economics and Business) and Permanent Visiting Professor at the Department of Organization, Copenhagen Business School. She has been a member of the EGOS (European Group for Organization Studies) Executive Board since 2008. She works mainly from a phenomenological perspective on institutions, and has recently focused on framing and legitimation strategies, visual rhetoric, identities and new organizational forms. Renate has published her work in academic journals such as *Academy of Management Journal, Academy of Management Annals, Organization Studies, Journal of Management Studies, Critical Perspectives on Accounting, Research in the Sociology of Organizations, Journal of Management Inquiry, Organization, or Public Administration*. Renate has also (co-)authored several books and book chapters.

Email: renate.meyer@wu.ac.at

Martin Reisigl has a PhD in Applied Linguistics and is currently Assistant Professor for Sociolinguistics at the Institute for German Studies of the University of Bern. From October 2009 until September 2010 he was Substitute Professor for German Linguistics at the University of Hamburg. Between 2009 and 2011 he was a visiting professor at the Central European University/CEU in Budapest (Nationalism Studies). For many years, he was a lecturer for Applied Linguistics at the University of Vienna. From May 2006 until February 2007 he was a visiting professor at the university 'La Sapienza' in Rome. From February until June 2007 he was a visiting fellow at the Institute for Human Sciences (IWM) in Vienna. His research interests include (critical) discourse analysis and discourse theory, text linguistics, sociolinguistics, pragmatics, politolinguistics, rhetoric, language and history, linguistics and literature, argumentation analysis and semiotics.

Email: martin.reisigl@germ.unibe.ch

Johann W. Unger is a Lecturer and Academic Director of Summer Programmes at Lancaster University's Department of Linguistics and English Language. He researches mainly in the areas of language policy and digitally mediated politics from a critical discourse studies perspective. His recent publications include 'Rebranding the Scottish Executive' in the *Journal of Language and Politics*, the book *The Discursive Construction of Scots: Education, Politics and Everyday Life*, the co-edited book *Multilingual Encounters in Europe's Institutional Spaces* and the co-authored textbook *Researching Language and Social Media: A Student Guide*. He is an Editor of the book series *Discourse Approaches to Politics, Society and Culture*.

Email: j.unger@lancaster.ac.uk

Teun A. van Dijk was Professor of Discourse Studies at the University of Amsterdam until 2004 and at Universitat Pompeu Fabra, Barcelona, from 1999. After earlier work on generative poetics, text grammar, and the psychology of text processing, his work since 1980 takes a more critical perspective and deals with discursive racism, news in the press, ideology, knowledge and context. He is the author of several books in most of these areas, and he founded and edited six international journals, of which he still edits four, *Discourse & Society*, *Discourse Studies*, *Discourse & Communication* and the electronic journal *Discurso & Sociedad* (www.dissoc.org). He has three honorary doctorates, and founded with Adriana Bolivar the Asociación Latino-americana de Estudios del Discurso (ALED), in 1995. His last monographs in English are *Ideology* (1998), *Racism and Discourse in Spain and Latin America* (2005), *Discourse and Power* (2008), *Discourse and Context* (2008), *Society and Discourse* (2009) and *Discourse and Knowledge* (2014). For a complete list of his publications, see www.discourses.org.

Email: vandijk@discourses.org

Theo van Leeuwen is Emeritus Professor at the University of Technology, Sydney, and Professor of Language and Communication at the University of Southern Denmark. He has published widely on critical discourse analysis, multimodality and visual semiotics. His books include *Reading Images* (with Gunther Kress) and *Discourse and Practice*. He is a founding editor of the journal *Visual Communication*.

Email: theodoorjacob@gmail.com

Ruth Wodak is Distinguished Professor of Discourse Studies at Lancaster University, UK. Her research interests focus on discourse studies, identity politics, language and/in politics, prejudice and discrimination. She is co-editor of the journals *Discourse & Society*, *Critical Discourse Studies* and *Language and Politics*. Recent book publications include *The Politics of Fear: What Right-Wing Populist Discourses Mean* (SAGE, 2015), *Analysing Fascist Discourse: European Fascism in Talk and Text* (with John Richardson; Routledge, 2013), *Right Wing Populism in Europe: Politics and Discourse* (with Majid KhosraviNik and Brigitte Mral; Bloomsbury Academic, 2013) and *The Discourse of Politics in Action: Politics as Usual* (Palgrave, 2011).

Email: r.wodak@lancaster.ac.uk

PREFACE

The third edition of *Methods of Critical Discourse Studies* marks a huge achievement in the vast field of critical social sciences.

We are very grateful to all contributors who agreed to revise their chapters and update them or even write a new version of their approach (Teun van Dijk, Siegfried Jäger and Florentine Maier, Martin Reisigl and Ruth Wodak, and Gerlinde Mautner). Indeed, we are really pleased that we were able to attract two new chapters on social media and how to analyse these from a critical discourse-oriented perspective (Majid KhosraviNik and Johann Unger), and a second chapter on multimodal genres and critical approaches to analysing multimodality (Dennis Jancsary, Markus Höllerer and Renate Meyer). We also changed and revised the Introduction accordingly, in order to accommodate the new and revised chapters. Two chapters have remained in their previous version (Theo van Leeuwen and Norman Fairclough). Moreover, we integrated the suggestions made by the reviewers and by SAGE to provide more readability, new examples, new approaches and some didactic features.

Thus, we would like to thank the anonymous reviewers for their constructive suggestions; and we are very grateful to SAGE, to Lily Mehrbod, Katie Metzler and Mila Steele, for supporting us through the difficult process of collecting all the chapters, and for their patience, in waiting for the revised manuscript. Gerard Hearne edited the papers written by non-native speakers of English and – last but not least – Martha Schöberl copy-edited and formatted all the chapters very carefully.

To date, the book has been translated into Spanish, Japanese and Arabic. The translations illustrate the wide international recognition for this book and the need for exemplary and didactic introductions to complex theories, methodologies and methods in critical discourse studies.

We hope that the new edition, which is even more comprehensive and contains many new didactic features, will provide an updated, better and easier entry point to CDS, a field that, we believe, is currently even more necessary than some years ago – in order to deconstruct, understand and explain the many complex phenomena of our globalized societies.

Ruth Wodak, Michael Meyer

Vienna and Lancaster, January 2015

1

CRITICAL DISCOURSE STUDIES: HISTORY, AGENDA, THEORY AND METHODOLOGY

RUTH WODAK AND MICHAEL MEYER

CONTENTS

Keywords

ideology, power, discourse, critique, methodology, levels of theory, approaches to critical discourse studies

---

CDS – What is it all about?

The manifold roots of critical discourse studies lie in rhetoric, text linguistics, anthropology, philosophy, social psychology, cognitive science, literary studies and sociolinguistics, as well as in applied linguistics and pragmatics. Teun van Dijk (2008) provides a broad overview of the field of discourse studies and identifies the following developments: between the mid-1960s and the early 1970s, new, closely related disciplines emerged in the humanities and the social sciences. Despite their different disciplinary backgrounds and a great diversity of methods and objects of investigation, some parts of the new fields/paradigms/linguistic subdisciplines of *semiotics, pragmatics, psycho- and sociolinguistics, ethnography of speaking, conversation analysis* and *discourse studies* all dealt and continue to deal with discourse and have at least seven dimensions in common (see also Angermuller et al. 2014):

- An interest in the properties of *'naturally occurring' language use* by real language users (instead of a study of abstract language systems and invented examples).
- A focus on *larger units than isolated words and sentences*, and hence, new basic units of analysis: texts, discourses, conversations, speech acts, or communicative events.
- The extension of linguistics *beyond sentence grammar* towards a study of action and interaction.
- The extension to *non-verbal (semiotic, multimodal, visual) aspects* of interaction and communication: gestures, images, film, the internet and multimedia.
- A focus on dynamic (socio)-cognitive or interactional moves and strategies.
- The study of the functions of (social, cultural, situative and cognitive) *contexts of language use*.
- Analysis of a vast number of *phenomena of text grammar and language use*: coherence, anaphora, topics, macrostructures, speech acts, interactions, turn-taking, signs, politeness, argumentation, rhetoric, mental models and many other aspects of text and discourse.

The significant difference between discourse studies and critical discourse studies lies in the *constitutive problem-oriented, interdisciplinary approach* of the latter, apart from endorsing all of the above points. *CDS is therefore not interested in investigating a linguistic unit per se but in analysing, understanding and explaining social phenomena that are necessarily complex and thus require a multidisciplinary and multi-methodical approach* (Wodak 2012c; van Dijk 2013). The objects under investigation do not have to be related to negative or exceptionally 'serious' social or political experiences or events: this is a frequent misunderstanding of the aims and goals of CDS and of the term 'critical' which, of course, does not mean 'negative' as in common sense usage (see below; Chilton et al. 2010). Any social phenomenon lends itself to critical investigation, to be challenged and not taken for granted. We will return to this important point and other common misunderstandings of CDS below. To quote Teun van Dijk (2013) in this respect:

> Contrary to popular belief and unfortunate claims of many papers submitted to discourse journals, CDA is *not a method of critical discourse analysis*. This may sound paradoxical, but I am afraid it isn't. Think about it. Indeed, what would be the systematic, explicit, detailed, replicable procedure for doing 'critical' analysis? There is no such method. Being critical, first of all, is a state of mind, an attitude, a way of dissenting, and many more things, *but not an explicit method for the description of the structures or strategies of text and talk*. So, in that sense, people who want to practice CDA may be supposed to do so from a perspective of opposition, for instance against power abuse through discourse. [....]. Methodologically, *CDA is as diverse as DA in general*, or indeed other directions in linguistics, psychology or the social sciences. Thus, CDA studies may do so in terms of grammatical (phonological, morphological, syntactic), semantic, pragmatic, interactional rhetorical, stylistic, narrative or genre analyses, among others, on the one hand, and through experiments, ethnography, interviewing, life stories, focus groups, participant observation, and so on, on the other hand. *A good method is a method that is able to give a satisfactory (reliable, relevant, etc.) answer to the questions of a research project.* It depends on one's aims, expertise, time and goals, and the kind of data that can or must be generated – that is, on the *context* of a research project. [...] So, there is not 'a' or 'one' method of CDA, but many. Hence, I recommend to use the term *Critical Discourse Studies* for the theories, methods, analyses, applications and other practices of critical discourse analysts, and to forget about the confusing term 'CDA'. *So, please, no more 'I am going to apply CDA' because it does not make sense.* Do critical discourse analysis by formulating critical goals, and then explain by what *specific* explicit methods you want to realize it. (emphasis added)

In this volume, we take Van Dijk's proposal very seriously: we would like to emphasize that each of the approaches introduced in this book cannot be isolated from specific complex social issues under investigation, from research questions and research interests. Below, we elaborate what the concept of 'critique' implies for the social sciences, and thus also for critical discourse studies.

The notions of *text* and *discourse* have to be discussed thoroughly in this context; they have been subject to a hugely proliferating number of usages in the social sciences. Almost no paper or article is to be found that does not revisit these notions, quoting Michel Foucault, Jürgen Habermas, Chantal Mouffe, Ernesto Laclau, Niklas Luhmann, or many others. Thus, *discourse* means anything from a historical monument, a *lieu de mémoire*, a policy, a political strategy, narratives in a restricted or broad sense of the term, text, talk, a speech, topic-related conversations, to language *per se*. We find notions such as racist discourse, gendered discourse, discourses on un/employment, media discourse, populist discourse, discourses of the past, and many more – thus stretching the meaning of *discourse* from a genre to a register or style, from a building to a political programme. This causes and must cause confusion – which leads to much criticism and more misunderstandings (see Flowerdew 2014; Hart and Cap 2014; Richardson et al. 2013; Wodak 2012a). This is why the contributors to this volume were asked to define their use of the term as integrated in their specific approach.

A brief history of 'the Group'

CDS as a network of scholars emerged in the early 1990s, following a small symposium in Amsterdam, in January 1991. Through the support of the University of Amsterdam, Teun van Dijk, Norman Fairclough, Gunther Kress, Theo van Leeuwen and Ruth Wodak spent two days together, and had the opportunity to discuss theories and methods of discourse analysis, specifically critical discourse analysis (CDA) (which was the term used in the 1990s and 2000s). The meeting made it possible to confront the very distinct and different approaches and discuss these with each other, all of which have, of course, changed significantly since 1991 but remain important, in many respects. In this process of group formation, differences and sameness were laid out: differences with regard to other theories and methodologies in discourse analysis (Renkema 2004; Titscher et al. 2000; Wetherell et al. 2001; Wodak and Krzyżanowski 2008) and sameness in a more programmatic way, both of which frame the range of theoretical approaches (Wodak 2012a). In the meantime, some of the scholars previously aligned with CDS have chosen other theoretical frameworks and have distanced themselves from CDS (such as Gunther Kress and Ron Scollon [who unfortunately died in 2008]); on the other hand, new approaches have been created which frequently find innovative ways of integrating the more traditional theories or of elaborating them (see below).

> In general, CDS as a school or paradigm is characterized by a number of principles: for example, all approaches are problem-oriented, and thus necessarily interdisciplinary and eclectic. Moreover, CDS approaches are characterized by the common interests in deconstructing ideologies and power through the systematic and retroductable investigation of semiotic data (written, spoken or visual). CDS researchers also attempt to make their own positionings and interests explicit while retaining their respective scientific methodologies and remaining self-reflective of their own research process.

The start of the CDS network was marked by the launch of van Dijk's journal *Discourse & Society* (1990) as well as by several books that coincidentally or because of a *Zeitgeist* were published simultaneously and were led by similar research goals.[1] The Amsterdam meeting determined an institutional start, an attempt both to constitute an exchange programme (ERASMUS for three years)[2] as well as joint projects and collaborations between scholars of different countries. A special issue of *Discourse & Society* (1993), which presented the above mentioned approaches, was the first visible and material outcome. Since then new journals have been launched, multiple overviews have been written, handbooks and readers commissioned and nowadays critical discourse studies is an established paradigm in linguistics; currently, we encounter *Critical Discourse Studies, The Journal of Language and Politics, Discourse & Communication, Discourse & Society* and *Visual Communication*, among many other journals; several e-journals also publish critical research, such as *CADAAD*. Book series attract much critically oriented research (such as *Discourse Approaches to Politics, Culture and Society*), regular CDS meetings and conferences take place and collaborative interdisciplinary projects are under way. In sum, CDS has become an established discipline, institutionalized across the globe in many departments and curricula.

The common ground: discourse, critique, power and ideology

When deconstructing the label of this research programme, we necessarily have to first define what CDS means when it employs the terms 'critical' and 'discourse'. It is important to stress that CDS has never been and has never attempted to be or to provide one single or specific theory. Neither is one specific methodology characteristic of research in CDS. Quite the contrary, studies in CDS are multifarious, derived from quite different theoretical backgrounds, oriented towards different data and methodologies. Researchers in CDS also rely on a variety of grammatical approaches. The definitions of the terms 'discourse', 'critical', 'ideology', 'power' and so on are therefore manifold. Thus, any criticism of CDS should always specify which research or researcher they relate to. Hence, we suggest using the notion of a 'school' for CDS, or of a programme, which many researchers find useful and to which they can relate. This programme or set of principles has, of course, changed over the years (see Fairclough and Wodak 1997; Wodak 1996, 2012a).

Such a heterogeneous school might be confusing for some; on the other hand, it allows for continuous debates, for changes in the aims and goals, and for innovation. In contrast to 'closed' theories, for example Chomsky's Generative Transformational Grammar or Michael Halliday's Systemic Functional Linguistics, CDS scholars have never had the reputation of being a dogmatic 'sect' and – as far as we are aware – do not want to have such a reputation.

This heterogeneity of methodological and theoretical approaches that can be found in this field confirm Van Dijk's point that CDS and critical linguistics 'are at most a shared perspective on doing linguistic, semiotic or discourse analysis' (van Dijk 1993: 131; see also above). Below, we summarize some of these principles, which are adhered to by most researchers.

The notion of discourse

Critical discourse studies see 'language as social practice' (Fairclough and Wodak 1997), and consider the 'context of language use' to be crucial. We quote one definition which has become 'very popular' amongst CDS researchers:

CDS see discourse – language use in speech and writing – as a form of 'social practice'. Describing discourse as social practice implies a dialectical relationship between a particular discursive event and the situation(s), institution(s) and social structure(s), which frame it: The discursive event is shaped by them, but it also shapes them. That is, discourse is socially constitutive as well as socially conditioned – it constitutes situations, objects of knowledge, and the social identities of and relationships between people and groups of people. It is constitutive both in the sense that it helps to sustain and reproduce the social status quo, and in the sense that it contributes to transforming it. Since discourse is so socially consequential, it gives rise to important issues of power. Discursive practices may have major ideological effects – that is, they can help produce and reproduce unequal power relations between (for instance) social classes, women and men, and ethnic/cultural majorities and minorities through the ways in which they represent things and position people. (Fairclough and Wodak 1997: 258)

Thus CDS approaches understand discourses as relatively stable uses of language serving the organization and structuring of social life. However, in the German and Central European context, distinctions are made between 'text' and 'discourse' relating to the tradition in text linguistics as well as to rhetoric (see Angermuller et al. 2014; Wodak 1996). In contrast to the above, in the English-speaking world, 'discourse' is often used both for written and oral texts (see Gee 2004; Schiffrin 1994). Other researchers distinguish between different levels of abstractness: Lemke (1995) defines 'text' as the concrete realization of abstract forms of knowledge ('discourse'), thus adhering to a more Foucauldian approach (see also Jäger and Maier in this volume). van Leeuwen (this volume) emphasizes the practice-dimension of the concept of discourse whereas the discourse-historical approach views 'discourse' as structured forms of knowledge and 'text' refers to concrete oral utterances or written documents (Reisigl and Wodak in this volume).

The critical impetus

The shared perspective and programme of CDS relate to the term 'critical', which in the work of some 'critical linguists' can be traced to the influence of the *Frankfurt School* and Jürgen Habermas (Anthonissen 2001; Fay 1987: 203; Thompson 1988: 71ff.). 'Critical theory' in the sense of the *Frankfurt School*, mainly based on the seminal 1937 essay by Max Horkheimer, means that social theory should be oriented toward critiquing and changing society as a whole, in contrast to traditional theory oriented solely to understanding or explaining it. Core concepts of such an understanding of Critical Theory are: (1) Critical Theory should be directed at the totality of society in its historical specificity, and (2) Critical Theory should improve the understanding of society by integrating all the major social sciences, including economics, sociology, history, political science, anthropology and psychology.

What is rarely reflected in this understanding of critique is the analyst's position itself. The social embeddedness of research and science, the fact that the research system itself and thus CDS are also dependent on social structures, and that criticism can by no means draw on an outside position but is itself well integrated within social fields, has been emphasized by Pierre Bourdieu (1984). Researchers, scientists and philosophers are not situated outside the societal hierarchy of power and status but subject to this structure. They have also frequently occupied and still occupy rather superior positions in society.

In language studies, the term 'critical' was first used to characterize an approach that was called Critical Linguistics (Fowler et al. 1979; Kress and Hodge 1979). Among other ideas, those scholars maintained that the use of language could lead to mystification of social events which systematic analysis could elucidate. 'For example, a missing by-phrase in English passive constructions might be seen as an ideological means for concealing or "mystifying" reference to an agent' (Chilton 2008). One of the most significant principles of CDS is the important observation that use of language is a 'social practice' that is both determined by social structure and contributes to stabilizing and changing that structure simultaneously.

Critical theories, thus also CDS, want to produce and convey critical knowledge that enables human beings to emancipate themselves from forms of domination through self-reflection. Thus, they are aimed at producing 'enlightenment and emancipation'. Such theories seek not only to describe and explain, but also to root out a particular kind of delusion. Even with differing concepts of ideology, Critical Theory seeks to create awareness in agents of their own needs and interests. This was, of course, also taken up by Pierre Bourdieu's concepts of '*violence symbolique*' and '*méconnaissance*' (Bourdieu 1989).

In agreement with its Critical Theory predecessors, CDS emphasizes the need for interdisciplinary work in order to gain a proper understanding of how language functions in constituting and transmitting knowledge, in organizing social institutions or in exercising power. In any case, CDS researchers have to be aware that their own work is driven by social, economic and political motives like any other academic work and that they are not in any superior position. Naming oneself 'critical' only implies specific ethical standards: an intention to make one's position, research interests and values explicit and their criteria as transparent as possible, without feeling the need to apologize for the critical stance of their work (van Leeuwen 2006: 293).

Following Andrew Sayer (2009), there are different concepts of critique in social sciences:

In a simple way, critique could merely indicate a critical attitude to other, earlier, approaches to the study of society. Hence all social science should be critical. If it goes further, critique shows that some of the concepts that are influential in explaining social phenomena are false or ignore something significant. In this sense, critical research is oriented towards the *reduction of illusion* in society itself. It supports 'subjugated knowledge' against 'dominant knowledge'. This kind of critique implies a *minimalist normative standpoint*. The idea of explanatory critique goes another step further as it explains why specific false beliefs and concepts are held.

Critique in this sense implies that social phenomena could be different – and can be altered. Societies are changeable, human beings are meaning-makers, and the critical subject is not a detached observer but s/he looks at society with a fresh and sceptical eye. Thus the subject is not external to discourses on which s/he reflects. From this viewpoint, reflexivity has received increased attention.

Nevertheless, many scholars have difficulties in taking an explicit critical standpoint nowadays (Sayer 2009): it is not only worries about essentialism and ethnocentrism, it goes much deeper to the fact–value, science–ethics, positive–normative dualisms of modernist thought. 'The crisis of critique stems from an evasion of the issue of conceptions of the good, and ethics' (2009: 783).

Ideology and power – a kaleidoscopic view

The critical impetus of CDS is the legacy of enlightenment (Horkheimer and Adorno 1991 [1969; 1974]). Critique regularly aims at revealing structures of power and unmasking ideologies. Ideology is then not understood in a positivistic way, i.e. ideologies cannot be subjected to a process of falsification. Nor is it the Marxian type of ideology according to the economic base/superstructure dichotomy that is of specific interest for CDS.

> Political scientists name four central characteristics of ideologies:
>
> 1. Ideology must have power over cognition,
> 2. it is capable of guiding individuals' evaluations,
> 3. it provides guidance through action, and
> 4. it must be logically coherent (Mullins 1972).

Although the core definition of ideology as a *coherent and relatively stable set of beliefs or values* has remained the same in political science over time, the connotations associated with this concept have undergone many transformations. During the era of fascism, communism and cold war, totalitarian ideology was confronted with democracy, the evil with the good. If we speak of the 'ideology of the new capitalism' (see Fairclough in this volume), ideology once again has a 'bad' connotation. Clearly it is not easy to capture ideology as a belief system and simultaneously to free the concept from negative connotations (Knight 2006: 625).

It is, however, not that explicit type of ideology that interests CDS, it is rather the more hidden and latent inherent in everyday-beliefs, which often appear disguised as conceptual metaphors and analogies, thus attracting linguists' attention: 'life is a journey, social organizations are plants, love is war' and so on (Lakoff 1987; Lakoff and Johnson 1980, 1999). In everyday discussions, certain ideas emerge more commonly than others. Frequently, people with diverse backgrounds and interests may find themselves thinking alike in surprising ways. Dominant ideologies appear as 'neutral', linked to assumptions that remain largely unchallenged. When most people in a society think alike about certain matters, or even forget that there are alternatives to the status quo, we arrive at the Gramscian concept of 'hegemony'. In respect to this key concept of ideology, van Dijk (1998) sees ideologies as the 'worldviews' that constitute 'social cognition': 'schematically organized complexes of representations and attitudes with regard to certain aspects of the social world, e.g. the schema ... whites have about blacks' (van Dijk 1993: 258).

Furthermore, it is the functioning of ideologies in everyday life that intrigues CDS researchers. Fairclough has a more Marxist view of ideologies and conceives them as constructions of practices from particular perspectives:

> Ideologies are representations of aspects of the world which contribute to establishing and maintaining relations of power, domination and exploitation. They may be enacted in ways of interaction (and therefore in genres) and inculcated in ways of being identities (and therefore styles). Analysis of texts ... is an important aspect of ideological analysis and critique ... (Fairclough 2003: 218)

It is important to distinguish between ideology (or other frequently used terms such as stance/beliefs/opinions/*Weltanschauung*/positioning) and discourse (Purvis and Hunt 1993: 474ff.). Quite rightly, Purvis and Hunt state that these concepts 'do not stand alone but are associated not only with other concepts but with different theoretical traditions'. Thus, 'ideology' is usually (more or less) closely associated with the Marxist tradition, whereas 'discourse' has gained much significance in the linguistic turn in modern social theory 'by providing a term with which to grasp the way in which language and other forms of social semiotics not merely convey social experience but play some major part in constituting social objects (the subjectivities and their associated identities), their relations and the field in which they exist' (Purvis and Hunt 1993: 474). The conflation of 'ideology' and 'discourse' thus leads, we believe, to an inflationary use of both concepts. They tend to become empty signifiers simultaneously indicating texts, positioning and subjectivities as well as belief systems, structures of knowledge and social practices (see Wodak 2012a). Discussions about the – various and interdisciplinary – epistemological underpinnings of CDS approaches are part and parcel of the chapters presented in this book (see also Wodak 2012c; Hart and Cap 2014).

Power is another concept that is central for CDS. Typically CDS researchers are interested in the way discourse (re)produces social domination, that is mainly understood as power abuse of one group over others, and how dominated groups may discursively resist such abuse (e.g. van Dijk in this volume). This raises the question of how CDS understands power and what normative standpoints allow researchers to differentiate between power use and abuse – a question that has so far remained unanswered (Billig 2008).

Power is one of the most central – and contentious – concepts in the social sciences. There is almost no social theory that does not contain, suggest or imply a specific notion of power.

Max Weber's notion of power serves as a common denominator: power as the chance that an individual in a social relationship can achieve his or her own will even against the resistance of others (Weber 1980: 28).

Concerning the source of power, at least three different concepts should be distinguished:

1. Power as a result of specific *resources* of individual actors (e.g. French and Raven 1959).
2. Power as a specific attribute of *social exchange* in each interaction (e.g. Blau 1964; Emerson 1962, 1975), depending on the relation of resources between different actors.
3. Power as a widely invisible systemic and constitutive characteristic of society (e.g., from very different angles, Foucault 1975; Giddens 1984; Luhmann 1975).

As far as the results of power are concerned (which – according to Max Weber's view – are named *domination*), again three dimensions should be distinguished (Lukes 1974, 2005):

1. *Overt power*, typically exhibited in the presence of conflict in decision-making situations, where power consists in winning, that is prevailing over another or others.
2. *Covert power*, consisting in control over what gets decided, by ignoring or deflecting existing grievances.
3. The *power to shape desires and beliefs*, thereby precluding both conflict and grievances.

From these perspectives, discourse is Janus-headed: it is a consequence of power and domination, but also a technology to exert power.

Michel Foucault, who introduced the conjunction of power and discourse, focuses on 'technologies of power': *discipline* is a complex bundle of power technologies developed during the eighteenth and nineteenth centuries. Power is thus exercised with intention – but this is not individual intention. Foucault focuses on what is accepted knowledge about how to exercise power. One way of doing this is by threatening somebody or something with violence. However, when suggesting how happy people would be if they would finally buy specific consumer products, should also be perceived as an exercise of power; marketing currently provides us with much knowledge of powerful techniques. Although Foucault also combines the notions of power and domination in a Weberian tradition, he focuses primarily on the structural dimension. Thus domination is not only the overt pressure that one person exercises over others. Manifold forms of domination might be exercised within society simultaneously, by various actors and without subjects being aware of this (Foucault 1975).

In modern societies, power and domination are embedded in and conveyed by discourses. Discourses are not only coherent and rational bodies of speech and writing, but play an important role as discursive formations in conveying and implementing power and domination in society (e.g. Hall 1992). Consequently, discourses and dispositives (see Jäger and Maier in this volume) are core elements of a 'microphysics of power' (e.g. Foucault 1963, 1975, 2004; Sauvêtre 2009) that permeate society like an invisible cobweb.

More recently, Holzscheiter has introduced an instrumental, optimistic and emancipatory conception of the power–discourse interplay (e.g. Holzscheiter 2005, 2012). She frames discourses as effective social and linguistic practices that are based on immaterial capabilities. She argues that in the quest for non-material power resources, subordinated actors – in her research, NGOs in the field of international relations – may dispose of discourses to generate power positions. Conventional power theories are of limited use as, 'They insufficiently take into account the role of language – as both a means for communication and as collectively shared meaning-structures – in the establishment and persistence of intersubjective power relations' (Holzscheiter 2005: 723).

A framework capable of integrating most of the diverse concepts of power mentioned above is provided by Pierre Bourdieu, who offers a multifaceted view on the language–power-relation (e.g. Bourdieu 1982, 1991). According to Bourdieu, all *social fields* are structured by relations of power and domination (Bourdieu 1977, 1980). Social fields are dynamic systems, characterized by struggles among the actors within this field over the distribution of resources; the latter account for the attribution of status in the field and – power. Furthermore, the notion of social field corresponds to a distinct logic of practice, a constellation of rules, beliefs and practices.

Bourdieu thus takes a resource- and interaction-oriented standpoint: the resources at stake in social fields are economic, cultural, and social capital (Bourdieu 1986), they are acquired through heritage or struggle, and social fields differ in how they assess/rank actors' equipment of capitals (e.g. Bourdieu and Passeron 1977). Actors' capitals are partly institutionalized (property, academic titles, group memberships) and partly incorporated.

To explain the 'incorporation' of capitals, Bourdieu introduces his most intriguing concept: *habitus*. It is regarded as a durable but also evolving system of dispositions which could be potentially activated and should ideally fit to a particular social field. A particular habitus ensures that an actor acts, perceives and thinks according to the rules of the field, and his or her movements within the respective field of career appear as 'natural'. S/he acts 'intentionally without intention' (Bourdieu 1987; 1990: 12). Actors take part in discourses that follow the rules of discursive games that are relevant in a social field. They are equipped with their linguistic habitus, which comprises their linguistic competencies, based on their capitals. Within this normative framework, there exist certain degrees of freedom for such actors, allowing them to act strategically and to also change power relations. In this sense, actors might also apply the emancipatory function of discourse mentioned above.

Within CDS, power is usually perceived in the Foucauldian sense, and discourse is widely regarded as a manifestation of social action which is determined by social structure and simultaneously reinforces or erodes structure.

Consequently it is not the individual resources and not the specifics of unique interactions that are crucial for CDS analyses, but overall structural features in social fields or in society. Power is central for understanding the dynamics and specifics of control (of action) in modern societies, but power remains mostly invisible. The linguistic manifestations, however, are analysed in CDS. The interdependence between social power and language is a continual and persistent topic not only in CDS (Fairclough 1991; Wodak 1989) but also in sociology (Bourdieu 1991) and sociolinguistics (e.g. Talbot 2003; Young and Fitzgerald 2006).

Discursive differences are negotiated in many texts. They are governed by differences in power that is in part encoded in and determined by discourse and by genre. Therefore texts are often sites of struggle in that they show traces of differing discourses and ideologies contending and struggling for dominance.

In sum, defining features of CDS are its concern with power as a central condition in social life, and its efforts to develop a theory of language that incorporates this phenomenon as a major premise. Not only the notion of struggles for power and control, but also the intertextuality and recontextualization of competing discourses in various public spaces and genres are considered important (Iedema 1997; Iedema and Wodak 1999; Muntigl et al. 2000; see Fairclough, Reisigl and Wodak, and van Leeuwen in this volume). Power is about relations of difference, and particularly about the effects of differences in social structures. Language is entwined in social power in a number of ways:

- Language indexes and expresses power.
- Language is involved where there is contention over and a challenge to power.
- Power does not necessarily derive from language, but language can be used to challenge power, to subvert it, to alter distributions of power in the short and the long term.
- Language provides a finely articulated vehicle for the expression of differences in power in hierarchical social structures.

> CDS can be defined as fundamentally interested in analysing hidden, opaque, and visible structures of dominance, discrimination, power and control as manifested in language. In other words, CDS aim to investigate critically social inequality as it is expressed, constituted, legitimized, and so on, by language use (or in discourse). Most critical discourse analysts would thus endorse Habermas's claim that 'language is also a medium of domination and social force. It serves to legitimize relations of organized power. Insofar as the legitimizations of power relations ... are not articulated ... language is also ideological' (Habermas 1967: 259).

Research agenda and challenges

In this section, we summarize some important research agendas and challenges for research which currently characterize CDS. Although we, of course, encounter a vast amount of research and also many methodological and theoretical approaches and proposals, we have decided to restrict ourselves to six major areas and related challenges:

- Analysing, understanding and explaining the impact of *neoliberalism* and the *knowledge-based economy* (KBE) on various domains of our societies; related to this, the recontextualization of KBE into other parts of the world and other societies (e.g. Drori et al. 2006).
- Analysing, understanding and explaining the impact of *globalization* in most domains of our lives – as well as the contradictory tendencies of glocalization and renationalization which can be observed in many parts of the world. Interestingly, although we are confronted with ever-faster and all-encompassing communication and related networks 24/7 (Hassan and Purser 2007), simultaneously, anachronistic nationalistic and even nativist imaginaries of homogeneous communities are becoming stronger worldwide.
- Analysing, understanding and explaining climate change and the many controversial debates surrounding the production of alternative energy sources and so forth.
- Analysing, understanding and explaining the use of digitally mediated communication and its impact on conventional and new modes of communication which seem to open up new modes of participation and new public spaces. However, new studies should explore what impact the new communication networks really have on social and political change in systematic detail.
- Integrating approaches from cognitive sciences into CDS; this requires complex epistemological considerations and the development of new theories, methodologies and tools.
- Analysing, understanding and explaining the relationship between complex historical processes and hegemonic narratives. Identity politics on all levels always entails the integration of past experiences, present events and visions of the future in many domains of our lives.

Methodological issues: theory, methods, analysis, interpretation

CDS view themselves as strongly grounded in theory. Yet we find no dominant theories but rather eclectic approaches in CDS. To which theories do the different methods refer? Here we detect a huge variety of theories, ranging from theories on society and power in Michel Foucault's tradition, theories of social cognition, and theories of functional grammar as well as individual concepts that are borrowed from larger theoretical traditions. Initially, this section aims to systematize these different theoretical influences (see also Figure 1.4).

A second part in this section is devoted to the operationalization of theoretical concepts. The primary issue at stake is to understand and challenge how the various approaches to CDS are able to translate their theoretical claims into instruments and methods of analysis. In particular, the emphasis is on the mediation between Grand Theories as applied to society, and concrete instances of social interaction that result in texts (to be analysed). With regard to methodology, there are several perspectives within CDS: in addition to what can be described primarily as variations from hermeneutics, we are confronted with interpretative perspectives with differing emphases, among them even quantitative procedures (see Mautner in this volume).

Particularly worthy of discussion is the way in which sampling is conducted and justified in CDS. Most studies analyse 'typical texts'. What is typical in which social situation, and for which aspect of a social problem, frequently remains vague. The possibilities and limitations in respect to the specific units of analysis will be discussed within the context of theoretical sampling. Some authors explicitly refer to the ethnographic tradition of field research (e.g. Reisigl and Wodak in this volume).

The connection between theory and discourse in CDS can be described in terms of the model for theoretical and methodological research procedures illustrated in Figure 1.1. Hereby theory is not only essential to formulate research questions that guide the data selection, data collection, analysis of data and interpretation. It should also be grounded in prior interpretations of empirical analyses. Thus CDS imply a circular and recursive–abductive relationship between theory and discourse.

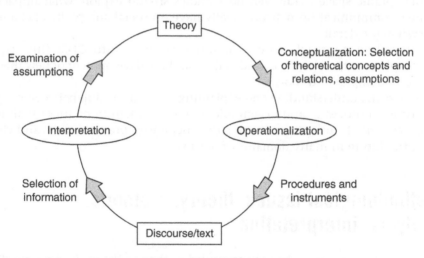

Figure 1.1   Critical discourse studies as a circular process

In CDS, as in all social research, theory, methods and analysis are closely interrelated, and decisions about the one affect the others. Data, i.e. in the case of CDS discourses and texts, are never theory-neutral. Which data are collected and how they are interpreted depends on the theoretical perspective. Theories, concepts and empirical indicators are systematically related: in theories, we link concepts, e.g. by functional or casual relationships. To observe and operationalize these concepts, we use empirical indicators (Gilbert 2008: 22).

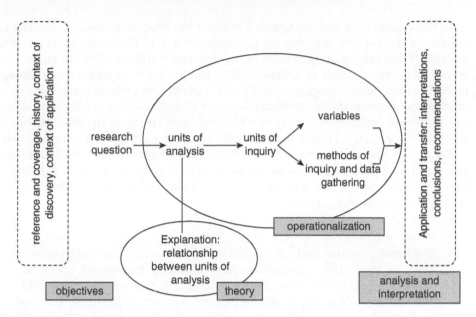

Figure 1.2 The research process (adapted from Titscher, Meyer and Mayrhofer 2008: 308)

Figure 1.2 illustrates the typical stages of the research process in empirical social research. In the context of discovery, we decide about and select *research objectives*. These may include the development of theoretical approaches, but also empirical coverage and the potential application of results. Hereby, we also decide whether findings and interpretations/explanations are valid only in respect to the units of analysis or beyond (generalizability).

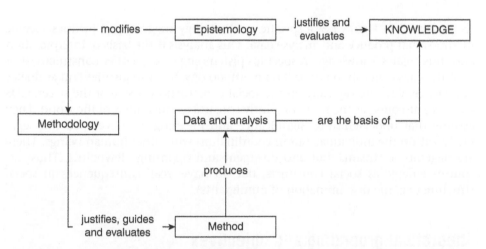

Figure 1.3 The simple relationship between epistemology, methodology and method (adapted from Carter and Little 2007: 1317)

In both qualitative and quantitative research the process of *operationalization* is crucial for the validity, but also for the auditability and the justification of CDS research. What are the units of analysis (e.g. ingroup/outgroup differentiation, discrimination, social status of speaker), what are the units of inquiry (e.g. group meetings, interviews, newspapers) and which variables are collected (e.g. indicators of ingroup/outgroup differentiation, indicators of discrimination, educational status of speakers/writers) by means of which methods (content analysis, rhetorical analysis, surveys, etc.). Finally, data are analysed and results have to be interpreted.

Figure 1.3 shows the simple relation between methodology, epistemology and method. These three notions are defined in conflicting ways in the literature. For this volume, we will try to clarify these ambiguities by introducing simple and precise definitions:

- *Epistemology* is the study of the nature of knowledge and justification. It tries to clarify the antecedents, conditions and boundaries of human knowledge; it, for instance, answers the question of whether social phenomena are real or just a construct of the observer, and, should these be real, whether we can observe this social reality adequately.
- *Methodology* is defined as a (normative) theory of how research should be conducted to generate knowledge. It tells us how research should proceed; it deals with the study (description, explanation, justification) of methods, but does not indicate the methods themselves. For instance, methodology yields process models such as the one presented in Figure 1.2.
- *Methods* are techniques for gathering evidence, e.g. for collecting and selecting data (cases, units of analysis), but also for explaining relationships (e.g. dependent by independent variables), for conducting interpretations in a transparent and retroductable way, etc.: 'Methods can be thought of as research action' (Carter and Little 2007: 1317).

As illustrated in Figure 1.3, a specific methodology suggests and justifies specific methods that produce and analyse data. This analysis is the basis of interpretation and thus creates knowledge. A specific epistemology – e.g. either constructivist or realistic – has a modifying impact on methodology, but also justifies and evaluates knowledge. CDS are typically on the social constructionist side of the street: CDS conceive discourse as the result of jointly constructed meanings of the world. They assume that understanding, significance and meaning are developed not separately within the individual, but in coordination with other human beings. There are hegemonic streams, but also divergent and opposing viewpoints. Thus discourses emerge as social constructs, but do have 'real' consequences in social structure (e.g. the discrimination of immigrants).

Theoretical grounding and objectives

Among the approaches presented in this book, scholars use theoretical cornerstones of very different origins in order to 'build their CDS-castles'. Neither is there any guiding theoretical viewpoint that is used consistently within CDS, nor do the CDS protagonists proceed consistently from the area of theory to the field of discourse and back to theory (see Figure 1.3).

Within the CDS approaches presented here, various theoretical levels of sociological and sociopsychological theory (the concept of different theoretical levels draws on the tradition of Merton [1967: 39–72]) can be detected:

- **Epistemology**, i.e. theories that provide models of the conditions, contingencies and limits of human perception in general and scientific perception in particular. Simplified, these theories lie between the poles of realism and constructivism.
- **General social theories**, often called 'Grand Theories', conceptualize relations between social structure and social action and thus link micro- and macro-sociological phenomena. Within this level we distinguish between more structuralist and the more individualist approaches. The former provide rather deterministic top-down explanations (structure → action), whereas the latter prefer bottom-up explanations (action → structure). Most modern theories reconcile these positions and imply some kind of circular relationship between social action and social structure (e.g. Pierre Bourdieu, Antony Giddens, Niklas Luhmann).
- **Middle-range theories** focus either upon specific social phenomena (e.g. conflict, cognition, social networks) or on specific subsystems of society (e.g. economy, politics and religion).
- **Microsociological theories** try to make sense of and explain social interaction, for example the resolution of the double contingency problem (Parsons and Shils 1951: 3–29) or the reconstruction of everyday procedures which members of a society use to create their own social order (ethnomethodology).
- **Sociopsychological theories** focus on the social conditions of emotion and cognition, and prefer, compared to microsociology, causal explanations to a hermeneutic understanding of meaning.
- **Discourse theories** aim at the conceptualization of discourse as a social phenomenon and try to explain its genesis and its structure.
- **Linguistic theories**, e.g. theories of semantics, pragmatics, of grammar or of rhetoric, describe and explain the patterns specific to language systems and verbal communication.

As all these theoretical levels can be found in CDS, it seems that the unifying parameters of CDS are rather the specifics of research questions (*critique*) than the theoretical positioning. In the following we present a short outline of the theoretical positions and methodological objectives of the CDS approaches presented in the volume.

Major approaches to CDS

The differences between CDS and other discourse analysis (DA), pragmatic and sociolinguistic approaches may be most clearly established in respect to the general principles of CDS. Firstly, the nature of the problems with which CDS are concerned is significantly different from all those approaches that do not explicitly express their research interest in advance. In general, critical discourse studies ask different research questions, and some CDS scholars play an advocatory role for socially discriminated groups. When viewing the CDS contributions assembled in this volume it also becomes evident that sometimes the distinctions between social scientific research, which ought to be intelligible and retroductable, and political argumentation become blurred.

Specifically, we distinguish between approaches that proceed *deductively* and those that choose a more *inductive* perspective. Linked to this distinction is the choice of objects under investigation: more deductively oriented theories that also propose a closed theoretical framework are more likely to illustrate their assumptions with a few examples that seem to best fit their claims (e.g. the dialectical-relational approach and sociocognitive approach in this volume). More inductively oriented approaches usually remain at the 'meso-level' and select problems they are 'curious' about and where they attempt to discover new insights through in-depth case studies and ample data collection (for example the discourse-historical approach, social actors approach, corpus linguistics approach, dispositive analysis in this volume). Of course, all approaches proceed *abductively*, i.e. oscillate between theory and data analysis in retroductive ways. However, on a continuum, we are able to distinguish obvious priorities in choosing entry points and themes.

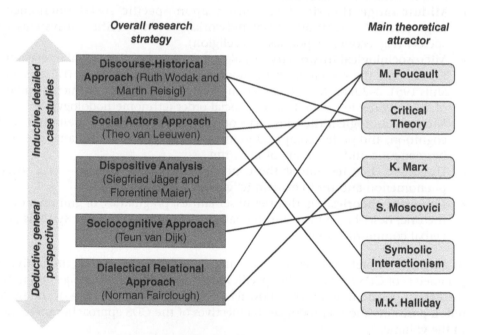

Figure 1.4 Overall research strategies and theoretical background

Figure 1.4 does not cover all the approaches presented in this volume, as the chapters presented by Mautner on corpus linguistics, KhosraviNik and Unger on social media and by Jancsary, Höllerer and Meyer on multimodal texts offer methodologies and methods for analysing specific data sets without relying strongly on specific theoretical attractors.

It has been criticized with good reason that each systematization of different approaches necessarily neglects the interconnectedness of particular approaches (Hart and Cap 2014, in their introduction). CDS emerged as a mixture of social and linguistic theories, and Halliday's systemic functional grammar was very influential. Hart and Cap (2014) further rightly state that different approaches to CDS rely on various linguistic theories: Halliday's systemic functional grammar (Halliday 1985), pragmatics, cognitive linguistics, corpus linguistics – and also rather generic theories such as post-structuralism and cognitive psychology. To cut a long story short: mapping different approaches to CDS has become more complex, as different authors use theoretical entry-points in a rather eclectic way depending on their specific interests and research questions.

Related to the choice of more 'macro-'or 'meso-topics' (such as 'globalization' or 'knowledge' versus 'un/employment' or 'right-wing populism'), we encounter differences in the evaluation of the chosen topics and objects under investigation. Macro-topics are relatively uncontroversial in the respective national or international academic contexts; some meso-topics, however, touch the core of the respective national community to which the researcher belongs. For example, research on concrete antisemitic, xenophobic and racist occurrences is much more controversial in certain academic and national contexts and is sometimes regarded as 'unpatriotic', or hostile. This explains the serious problems which some critical scholars have encountered when venturing into such sensitive fields (Heer et al. 2008).

In any case, it remains a fact that critical discourse studies follow a different and critical approach to problems, since CDS endeavours to make power relations explicit that are frequently obfuscated and hidden, and to derive results which are also of practical relevance.

Furthermore, one important assumption characterizes some CDS approaches that all *discourses are historical* and can therefore only be understood with reference to their context. Hence, the notion of context is crucial for CDS, since this explicitly includes sociopsychological, political, historical and ideological factors and thereby postulates an interdisciplinary procedure.

Interdisciplinarity is implemented in many different ways in the CDS approaches in this volume: in some cases, interdisciplinarity is characteristic of the theoretical framework (dispositive approach, dialectical-relational approach, sociocognitive approach); in other cases, interdisciplinarity also applies to team research and to the collection and analysis of data (social actors approach, discourse-historical approach). Moreover, CDS approaches use the concepts of intertextuality and interdiscursivity and analyse the intricate and complex relationships with other texts; in sum, it may be concluded that critical discourse studies are open to a broad range of factors exerting an influence on meaning-making.

CDS and other DA approaches also differ in respect to constitutive assumptions about the *relationship between language and society*. CDS do not believe this relationship to be simply deterministic but invoke the concept of *mediation*. The dialectical-relational approach draws on Halliday's multifunctional linguistic theory (Halliday 1985) and the concept of orders of discourse according to Foucault, while the discourse-historical approach and the sociocognitive approach make use of theories of social cognition (e.g. Moscovici 2000). Reflection on the mediation between language and social structure is absent from many other linguistic approaches, for example from conversation analysis. This is somewhat related to the level of social aggregation: although CDS approaches focus on social phenomena such as ideology or power, scholars select different units of analysis: the way in which individuals (or groups) mentally (cognitively), perceive, or the way social structures determine, discourse (see Figure 1.5). In other words: we distinguish between more cognitive–sociopsychological and more macro-sociological–structural approaches – although admittedly this is a rough distinction.

Moreover, most researchers integrate linguistic categories into their analyses – but to a different extent and with a different focus and intensity. Critical discourse studies do not necessarily include a broad range of linguistic categories in each single analysis; one might get the impression that only few linguistic devices are relevant. For instance, many CDS scholars consistently use social actor analysis by means of focusing upon pronouns, attributes and the verbal mode, time and tense; Hallidayan transitivity analysis and the analysis of *topoi* are employed frequently by social scientists because these concepts – quite wrongly – seem to be easy to apply without much linguistic background knowledge. Exceptions always prove the point: Reisigl and Wodak (this volume) and van Dijk (this volume) illustrate how a broad range of macro- and micro-linguistic, pragmatic and argumentative features can be operationalized and integrated in the analysis of texts (Figure 1.5).

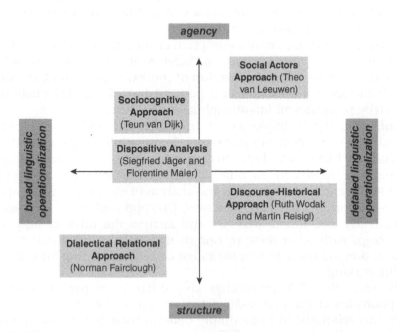

Figure 1.5 Linguistic involvement and level of aggregation

CDS generally perceive their procedure as a *hermeneutic process*, although this is not always evident in the positioning of every author. As an opponent to (causal) explanations of the natural sciences, hermeneutics can be understood as the method of understanding and producing meaning relations. The *hermeneutic circle* – i.e. the meaning of one part can only be understood in the context of the whole, but this in turn is only accessible from its component parts – indicates the problem of intelligibility of a hermeneutic interpretation. Therefore a hermeneutic interpretation specifically requires detailed documentation. Indeed, the details of the hermeneutic interpretation procedure are not always made transparent by many CDS-orientated studies.[3] If a crude distinction were to be made between *'text-extending'* and *'text-reducing'* methods of analysis, then CDS, on account of their focus on distinct formal properties and the associated compression of texts during analysis, might be characterized as 'text-reducing'.

Data collection

We concluded above that CDS does not constitute a well-defined empirical method but rather a bulk of approaches with theoretical similarities and research questions of a specific kind. But there is no CDS-way of collecting data, either. Some authors do not even mention data sampling methods, other scholars strongly rely on traditions based outside the sociolinguistic field.[4] In any case, similar to Grounded Theory (Glaser and Strauss 1967), data collection is not considered to be a specific phase that must be completed before the analysis can be conducted: after the first data collection one should perform first pilot analyses, find indicators for particular concepts, expand concepts into categories and, on the basis of these first results, collect further data (*theoretical sampling*). In this procedure, data collection is never completely concluded nor excluded, and new questions may always arise that require new data or re-examination of earlier data (Strauss 1987; Strauss and Corbin 1990).

Most CDS approaches do not explicitly explain or recommend data sampling procedures. Obviously corpus linguistics specifically refers to large corpora of texts. Other approaches introduced in this volume rely on existing texts, such as mass media communication or organizational documents. Beyond this, some of them – especially the DHA – additionally propose incorporating fieldwork and ethnography, if possible, in order to explore the object under investigation as a precondition for any further analysis and theorizing. Focusing on existing texts, however, does imply specific strengths (e.g. providing non-reactive data, see Webb et al. 1966) but also limitations in respect to necessary context knowledge and information about conditions of text production and reception.

Summary

The aims of this chapter were to provide a summary of CDS approaches and to discuss their similarities and differences. CDS are characterized by their diversity and their continuous development and elaboration. Therefore, this chapter does not claim to provide a complete overview of CDS; we obviously focus on the approaches assembled in this volume. Nevertheless, a few general points can be made within this diversity:

- Concerning the theoretical background, CDS work eclectically in many aspects. The entire range from Grand Theories to micro-linguistic theories are touched upon, although each single approach emphasizes different levels.
- There is no accepted canon of data sampling procedures; indeed many CDS approaches work with existing data, i.e. texts not specifically produced for the respective research projects.
- Operationalization and analysis are problem-oriented and imply linguistic expertise.

The most evident similarity is a shared interest in social processes of power, inclusion, exclusion and subordination. In the tradition of Critical Theory, CDS aims to shed light on the discursive aspects of societal disparities and inequalities. Critical discourse studies frequently explore the linguistic means used by the elites to reinforce and intensify inequalities in society. This entails careful and systematic analysis, self-reflection at every point of one's research, and distance from the data which are being investigated. *Description, interpretation* and *explanation* should be kept apart, thus enabling *transparency* and *retroductability* of the respective analysis. Of course, not all of these recommendations are consistently followed, and they cannot always be implemented in detail because of time pressures and similar structural constraints.

Therefore some critics will continue to state that CDS constantly sits on the fence between social research and political activism (Widdowson 2004a; Wodak 2006a); others accuse some CDS research of being too linguistic or not linguistic enough. In our view, such criticism keeps a field alive because it necessarily triggers more self-reflection and encourages new responses and innovative ideas.

Notes

1 See Fairclough 1991; van Dijk 1984; Wodak 1989.
2 The Erasmus network consisted of cooperation between Siegfried Jäger, Duisburg; Per Linell, Linkoeping; Norman Fairclough, Lancaster; Teun van Dijk, Amsterdam; Gunther Kress, London; Theo van Leeuwen, London; Ruth Wodak, Vienna.
3 The question whether it is possible to make hermeneutic processes transparent and intelligible at all remains undecided, although some authors (Oevermann et al. 1979) developed a hermeneutically oriented method with well-defined procedures and rules.
4 A general overview on sampling and the problem of text selection is provided by Titscher et al. (2000).

2

THE DISCOURSE-HISTORICAL APPROACH (DHA)

MARTIN REISIGL AND RUTH WODAK

CONTENTS

Keywords

argumentation, climate change, context, discourse-historical approach, discourse strategy, field of action, online news reporting, posting, topos, validity claim

Introducing key concepts and terms

We start our chapter by introducing the notions of 'critique', 'ideology' and 'power'. These three concepts are constitutive of every approach in CDS/CDA, though frequently employed with different meanings. Therefore, it is important to clarify how they are conceptualized in the discourse-historical approach (DHA). We then proceed to definitions of other salient terms, such as 'discourse', 'genre', 'text', 'recontextualization', 'intertextuality' and 'interdiscursivity'.

The second section summarizes some analytical tools and the general principles of the DHA. In the third section, we illustrate our methodology, step by step, by focusing on 'discourses about climate change'. In the final section, we mention the strengths and limitations of the DHA and point to future challenges for the field.

'Critique', 'ideology' and 'power'

Three concepts figure in all variants of CDS: critique, ideology and power.

'Critique' carries many different meanings: some adhere to the Frankfurt School, others to a notion of literary criticism, and some to Marxist theory. Adhering to a 'critical' stance should be understood as getting closer to the data (despite the fact that critique is mostly 'situated critique'), embedding the data in a social context, clarifying the positioning of the discourse participants, and engaging in continuous self-reflection while undertaking research. Moreover, our understanding of critique often implies that the results of research should be applied, be it in practical seminars for teachers, doctors and bureaucrats, in the writing of expert opinions or in the production of schoolbooks.

> *Critique* refers to the examination, assessment and evaluation, from a normative perspective, of persons, objects, actions, social institutions and so forth. Critique can relate to a quest for truth, to specific values and ethics, to appropriate text exegesis, to self-reflection, to enlightenment and emancipation, to specific aspects of social change, to ecological protection and to aesthetic orientation. Following Kant, 'critique' also refers to a propaedeutic ('preliminary') investigation into the conditions and possibilities of knowledge. The term acquired political prominence during the French Revolution and with the emergence of Marxism. Ever since, social critique has assessed the political and social status quo from the point of view of an ideal standard or alternative, in order to diagnose shortcomings and contradictions (see Chilton, Tian and Wodak 2010). At this point, critique can merge with resistance; here, we are also reminded of Foucault's conception of critique as 'the art of not being governed in this specific way and at this specific price' (Foucault 1990: 12).

The DHA adheres to the socio-philosophical orientation of Critical Theory.[1] As such, it follows a concept of social critique that integrates three related aspects:[2]

1. *'Text or discourse immanent critique'* aims to discover inconsistencies, (self)-contradictions, paradoxes and dilemmas in text-internal or discourse-internal structures.
2. *'Socio-diagnostic critique'* is concerned with uncovering the – particularly latent – persuasive or 'manipulative' character of discursive practices. Here, we rely on our contextual knowledge and draw on social theories and other theoretical models from various disciplines to interpret discursive events.
3. Future-related *prospective critique* seeks to improve communication (e.g. by elaborating guidelines against sexist language use or by reducing 'language barriers' in hospitals, schools and so forth).

It follows from our understanding of critique that the DHA should make the object under investigation and the analyst's own position transparent and then justify, theoretically, why certain interpretations and readings of discursive events seem more valid than others.

Thompson (1990) discusses the concept of ideology and its relationships to other concepts, especially aspects of mass communication in great detail. He points out that the notion of ideology has been given a range of functions and meanings since it first appeared in late eighteenth-century France. For Thompson, ideology refers to social forms and processes within which, and by means of which, hegemonic symbolic forms circulate in the social world.

Ideology, in the DHA's view, is seen as a perspective (often one-sided), i.e. a worldview and a system composed of related mental representations, convictions, opinions, attitudes, values and evaluations, which is shared by members of a specific social group. Fully developed ideologies (often labelled 'grand narratives'), such as communism, socialism, conservatism or liberalism, include three inter-related imaginaries: (1) a representational model of what a society looks like, i.e. a model of the status quo (e.g. a communist model of a capitalist exploit-ative society); (2) a visionary model of what a society should look like in the future (e.g. a communist model of a classless society); and (3) a programmatic model of how the envisioned society could be achieved 'on the path' from the present to the future (e.g. a communist model of a proletarian revolution). Ideologies serve as important means of creating shared social identities and of establishing and maintaining unequal power relations through discourse, e.g. by establishing hegemonic identity narratives or by controlling the access to specific discourses or public spheres ('gate-keeping'). In addition, ideologies also function as a means of transforming power relations.

We take a particular interest in the ways in which linguistic and other semiotic practices mediate and reproduce ideologies in a range of social institutions. One of the aims of the DHA is to deconstruct the hegemony of specific dis-courses by deciphering the ideologies that serve to establish, perpetuate or resist dominance.

For the DHA, language is not powerful on its own – it is a means to gain and maintain power via the use that powerful people make of it, and an expression of power relations.

> *Power* relates to an asymmetric relationship among social actors who have different social positions or who belong to different social groups. Following Weber (1980), 'power' can be defined as the possibility of enforcing one's own will within a social relationship against the will or interests of others. Furthermore, power can be described in terms of social relations and their attributes, i.e. of 'ties of mutual dependence between parties' (Emerson 1962: 32), and in terms of power networks, i.e. of 'two or more power-dependence relations' (Emerson 1962: 32). Fundamental ways in which power is implemented are 'actional power' (physical force and violence), the control of people through threats or promises, the attachment to authority (the exertion of authority and submission to authority) and technical control through objects, e.g. means of production, means of transportation, weapons and so on (Popitz 1992).

Power is socially ubiquitous. It can be productive, but it is often destructive. Power is legitimized or de-legitimized in discourses, but power relations also limit and regulate discourses by various types of controlling procedures. Texts are frequently sites of social struggle, in that they manifest traces of a range of ideological struggles for dominance and hegemony. We focus on the ways in which linguistic forms are used in various expressions and manipulations of power. Power is discursively realized not only by grammatical forms, but also by a person's control of the social occasion, by means of the genre of a text, or by the regulation of access to specific public spheres.

'Discourse', 'text' and 'context'

By employing the DHA, we investigate multifaceted phenomena in our societies. This implies that the study of (oral, written, visual) language use remains only one of many aspects of the whole enterprise. Hence, our research is interdisciplinary. Moreover, in order to *analyse, understand* and *explain* the complexity of the objects under investigation, we consider many different and accessible sources of data (always depending on external constraints, such as available time, funding etc.) from various analytical perspectives. We follow the *principle of triangulation*, which implies taking a whole range of empirical observations, theories from various disciplines and methods, as well as background information, into account (see, for example, Heer et al. 2008; Wodak 2011b, 2015b; Wodak et al. 2009). The specific choices depend on the specific problem – in this chapter, on controversies about climate change.

We consider 'discourse' to be:

- a cluster of context-dependent semiotic practices that are situated within specific fields of social action;
- socially constituted and socially constitutive;
- related to a macro-topic;
- linked to argumentation about validity claims, such as truth and normative validity involving several social actors with different points of view.

Thus, we regard (a) macro-topic relatedness, (b) pluri-perspectivity and (c) argumentativity as constitutive elements of a discourse. Other approaches to CDS do not explicitly link 'discourse' with a macro-topic or with more than one perspective (see Reisigl 2003: 91ff.; 2014: 71ff.); frequently 'discourse' is also equated with 'ideology' or 'stance' (see the discussion in Wodak 2012b).

It is important to consider how one can identify and delimit the borders of a discourse, and how one can differentiate a specific discourse from other discourses: the boundaries of a discourse, such as the one on global warming or climate change, are partly fluid. As an analytical construct, a discourse always depends on the discourse analyst's perspective. As an object of investigation, a discourse is not a closed unit, but rather a dynamic semiotic entity that is open to reinterpretation and continuation.

We distinguish between 'discourse' and 'text': texts are parts of discourses. They make speech acts durable over time and thus bridge two dilated speech situations, i.e. the situation of speech production and the situation of speech reception. In other words, texts – be they visualized, written or oral – objectify linguistic actions (Ehlich 1983). Texts can be assigned to genres. A 'genre' can be characterized as a socially conventionalized type and pattern of communication that fulfils a specific social purpose in a specific social context. In addition, a genre can be seen as a mental scheme that refers to specific procedural knowledge about a specific text function and the processes of text production, distribution and reception.

Consequently, a manifesto on combating global warming proposes certain rules and expectations according to social conventions, and has specific social purposes. A discourse on climate change is realized through a range of genres and texts, e.g. TV debates on the politics of a particular government on climate change, guidelines to reduce energy consumption, speeches or lectures by climatologists, online comments about newspaper articles, and so forth.

The DHA also investigates *intertextual* and *interdiscursive relationships* between utterances, texts, genres and discourses, as well as extra-linguistic social/sociological variables, the history of an organization or institution, and situational frames. While focusing on all these relationships, we explore how discourses, genres and texts change in relationship to sociopolitical change.

- 'Intertextuality' means that texts are linked to other texts, in both the past and the present. Such connections are established in different ways: through explicit reference to a topic or main actor; through references to the same events; by allusions or evocations; by the transfer of main arguments from one text to the next, and so forth. The process of transferring given elements to new contexts is labelled 'recontextualization': if an element is taken out of a specific context, we observe a process of 'de-contextualization'; if the respective element is then inserted into a new context, we witness a process of recontextualization. The element (partly) acquires a new meaning, since meanings are formed in use (see Wittgenstein 1989 [1952]). Recontextualization can, for instance, be observed when contrasting a political speech with the reporting of that speech in various newspapers. A journalist will select specific quotes that best suit the general purpose of an article (e.g. commentary). The quotations are thus de- and re-contextualized, i.e. newly framed. They can in part acquire new meanings in the specific context of press coverage.
- 'Interdiscursivity' signifies that discourses are linked to each other in various ways. If we conceive of 'discourse' as primarily topic-related (as 'discourse about x'), then we are able to observe that, for instance, the discourse about climate change frequently refers to topics or subtopics of other discourses, such as international competition or health. Discourses are open and often hybrid; new subtopics can be created at many points.
- 'Field of action' (Girnth 1996) indicates a segment of social reality that constitutes a (partial) 'frame' of a discourse. Different fields of action are defined by different functions of discursive practices. For example, in the arena of *political action* we differentiate between eight different political functions as eight different fields (see Figure 2.1). A 'discourse' about a specific topic can find its starting point within one field of action and proceed through another one. Discourses then 'spread' to different fields and relate to or overlap with other discourses.

We represent the relationship between fields of action, genres and macro-topics in the area of *political action* as shown in Figure 2.1.[3]

Figure 2.2 further illustrates the interdiscursive and intertextual relationships between discourses, discourse topics, genres and texts. In this diagram, interdiscursivity is indicated by the two large overlapping ellipses. Intertextual relationships are represented by simple bold arrows. The assignment of texts to genres is marked by simple arrows. The topics to which a text refers are indicated by small ellipses with simple dotted arrows; the topical intersection of different texts is indicated by the overlapping small ellipses. Finally, a specific intertextual relationship, of the thematic reference of one text to another, is indicated by simple broken arrows.

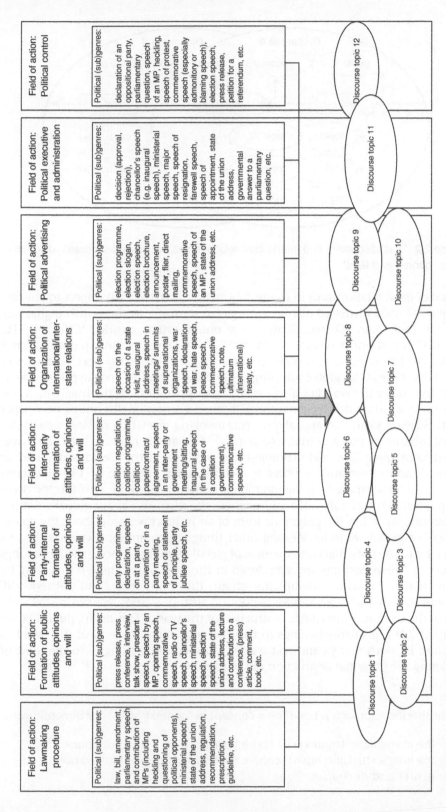

Figure 2.1 Fields of political action, political genres and discourse topics (see Reisigl 2007: 34–5)

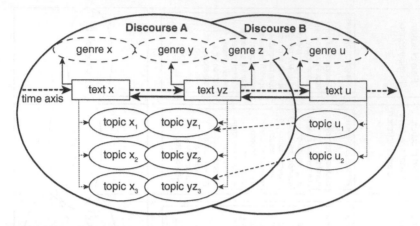

Figure 2.2 Interdiscursive and intertextual relationships between discourses, discourse topics, genres and texts

Several of these relationships in Figure 2.2 can be illustrated with respect to our case study – the mass-mediated discourse on global warming in the British digital tabloid the *Daily Star*. We will analyse one online article entitled 'END OF THE WORLD? Top scientist reveals "We're f*****!"'' by Dave Snelling, published on 8 August 2014 in the online version of the *Daily Star*. This text (= text yz) relates to both a discourse about global warming (= discourse A) and an apocalyptic discourse about the end of the world (= discourse B), as is apparent from the title (which was probably not formulated by the author). It mixes a sensationalist online newspaper report (= genre y) and an apocalyptic, fear invoking revelation realized as a multi-modal mixture of text and image (= genre z). This article refers to a specific tweet (= text x) by Jason Box, a climatologist and professor at the Geological Survey of Denmark and Greenland. A tweet is a short digital message of 140 characters posted and disseminated via the microblog Twitter (= genre x). This specific tweet was published on 29 July 2014 and refers to the discourse about global warming (= discourse A). It has the pragmatic form of an indirect warning about the consequences of global warming. Among other things in common, text z and text yz both refer to the potential consequences of global warming. Among the 24 postings on text yz (these postings are reproduced in the Appendix), there is a posting by commentator 3, which complains about the numerous 'end-of-the-world' announcements and takes a more hedonistic attitude ('enjoy your lives, folks') in view of the seemingly inevitable destruction of the world. This text u, published on 8 August 2014, primarily belongs to the discourse about the end of the world (= discourse B). Both text yz and text u refer – among other things – to the topic of predicting the potential destruction of the world.

Our specific approach is based on a concept of 'context' with four dimensions:

1. the immediate, language or text-internal co-text and co-discourse;
2. the intertextual and interdiscursive relationships between utterances, texts, genres and discourses;

3. the social variables and institutional frames of a specific 'context of situation';
4. the broader sociopolitical and historical context, which discursive practices are embedded in and related to.

In our analysis, we orient ourselves to all four dimensions of context in a recursive manner (see also Wodak 2007, 2011b).

Some principles of the DHA and tools of analysis

The study for which the DHA was first developed analysed the emergence of antisemitic stereotypical images in public discourses in the 1986 Austrian presidential campaign of former UN Secretary General Kurt Waldheim who, for a long time, had kept secret his National-Socialist past (Wodak et al. 1990).[4] In this research project, several salient characteristics of the DHA were first established: (1) interdisciplinary research with a special focus on historical embedding; (2) multiple triangulation as a methodological principle combining various perspectives on the research object by including different data (data triangulation), different theories (theory triangulation), different methods (triangulation of methods) and different researchers (investigator triangulation) conducting teamwork (Flick 2004); and (3) orientation towards the practical application of results.

This interdisciplinary study combined linguistic analysis with historical and sociological approaches. Moreover, the researchers presented an exhibition about 'Post-war antisemitism' at the University of Vienna in the spring term 1987, based on the analysis of the many genres and texts analysed in the research project.

The DHA was further elaborated in a number of studies on, for example, racist discrimination against migrants from Romania after the fall of the so-called Iron Curtain, 1989, and the discourse about nation and national identity in Austria (Matouschek et al. 1995; Reisigl 2007; Wodak et al. 2009). The research centre 'Discourse, Politics, Identity' (DPI) in Vienna allowed for a shift to comparative interdisciplinary and transnational projects relating to the study of European identities and European politics of the past (Heer et al. 2008; Kovács and Wodak 2003).

Various principles characterizing this approach have evolved over time since the study on Austrian post-war antisemitism. Here, we summarize 10 of the most important principles:

1. The approach is interdisciplinary. Interdisciplinarity involves theory, methods, methodology, research practice and practical application.
2. The approach is problem-oriented.
3. Various theories and methods are combined, wherever integration leads to an adequate understanding and explanation of the research object.

(Continued)

(Continued)

4. The research incorporates fieldwork and ethnography (study from 'inside') if these are required for a thorough analysis and theorizing of the object under investigation.
5. Research necessarily moves recursively between theory and empirical data. Therefore, we endorse a complex research strategy that combines abductive reasoning (the construction of explanatory hypotheses by observing data and relating them tentatively to previous theoretical models), inductive procedures (an empirical examination of the strength of these hypotheses) and – if possible – deduction (drawing a prognostic conclusion on the basis of a theory).
6. Numerous genres and public spaces as well as intertextual and interdiscursive relationships are studied.
7. The historical context is taken into account when interpreting texts and discourses. The historical orientation permits the reconstruction of how recontextualization functions as an important process of linking texts and discourses intertextually and interdiscursively over time.
8. Categories and methods are not fixed once and for all. They must be elaborated for each analysis according to the specific problem under investigation.
9. 'Grand theories' often serve as a foundation. In specific analyses, however, 'middle-range theories' frequently offer a better theoretical basis (Weick 1974).
10. The application of results is an important aim. Results should be made available to and applied by experts and be communicated to the public.

The DHA is three-dimensional: (1) having identified the specific *content* or *topic(s)* of a specific discourse, (2) *discursive strategies* are investigated. Then (3), *linguistic means* (as types) and context-dependent *linguistic realizations* (as tokens) are examined.

There are strategies that deserve special attention when analyzing a specific discourse (see Step 5 below). When approaching these strategies in our analyses, within the framework of our methodology, we frequently orient ourselves to five questions:

1. How are persons, objects, phenomena/events, processes and actions named and referred to linguistically?
2. What characteristics, qualities and features are attributed to social actors, objects, phenomena/events and processes?
3. What arguments are employed in the discourse in question?
4. From what perspective are these nominations, attributions and arguments expressed?
5. Are the respective utterances articulated overtly, intensified or mitigated?

According to these five questions, we elaborate five types of discursive strategies.

By 'strategy' we mean a more or less intentional plan of practice (including discursive practices) adopted to achieve a particular social, political, psychological or linguistic goal. Discursive strategies are located at different levels of linguistic organization and complexity.[5]

Table 2.1   A selection of discursive strategies

Strategy	Objectives	Devices
NOMINATION	discursive construction of social actors, objects, phenomena, events, processes and actions	• membership categorization devices, deictics, anthroponyms, etc. • tropes such as metaphors, metonymies and synecdoches (*pars pro toto, totum pro parte*) • verbs and nouns used to denote processes and actions, etc.
PREDICATION	discursive qualification of social actors, objects, phenomena, events, processes and actions (positively or negatively)	• (stereotypical) evaluative attributions of negative or positive traits (e.g. in the form of adjectives, appositions, prepositional phrases, relative clauses, conjunctional clauses, infinitive clauses and participial clauses or groups) • explicit predicates or predicative nouns/ adjectives/pronouns • collocations • comparisons, similes, metaphors and other rhetorical figures (including metonymies, hyperboles, litotes, euphemisms) • allusions, evocations, presuppositions/ implicatures, etc.
ARGUMENTATION	justification and questioning of claims of truth and normative rightness	• topoi (formal or more content-related) • fallacies
PERSPECTIVIZATION	positioning the speaker's or writer's point of view and expressing involvement or distance	• deictics • direct, indirect or free indirect speech • quotation marks, discourse markers/ particles • metaphors • animating prosody, etc.
INTENSIFICATION OR MITIGATION	modifying (intensifying or mitigating) the illocutionary force and thus the epistemic or deontic status of utterances	• diminutives or augmentatives • (modal) particles, tag questions, subjunctives, hesitations, vague expressions, etc. • hyperboles or litotes • indirect speech acts (e.g. question instead of assertion) • verbs of saying, feeling, thinking, etc.

The analysis of 'discourses about climate change'

The DHA in eight steps

A thorough, ideal-typical discourse-historical analysis should follow an eight-step programme. Typically, the eight steps are implemented recursively:

1. Activation and consultation of preceding theoretical knowledge (i.e. recollection, reading and discussion of previous research).
2. Systematic collection of data and context information (depending on the research questions, various discourses and discursive events, social fields as well as actors, semiotic media, genres and texts).
3. Selection and preparation of data for specific analyses (selection and downsizing of data according to relevant criteria, transcription of tape recordings, etc.).
4. Specification of the research question/s and formulation of assumptions (on the basis of a literature review and a first skimming of the data).
5. Qualitative pilot analysis, including a context analysis, macro-analysis and micro-analysis (allows testing categories and first assumptions, as well as the further specification of assumptions; see the pilot analysis below).
6. Detailed case studies (of a whole range of data, primarily qualitatively, but in part also quantitatively).
7. Formulation of a critique (interpretation and explanation of results, taking into account the relevant context knowledge and referring to the three dimensions of critique).
8. Practical application of analytical results (if possible, the results may be applied or proposed for practical application targeting some social impact).

This ideal-typical list is best realized in a large-scale interdisciplinary project with sufficient resources in the form of time, personnel and money. Depending on the funding, time and other constraints, smaller studies are, of course, useful and legitimate. In any case, it makes sense to be aware of the thorough overall research design, and thus to make explicit choices when devising one's own project such as a PhD thesis. For the purpose of a PhD project one can, of course, conduct only a few case studies and necessarily restrict the range of the data collection (to a few genres). Sometimes a pilot study can be extended to more comprehensive case studies, and occasionally case studies planned at the very beginning must be left for a follow-up project.

Below, we focus on four of the eight research stages (1, 2, 4 and especially 5). Among the discursive strategies listed in Table 2.1, we will specifically illustrate the *analysis* of *argumentation* in this pilot study,[6] since other strategies such as nomination and predication (which we also take into consideration) are integrated into argumentation and subordinated under the persuasive aims of the text(s) we analyse below. Our observations on argumentation analysis exemplify how a normative middle-range theory that transcends a purely linguistic horizon can be applied to a concrete analysis.

> Argumentation is a linguistic as well as a cognitive pattern of problem-solving that manifests itself in a (more or less regulated) sequence of speech acts which form a complex and more or less coherent network of statements. Argumentation serves the methodical/systematic challenging or justification of validity claims, such as truth and normative rightness (Kopperschmidt 2000: 59f.). Its purpose is to persuade recipients via convincing (sound) arguments and/or suggestive fallacies. Whereas the *validity claim of truth* relates to questions of knowledge, degrees of certainty and theoretical insights, the *validity claim of normative rightness* relates to questions of what should be done or not or what is recommended or forbidden, i.e. to questions of practical norms or ethical and moral standards.[7]

A comprehensive analysis of argumentation includes at least the following dimensions:

a. functional categories (e.g. claim, argument/premise, conclusion rule, modality);
b. formal categories (formal topoi/fallacies, such as the scheme of definition, the scheme of authority, the scheme of comparison and the scheme of example; see below for an explanation of the concepts of 'topos' and 'fallacy');
c. content-related categories (content-related topoi/fallacies such as the scheme of ignorance, the scheme of nature and the scheme of manipulation);
d. categories for describing argumentative meso- and macro-structures (such as stages of argumentation, the complexity of argumentation and the [inter]-dependency of arguments). In the present context, we will focus especially on content-related topoi and fallacies.

> 'Topoi' (singular 'topos', the Greek word for 'place') can be understood as parts of argumentation that belong to the required premises. They are formal or content-related warrants or 'conclusion rules'. As such, they connect the argument(s) with the conclusion, the claim. In this way, they justify the transition from the argument(s) to the conclusion (Kienpointner 1992: 194). Topoi are socially conventionalized and recur habitually. They are not always expressed explicitly, but can always be made explicit as conditional or causal paraphrases, such as 'if x, then y' or 'y, because x' (for more details see Reisigl 2014; Reisigl and Wodak 2001: 69–80; see also Rubinelli 2009; Wengeler 2003; Wodak 2014, 2015b).

Topoi are reasonable or fallacious. If the latter is the case, we label them *fallacies*. There are 10 rules for rational disputes and constructive arguing that allow discerning topoi from fallacies (see the *pragma-dialectical approach* of Van Eemeren and Grootendorst 1992; Van Eemeren et al. 2009):

1. Freedom of arguing – parties must not prevent each other from advancing or challenging claims.
2. Obligation to give reasons – parties that advance a claim may not refuse to defend that claim when requested to do so.
3. Correct reference to the previous discourse by the antagonist – attacks on claims may not bear on a claim that has not actually been put forward by the other party.
4. Obligation to 'matter-of-factness' – claims may not be defended by non-argumentation or argumentation that is not relevant to the claim.
5. Correct reference to implicit premises – parties may not falsely attribute unexpressed premises to the other party, nor disown responsibility for their own unexpressed premises.
6. Acceptance of shared starting points – parties may not falsely present something as an accepted starting point or falsely deny that something is an accepted starting point.
7. Use of plausible schemes of argumentation – claims may not be regarded as conclusively defended if the defence does not take place by means of an appropriate argumentation scheme correctly applied.
8. Logical validity – an argumentation that is presented in an explicit and complete way must not contradict the rules of logic.
9. Acceptance of the discussion's results – inconclusive defences of claims may not lead to maintaining these claims, and conclusive defences of claims may not lead to maintaining expressions of doubt concerning these claims.
10. Clarity of expression and correct interpretation – parties may not use any formulations that are insufficiently clear or ambiguous, and they may not deliberately misinterpret the other party's formulations.

If these rules are violated, fallacies will occur. It is not always easy, however, to decide without precise context knowledge whether an argumentation scheme has been employed as a reasonable topos or as a fallacy.

A pilot study on online news reporting on climate change

Step 1: Activation and consultation of preceding theoretical knowledge

The overarching research question of 'global warming' can be approached in various ways:

a. What does 'climate change' mean according to the existing (scientific) literature, i.e. how is 'climate change' defined?
b. What does relevant literature convey about the relationship between 'climate change' and modern societies, i.e. the influence of human behaviour on the global climate?

To approach these questions, we must first consult relevant literature. Which literature may be relevant depends on the research interests. The two questions refer to scientific knowledge (thus, climatology literature is relevant) and to knowledge about the relationship between climate change and society (thus, social science literature is relevant). Furthermore, a linguistic approach to the semantics of 'climate change' should also discuss the meanings of 'ordinary language use (or 'common sense')'. A first consultation of the respective literature supplies the following answers:

a. In 'everyday' language, 'climate change' predominantly means 'global warming', although other meanings can also be found: 'climate change' sometimes denotes 'global cooling towards a new ice age' and sometimes relates to a 'natural climatic variation which temporarily leads to a warming or cooling'. In scientific terms, 'climate change' refers to the change of the medial annual temperature over a longer period (e.g. of 30 years), but also to various climatic alterations during this period, including precipitation change, sea-level rise, an increase in extreme weather events, ozone depletion and so forth. A historical semantic reconstruction reveals that the scientific and political meaning of the phrase has been extended. According to the Intergovernmental Panel on Climate Change (IPCC), '[c]limate change refers to a change in the state of the climate that can be identified (e.g. by using statistical tests) by changes in the mean and/or the variability of its properties, and that persists for an extended period, typically decades or longer. Climate change may be caused by natural internal processes or external forces such as modulations of the solar cycles, volcanic eruptions and persistent anthropogenic changes in the composition of the atmosphere or in land use.' In contrast to this broad conception, Article 1 of the United Nations Framework Convention on Climate Change (UNFCCC) of 1992 contains a restricted understanding that relates the term exclusively 'to a change of climate that is attributed directly or indirectly to human activity that alters the composition of the global atmosphere', whereas the natural climate alteration observable over comparable time periods is termed 'climate variability' (NN 2013: 1450).
b. Most scientists consider the relationship between 'climate change' and modern societies to be a causal one, in the sense that nature becomes more and more dependent on human civilization, global warming being – to a large extent – the anthropogenic consequence of the greenhouse effect caused by the worldwide increase in the output of carbon dioxide and other greenhouse gases.[8]

After this first orientation, we are now able to formulate a more general discourse-related research question: What does 'climate change' mean in the specific public discourse that we focus on and how is human influence on climate represented and discussed in this discourse?

Assumptions related to this question are, for example, that the discourse will comprise different and perhaps contradictory interpretations of the 'nature' of climate change (of its existence, origins and consequences), of the relationship between climate and civilization, and of possible measures to be taken against climate change. If this should be the case, then we assume that such differing discursive representations of and attitudes to climate change might make it difficult to achieve a political compromise as a precondition for political decisions. Viewed from a historical perspective, we assume that the discourse (or some facets of the discourse) will have changed over time, depending on a range of factors to be identified in our analyses.

Step 2: Systematic collection of data and contextual information

Depending on what data are accessible (by observations, audio-visual recording, interviews, research in archives and digital internet sources) and on how much data can be analysed within the respective research project, a range of empirical data can be collected, while considering the following criteria:

- *specific political units* (e.g. region, nation state, international union) or *language communities*;
- *specific periods of time* relating to *important discursive events*, which are connected with the issue in question, e.g. climate summits or publications of reports issued by the Intergovernmental Panel on Climate Change and their discussion in public;
- *specific social and especially political and scientific actors* (individual and 'collective' actors or organizations, e.g. politicians with different party-political affiliations, environmentalists, climatologists, national and international councils on climate change, oil companies, car companies and so forth);
- *specific discourses*, in our case, discourses about climate change and particularly about global warming;
- *specific fields of political action* (see Figure 2.1 above), especially the formation of public attitudes, opinions and will (e.g. related to media coverage), the management of international relations (e.g. related to international summits and agreements), the fields of political control (e.g. related to environmentalist actions), political advertising (e.g. related to promotion of the energy business), the inter-party formation of attitudes, opinions and will (e.g. related to the inter-party coordination of environmental policy), the law-making procedure (e.g. related to tax laws on carbon emissions) and *specific policy fields* such as environmental policy, energy policy, economic policy, health policy or migration policy;
- *specific semiotic media* and *genres* related to the scientific study of climate developments, to environmental policy and so on (expert reports, election manifestos, political debates inside and outside parliament, scientific articles, press articles as well as comments, TV interviews and TV discussions, leaflets, car advertisements, popular scientific texts, etc.).

In this chapter, we restrict the broad research question formulated above as follows: 'What does "climate change" mean in the specific sequence of public discourse fragments (press article and postings) under investigation? How is human influence on climate represented and discussed in these discourse fragments?' In other words: We focus on one single *discourse fragment* (a multimodal online press article written by the journalist Dave Snelling and published in the *Daily Star* on 8 August 2014) and *some readers' reactions to it* (i.e. 24 postings, from 8 August 2014 onwards). We chose this article and the related postings because they are rather brief and easily accessible on the internet, because internet media use (including postings) is considered to be an important source of information with respect to the topic of climate change, and because the discursive dynamic between a press article and its reception via postings is an interesting source for a CDA 2.0 interested in critical reception research and the deliberative potential of new media, see Angouri and Wodak (2014), Dorostkar and Preisinger (2012, 2013), KhosraviNik and Unger (this volume). In step 5, we will take a closer look at the online article and some discursive features of the respective postings.

Step 3: Selection and preparation of data for specific analyses

When preparing the corpus for analysis, the collected data are downsized according to specific criteria such as frequency, representativity,[9] (proto) typicality, intertextual or interdiscursive scope, salience, uniqueness and redundancy. If necessary, oral data have to be transcribed according to the conventions determined by the research question. As we focus on a single textual chain (a news report and related postings), there is no need to continue the discussion of this step.

Step 4: Specification of the research question and the formulation of assumptions

The research question can now be further specified with regard to the following dimensions, i.e.:

a. whether global warming can be undisputedly perceived by the discourse participants;
b. whether climate change is seen as a natural process or co-caused by human beings.

Moreover, the research question should also consider agonistic political accusations of abuse and manipulation, and alternative appeals for action (Gore 2007: 268f.; Oreskes and Conway 2010: 169–215; in contrast to Klaus 2007: 79, 95, 97f.). Hence, a possible point of departure for further elaboration of our research question could be the analysis of such controversial and conflicting positions. As critical discourse analysts, we describe and assess such contradictory positions and their persuasive character on the basis of principles of rational argumentation mentioned above, and with regard to underlying manipulative strategies.

A second point of departure could be the analysis of media coverage and the relationship between scientific statements about global warming and the media recipients' knowledge. Indeed, Allan Bell (1994) already focused on such issues many years ago. In his case study of the discourse about climate change in New Zealand, he analysed the relationship between the media coverage of scientific explanations and laypersons' understanding of this coverage. Bell's research, which illustrated convincingly that knowledge about climate change is greater among socially advantaged than among socially disadvantaged media users (Bell 1994), could be compared with the situation in 2015.[10] The DHA pays special attention to such comparisons over time.

Should we conduct a comprehensive study on discourses about climate change while accounting for all these dimensions, then our research question could be divided into a much more detailed set of questions.

- What kind of social actors participate in the specific discourse on climate change? What kinds of positions are adopted in the different fields of political action? (*We assume that different actors pursue different and often conflicting interests.*)
- What role do scientists play in the triangle of science, policy/politics and the mass-mediated public sphere? How do they 'translate', i.e. recontextualize, their expert knowledge for laypeople? How reliable are the statements of scientists as epistemic and deontic authorities? How are scientists 'controlled' in modern democratic societies? On the basis of what criteria do laypeople judge scientific statements? (*Here, we assume that scientists play an important role as experts, both in processes of political decision-making and in the formation of public attitudes, opinions and will.*)
- What role do the mass media play in the 'translation' of expert knowledge for laypeople? Which experts are chosen by the media, which expert voices remain silent in the media? How are the media controlled in democratic societies? Is it difficult to understand mass media texts on climate change? Which social actors have access to the media? (*We assume that the media play a crucial role in the formation of public attitudes, opinions and will, as well as in the field of political control.*)
- What validity claims of truth and normative rightness are explicitly made or presupposed in the discourse under investigation? How are these claims related to party-political and – in a wider sense – ideological alignments? (*We assume that different discourse participants will make different and often contradictory, ideology-dependent claims about climate change.*)
- What are the main topics of the discourse? Is the influence of human beings on the global climate represented and, if so, how is it discussed? In more linguistic terms: what descriptions, explanations, argumentation and narratives about the genesis, diagnosis, prognosis and avoidance of climate change are represented or reported in order to support the presupposed validity claims? What semiotic (especially linguistic and visual) means are employed to persuade recipients? What contradictions are constructed in the discourse? (*A basic assumption is that we will find a wide range of differing representations and argumentation.*)
- What aspects of the discourse change over time? What are the reasons for change? (*This question presupposes that there is diachronic change involving partial continuities and new developments.*)
- What other discourses does the discourse intersect with and relate to? (*We assume that the specific discourse has interdiscursive links to other discourses.*)

Of course, we cannot respond adequately to all these questions in this chapter. Only large-scale interdisciplinary research projects would be able to investigate the aforementioned complexities in a comprehensive way. Smaller projects and pilot studies will necessarily focus on some selected aspects.

Step 5: Qualitative pilot analysis

Our pilot study seeks to explore the assumptions mentioned above. Accordingly, we restrict this qualitative pilot study to one article written by the journalist Dave Snelling for the online version of the *Daily Star*. Briefly, we will also consider the 24 comments posted in reaction to that online article (they are reproduced in the Appendix). Let us, first of all, reproduce the article: see Figure 2.3.

END OF THE WORLD? Top scientist reveals "We're f*****!"

TERRIFYING discovery could see the Earth warming to devastating levels in just a few years

By Dave Snelling / Published 8 August 2014

It's probably not the words you want to hear from a leading figure on climate change.

But Jason Box, a professor at the Geological Survey of Denmark and Greenland, reckons, "We're f**ked".

He made the remarks on his twitter account after a team of scientists made an alarming discovery.

It appears that huge quantities of methane gas are leaking from the sea floor under the Arctic and rising into the atmosphere.

GLOBAL WARMING: The Earth is heating at an alarming rate [GETTY]

Methane is one of the most dangerous greenhouse gases as it traps far more heat than other gases, such as carbon dioxide.

Jason Box
@climate_ice

If even a small fraction of Arctic sea floor carbon is released to the atmosphere, we're f'd.

5:43 PM · 29 Jul 2014

1,116 RETWEETS 424 FAVORITES

(Continued)

(Continued)

And this increased temperature is helping to warm up parts of the Earth at an alarming rate.

Box told website Motherboard, "Even if a small fraction of the Arctic carbon were released to the atmosphere, we're f**ked."

"Methane is more than 20 times more potent than CO_2 in trapping infrared as part of the natural greenhouse effect."

"Methane getting to the surface—that's potent stuff."

"The conventional thought is that the bubbles would be dissolved before they reached the surface. [*sic*]

"But if the plumes are making it to the surface, that's a brand new source of heat-trapping gases that we need to worry about."

What makes this news even more concerning is that the Arctic is warming faster than anywhere else on earth.

And, as the ocean gets hotter, more methane gets pumped into the atmosphere.

It's all happening fast and Box thinks things could change very rapidly, "I may escape a lot of this, but my daughter might not. She's 3 years old."

This news comes as giant sinkholes discovered in Siberia have been linked to changing temperatures on the planet.

The holes are forming as long-frozen permafrost thaws due to increased heat, the earth around it then collapses.

And given the right conditions, some scientists are concerned that something similar could happen in other places around the globe.

Carolyn Ruppel, chief of the U.S. Geological Survey's Gas Hydrates Project, told NBC News, "Global warming is happening, and it's exacerbated in the Arctic. [*sic*]

"And if these craters are related to permafrost thaw, it's a very visible effect of what's happening to the Earth."

Figure 2.3 Article by Dave Snelling, 8 August 2014, online version, *Daily Star*

We will analyse this article with respect to its macrostructure (macro-analysis), its microstructure (micro-analysis) and its context (context analysis). Before starting this analysis, however, we provide an overview of the basic analytical tools for the specific (micro-)analysis of the discourse about climate change by adapting the heuristic questions and strategies presented above. They are summarized in Table 2.2 (the right-hand column contains some excerpts from the online article and the postings).

Table 2.2 Important categories for the analysis of discourses about climate change

Discursive strategies	Purpose
Nomination strategies:	**Discursive construction of social actors:**
How are persons, objects, phenomena, events, processes and actions related to climate change named and referred to linguistically?	• *proper names*: Jason Box/Dr. Box, Carolyn Ruppel, Svante Arrhenius • *deictics and phoric expressions*: I, we, you, they • *generalizing anthroponyms*: humans, folks • *professional anthroponyms*: professor, scientists • *relational anthroponyms*: my daughter, your kids, mother nature • *ideological anthroponyms*: oil billionaire, my own countrymen

Discursive strategies	Purpose

	• *collectives, including metonymic toponyms*: man, our species, human race, fossil fuel industry, carbon corporations
	• *economic anthroponyms*: taxpayers
	• *anthroponyms referring to geopolitical units*: Europeans, Russians
	
	Discursive construction of objects/phenomena/events:
	• *concrete*: world/Earth/planet, sea floor, ocean, Arctic, iceberg, Siberia, methane, (methane) gas, bubble, carbon dioxide, greenhouse gases, atmosphere, permafrost, sunshine, sunstorm, tsunami, eruptions, meteor, surface
	• *abstract*:
	  ○ *natural/environmental*: nature, climate, stuff, greenhouse effect
	  ○ *mental object/feelings*: thought, threat, fear, worrying
	  ○ *economic matters*: agrarian economy, agrarian society, carbon tax scheme, fossil-fuel industry, credit card
	  ○ *political matters*: green taxes, regulation/measure, precautionary principle, emission reduction scheme, welfare
	  ○ *ideological matters*: fantasy religion, enlightment [sic], 'end-of-the-world' announcement
	
	Discursive construction of processes and actions:
	• *material*:
	  ○ *natural/environmental*: climate change, global warming, Earth warming, greenhouse effect, emissions, release of methane, equilibrium, collapse
	  ○ *economic*: repaments [sic], consumption
	• *mental*: discovery, reasoning, thinking, belief
	• *verbal*: announcement, response, Lalalalala

Predication strategies: What characteristics, qualities and features are attributed to social actors, objects, phenomena/events and processes?	**Discursive characterization/qualification of social actors, objects, phenomena, events processes and actions** (positively or negatively): • *social actors*, e.g. we (= humans): fucked, all going to die, ignorant, not needing to keep paying all these green taxes, not deserving the Earth, being in the same boat, not knowing what we can do unless we try • *natural/environmental processes*, e.g. climate change: leading to the end of the world/to collapse, having devastating effects, reaching an alarming rate
Argumentation strategies: What arguments are employed in discourses about climate change?	**Persuading readers of the validity of specific claims of truth and normative rightness:** • *claims of truth* regarding the existence, causes, effects and avoidance of climate change • *claims of rightness* regarding human action related to climate change
Perspectivization strategies: From what perspective are these nominations, attributions and arguments expressed?	**Positioning speaker's or writer's point of view and expressing involvement or distance:** • *ideological perspectives*: neoliberal and capitalist-consumerist, apocalyptic (doomsday-oriented)

(Continued)

Table 2.2 *(Continued)*

Discursive strategies	Purpose

Mitigation and intensification strategies:
 	
Are the respective utterances articulated explicitly, are they intensified or mitigated?
	Modifying the illocutionary force of utterances in respect of their epistemic or deontic status:
	
	• *epistemic*:
	  o *mitigation*: fallacy of scientific uncertainty
	  o *intensification*: 'If even a small fraction of Arctic sea floor carbon is released, we are f'd' (but at the same time mitigation by the omission of letters for the four-letter word)
	
	• *deontic*:
	  o *mitigation*: 'the Arctic has been ice free numerous times in the past and yet we are here. I wouldn't worry too much.'
	  o *intensification*: hasty generalization ('If it doesn't level off then – yes – we are all going to die')

First, we identify the main discourse topics of the text. Most of them relate to the processes and (potential) effects of global warming. They are:

- the end of the world
- the terrifying scientific discovery of huge quantities of Arctic methane gas
- methane as one of the most dangerous greenhouse gases
- the warming of the atmosphere
- the fast and disconcerting warming of the Arctic
- methane leaking from the seafloor under the Arctic
- methane getting pumped into the atmosphere
- the warming of the ocean
- the thawing of long-frozen permafrost
- escaping the effects of global warming (scientist and his daughter).

These main discourse topics are closely interrelated.[11] They are not explicitly connected to fields of political action, since nowhere in the text do we find an overt reference to policy and politics. However, they have implicit political implications, because they refer to utterances of scientists (climatologists) such as Jason Box and Carolyn Ruppel, who pursue political aims resulting from their scientific work: these scientists want to warn everybody about the (potentially) negative consequences of anthropogenic global warming. This political implication is not apparent in Snelling's text, which is fatalistic in tone, but it can be inferred from the readers' background knowledge, based on intertextual and interdiscursive experience, and from the postings following publication of the article.

The text is primarily located within the field of the formation of public attitudes, opinion and will, and within the field of political control ('political' in a wider sense that transcends the area of professional policy and reaches into the 'private' life of individuals who consume goods and cultivate a specific lifestyle). This characterization results from the functions of mass media such as newspapers. They serve the constitution of a public that allows for the exchange and discussion of opinions. In addition, they establish a platform for political control, protest and critique. Furthermore, and this aspect is relevant for the present case, they follow their own 'logic' of news values, of receiving and keeping the attention by presenting sensational, negative and unexpected events and mixing information with entertainment (Street 2001).

The journalist is asking whether the end of the world is nigh. Thus, he is connecting the discourse about global warming (= discourse A) to an apocalyptic discourse about the end of the world (= discourse B). More specifically, he is mixing the registers of a scientific language, a tabloid sensationalist and hyperbolic media language and a colloquial, quite vulgar slang.

The macrostructure of the article consists of a combination of description, explanation and argumentation. The description and explanation are not oriented towards a precise and clear scientific representation (as the topic might suggest), but rather deliver an exaggerated and strongly evaluative report. Correspondingly, the argumentation is not composed of a concise sequence of arguments leading to a sound conclusion, but rather of a list of similar arguments leading to a fallacious overall claim ('end of the world?') (see also below).

With respect to its generic macrostructure, the multimodal newspaper text contains eight elements:

- bipartite title
- one-line lead
- identification of the author by his full name and date of publication
- line with six hyperlinks for readers (recommended for Facebook, Twitter, share on google+, share on one of 12 [iconically indicated] media, mail, print)
- coloured picture of a spherical cap of the globe (probably depicting the Arctic zone) and a steaming atmosphere above this cap
- main text consisting of 19 sentences that are not segmented into paragraphs
- insertion 1 into the text: insertion of a tweet with a small portrait photograph (colour representation)
- insertion 2 into the text (this insertion is not represented in Figure 2.3): insertion of a red-coloured quotation and professional data about the quoted person (the scientist Jason Box).

The article with its eight functional sections is embedded within the layout of an online newspaper that has the hyper-function of a communication portal. The text environment includes a series of advertisements on the left and a series of announcements for 'more stories' with lucid short headings and voyeuristic photographs (often of half-naked women). The thread consists of 24 postings.

The text itself (without the two insertions) consists of 370 words, 37.5% of the text, i.e. 139 words, consists of quotations. This high level of discourse representation in the form of direct speech serves – among other things – to legitimize the content of the text by scientific authority. The quotations are sometimes listed one after the other without being framed by verbs of saying. Twice, closing quotation marks are missing, and intertextual research implies that the quotations are not always reproduced literally. This points to a lack of journalist accuracy. The last observation already links the macro-analysis to the micro-analysis and the context analysis.

Analysis of the microstructure (micro-analysis)

In this pilot study, we can only address a few aspects of the text's microstructure: a small number of nominations, predications and perspectivizations as well as the overall argumentation, with respect to the text and the picture.

The picture shows (visually 'nominates') a spherical cap of the earth, probably the Arctic with a cover consisting of white-coloured ice and Greenland on the left. This segment of the globe is characterized – via visual predication – as a strongly warming zone with a steaming atmosphere. The process of warming is symbolized – also metaphorically – by the red and orange that cover most of the atmosphere. Reading the picture from left to right – according to social semiotics (Kress and van Leeuwen 2006) – the left part with the blue planet represents 'the given' (the present) that develops into 'the new' (the future). The new is represented by the big red and orange zone as well as the bright aura and radiating vectors running from the surface of the globe more or less vertically to the top. The picture thus states that the Arctic zone is undergoing a drastic process of warming. The caption emphasizes this statement: 'GLOBAL WARMING: The Earth is heating at an alarming rate'. Linking it to the content of the text, the radiating steam could also symbolize the greenhouse gases (particularly methane and carbon dioxide) rising from the Arctic seafloor into the atmosphere. It is important to note that the picture has not been produced within any context of scientific research. The highly suggestive ready-made picture has been intentionally chosen from the image-company Getty as the small caption indicates (the respective link is http://cache3. asset-cache.net/xt/174694000.jpg?v=1&g=fs1|0|EPL|94|000&s=1, accessed on 22 August 2014). It is important to consider in respect of the context analysis that nowadays journalists frequently resort to generic pictures offered by globalizing media industries such as Getty (Machin and van Leeuwen 2007). However, such a prefabrication clearly contradicts the potential news value of novelty and might seriously undermine the journalist's credibility.

A propos credibility: the trustworthiness of the journalist (who is not necessarily the author of the title) could be perceived as challenged by the title of the article: 'END OF THE WORLD? Top scientist reveals "We're f*****!"'. Here, the two most important social actors of the text are mentioned, i.e. the scientist Jason Box, who is presented as a top scientist in a positive way, and the 'we-group', which is supposed to extend referentially to the global level of all (living) human beings. The globalizing interpretation can co-textually be inferred, if 'we' is connected with 'world', mentioned in the first part of the title. 'The world' is one of the most important objects that are discursively constructed in the text, together with 'methane gas'. Three predications can be identified in the bi-partite title: the 'scientist' is attributed the quality of being 'at the top', 'the world' is attributed the feature of possibly being close to its terminal stage, and the 'global-we' is attributed the characteristic of being fucked, i.e. of being in the midst of unfortunate and inevitable circumstances. The journalist's credibility should be challenged because the scientist's rude predication of 'being fucked' (the rudeness is mitigated by substitution of the five letters 'ucked' by five asterisks) was originally embedded into a conditional if–then formula. The 'if' part of this formula does not appear in the title. Further, it is obvious that the scientist's statement does not allow a conclusion as to whether the end of the world is imminent or not. Only sloppy journalism can construe such an untenable claim (the claim is intensified by the capital letters in addition to the bold style) from what the scientist actually wrote (see below). In this sense, the title contains an argument from authority that assumes the character of a fallacious reference to a 'top scientist'. In other words: we are confronted with the fallacy of an *argumentum ad verecundiam* that goes: 'Since a top scientist says "we are fucked", the question arises as to whether the end of the world is approaching.' This argumentation violates the pragma-dialectical rule of using plausible argumentation schemes as well as the rule of correct reference to the previous discourse, since the scientist's standpoint is misrepresented, i.e. oversimplified. The structure of the argumentation can be explicated as follows:

Argument:	Top scientist reveals 'We're f*****!'
Conclusion rule:	If a top scientist says 'We're f*****!', the question arises whether the end of the world is approaching.
Truth claim:	We have to ask whether the end of the world is approaching.

In this argumentation, the conclusion rule does not guarantee the transition from the first premise (argument) to the claim. The conclusion rule cannot be backed up by the scientist's statement, which the journalist has distorted in his discourse representation. The claim itself is mitigated by the journalist's decision to select an interrogative speech act and not an assertive speech act.

It is the vulgar language use by the scientist ('we're fucked') that is certainly one of the main reasons why the journalist quotes Jason Box. The sexual metaphor 'to be fucked', literally denoting sexual domination and figuratively meaning 'to be in serious trouble with far-reaching consequences', does not belong to the register of scientific language use. Thus, its contrast to the 'serious' language of science seems to work better for tabloid journalists. The contrast between such a metaphor and 'normal' scientific language use also exists in the semantic vagueness of 'to be fucked' and the expectation that academic language would be more precise. There is considerable scope for interpretation with respect to the meaning of the 'four-letter word'. The verb is semantically open and does not specify the consequences of the Arctic greenhouse gases potentially rising into the atmosphere. The drastic, but vague vulgarity follows a discursive intensification strategy. Its use may result from the scientist's desire to use everyday language that resonates with 'normal' people in order to stress the relevance of the problem and the urgency of finding a solution. These motifs are, of course, comprehensible, since climatologists have been warning for many years about the terrible and threatening effects of global warming. However, the price of such drastic metaphors is semantic under-determination. Thus, we are confronted with the problem of communicating scientific knowledge to the greater general public. A more adequate way of communication should allow for a compromise between the highly complex scientific information and simplistic representations that are susceptible to misinterpretation and – as in the present case – alarmist exaggeration.

Alarmist exaggeration can also be detected in the short lead: 'TERRIFYING discovery could see the Earth warming to devastating levels in just a few years'. Here, the overstatement is even more intensified by the capital letters of the evaluative and fear-mongering predication 'terrifying'. Interestingly, 'discovery' is personified as a sensual perceiver of global warming in the near future that could have destructive effects. Thus, any social actors behind this alleged finding are linguistically backgrounded. Consequently, the journalist does not need to refer to scientists, who most probably would not subscribe to this alarmist over-statement, even though the statement is mitigated by the subjunctive ('could') and a modal verb with a middle deontic degree ('can').

The main text after the suggestive Getty image contains 19 sentences. It starts with a focus on the most important social actor of the text, Jason Box, who is represented as an important scientist (by the predication 'a leading figure on climate change'). This focus serves the further development of the argument from authority in the title. The emphasis on the leading role of the scientist functions as backing that aims to support the argument from authority. Then, the scientist's rude word choice is repeated and identified as a tweet on Twitter. After the fifth sentence, this tweet is also visualized as multimodal insertion 1. When deconstructing the tweet from 29 July 2014, we are able to detect that – before the insertion of the tweet – the journalist had twice decided to delete the 'if' part of the tweet, which originally stated: 'If even a small fraction of Arctic sea floor carbon is released to the atmosphere [...]'. However, this if-clause is reproduced in the seventh sentence, but not correctly. It is informative and an important procedure in the DHA to compare the original with the direct speech reproduced by the journalist. It reads as follows: 'Even if a small fraction of the Arctic carbon were released to the atmosphere, we're f**ked.' Obviously, five differences can be observed in the recontextualization of the tweet: (1) The order of the first two words has been reversed. (2) The definite article 'the' has been inserted. (3) The specification of the carbon ('sea floor') has been deleted. (4) The mood has been changed from indicative ('is') to subjunctive ('were'). (5) The euphemistic deletion 'f'd' is partly annulled ('ke' is inserted) and partly marked ('**'). It is quite surprising that a journalist changes so much in such a short direct quotation, especially within the given context, where every reader has the possibility to compare the literal wording reproduced in insertion 1 with the journalist's wording. More evidence for the rather hasty production of the article is probably also the omission of the closing quotation marks in sentences 10 and 18.

The eight direct quotations in the text all serve to support the argument from authority. However, Box also refers to another authority in order to develop his argument. This source is mentioned in the third sentence. Box made his rude remarks 'after a team of scientists made an alarming discovery'. In sentences 5, 6 and 7, the discovery is specified. Vast amounts of methane gas, which is one of the most potent greenhouse gases, seem to be leaking from the seafloor under the Arctic and rising into the atmosphere; this may contribute to the warming of other parts of the world at an alarming rate. That the consequence of this process may be very dramatic is expressed in sentence 7 by the already analysed quotation of Box. In sentence 7, the journalist indicates the source of his quotation: the 'Motherboard'. Following this intertextual reference, the reader might notice that the quotations in sentences 8, 9, 10, 11 and 14 are all taken from a text written by Brian Merchant (see http://motherboard.vice.com/read/if-we-release-a-small-fraction-of-arctic-carbon-were-fucked-climatologist, accessed on 27 August 2014). The four quotations in sentences 8, 9, 10 and 11 are listed sequentially, without any framing by a verb of saying. In these quotations, the climatologist Box explains to the interviewer Brian Merchant, from the website 'Motherboard', that methane is 20 times more potent than CO_2 in contributing to the greenhouse effect and that this new source of methane plumes reaching the surface and then rising into the air in Arctic zones should make 'us' (= global we) concerned. Sentences 12 and 13 intensify these concerns by arguments presented in indicative, thus seemingly conveying facts. These arguments emphasize that the Arctic is warming faster than any other zone on earth and that the ocean, in becoming hotter, would lead to more methane in the atmosphere. In sentence 14, the journalist again refers to Box, who is alleged to think that these processes are rapid and everything could change quickly. The focus on the temporal dimension is maintained and specified by a quotation with a personal character: Box himself may not be affected by many of these processes and their effects, but his 3-year-old daughter may have to face them. Linking this statement to the content of the lead, we notice a contrast with respect to the temporal predication. Box introduces the time measure of a biological generation ('my daughter'), the lead speaks about devastating levels of global warming in just a few years. This text-internal contradiction is not diluted. The focus on it highlights the fallacious character of the alarmist lead and title.

In sentences 15 and 16, the argument from example, which until now has focused on the Arctic, is extended to other examples. First, the focus is shifted to huge sinkholes in Siberia that are forming because the long-frozen permafrost is thawing due to global warming (and releasing greenhouse gases) and the earth around the permafrost collapsing – it is assumed that this process will accelerate the heating of the earth in the future. The two sentences remain without any expert actors who could be quoted as epistemic authorities, i.e. sources of this scientific knowledge. In sentence 15, the 'news comes' (utterance autonomization), the sinkholes are 'discovered' and 'have been linked' (double passivation). The explanation in sentence 16 is formulated from an apodictic standpoint. Then, in sentence 17, the argument from example is continued and scientists come into play again as sources of knowledge. They are quantified vaguely as 'some scientists' who are concerned that similar developments might materialize in other regions around the globe. Neither the reference to the scientists nor to other places is put in concrete terms. The last two sentences (18 and 19) are dedicated to a second climatologist identified by name: Carolyn Ruppel. This geologist is quoted twice by reference to her contribution to the American broadcasting network NBC. The quotation functions as an authoritative general summary of the main topic of the article.

To sum up briefly: the most important phenomenon in the text is 'global warming' caused by the rise of greenhouse gases into the atmosphere, particularly of methane gas in addition to carbon dioxide in the Arctic, in Siberia and probably also in other regions of the world. This complex process is primarily qualified with predications such as being 'dangerous', 'alarming', 'devastating in just a few years', 'becoming faster', 'soon reaching a natural tipping point', 'exacerbating in the Arctic' and 'inescapable for future generations represented by "my daughter"'. The text is not dealing with the question of to what extent global warming is actually caused by human behaviour. Nor does it deal with the political dimension of the problem or its possible solution.

The various predications and nominations identified in the microanalysis are relevant elements of the text's argumentation structure. They are linked to and form the basis for the argumentation schemes. With respect to argumentation, the text is highly alarmist, particularly at the beginning, mostly in the title and the lead.

The overall structure of argumentation is a mix of causal arguments supported by arguments from authority and arguments from example. In sum, the text forms a fallacious causal scheme termed *argumentum ad consequentiam*. It goes: '*Since the top scientist Jason Box as well as other scientists warn us against the huge quantities of greenhouse gases which are leaking from the sea floor under the Arctic as well as other regions of the world and rising into the atmosphere, thus contributing to global warming, the question has to be asked whether the world is in danger of soon being destroyed or not.*'

This causal fallacy contains an implicit fallacy of composition that violates the pragma-dialectical rule of logical validity in combination with a slippery-slope fallacy that violates the rule of using appropriate (causal) argumentation schemes. The generalizing fallacy of composition goes: If something (the collapse) is true for some parts of the world, it is true for the whole world. The slippery slope fallacy goes: If an initial cause arises, a chain reaction will be triggered that leads to an all-encompassing effect (i.e. if a new source of potent and harmful greenhouse gases is accelerating global warming, the whole world may be destroyed).

The overall structure of the argumentation schemes can be formally represented as follows:

1 Argument from authority (general pattern)

Argument: Leading scientists (Box, Ruppel etc.) say X.

Conclusion rule: If leading scientists say X, then X is true.

Claim: X is true.

Title (fallacy of *argumentum ad verecundiam*)

Argument: Top scientist reveals 'We're f*****!'

Conclusion rule: If a top scientist says 'We're f*****!', the question arises of whether the end of the world is imminent.

Truth claim: We have to ask whether the end of the world is imminent.

Sentences 1–3

Argument: After the scientists' discovery in the Arctic, Box uses an obscene metaphor to depict serious consequences following that discovery.

Conclusion rule: If a top scientist counters the expectation not to use a negative vulgarism when talking about his topic, the topic he is talking about must be very serious.

Truth claim: The topic is very serious.

2 Causal schemes (= part of X)

Argument: Cause C.

Conclusion rule: If cause C, then effect E.

Claim: Effect E.

Sentences 4 and 5

Argument: Huge quantities of Arctic methane are leaking into the atmosphere.

Conclusion rule: If huge quantities of Arctic methane leak into the atmosphere, this will contribute to global warming.

Truth claim: The huge quantities of Arctic methane will contribute to global warming.

Sentences 5 and 8

Argument: Methane traps far more heat than other gases, such as CO_2.

Conclusion rule: If methane traps far more heat than other gases, such as CO_2, methane is one of the most dangerous greenhouse gases.

Truth claim: Methane is one of the most dangerous greenhouse gases.

Sentences 4 and 11

Argument: Arctic methane seems to be leaking to the surface.

Conclusion rule: If Arctic methane is leaking to the surface, it becomes a new source of heat-trapping gases.

Truth claim: Arctic methane seems to have become a new source of heat-trapping gases.

(Continued)

(Continued)

Sentences 4 and 11

Argument:	Arctic methane may be making it to the surface and will become a new source of heat-trapping gases.
Conclusion rule:	If Arctic methane makes it to the surface and becomes a new source of heat-trapping gases, we need to worry about this.
Rightness claim:	We need to worry about Arctic methane (possibly) making it into the atmosphere.

Sentence 12

Argument:	The Arctic is warming faster than elsewhere in the world.
Conclusion rule:	If the Arctic is warming faster than elsewhere in the world, this news about Arctic methane is even more worrying.
Truth claim:	This news about Arctic methane is even more worrying.

Overall fallacy (slippery slope fallacy and fallacy of composition)

Argument:	Many newly discovered greenhouse gases leaking into the atmosphere in several places in the world are accelerating global warming.
Conclusion rule:	If many greenhouse gases leaking into the atmosphere in several places in the world are accelerating global warming, we have to ask whether the end of the whole world is imminent.
Truth claim:	We have to ask whether the end of the whole world is imminent.

3 Argument from the illustrative example

Conclusion rule:	If X is the case in many regions of the world, then effect E will be strong.
Argument:	X is the case in the Arctic. X is the case in Siberia. X is also the case in other regions of the world.
Claim:	Effect E will be strong.

Conclusion rule:	If heat-trapping gases reach the surface and get into the atmosphere in many parts of the world, the heat-trapping effect will be strong.
Argument:	Heat-trapping gases are leaking into the atmosphere in the Arctic. Heat-trapping gases are leaking into the atmosphere in Siberia. Heat-trapping gases are leaking into the atmosphere in other regions of the world.
Claim:	The heat-trapping effect will be strong.

What do we learn from this overview? Had the journalist Dave Snelling avoided constructing the three fallacies of *argumentum ad verecundiam*, slippery slope and generalizing composition, the article could have had a sound argumentation structure.

Analysis of the context (context analysis)

At several points in the previous macro- and micro-analyses we could not avoid focusing on the context of the discourse fragment. This was the case for the analysis of intertextual and interdiscursive relationships, especially with respect to the argumentation analysis. Thus, the macro-, micro- and context analyses have to be seen as interdependent.

The systematic argumentation analysis within the framework of the DHA also focuses on the content of argumentation in a sequence of discourse fragments belonging to the same discourse, e.g. a discourse about climate change. The analysis of typical content-related topoi and fallacies depends on the macro-topics of a discourse. There is an impressive amount of literature dealing with field- and content-related argumentation schemes in various discourses (see, for example, Kienpointner 1996; Kienpointner and Kindt 1997; Kindt 1992; Reeves 1983; Wengeler 2003). In the present context, we refer to several topoi discussed elsewhere, but we would also have to coin new topoi and fallacies should they occur in our data.

When looking at the 24 postings in response to the online article, we identify argumentation schemes that are repeatedly employed in mass-mediated discourses on climate change. Here, we mention only two of them:

- The *argument from nature* (topos or fallacy of nature) is frequently employed from a sceptical perspective in order to challenge the existence of anthropogenic climate change or the negative effects of global warming: Since nature/natural processes shows/show a cyclical or recursive character of rising and falling temperatures, 'we' do not have to worry (too much). Accordingly, a commentator writes: 'the Arctic has been ice free numerous times in the past and yet we are here. I wouldn't worry too much.'
- The *argument from ignorance* (topos or fallacy of ignorance) stresses the lack of (scientific) understanding of the issue under discussion. A special version

of this argument scheme is realized – together with an argument from comparison – in a sceptical posting that emphasizes that, already, former apocalyptic predictions or prophecies were proven wrong: 'Not another "end-of-the-world" announcement! We've recently been told that a super solar sunstorm is going to end the world. We've been warned of a meteor that will devastate the earth, and then there are tsunami, eruptions, and heaven knows what else that the scientists will scare the living daylights out of us and end life as we know it ON TOP OF ALL THOSE!'

A thorough case study would certainly benefit from detailed analysis of the online postings and conduct reception research, in order to detect which arguments on the topic in question ('climate change') are important in this context (see Angouri and Wodak 2014). In the present case, several commentators accept the apocalyptic tone of the article, especially the most active poster who produces six (some very long) comments (one of these has been deleted and is no longer visible on the website). They seem to come to terms with their alleged fate. Two of them draw the hedonistic conclusion that the best way of dealing with the approaching catastrophe is not to care what happens when 'I am out of the way' (e.g. 'to apply for as many credit cards as possible!! Repaments [sic] won't be a problem if were [sic] all going to cook!' and 'So enjoy your lives folks – the scientists would have us all giving up the ghost!!'). Two other posters are more fatalistic. They claim that – if one looks at the way people treat each other – 'man' does not deserve to live. However, there are also a few voices that at least partly deconstruct the fallacious arguments in Snelling's text. They either (1) stress that the development will not lead to the end of the world, but only to a major setback for 'our civilization' or emphasize (2) that 'mother nature will win all the time as it will just reset it self [sic] and evolve again over millions of years', or claim (3) that the expected negative consequences will not materialize as fast as suggested by the article. Only one commentator explicitly challenges defeatism: 'I might not be getting any younger, but we never know WHAT we can do unless we try – but most important you should never just give up' (see the Appendix).

Due to space restrictions, we cannot continue with our analysis. We would, however, like to indicate which features we would investigate in a larger study. For example:

- intertextual and interdiscursive relationships, e.g.:
  - How does the text relate to other texts in the specific issue of the newspaper and to former texts on 'global warming' in the *Daily Star*?
  - What other discourse fragments on the topic have been published by the social actors and communication platforms mentioned in the article (e.g. by Snelling, Box, Ruppel, Motherboard), but also by the online commentators (at least one commentator seems to post regularly on the topic of global warming).

o How does the text relate to others texts on global warming published in the online version of the newspaper? Which [parts] of these texts have also been published in the printed version, and which not?

- the tabloid format of the newspaper (regular and irregular features with respect to its multimodal and multimedia realization on the internet)[12]
- the genre of a tabloid and its positioning (from this analysis we would learn that this tabloid usually neglects explicit political issues, which might be the reason why the fatalistic tone dominates)
- the circulation of the print and online version of the newspaper
- the *Daily Star*'s relationship to other newspapers in Great Britain
- the author of the text (e.g. Are there other texts by the same author dealing with global warming?)
- the consequences of the postings as a genre (virtual identities, restricted space to answer, interactive functions, type of moderation, type of hierarchical organization of postings, etc.; see Dorostkar and Preisinger (2012)
- the wider social, political, economic, psychological and historical context of the discourse on global warming in Great Britain, in the European Union and on a global level (NN 2013).

However, we have to interrupt our pilot analysis here. In sum, we conclude that Dave Snelling's argumentation is fallacious, though it could easily be transformed into a rather sound argumentation, if the fallacies of *argumentum ad verecundiam*, slippery slope and composition were substituted by sound arguments.

Step 6: Detailed case studies

This step consists of detailed case studies on the macro-, meso- and micro-levels of linguistic analysis, as well as on the level of context. This step would allow interpreting the different results within the social, historical and political contexts of the discourse(s) under consideration.[13]

In the present case, this step would lead to general descriptions of the discourse about climate change in respect to:

- social actors and fields of political action
- communication obstacles and misunderstandings
- contradictory validity claims imbued by political or ideological orientations
- salient topics and discursive features
- aspects of historical change
- interdiscursive relationships, particularly overlaps with other discourses (such as discourses about globalization, migration, economy or freedom/liberalism).

The overall interpretation would, for example, consider the question of whether the mass-mediated discourse(s) on climate change and global warming resemble(s) the discourses in the USA until 2005, where company lobbying frequently led to a 'balance as bias' in media coverage: the prevailing scientific consensus on the anthropogenic influence on global warming was not represented adequately in the media. In contrast, media coverage seemed to suggest that scientists do not agree on this issue.[14]

The overall interpretation could further refer to research by Weingart et al. (2008) and Viehöver (2003/2010) on various discourses about climate change. Viehöver investigated media coverage from 1974 to 1995. On the basis of this comprehensive case study, he distinguished between six 'problem narratives' about global climate change and its definition, causes, (moral) consequences and possible reactions to it. According to Viehöver, these 'narratives' gained different salience at different times; currently, the predominant 'narrative' seems to be the 'global warming story'. 'Stories' competing with this 'narrative' were and still are 'the global cooling story', 'the story of a climatic paradise', 'the story of cyclical sunspots', 'the story of climatic change as scientific and media fiction' and the 'story of a nuclear winter' (see Viehöver 2003/2010).

Step 7: Formulation of critique

Our 'critique' is based on ethical principles such as democratic norms, human rights, the principle of empathy with socially disadvantaged groups of people and criteria of rational argumentation (Reisigl 2014). It points to intentional bias(es) in representations (especially media coverage) and to contradictory and manipulative relationships between discourses and power structures.

In a theoretical sense, the critique – based on our empirical analysis and a theory of discursive/deliberative democracy – offers analytical parameters that evaluate the 'quality' of public political discourses in which 'collective' learning and decision-making are at stake.

In a practical sense, the critique could – we hope – influence current discourses about global warming and raise the awareness of involved social actors about the problem and fallacious argumentation schemes.

Step 8: Application of the detailed analytical results

The application of analytical results is based on the formulation of critique. The application should not only consist of the scholarly publication of the results. In addition, we think that our insights should also be made accessible to the 'general public' (e.g. via recommendations, newspaper commentaries, training seminars, radio broadcasts and political advising). Such knowledge 'transfer' requires the recontextualization of theory, methodology, methods and empirical results into other genres and communicative practices. This is, of course, a challenging task for academics not used to writing in an accessible way.

Summary

The strengths of the *discourse-historical approach* include:

- its *interdisciplinary orientation*, which allows avoiding disciplinary restrictions;
- the *principle of triangulation*, which implies a quasi-kaleidoscopic approach to the research object and enables grasping many different facets of the object under investigation;
- its *historical analysis*, which allows focusing on the diachronic reconstruction and explanation of discursive change;
- *practical application* of the results for emancipatory and democratic purposes.

The DHA – like any inter- or multidisciplinary enterprise – should avoid the combination of theoretically incompatible approaches. This caveat remains one of the main theoretical challenges. Furthermore, many complex social phenomena (such as the one discussed in the present chapter) need to be investigated in more systematic and detailed ways in the future.

Further reading

Reisigl, M. (2014) Argumentation analysis and the Discourse-Historical Approach: A methodological framework. In: C. Hart and P. Cap (eds), *Contemporary Critical Discourse Studies*. London: Bloomsbury. pp. 67–96.
Reisigl, M. and Wodak, R. (2001) *Discourse and Discrimination: Rhetorics of Racism and Antisemitism*. London: Routledge.
Wodak, R. (2011) *The Discourse of Politics in Action: Politics as Usual*, 2nd rev. edn. Basingstoke: Palgrave.
Wodak, R. (2014) Political discourse analysis – distinguishing frontstage and backstage contexts: A discourse-historical approach. In: J. Flowerdew (ed.), *Discourse in Context*. London: Bloomsbury. pp. 522–49.
Wodak, R. (2015) *The Politics of Fear: What Right-wing Populist Discourses Mean*. London: Sage.
Wodak, R., De Cillia, R., Reisigl, M. and Liebhart, K. (1999/2009) *The Discursive Construction of National Identity*. Edinburgh: Edinburgh University Press.

Tasks

1. Design a pilot study that should explore 'the discourse about austerity'. Choose some editorials in important broadsheets and analyse the various arguments (topoi and fallacies) and underlying ideologies informing the articles in detail.
2. Choose a recent parliamentary debate in your country which focuses on issues of security and migration. Analyse the different for and against arguments related to immigration and the manifold ways these are expressed in statements, speeches and polemic/agonistic struggles. How do these arguments (content-related topoi) relate to various political parties and speakers? Explore the recent sociopolitical context informing the respective debate.

3. Choose a recent interview with an important politician on TV prime-time news and analyze a question–answer sequence. Which discursive strategies can be identified? Can various blame-avoidance strategies be detected? What are the main arguments put forward by the interviewee and interviewer? Relate the interview to respective political issue(s) and discourse(s) it belongs to.

Appendix: 24 postings

1	Commentator 1
	I would like to see all human life die we dont deserve the earth ... Look how we treat it and each other ...
	3 replies to 1
2	Commentator 2 (reply 1 to 1)
	So basically you are saying you would like to see yourself die?
3	Commentator 3 (reply 2 to 1)
	Commentator 11 [anonymized by M.R. and R.W.] – We may not deserve the earth, as you put it, but it's the only planet we've got to live on. If a catastrophe hits, we'll all be in the same boat, so to speak, and I for one do not intend to lie down and play doggo!!
	I might not be getting any younger, but we never know WHAT we can do unless we try – but most important you should never just give up. :)
4	Commentator 4 (reply 3 to 3)
	Speak for yourself, i'm not the one murdering my own countrymen over a fantasy religion, unlike some people i could mention!
5	Commentator 3
	Not another 'end-of-the-world' announcement! We've recently been told that a super solar sunstorm is going to end the world. We've been warned of a meteor that will devastate the earth, and then there are tsunami, eruptions, and heaven knows what else that the scientists will scare the living daylights out of us and end life as we know it ON TOP OF ALL THOSE!
	WHAT ARE WE SUPPOSED TO DO? COWER IN FEAR AND SPEND OUR LIVES WORRYING ABOUT SOMETHING THAT WE CANNOT DO ANYTHING ABOUT??
	If the end comes, it will come – there isn't ONE LITTLE THING that any of us can do to prevent what happens. So enjoy your lives, folks – the scientists would have us all giving up the ghost!!
	1 reply to 5
6	Commentator 5 (reply 1 to 5)
	No – the solar storm would only wipe out most of our electronic systems.
	Again, our civilisation would suffer a major set back and probably billions would die. I mean it's hard to run a global agrarian economy without computers and phones. But we wouldn't all die and society would eventually recover I suspect.
	And of course we could get struck by a meteor at any time – it's realy not a question of if but 'when'. Might not be for another 50 million year or it could be within a century. Who knows? Certainly not you – that much is obvious.
	But with regard to the methane cathrates – we DO have a choice. We could switch to carbon free power sources as soon as humanly possible. Something we should have begun doing 40 years ago when it first became obvious what was happening to the climate. In fact we should have started taking it into account way back in 1896 when Svante Arrhenius first demonstrated that CO_2 increases would warm the Earth.

	So we CAN do something about this particular threat. It's up to us if we wan't to use carbon fuels more than we want the human race to survive. Myself I'm not particularly bothered one way or the other.
7	Commentator 6
	i be-leave this story mother nature will win all the time as it will just reset it self and evolve again over millions of years but humans will not see it as we be with the dinosaurs
8	Commentator 7
	[this comment has not always been visible on the website, M.R. and R.W.]
	Politicians are refusing to look at near-zero CO2 plans, that can prevent any more warming. The first of it's kind was self-funding, generating self billion a year, and can be seen at: http://www.kadir-buxton.com/page2.htm
9	Commentator 8
	we are all going to die captain meanwearing dont panic dont panic dont panic lol
	2 replies to 9
10	Commentator 3 (reply 1 to 9)
	sunshine - That's chuckle time. Lol
11	Commentator 5 (reply 2 to 9)
	Yep – we are all going to die. Well – probably about 90% of our species anyway. It depends if we get a runaway greenhouse effect from the release of the methane or if it levels out at some now equilibrium. Frankly – we just don't know.
	If it doesn't level ot then – yes – we ARE all going to die.
	Luckily most of us are too ignorant to even realise this yet.
	I'll give it another 30 years before we start seeing the collapse – but then again – no-one really knows.
12	Commentator 9
	Im off to apply for as many credit cards as possible!! Repaments wont be a problem if were all going to cook!
	2 replies to 12
13	Commentator 3 (reply 1 to 12)
	Ron007 – Won't the cards melt?
14	Commentator 5 (reply 2 to 12)
	It's going to take at least another 20 years or more before large regions of the world become uninhabitable and probably at least a century before most of humanity has died off so I wouldn't be too quick to apply for those credit cards.
15	Commentator 10
	This might be the thing to happen because MAN has done this to his world – Look at the way people treat each other they DO NOT deserve to live – So if nature takes over then all well and good they deserve it AND they will NOT listen and change their ways
16	Commentator 11
	Ok then no need to keep paying all these green taxes, give us it all back before it's too late to enjoy it.
	1 reply to 16
17	Commentator 5 (reply 1 to 16)
	Personaly I would rather have some of the 520 billion dollars per year that goes to subsidise the fossil fuel industry. But that's just me.

(Continued)

(Continued)

	And by the way – a carbon tax is fiscaly neutral so unless you are an oil billionaire you would get a rebate under a carbon tax scheme.
	That's the whole point – but of course the carbon corporations dont want you to know that.
18	Commentator 12
	Still, at least it will kill all those man-eating spiders, rats, killer wasps etc and all the nasty diseases ... that are not going to happen either!
19	Commentator 13
	[this comment has not always been visible on the website, M.R. and R.W.]
	This would be a headline news and front page if it was true and backed up, yet this is just a typical Daily Star article to create fanfare ... no reliable scientific evidence backs these claims.
20	Commentator 14
	The truly sad part about all this is that Dr. Box truly believes the end is nigh. Alas, the Arctic has been ice free numerous times in the past and yet here we are. I wouldn't worry too much.
	You have a greater chance of slipping in the shower and dying than being released from this mortal coil because of climate change.
	1 reply to 20
21	Commentator 5 (reply to 20)
	[this comment has been removed, M.R. and R.W.]
	No – what Dr Bos actualy said – and it's right there in front of you in black and white if you notice – is that 'if even a small part of the methane is released then were' f*****d'
	And that is perfectly true. It's a big 'if' I'll grant you that. But at the moment it is being released as the sea off the north of Siberia warms and the sea off the north of Siberia has been steadily warming for decades now so it's not likely that it will suddenly reverse that trend any time soon.
	In fact the northern hemisphere sea surface temperatures are currently at a new record high of 1.47C above the the already warm 1980 to 200 average and the seas north of Scandinavia are currently at 3C above that average. And rising.
	And of course the last time the Arctic was ice free was 120,000 years ago and there was no global human civilisations of billions of people based predominately at less than 20 feet above sea level.
	So – big difference there.
	And your analogy of chance is waaay out I'm afraid. Over 100,000 Europeans and Russians alone have already died as a result of climate change in the last decade alone – mainly during the 2003 and 2010 heat waves.. I'm sure your response to that fact will be to yell 'Lalalalala I can't hear you' but that doesn't change the facts.
	The laws of physics dont give a damn who you vote for or what you think and believe.
	CO2 levels rise – the Earth warms.
	Always has – always will.
	Whether you think billions dying is a big deal or not – the laws of physics couldn't care less.
22	Commentator 5
	No – it won't 'end the world' but it will destroy most of the trappings of civilisation. Pretty obvious really.
	Our civilisation took thousands of years to build up based on the last 7,000 years of a relatively stable climate and progress in agricultural techniques.
	If the Earth warms by 3C or more by the end of the century then our agricultural system will only be able to support about one billion people.

	I don't really care as I won't be here but your kids will witness the deaths of billions of people (if they live) and the collapse of agrarian society. Maybe you don't think that's a big deal but I expect your kids might.
	And make no mistake – this methane release is probably the most important bit of news on the planet today. If it does continue – and I don't know of any mechanism that can prevent it – then he is perfectly correct – we're f****d!
23	Commentator 15
	Where I live, during the ice age, this place was full of icebergs … Now,!!! It's full of, Goldgerg's, Bloombergs's, Mossberg's, Sternberg's etc. !!!!!!!!!
24	Commentator 16
	who cares!!

Notes

1 See Horkheimer and Adorno (1991 [1969; 1974]); Habermas (1996).
2 See Reisigl and Wodak (2001: 32–5), Reisigl (2003: 78–82), Reisigl (2011: 483–7) for extended discussions.
3 In three of the eight fields, we distinguish between attitudes, opinions and will. This distinction emphasizes differences in the emotional, cognitive and volitional dimensions.
4 The very first critical study which inspired the development of the DHA was the project on postwar antisemitism in Austria (Wodak et al. 1990).
5 Many of these strategies are illustrated in Reisigl and Wodak (2001). In this chapter, we primarily focus on nomination, predication and argumentation strategies.
6 See also Forchtner and Tominc (2012), Boukala (2013), Reisigl (2014) and Wodak (2014, 2015b).
7 The concept of 'validity claims' is already discussed in Habermas (1972: 137–49). He introduces four types of validity claims: the claim of truth, the claim of normative rightness, the claim of sincerity and the claim of understandability.
8 See IPCC (2013: 13–19). See also Rahmstorf and Schellnhuber (2012) and Latif (2012).
9 The question of 'representativity' is a tricky one. In general, 'representativity' refers to the ability of a random sample to mirror the structure of the totality of data (which can hardly ever be delimited in the social sciences). Many discourse studies do not rely on such a statistical criterion of 'representativity'. Rather, they refer to 'representative data' in the sense of 'typical cases' within a more or less well-defined corpus. All in all, the concept of 'representativity' is not operationalized in a clear way, and thus of minor importance for the majority of empirical research on discourse. The data in our case study are not representative.
10 See, for instance, Boykoff (2011), Carvalho (2005, 2008), Carvalho and Burgess (2005).
11 For the concept of 'topic of discourse', see van Dijk (1980: 44ff.).
12 Visual and multimodal argumentation in discourses about climate change is becoming more and more important in critical discourse studies. See, for example, Sedlaczek (2012, 2014).
13 See, for example, Muntigl et al. (2000), Reisigl and Wodak (2001) and Wodak et al. (2009) for such comprehensive studies.
14 See Boykoff (2011), Boykoff and Boykoff (2004), Oreskes (2004) and Oreskes and Conway (2010).

3

CRITICAL DISCOURSE STUDIES: A SOCIOCOGNITIVE APPROACH

TEUN A. VAN DIJK

CONTENTS

Keywords

discourse, critical discourse studies, sociocognitive approach, cognition, mental model, ideology, knowledge, context, racism, anti-racism, Brazil

Terminology and definitions

This chapter introduces the sociocognitive approach in critical discourse studies (CDS), more traditionally called critical discourse analysis (CDA). I avoid the term CDA because it suggests that it is a *method* of discourse analysis, and not a critical *perspective* or *attitude* in the field of discourse studies (DS), using many different methods of the humanities and social sciences.

The critical approach of CDS characterizes scholars rather than their methods: CDS scholars and their research are sociopolitically committed to social equality and justice. They are specifically interested in the discursive (re)production of power abuse and the resistance against such domination. Their goals, theories, methods and data and other scholarly practices are chosen as academic contributions to such resistance. CDS is more problem-oriented than discipline-oriented, and requires a multidisciplinary approach.

A critical approach to discourse presupposes an ethics. Its research may conclude that some forms of dominant text or talk are unjust or illegitimate, for instance because they violate human and social rights. For example, sexist or racist discourse may be found to flout basic norms and values of gender and ethnic equality and justice.

The Discourse–Cognition–Society triangle

Within the broader framework of critical discourse studies my sociocognitive approach to discourse is characterized by the Discourse–Cognition–Society triangle.

Whereas all approaches in CDS study the relations between discourse and society, a sociocognitive approach claims that such relations are cognitively mediated. Discourse structures and social structures are of a different nature, and can only be related through the mental representations of language users as individuals and as social members.

Thus, social interaction, social situations and social structures can only influence text and talk through people's interpretations of such social environments. And conversely, discourse can only influence social interaction and social structures through the same cognitive interface of mental models, knowledge, attitudes and ideologies.

For most psychologists such cognitive mediation is as obvious as it is fundamental. Yet, many interactionist approaches to discourse today still tend to be as anticognitivist as behaviorism many decades ago, while limiting their analysis to what is believed to be directly 'observable' or socially 'available'. Such an empiricist limitation ignores that grammatical and other discourse structures, and especially the semantic, pragmatic and interactional ones, are not observable at all, but language users' cognitive representations or inferences from actually occurring discourse or conduct. Indeed, language users not only act (communicate, talk, write, listen, read, etc.), but also *think* when they do so.

A triangular sociocognitive account of racist discourse

The relevance of a triangular sociocognitive approach may be illustrated with reference to the study of racist discourse. First of all, the discursive component of the theory deals with the many structures of racist text and talk, such as specific topics, negative descriptions of minorities or immigrants, disclaimers, the lexicon and other grammatical structures, topoi, argumentation or metaphors, among many other structures of ideological polarization between 'Us' and 'Them'. Secondly, such discourse structures are interpreted and explained in terms of underlying, socially shared ethnic prejudices and racist ideologies and the ways they influence the mental models of individual language users. Thirdly, such discourses and their underlying cognitions are socially and politically functional in the (re)production of ethnic domination and inequality by white dominant groups against minority groups or immigrants. They are controlled by powerful symbolic elites and organizations, e.g. those of politics, mass media and education, who have privileged access to public discourse. Each of these components of the theory and the analysis is necessary to account for racist discourse in society. We shall show below that a similar triangular approach is necessary for the study of racism and anti-racism.

An example: Racist propaganda in the European Parliament elections of 2014

In the elections for the European Parliament (EP) in 2014 many political parties, and not only at the extreme right, more or less blatantly engaged in racist and xenophobic propaganda to win votes. In Britain, the United Kingdom Independence Party (UKIP), for instance, used billboards such as in Figure 3.1.

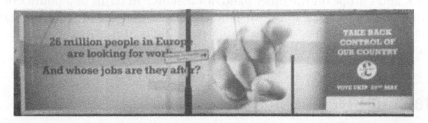

Figure 3.1   Election billboard used by UKIP in the 2014 European Parliament elections

A critical sociocognitive analysis of this billboard will first analyse its **discursive and semiotic structures**, such as the strategic use of numbers (*26 million people*), rhetorical questions (*whose jobs are they after?*), commands or recommendations (*take back, vote*), possessive pronouns (*our country*), on the one hand, and the image of a finger pointing at the readers and different colours on the other hand. Part of such a discursive-semiotic analysis is the study of the implied and implicated meanings of this propaganda, namely that the unemployed in Europe (which in the UK means the European mainland) are after British jobs, an implication semiotically expressed by the finger pointing at *you*, readers of the billboard in the UK. Similarly *our country* contextually refers to Britain, and *take back* presupposes that 'we' have lost control of 'our' country.

Already in this brief discourse analysis of the billboard the very interpretation of this message requires various **cognitive structures**. For instance, the message does not make sense without shared *sociocultural knowledge*, for instance about current unemployment in the UK and the arrival of many immigrant workers from (mostly) Eastern Europe, as well as the ongoing debate on immigration and the claims of the Right that such immigration is out of control. The billboard also expresses a xenophobic *attitude* of UKIP, featuring, among many other norms and values, that British workers should have priority over foreign workers. This attitude is based on a more fundamental racist *ideology* polarizing ingroups and outgroups, and enhancing the superiority or priority of (ethnic) ingroups, also in many other social and political domains, and specified in many other xenophobic or racist attitudes – such as associating immigrants or minorities with crime.

Finally, these discursive and cognitive structures function as such in the communicative **interaction** between UKIP and readers of the billboard, especially (white) British citizens, as addressed by the deictic expression *our* (*country*), as it is based on the context model (see below) of the participants, featuring the Setting (Time: expressed by the date of the elections – *22nd May*; Space: expressed by *our country*), Participants (and their identities: UKIP, British citizens), Actions (election advertising and the commands *take back*) and Aims (getting votes for UKIP). The context model of readers in the UK may also feature emotions such as anger or fear. This advertising action of UKIP, at the level of **societal and political macrostructures**, is a form of organizational communicative action (propaganda) of a political party, part of a political system, and as part of a state (the UK) and an organization of states (the European Union) and its organization (the European Parliament), on the one hand, and of white dominant racism in the UK and Europe on the other hand, for instance in terms of a politics of fear.

After this very brief analysis (summarizing *How to do sociocognitive critical discourse analysis*) let us now examine these three different dimensions of a sociocognitive analysis of discourse in more detail.

The cognitive component

While less generally recognized to be crucial, as is also the case in CDS studies, let us pay special attention to the cognitive component of the sociocognitive approach to discourse. Such a component deals with the mind, memory and especially with the cognitive processes and representations involved in the production and comprehension of discourse.

Cognitive structures

Memory. Memory or Mind, as implemented in the brain, is usually divided into Working Memory (WM) – also called Short Term Memory (STM) – and Long Term Memory (LTM). LTM itself features remembrances of autobiographical experiences and knowledge stored in Episodic Memory (EM), on the one hand, and more general, socially shared knowledge, attitudes and ideologies in Semantic Memory (SM), on the other hand.

Mental models. Our personal experiences, as processed in Working Memory, are represented as subjective, unique, individual *mental models*, stored in Episodic Memory. Such mental models have a standard hierarchical structure of a spatiotemporal Setting, Participants (and their identities, roles and relations), Actions/Events, and Goals. Such categories also appear in the semantic structures of the sentences that describe such experiences. Mental models are multimodal and embodied. They may feature visual, auditory, sensorimotor, evaluative, and emotional information of experiences, as differentially processed in different parts of the brain.

Social cognition. Whereas mental models are personal and unique, human beings also have various forms of socially shared cognitions. Thus we all have generic and abstract *knowledge* of the world, shared with other members of the same epistemic community. And as members of specific social groups, we may also share *attitudes* (e.g. about abortion, immigration or the death penalty) or more fundamental *ideologies*, such as those of racism, sexism, militarism or neoliberalism, or opponent ideologies such as those of antiracism, feminism, socialism, pacifism or environmentalism. Our personal experiences are interpreted, and hence construed and represented as mental models, on the basis of these various forms of social cognition. Hence, unique, personal mental models may be more or less similar to those of other members of the same community or group. These crucial features of human cognition allow cooperation, interaction and communication, and hence discourse.

Discourse processing

Discourse is strategically produced and understood on the basis of these cognitive structures. Its words, phrases, clauses, sentences, paragraphs or turns are sequentially processed in WM and represented and controlled by the mental models, knowledge (and sometimes ideologies) in LTM.

We distinguish between two types of mental model in discourse processing:

a. **Situation models** represent the situation a discourse is *about*, refers to and hence may also be called **semantic models**. Thus, the UKIP poster is about the upcoming EP elections. These models account for the personal meaning or interpretation of discourse and define its meaningfulness and (local and global) coherence. Mental models are more complex and complete than the meaning explicitly expressed in discourse, because language users are able to infer relevant aspects of a situation model by applying their shared knowledge.

b. **Context models** ongoingly represent the dynamically changing communicative situation or experience *in which* language users are ongoingly involved. As all mental models, they are subjective and hence represent how each participant understands and represents the communicative situation. They define the *appropriateness* of discourse with respect to the communicative situation, and therefore may also be called **pragmatic models**. They not only control what information of the situation model (e.g. a personal experience) can or should be appropriately talked about, but especially also *how* this should be done. Indeed, we tell about the same experience (and hence the same mental model), for instance of a break-in, in a different way (or style) to our friends than to the police.

Thus, we have seen above what the parameters of the probable context models of the Participants (UKIP, UK citizens) of the propaganda billboard are (Setting, etc.). At the same time, this context model defines the *genre* of the billboard as a form of political election propaganda. These parameters of the context models of discourse participants can be established by the analysis of indexical expressions (such as *our country* or *22nd May, vote UKIP* in the UKIP text) referring to Setting, Participants, Actions and Aims of the communicative situation, as well as of speech acts (commands and advice: *Vote!*) and the analysis of *relevant* sociopolitical structures in which such political propaganda functions (elections, etc.).

This is why *understanding* text or talk involves a strategic process in which units of sentences and discourse are sequentially analysed and interpreted in WM in terms of semantic structures related to an underlying situation model in EM. Conversely, the *production* of discourse about a personal experience starts with a situation model of which pragmatically relevant information is selected for the semantic structure of a discourse, under the control of the context model – which also controls *how* such meanings are appropriately formulated and in what discourse *genre* (a conversation, an e-mail, a lecture, news report or police report).

Knowledge

The basis of all cognition, and hence of all thought, perception, understanding, action, interaction and discourse, is the system of knowledge accumulated during our lifetime, and as shared by the members of epistemic communities. Although the precise overall organization of the knowledge system is still unknown, it is assumed to be locally organized by hierarchical categories of concepts and schemas of different types, such as scripts of everyday episodes, schemas of objects, persons or groups of people, and many more. Knowledge is defined as beliefs that meet the (historically developing) epistemic criteria of each community, such as reliable perception, discourse or inference.

Generic, socially shared knowledge is 'instantiated' (applied) in the construction of personal mental models that represent our individual experiences, perceptions and interpretations of events and situations. It is partly acquired and extended by the generalization and abstraction of these mental models, by discourses about such experiences (stories, news) as well as by pedagogical and expository discourse that expresses such knowledge directly, for instance in parent–child discourse, textbooks or the mass media.

The relations between knowledge and discourse are crucial for both: Most of our non-experience-based knowledge is acquired by discourse, and the production and comprehension of discourse requires vast amounts of socially shared knowledge. Many structures of discourse require description and explanation in epistemic terms, as is the case for the topic-focus articulation of sentences, (in) definite articles, evidentials (indicating the source of our knowledge), implications, implicatures, presuppositions, argumentation, among many others.

Since knowledge of participants is crucial for all discourse processing as well as for all talk in interaction, its use is part of the communicative situation. Hence, context models have a special *knowledge device* (K-device), which at each moment of discourse processing 'calculates' what knowledge is (already) shared by the recipients, and hence is common ground that may be presupposed, and which knowledge or information is (probably) new, and hence needs to be asserted. This K-device controls the vast number of epistemically relevant structures of discourse mentioned above.

Especially relevant for CDS is that knowledge is a power resource. Some groups or organizations in society have privileged access to specialized knowledge and may thus manipulate or otherwise control public discourse and the subsequent actions of others. Thus, in the billboard analysed above, UKIP uses knowledge about unemployment statistics in the EU to manipulate UK citizens, e.g. by the implication that all those millions of unemployed would want to come to the UK and take jobs there.

Attitudes and ideologies

Whereas social knowledge is defined as beliefs shared by all or most members of epistemic communities or cultures, there are forms of social (often evaluative) beliefs that are only shared by specific groups: attitudes and ideologies. Thus, most people know what abortion or immigration is, but some groups may have different attitudes about them — for instance as being good or bad, prohibited or allowed, depending on their underlying ideologies.

Although the precise mental structure of such socially shared attitudes is still unknown, it is likely that they are also schematically organized, as is the case for most of our beliefs. For instance, an attitude about immigration may feature beliefs about the identity, origin, properties, actions and goals of immigrants, their relations with 'our own' group, each associated with positive or negative evaluations based on norms and values. Thus UKIP propaganda uses a xenophobic attitude about foreigner unemployed 'taking *our* jobs'.

Attitudes tend to be based on or organized by more fundamental ideologies that control the acquisition and change of more specific attitudes. Thus, a racist ideology may control negative attitudes about immigration, affirmative action, quotas, ethnic diversity, cultural relations and many more.

As is the case for much social cognition, we still ignore the precise mental organization of ideologies, but some of their general categories often appear in ideological-based discourse: identity, activity, goals, relations to other groups and resources or interests. These are all crucial for the social definition of groups, and especially of Us vs Them, a polarized structure controlling power abuse, domination, competition and cooperation among groups, as well as all ideological discourse.

General ideologies, as well as their more specific attitudes, also control the personal experiences, that is, the mental models of the members of ideological groups. And if these (biased) models control discourse, they are often expressed in polarized ideological discourse structures. Hence, in such ideological discourse we may observe a positive representation of 'Our' group, and a negative representation of the 'Others' — always depending on the communicative situation, that is, our context models — at all levels of text or talk: topics, lexicon, descriptions, argumentation, storytelling, metaphors and so on. The UKIP billboard does just that: the Others are represented as a menace to Us.

The relevance of the cognitive component

From the brief summary of personal and social cognition we may already conclude that the cognitive component is crucial for a theory of discourse in general, and for critical studies in particular. Power and power abuse, domination and manipulation, as well as all other illegitimate forms of discourse, interaction and communication are rooted in social structure and relations between social groups. Yet, in order to explain how such complex societal structures influence the actual structures of text and talk, and vice versa, we need cognitive mediation. Such mediation is defined in terms of the shared knowledge and ideologies of group members and how these influence mental models that finally control the structures of individual discourse. If discourse were directly dependent on social structure, instead on mediating (personal and social) cognitive representations, all discourses in the same social situation would be the same. Semantic and pragmatic models, thus, define the uniqueness of all text and talk.

Since underlying cognitive structures in many ways are expressed in, or control, discourse structures, detailed discourse analysis may in turn be used as a valid and sensitive method for the assessment of such cognitive structures, for instance in cognitive and social psychology and the social sciences. Such a method is not circular, because underlying cognitive structures are not only manifest in discourse but also in other social practices, such as discrimination, exclusion or violence. Also, such cognitive structures may remain implicit (as is the case for much knowledge) or be transformed in text and talk – depending on the context models of the participants. For instance, racist ideologies and attitudes are not always expressed in discourse, or they may be strategically adapted or denied in specific communicative situations, for instance in disclaimers ('I am not a racist, but ...!).

The social component

Obviously, the critical study of discourse needs an important social component. We are dealing with power abuse of dominant groups or the resistance of dominated groups, as well as with organizations, institutions, enterprises and nation states, among other societal macrostructures. In CDS we are especially interested in the groups and organizations that directly or indirectly control public discourse, as well as their leaders, the Symbolic Elites, for instance in politics, the mass media, education, culture and business corporations.

Part of this societal account of discursive domination and resistance has been formulated in terms of *social cognition*, that is, as the specific knowledge, attitudes and ideologies shared by the members of these societal organizations.

A more sociological approach focuses on the micro-level of everyday interaction of social members on the one hand, and on the macro-level of the overall structures and relations of groups and organizations on the other. For instance, much of the information we read in the paper or see on television depends on the internal organization of news production within media organizations on the one hand, as well as on the relations between such corporations and the government, political parties or social groups, on the other hand.

Such high-level societal macrostructures are actually implemented and reproduced by the everyday actions and interactions of their members at the basic micro-level of the social order. And much of such local (inter-)actions are carried out by text and talk.

The overall structure of the sociocognitive account of the relations between discourse, cognition and society may now be summarized in Table 3.1.

Table 3.1 The organization of the sociocognitive approach of discourse

Level of structure	Cognition	Society
Macro	Socially shared knowledge, attitudes, ideologies, norms, values	Communities, groups, organizations
Micro	Personal mental models of (experiences of) social members	Interaction/discourse of social members

Power and domination

Since CDS is specifically interested in the critical analysis of discursive power abuse or domination, we briefly need to define these complex concepts of the social component of the theory.

Power and domination are here defined as a specific relationship of *control* between social groups or organizations – and not as a property of interpersonal relations. Consistent with the overall system presented here, such control has a social and a cognitive dimension: control of the actions (and hence discourses) of dominated groups and their members, on the one hand, and control of their personal and socially shared cognitions – mental models, knowledge, attitudes and ideologies – on the other.

Discourse plays a pivotal role in the exercise of power. It is like any other social action that may control (members of) dominated groups, for instance by laws, commands and prohibitions, as well as their discourses. But discourse also expresses social cognition and may thus 'manage the minds' of other groups and their members.

Group power is based on material power resources, such as property or capital, and also on symbolic power resources, such as knowledge, status, fame and access to public discourse. In ethnic relations, such symbolic power resources may be skin colour, origin, nationality or culture.

We see that in the definition of the crucial notion of power we again need the three main components of the theory: (i) society defined in terms of controlling groups and organizations at the macro-level, and members and controlling interactions at the micro-level; (ii) cognition in terms of the personal mental models of members, or the shared knowledge and ideologies of groups and organizations; and (iii) discourse of members of groups or organizations as forms of controlling interaction and as expression and conducive of underlying personal and social cognition.

Whereas power in general may well be legitimate, for instance in democratic societies or between parents and children in families, CDS is more specifically interested in **power abuse** or **domination**. Such a 'negative' social relationship of power may be defined in terms of legitimacy, and the violation of social norms and human rights. This typically involves that control is in the *interest* of the powerful group, and against the interest of the less powerful group. Thus, racism is a social system of domination that favours the interests of white (European) people and that is against the interests of non-white (non-European) people.

The discourse component

Whereas the details of the cognitive and social components of the theory presented here need to be specified in cooperation with psychologists and sociologists, the discourse component is obviously the main task of critical discourse analysts. These often also need to establish the relations with the other components — as is also the case for linguists in their research in psycho- and sociolinguistics.

Critical discourse analysts do not need their own theory of the *structures* of discourse, which they may largely share with other discourse analysts. However, they typically go beyond such structural theories of discourse. They also describe and explain how discourse may be involved in the (re)production of power abuse, or against such domination, in society. In the approach presented here, this also involves a cognitive component that is necessary to account for the role of knowledge, attitudes and ideologies in such discursive domination.

Structures of discourse

While not specific for CDS, we shall be brief about the structural account of discourse. Such an account was initially formulated as an extension of structural, functional or generative grammars of the phonological, morphological, syntactic and semantic structures of sentences. For instance, it was shown that the intonation or syntax of sentences may depend on the structure of previous sentences or turns of text and talk.

More specific of such text or discourse grammars was the account of semantic local and global coherence of a discourse, for instance in terms of functional relations between its propositions (such as generalization or specification) on the one hand, and semantic macrostructures on the other. In a later stage, however, it was found that a fundamental notion such as coherence could not be accounted for only in terms of relations between propositions (meanings), but needed to be formulated in terms of the mental representation of what a discourse is about: mental models. For instance in such a mental model a causal or temporal relation between events may be represented and thus provide a basis for the local coherence of the discourse based on such a model.

After this early grammatical account of discourse structures beyond the level of the sentence, many other theories of discourse have introduced a host of other structures and strategies that cannot be described in terms of the usual linguistic categories of grammar. Thus, many genres of discourse have their own, overall schematic organization (or superstructure), with specific categories, as is the case for stories, news items in the press or scholarly articles, such as Summaries (Headlines, Titles, Abstracts, Announcements, etc.), Introductions or Orientations, Complications, Interesting Events or Experiments, and Resolutions, Commentary and Conclusions or Coda — depending on the genre. Similarly, argumentative genres, such as everyday debates, scientific articles, or editorials, may feature various kinds of Arguments and Conclusions.

Conversation Analysis introduced the specific units, structures and strategies of talk in interaction, such as turns, side sequences, topics, various forms of organization (e.g. how to start or terminate a conversation, or change topics) and how each turn or segment of talk may be related to previous or next ones, for instance by (dis) agreeing, aligning, or preparation.

In each of these fields, the last decade has seen the development of sophisticated structural accounts of text and talk, far beyond the grammar of sentences of traditional linguistics.

Ideological structures of discourse

More specific for research in CDS is the analysis of those structures of discourse that are specifically involved in the (re)production of power abuse. Since power and power abuse are defined in terms of the relations between social groups or organizations, such discourse generally will be ideologically based. Let us therefore briefly focus on those discourse structures that tend to exhibit underlying attitudes and ideologies of dominant social groups.

If ideologies have the schematic structure of fundamental categories postulated above (Identity, Activity etc.) for the identification of social groups, their properties and their relations (friends or enemies), as well as their interests, we may expect ideological discourses to feature pragmatically controlled expressions of such categories. Here are some of these ideological discourse structures:

- **Polarization**. Underlying ideologies are polarizing between a positive representation of the ingroup and a negative representation of the outgroup. Such polarization affects all levels of discourse.
- **Pronouns**. Language users (including collective ones such as organizations) speaking as members of ideological groups typically use the 'political' pronoun *We* (as well as *us*, *ours*, etc.) to refer to themselves and fellow group members. Similarly they refer to members of other, competing or dominated groups in terms of *They* (*theirs*, *them*). Given the overall polarization between ingroups and outgroups, its pronominal expression is the pair *Us* vs *Them*. Distance or a negative opinion about outgroups may also appear in possessives, such as *Those people ...*
- **Identification**. The main category of group ideologies is their identity. Members of ideological groups ongoingly identify with 'their' group, and express such identification in many ways, e.g. *As a feminist, I/we ... Speaking as a pacifist, I/we ...*
- **Emphasis of positive self-descriptions and negative other-descriptions**. Ideologies are often organized by a positive self-schema. Under the influence of ideological ingroup–outgroup polarization, we may typically expect an emphasis on positive self-descriptions (e.g. in nationalist discourse we typically find glorification of Our country) and an emphasis of negative other-descriptions, for instance in racist or xenophobic discourse. On the other hand Our negative properties (e.g. Our racism) will tend to be ignored or mitigated as is also the case of Their positive properties. This rhetorical

combination of hyperbolic emphasis and mitigation of good or bad things of ingroups and outgroups is called the **Ideological Square**.

- **Activities**. Ideological groups are often (self) identified by what they do, that is what their typical activities are. Hence we may expect that ideological discourse typically deals with what 'We' do and must do, e.g. to defend or protect the group (or the nation), or how to attack, marginalize or control the outgroup.
- **Norms and values**. Ideologies are built on *norms* of (good) conduct, or *values* of what should be striven for, as is the case for Freedom, Equality, Justice, Independence or Autonomy. These may be explicitly or implicitly expressed in many ways in discourse, especially in all evaluative statements about groups of people. They typically also appear in the Aims we want to reach.
- **Interests**. Ideological struggle is about power and interests. Hence, ideological discourse typically features many references to our interests, such as basic resources (food, shelter, and health) as well as symbolic resources such as knowledge, status, or access to public discourse.

For each of these ideological structures and strategies in discourse there may be many local units and moves that express them, depending on discourse genre. For instance, in order to emphasize Our good things and Their bad things, we may use headlines, foregrounding, topical word or paragraph order, active sentences, repetitions, hyperboles, metaphors and many more. Conversely, to mitigate Our bad things, we may use euphemisms, passive sentences, backgrounding, small letter type, implicit information and so on.

The integration of the components

The sociocognitive approach in CDS does not deal with the structures of discourse, cognition and society as independent components. Crucial, both in theory as well as in analysis, is their integration – an important characteristic of multidisciplinary research. Thus, for each discourse structure we not only need an explicit description in terms of a relevant theory, as well as a description of their relations with other structures of the same or different levels. At the same time, such a structure needs to be described and explained in terms of underlying mental representations, such as mental models, knowledge or ideologies, as part of their actual production and comprehension by language users. And finally, the structure and its cognitive basis is accounted for in terms of its sociopolitical or cultural functions in the communicative and social contexts, such as the (re)production of domination or resistance.

Illustration: Immigration as WAVE

A concrete example may illustrate the integration of the three components of the sociocognitive approach.

Much public discourse about immigration, for instance in politics and the media, is replete with metaphors emphasizing the negative aspect of the arrival of many immigrants, such as WAVE. Such lexical items are identified and described as metaphors, which in turn may be related to other metaphors (e.g. AVALANCHE, TSUNAMI, etc.) in the same discourse, or with other negative descriptions of immigrants — as part of a semantic or rhetorical analysis.

Next, such metaphors are cognitively interpreted as expressing underlying concepts, such as 'large quantities of people', represented in the multimodal mental model governing such discourse. At the same time, however, such a model explains the relevance of the metaphor, because it embodies and emphasizes the fear of drowning in so many immigrants. The WAVE metaphor thus cognitively concretizes the more abstract concept of massive immigration.

Finally, the use of such metaphors and their cognitive effects on recipients are not socially or politically innocent. On the contrary, if they indeed cause fear of immigrants among many people, these may develop an anti-immigrant attitude, e.g, by the generalization of concrete mental models of other negative properties attributed to immigrants. As is the case in Europe of the last decades, and especially the European Parliament elections of 2014, such fear and such negative attitudes are strategically used by many political parties to muster votes and to curb immigration. We thus link the use of a metaphor at the local level of discourse, via mental models of experience, with immigration policies and institutional practices of parties and parliament, and the reproduction of xenophobia or racism at the social macro-level.

Whereas discourse analysts may thus focus on some relevant aspect of discourse structure and then search for its discursive relations and functions, its mental basis and its social political functions, social scientists may primarily focus on a social phenomenon or problem, such as ethnic discrimination in many fields of social life. Besides describing the details of everyday discrimination and its links with other social actions, they may then search for an explanation in terms of the underlying ethnic prejudices shared by many people. And, finally, to study and explain the cause of such prejudices they may finally record and analyse discourse among white group members. We now also see in more detail how, via what stages and levels, a complex system of racism is discursively reproduced in society.

Discourses of resistance: anti-racist discourse in Brazil

In much of my earlier work of the last three decades I presented a systematic analysis of racist discourse in Europe and the Americas. To stress that CDS also deals with dissident discourse, the analysis of a concrete example in this chapter will focus on anti-racist discourse. More specifically, I examine some of the discursive strategies of anti-racist contributions to a parliamentary hearing on the Bill for Racial Equality in Brazil.

Racism

As we have seen above, I define racism as a social system of racial or ethnic domination, consisting of two major subsystems: racist social cognition (prejudices, racist ideologies) underlying racist practices (discrimination). Racist discourse is one of the discriminatory racist practices, and at the same time the major source of the acquisition and reproduction of racist prejudices and ideologies. Consistent with a sociocognitive approach, we thus account for racism in terms of the triangular relation between discourse, cognition and society.

The social component of the theory of racism is not limited to an account of everyday discriminatory practices in interaction, whether discursive or non-discursive, at the micro-level. More broadly it identifies the groups and organizations that control the public discourse on immigrants and minorities, that is, the main source of the reproduction of racist attitudes and ideologies. This control, and hence domination, is exercised by the Symbolic Elites, who have privileged access to the influential public discourses in politics, the media, education and business corporations.

Racism in Europe and the Americas has been a dominant system for centuries, legitimating colonialism and slavery in the past, to anti-immigration policies, xenophobia and racist parties in most European countries today.

Anti-racism

Many if not most systems of domination provoke dissent, resistance and opposition, first of all among the dominated groups, and secondly among dissident members of the dominant group. Thus, slavery was opposed, for various (also economic) reasons, by the anti-slavery movement. Colonialism was discredited and opposed by independence movements, as well as by anti-colonialist dissidents, both in the colonies as well as in the metropolis itself.

Anti-racist movements, actions and policies in Europe, today, continue a long tradition of resistance against racist and xenophobic power abuse. They vary from official organizations, such as the Commission for Racial Equality (CRE) in the UK, or the European Commission against Racism and Intolerance (ECRI) of the Council of Europe, to a vast number of grass-roots movements, such as SOS-Racism in France and Spain. Anti-racist aims and values can be found in many official documents, policies and the constitutions of many countries, both in Europe as well as the Americas.

Despite these official anti-racist organizations, discourses and grass-roots movements, however, it would be inconsistent with widespread discriminatory practices and racist prejudices to declare the system of anti-racism to be dominant in Europe and the Americas. Despite official anti-racist discourse, anti-immigrant legislation is increasingly harsh in most European countries, xenophobic and racist parties are getting around 25% of the vote in local, national and European elections, whereas conservative parties and newspapers, eager to compete with the racist extreme right, similarly express and stimulate prejudices against asylum seekers and immigrants.

In the USA, racism has often been declared a thing of the past, but anti-immigrant policies and practices are dominant, as well as a wide array of different forms of everyday discrimination against African and Latin Americans that continue to reproduce white-European hegemony.

The theory of anti-racism

If anti-racism is a system of resistance and opposition, the theory of anti-racism may be formulated in a complementary way to the system of racism. That is, the social system of anti-racism also consists of a subsystem of anti-racist social practices (protests, etc.) based on a subsystem of anti-racist social cognition (anti-racist ideology and anti-racist attitudes). Again, anti-racist discourse is a major anti-racist practice, which also is the way anti-racist cognitions are being acquired and reproduced. Indeed, anti-racism is no more innate than racism, and needs to be learned – largely by text and talk. Anti-racist ideologies – and hence their attitudes and discourses – are also polarized, but in this case the outgroup is defined as 'racist'. Associated to anti-racist ingroups, however, are allies such as the United Nations. The aim is to fight racism and the norms and values feature equality, justice, democracy and so on. As a system of opposition, anti-racism has no other resources than the legitimacy of generally recognized values, such as those of equality, and limited access to public discourse.

Racism in Brazil

Although discriminatory ethnic practices and prejudices in Latin America vary from country to country, for instance as a function of the presence of indigenous people or communities of African descent, white racism imported from Europe and locally adapted and reproduced is dominant. Blacks and indigenous people in Latin America, by any criterion of power, are economically, socially and culturally unequal to the people from European descent.

The same is also true in Brazil, where half of the population is of African descent. Slavery in Brazil was one of the harshest in the Americas, because slave-owners had such a vast supply of slaves that they could work them to death in a few years. Rio de Janeiro was the largest slave market worldwide.

As a consequence, until today, Afro-Brazilians have lower salaries, worse jobs, bad housing, less health care and education and are barely represented in local, regional or federal parliaments, or among judges, professors or the business elites. The ubiquitous telenovelas on TV show few black faces in leading roles. Students in the prestigious public universities are mostly white and mostly come from private (and hence expensive) secondary schools, which most parents of black students cannot afford. Official quotas to remedy such academic inequality may be seen as official forms of anti-racism but are vigorously opposed (e.g. as 'reverse racism' or as 'dividing the country') by much of the press and many academics. As part of the 'war on drugs', the police and military are 'pacifying' the slums, largely inhabited by black people, often with lethal consequences. In sum, Brazil not only is a fundamentally unequal country by social class, but also is characterized by pervasive racial inequality, from the time of the colony and slavery, until today.

Anti-racist discourse in Brazil

Brazil was one of the latest countries in the world to abolish slavery, abolition coming in 1888. Similarly, anti-racist discourse in the twentieth century had a hard time to delegitimize the pervasive myths of 'racial democracy' and 'cordial racism', celebrating the qualities of a 'mixed race' and ignoring the many forms of racial inequality and discrimination. It was only in the 1970s that a Black Movement, partly inspired by the Civil Rights Movement in the USA, began to claim its rights, first mostly in the cultural sphere, but later also in politics and the economy. At the same time quantitative social research finally started to document the facts of the many areas of racial inequality. But we still had to wait until the late 1990s before the government and official organizations and institutions began to formulate and implement policies intended to curb such inequality — such as imposing university quotas for black students.

The debate on the Law of Racial Equality

On 26 November 2007, the Câmara de Deputados held a special plenary session dedicated to the proposed Statute of Racial Equality. The current parliamentary Chair, Arlindo Chinaglia, MP for the State of São Paulo for the governing Partido de Trabalhadores (PT) [Workers' Party], declared the whole parliament to be a General Committee, so that MPs and invited experts could debate about:

> [a] luta do movimento negro; políticas públicas afirmativas nas áreas econômica, social, educacional, da saúde etc.; necessidade de aperfeiçoamento da legislação; mercado e relações de trabalho; sistema de cotas nas universidades públicas; regularização fundiária das comunidades quilombolas; resgate e preservação da memória e da cultura do povo negro no Brasil.

> *[[the] struggle of the black movement, affirmative public policies in the fields of the economy, society, education, health, etc.; [the] necessity to improve legislation; market and labour relations; quota system in public universities; regularization of Maroon communities; [the] recovery and preservation of memory and culture of black people in Brazil.]*[1]

This debate was published in 2008 in a special 81-page publication of the Câmara, a text of about 27,000 words, which serves as our corpus. Participants were not only MPs, but also invited experts and (other) representatives of Afro-Brazilian organizations.

The official focus of the plenary and committee debate was Bill no. 6.264, of 2005, of the Federal Senate, instituting the Statute of Racial Equality. The Bill was presented to the Senate on 11 November 2005 by famous Afro-Brazilian Senator (for the state of Rio Grande do Sul) Paulo Paim (born 1950), author of many political initiatives in favour of the Afro-Brazilian community, member of the governing PT, and just as the (then) president, Luis Ignacio Lula da Silva, originally a union leader and worker in the metallurgical industry.

The Bill itself may also be seen as a form of anti-racist discourse, despite the fact that some of the final amendments toned down some of its original intentions and formulations. The final version of the Statute was formulated in Law 12.288 of 20 July 2010, superseding various other laws, and signed by President Lula. Article 1 (of Title I) reads as follows:

[1]Esta lei institui o Estatuto da Igualdade Racial, destinado a garantir à população negra a efetivação da igualdade de oportunidades, a defesa dos direitos étnicos individuais, coletivos e difusos e o combate à discriminação e às demais formas de intolerância étnica.

[This law establishes the Statute of Racial Equality, which aims to ensure for the black population the realization of equal opportunities, the protection of individual, collective and diffuse rights and to combat ethnic discrimination and other forms of ethnic intolerance.]

The analysis of anti-racist discourse

Within a sociocognitive framework the analysis of the discourse of some of the participants in this debate first of all focuses on characteristic anti-racist discourse structures, such as topics, topoi, arguments, lexicon and metaphors, among others. Secondly, these structures are interpreted and explained in terms of underlying mental models, as well as their sustaining attitudes and ideologies. And finally, the social conditions and functions of such discourse and cognition are formulated as a contribution to the system of anti-racism in Brazil.

We shall ignore here the formal discourse structures that characterize most parliamentary debates and hearings, such a formal presentation of the speakers by the Chair, as well the initial greetings of speakers, mutual compliments and other moves of political politeness. Where relevant, we do examine relevant self-presentations of speakers, since they index their identities as social members and speakers.

Most of our analysis will be semantic, and focuses on topics and local descriptions of events and situations, experiences of Afro-Brazilian people, implications, presuppositions and metaphors, especially those related to underlying attitudes and ideologies.

The pragmatic context models of the speakers will generally be more or less the same, namely the spatiotemporal coordinates of parliament, the current date, the participants and their identities, roles and relations, the aims of the discourses as well as the ongoing action in which they participate. Relevant is also the vast social knowledge of the speakers about racism and inequality in Brazil. Ideologies and attitudes about such racism may, however, be different. Indeed, some speakers oppose the current Bill, although for different reasons. However, we only focus here on the anti-racist speakers, most of which support the Bill.

Self-presentations

Most speakers begin their speech with a self-presentation that tends to focus on their various social identities. Contextually, such presentations have as a primary function the legitimation of their current role as participant in the debate, namely as knowledgeable experts on the topic of racism in Brazil. Implicit or explicit initial self-definition as experts at the same time functions as a form of positive self-presentation and enhances their credibility. Finally, the legitimation also extends to their role of representatives of organizations, and hence as participants in a democratic hearing – e.g. as voices of the Afro-Brazilian community, or its allies. Here are some of these self-presentations:

> [2]... tenho bastante prazer de estar aqui representando o governo federal, na condição de ministra da Secretaria Especial de Políticas de Promoção de Igualdade Racial. (Ministra Matilde Ribeira)
>
> *[... I'm very pleased to be here representing the federal government, in my role of Minister of the Special Secretariat of Policies for the Promotion of Racial Equality.]*
>
> [3]Sou negro, ferroviário há 27 anos, militante do movimento operário e poderia começar a minha intervenção dizendo que estou extremamente feliz hoje porque estou vindo de Curitiba ... (Roque José Ferreira)
>
> *[I'm black, a 27- year-old rail worker, a militant of the labour movement and could start by saying that I am extremely happy today because I'm coming from Curitiba ...]*
>
> [4]Sr. Presidente, é uma grande honra poder representar a Universidade de Brasília ... (Timothy Mulholland)
>
> *[Mr. President, it is a great honour to represent the University of Brasilia ...]*

The self-presentations are couched in the usual politeness formulas (*it is an honour, it is a pleasure*, etc.) and focus on important functions (minister, university rector), on the one hand, and ethnic (black), professional (rail worker), political (militant) and age (27 years old) identities, on the other hand. All three speakers also present themselves as formal or informal representatives of relevant organizations (the government, a workers movement and a university). Hence, they define the still missing part, the identity of the Participant category of the provisional context models of the audience, which will guide the way the hearers will understand and interpret the discourses of the speakers: From a minister, rector or a black, young militant worker, different discourses will be expected.

Group description

Crucial in 'bottom-up' anti-racist discourse, as formulated by members of the Afro-Brazilian community, is the (self) description of the group – expressing underlying collective knowledge. Pragmatically, such fragments do not offer new knowledge, because all participants know the facts of the history of slavery, etc. Rather, they function as reminders and emphasis for the necessity of the current law now under debate – hence such fragments are both semantic (descriptions of the history of race relations in Brazil) as well as pragmatic (defining positions in the ongoing debate). After a brief summary by a black speaker as member (marked by the pronoun *nós* 'us') of the Afro-Brazilian community, also the (white) rector of the University of Brasilia contributes to such a group description, in more academic style (*data show ... marked by exclusion ... the effective enjoyment of ...*):

[5]... o racismo não foi criado por nós, mas pelos brancos. Quando disseram que tínhamos de ser escravos, criaram o racismo. (Luiz Oscar Mendes)

[... racism was not created by us but by whites. When they said we had to be slaves, they created racism.]

[6]Dados apontam com clareza que os brasileiros negros, descendentes de escravos africanos, historicamente foram os mais marcados pela exclusão, sendo mais acentuada a das mulheres negras. Há quase 120 anos da Lei Áurea, ainda temos muito o que fazer para garantir o efetivo gozo da igualdade assegurada pela Constituição Federal. (Timothy Mulholland)

[Data show clearly that black Brazilians, descendants of African slaves, were historically most marked by exclusion, and this is especially the case for black women. Almost 120 years ago the Lei Aurea [abolishing slavery] was adopted, but we still have much to do to ensure the effective enjoyment of equality guaranteed by the Constitution.]

Note that the denial of the speaker in example (5) has interactional functions: it responds to the opponents of the Statute, who argue that its opposition to racism and the self-identification of blacks recognizes 'race' as relevant in policy, and that such a recognition will cause racial antagonism. Thus instead of the assumed conflicts purportedly created by the Statute in terms of 'race' he focuses on what is relevant, namely racism, and the responsibility of the white descendants of Europeans.

Ideological polarization: Us vs Them

The speaker in example (5) already shows that anti-racist discourse is polarized, and especially directed against those who engage in, condone or refuse to act against racism. The same polarization and negation of the opinion of the opposition to the Bill is formulated by the following speaker, formulating in example [7], an **empirical counter-argument** against the denial of current division in terms of the 'apartheid' that can be observed in any city:

[7]Em absoluto, não fomos nós que criamos o racismo; não fomos nós que dividimos nada – a sociedade brasileira é dividida. Qualquer pessoa séria que andar por qualquer cidade do país vai constatar a cisão, vai constatar onde estão os negros e onde estão os brancos. E isso foi promovido pelo Estado. (Paulo César Pereira de Oliveira)

[It was not us at all who created racism; we did not create any division – Brazilian society is divided. Any serious person who would walk through any city in the country will observe the separation and will note where blacks are and where whites are. And that was promoted by the State.]

Although 'branding' others as 'racist' is usually fiercely resisted by anti-antiracists, and also by anti-racists as strategically hardly efficient as a form of persuasion, obviously there are many ways to convey the same by implication and implicature:

[8]Fomos arrancados da África, mulheres foram estupradas, fomos roubados, mutilados, e hoje dizem que não temos de falar em raça, senão vamos dividir o Brasil. Que falácia! Que falácia! O Brasil já foi dividido há muito tempo, desde que nos arrancaram da África e nos trouxeram para cá. Essa é a divisão, e agora não querem pagar a dívida secular que têm conosco (Luis Osmar Mendes)

[We were torn from Africa, women were raped, we were stolen, mutilated, and now they say we should not talk about race, because otherwise we divide Brazil. What a fallacy! What a fallacy! Brazil was divided long ago, since they tore us from Africa and brought us here. This is the division, and now they do not want to pay the secular debt they have with us.]

Thus, through a very concrete and dramatic description of the horrors of slavery, the opponents of the current Bill, merely identified by the pronoun *they* and their current position on the Bill, are negatively described as the ideological descendants of the slave-masters. On the other hand, the Afro-Brazilian ingroup is implicitly represented as the victims or survivors of slavery and as the contemporary victims or survivors of those who oppose the Bill because it allegedly promotes racial division. Besides an expression of the underlying ideological **polarization** between racists and anti-racists, and between black and white, this fragment also contributes to a major **counter-argument** in the argumentation against the Bill (its alleged divisiveness). Also, this argument denounces the **presupposition** of the opposition, namely that there was no racial division before this Bill or the current anti-racist policies of the government. At the same time the argument **implies** that the opposition is denying contemporary racism in Brazil and **implicates** that they are racist. Finally, the pragmatic function of the intervention is to **delegitimize** the opponents.

Norms and values

Anti-racist discourse exhibits the underlying **norms and values** of anti-racist ideologies. Thus, the very name of the proposed Statute features the crucial value of equality – as a major aim – while **presupposing** and then documenting that the current situation in Brazil is marked by racial or ethnic inequality:

[9]O movimento negro brasileiro transformou em uma ferramenta de luta aquilo que foi a causa da sua opressão. Imputaram-nos a pecha de seres inferiores por sermos negros, e o que fizemos? Dissemos: 'Somos negros. Somos negros e somos seres iguais, somos seres diferentes, somos portadores de valores, somos

portadores de uma história'. A partir desses valores e dessa história é que vamos reconstruir nossa existência no mundo. Vamos lutar por igualdade, estamos lutando por igualdade. Estamos lutando hoje aqui, estamos construindo essa igualdade. (Edna Maria Santos Roland)

[The Brazilian black movement turned into a weapon that was the cause of their oppression. They ascribed us the taint of lesser beings because we are black, and what did we do? We said: 'We are black. We are black and we are equal beings, we are different beings, bearers of values, we are bearers of history.' From these values and from this history we will rebuild our existence in the world. Let's fight for equality, we are fighting for equality. We are fighting here today, we are building this equality.]

This intervention combines various ideological-based elements of anti-racist discourse, such as the emphasis of the value of identity, the social group memory of oppression, the self-identity of the community in terms of colour, aims of current action and plans for the future, and so on. The persuasive rhetoric of struggle is at the same time marked by the usual **metaphors**, such as arguments are weapons, and the future of the group as a building.

Norms and values are general and abstract components of underlying ideologies. In more specific attitudes, they need to be translated into more concrete aims and values, as is the case in the following fragment defending the controversial quota policy of the government:

[10]Com efeito, os objetivos das cotas raciais são: a) reduzir as desigualdades raciais quanto ao acesso dos negros (as) ao ensino superior; b) promover a igualdade de oportunidade entre brancos e negros no mercado de trabalho formal; c) concretizar a democracia substantiva; d) dar oportunidade a negros (as) que serão modelos para outros negros das gerações futuras; e) corrigir os eixos estruturantes da reprodução da desigualdade social, isto é, de raça e de gênero. (Antônio Leandro da Silva)

[Indeed, the goals of racial quotas are: a) to reduce racial disparities in access of black men and women to higher education, b) to promote equality of opportunity between blacks and whites in the formal labour market, c) to achieve substantive democracy, d) to provide opportunities for black men and women to be models for other blacks of future generations, and e) to correct the structural axes of the reproduction of social inequality, that is, those of race and gender.]

Thus, equality is specified as reducing differences of access, as equality of students at the (future) labour market, as creating opportunities and as enhancing democracy. As elsewhere in anti-racist discourse, the systematic presupposition of such arguments is that at present there is no equality, equal access, opportunity and democracy for Afro-Brazilians.

Arguments

Debates in parliament are generally argumentative. Speakers defend their own position with arguments, and attack and delegitimize opponents with counter-arguments. We have seen already that one major counter-argument against the argument against the Bill (namely that differentiating between black and white in a largely racially mixed country leads to division and conflict) is that Brazil already was and is racially divided.

Throughout the debate there are, of course, many other argumentative moves, such as:

- **The number-game.** Repetition of the fact that blacks constitute 50% of the population. Numbers of how few black professors there are in the universities. The success of the quota system in terms of numbers of black students participating.
- **International comparisons.** Comparisons with the USA and other countries where quotas have been implemented successfully.

Summary

The sociocognitive approach in critical discourse studies advocates a multidisciplinary, triangular analysis of text and talk integrating a discursive, cognitive and social component. It is critical of CDS approaches that link discourse with society while ignoring the personal mental models of individual experiences and interpretations based on socially shared knowledge, attitudes and ideologies. Thus, the polarized and categorical structure of underlying ideologies also characterizes social attitudes, which in turn influence personal mental models and opinions that finally are expressed and reproduced by discourse.

Thus, a brief analysis of an example of xenophobic propaganda by UKIP (the UK Independence Party) in the UK and anti-racism as a system of opposition against racist domination, for instance in government policies in Brazil, shows how the polarization between Us vs Them (black vs white), as well as basic categories (Identity, Actions, Aims, Norms, Values, Allies/Enemies and Resources) shows in specific attitudes about quotas and finally in a series of discourse structures. The summary of the analysis of the UKIP billboard may be used as a brief *How to do sociocognitive discourse analysis*.

A detailed analysis of the cognitive interface between discourse and society not only provides methodological grounding for many discourse structures, but also explains how discourse is involved in the reproduction of domination and resistance in society.

Further reading

The number of relevant references for this chapter is so high, that I give only some suggestions for further reading on the topics presented in this chapter. (For general references to CDS and other approaches to CDS, see the other chapters of this book.)

van Dijk, T. A. (2008) *Discourse and Power*. Houndmills: Palgrave–Macmillan.
This collection of articles provides a good introduction to the sociocognitive approach, and mainly focuses on political discourse and political cognition, with many examples of critical analyses of racist political discourse, ideology and the definition of power and power abuse.

van Dijk, Teun A. (ed.) (2009) *Racism and Discourse in Latin America*. Lanham, MD: Lexington Books. This edited book features chapters on racism and discourse in Mexico, Colombia, Venezuela, Brazil, Argentina, Chile and Peru, written by local experts. It is the only study in English (translated from the Spanish and Portuguese) on discourse and racism in Latin America written by Latin American linguists and social scientists.

The sociocognitive approach to discourse analysis

van Dijk, T. A. (1998) *Ideology: A Multidisciplinary Approach*. London: Sage.
van Dijk, T. A. (2008) *Discourse and Context: A Sociocognitive Approach*. Cambridge: Cambridge University Press.
van Dijk, T. A. (2008) *Discourse and Power*. Houndmills: Palgrave–Macmillan.
van Dijk, T. A. (2009) *Society and Discourse. How Social Contexts Influence Text and Talk*. Cambridge: Cambridge University Press.
van Dijk, T. A. (2014) *Discourse and Knowledge: A Sociocognitive Approach*. Cambridge: Cambridge University Press.

On (anti)racism and discourse in the UK, Europe and Brazil

Bonnett, A. (2000) *Anti-racism*. London, New York: Routledge.
Guimarães, A. S. A. and Huntley, L. (eds) (2000) *Tirando a máscara. Ensaios sobre o racismo no Brasil*. São Paulo, SP: Paz e Terra.
Twine, F. W. (1998) *Racism in a Racial Democracy: The Maintenance of White Supremacy in Brazil*. New Brunswick, NJ: Rutgers University Press.
van Dijk, T. A. (1993) *Elite Discourse and Racism*. Newbury Park, CA: Sage.
van Dijk, T. A. (ed.) (2009) *Racism and Discourse in Latin America*. Lanham, MD: Lexington Books.
Wodak, R. and van Dijk, T. A. (eds) (2000) *Racism at the Top: Parliamentary Discourses on Ethnic Issues in Six European States*. Klagenfurt, Austria: Drava Verlag.
Wodak, R., KhosraviNik, M. and Mral, B. (eds) (2013) *Right-Wing Populism in Europe: Politics and Discourse*. London: Bloomsbury Academics.

Task

Collect 2014 European Parliament election manifestos and propaganda of a (especially right-wing) political party in your own country, and systematically analyse the relevant structures' discourse fragments dealing with immigration or immigrants, their communicative contexts, their underlying attitudes and ideologies and their sociopolitical functions.

Note

1   The translations of these examples are necessarily approximate and as close as possible to the original. Adequate translation would presuppose detailed knowledge of the social and political situation in Brazil.

4

A DIALECTICAL-RELATIONAL APPROACH TO CRITICAL DISCOURSE ANALYSIS IN SOCIAL RESEARCH

NORMAN FAIRCLOUGH

CONTENTS

Keywords

dialectical relations, explanatory critique, structures and strategies, political analysis, transdisciplinary research

In this chapter I introduce and illustrate a methodology for using a *dialectical-relational* version of CDA in transdisciplinary social research (Chouliaraki and Fairclough 1999; Fairclough 2003, 2006). I begin with a theoretical section explaining the dialectical-relational approach, including my view of discourse, of critical analysis and of transdisciplinary research. In the second section I briefly discuss fields of application of this approach, and in the third section I explain the methodology, presenting it as a series of stages and steps, and identify a number of core analytical categories. In the fourth section I present an example, showing the application of this methodology in researching a political topic, and illustrate the approach to political analysis in the fifth section, with respect to particular texts. The sixth section summarizes what can be achieved with this methodology, and discusses possible limitations.

Theory and concepts

First a terminological point. *Discourse* is commonly used in various senses including (a) meaning-making as an element of the social process, (b) the language associated with a particular social field or practice (e.g. 'political discourse'), (c) a way of construing aspects of the world associated with a particular social perspective (e.g. a 'neo-liberal discourse of globalization'). It is easy to confuse them, so to at least partially reduce the scope for confusion I prefer to use *semiosis* for the first, most abstract and general sense (Fairclough et al. 2004), which has the further advantage of suggesting that discourse analysis is concerned with various 'semiotic modalities' of which language is only one (others are visual images and 'body language').

Semiosis is viewed here as an element of the social process which is *dialectically* related to others – hence a 'dialectical-relational' approach. Relations between elements are dialectical in the sense of being different but not 'discrete', i.e. not fully separate. We might say that each 'internalizes' the others without being reducible to them (Harvey 1996) – e.g. social relations, power, institutions, beliefs and cultural values are in part semiotic, they 'internalize' semiosis without being reducible to it. For example, although we should analyse political institutions or business organizations as partly semiotic objects, it would be a mistake to treat them as purely semiotic, because then we could not ask the key question: what is the relationship between semiotic and other elements? CDA focuses not just upon semiosis as such, but on *relations between semiotic and other social elements*. The nature of this relationship varies between institutions and organizations, and according to time and place, and it needs to be established through analysis.

This requires CDA to be integrated within frameworks for *transdisciplinary* research such as the framework I have used in recent publications, 'cultural political economy', which combines elements from three disciplines: a form of economic analysis, a theory of the state and a form of CDA (Fairclough 2006; Jessop 2004). Transdisciplinary research is a particular form of interdisciplinary research (Fairclough 2005). What distinguishes it is that in bringing disciplines and theories together to address research issues, it sees 'dialogue' between them as a source for the theoretical and methodological development of each of them. For example, *recontextualization* was introduced as a concept and category within CDA through a dialogue with Basil Bernstein's sociology of pedagogy, where it originated (Chouliaraki and Fairclough 1999).

In what sense is CDA *critical*? Critical social research aims to contribute to addressing the social 'wrongs' of the day (in a broad sense – injustice, inequality, lack of freedom etc.) by analysing their sources and causes, resistance to them and possibilities of overcoming them. We can say that it has both a 'negative' and a 'positive' character. On the one hand it analyses and seeks to explain dialectical relations between semiosis and other social elements to clarify how semiosis figures in the establishment, reproduction and change of unequal power relations (domination, marginalization, exclusion of some people by others) and in ideological processes, and how in more general terms it bears upon human 'well-being'. These relations require analysis because there are no societies whose logic and dynamic, including how semiosis figures within them, is fully transparent to all: the forms in which they appear to people are often partial and in part misleading. On the other hand, critique is oriented to analyzing and explaining, with a focus on these dialectical relations, the many ways in which the dominant logic and dynamic is tested, challenged and disrupted by people, and to identifying possibilities which these suggest for overcoming obstacles to addressing 'wrongs' and improving well-being.

The social process can be seen as the interplay between three levels of social reality: social *structures*, *practices* and *events* (Chouliaraki and Fairclough 1999). Social practices 'mediate' the relationship between general and abstract social structures and particular and concrete social events; social fields, institutions and organizations are constituted as networks of social practices (see Bourdieu on social practices and fields; Bourdieu and Wacquant 1992). In this approach to CDA, analysis is focused on two dialectical relations: between structure (especially social practices as an intermediate level of structuring) and events (or: structure and action, structure and strategy); and, within each, between semiotic and other elements. There are three major ways in which semiosis relates to other elements of social practices and of social events – as a facet of action; in the construal (representation) of aspects of the world; and in the constitution of identities. And there are three semiotic (or: discourse-analytical) categories corresponding to these: genre, discourse and style.

Genres are semiotic ways of acting and interacting, such as news or job interviews, reports or editorials in newspapers, or advertisements on TV or the internet. Part of doing a job, or running a country, is interacting semiotically or communicatively in certain ways, and such activities have distinctive sets of genres associated with them.

Discourses are semiotic ways of construing aspects of the world (physical, social or mental) which can generally be identified with different positions or perspectives of different groups of social actors. For instance, the lives of poor people are not only construed through different discourses associated with different social practices (in politics, medicine, social welfare, academic sociology) but through different discourses in each which correspond to differences of position and perspective. I use 'construe' in preference to 'represent' to emphasize an active and often difficult process of 'grasping' the world from a particular perspective.

Styles are identities, or 'ways of being', in their semiotic aspect – for instance, being a 'manager' in the currently fashionable way in business or in universities is partly a matter of developing the right semiotic style.

The semiotic dimension of (networks of) social practices that constitute social fields, institutions, organizations etc. is *orders of discourse* (Fairclough 1992b); the semiotic dimension of events is *texts*. Orders of discourse are particular configurations of different genres, different discourses and different styles. An order of discourse is a social structuring of semiotic difference, a particular social ordering of relationships between different ways of making meaning – different genres, discourses and styles. So for example the network of social practices that constitutes the field of education, or a particular educational organization such as a university, is constituted semiotically as an order of discourse. Texts are to be understood in an inclusive sense, not only written texts but also, for example, conversations and interviews, as well as the 'multimodal' texts (mixing language and visual images) of television and the internet. Some events consist almost entirely of texts (e.g. a lecture or an interview), in others texts have a relatively small part (e.g. a game of chess).

Discourses that originate in some particular social field or institution (e.g. to anticipate the example, neo-liberal economic discourse, which originated within academic economics and business) may be *recontextualized* in others (e.g. in the political field, or the wider educational field). Recontextualization has an ambivalent character (Chouliaraki and Fairclough 1999): it can be seen as 'colonization' of one field or institution by another, but also as 'appropriation' of 'external' discourses, often incorporation of discourses into strategies pursued by particular groups of social agents within the recontextualizing field. For example, the 'transition' to a market economy and Western-style democratic government in the formerly socialist countries of Europe (e.g. Poland, Romania) has involved a 'colonizing' recontextualization of discourses (e.g. discourses of 'privatization') which were, however, incorporated differently into the strategies of new entrepreneurs, government officials, managers of state industries etc. (Fairclough 2006).

Discourses may under certain conditions be *operationalized*, 'put into practice', a dialectical process with three aspects: they may be *enacted* as new ways of (inter)acting, they may be *inculcated* as new ways of being (identities), they may be physically *materialized*, for example as new ways of organizing space, such as in architecture. Enactment and inculcation may themselves take semiotic forms: a new management discourse (e.g. the discourse of marketized 'new public management' which has invaded public sector fields such as education and health) may be enacted as management procedures that include new genres of interaction between managers and workers, or it may be inculcated as identities that semiotically include the styles of the new type of managers.

CDA oscillates as I have indicated between a focus on *structures* (especially the intermediate level of structuring of social practices) and a focus on the *strategies* of social agents, i.e. the ways in which they try to achieve outcomes or objectives within existing structures and practices, or to change them in particular ways. This includes a focus on shifts in the structuring of semiotic difference (i.e. shifts in orders of discourse) which constitute a part of social change, and on how social agents pursue their strategies semiotically in texts. In both perspectives, a central concern is shifting relations between genres, between discourses and between styles: change in social structuring of relations between them which achieves relative permanence and stability in orders of discourse, and the ongoing working and re-working of relations between them which is regarded in this approach to CDA as a normal feature of texts.

The term *interdiscursivity* is reserved for the latter: the interdiscursivity of a text is a part of its intertextuality (Fairclough 1992b), a question of which genres, discourses and styles it draws upon, and how it works them into particular articulations. Textual analysis also includes linguistic analysis, and analysis where appropriate of visual images and 'body language', and these features of texts can be seen as realizing its interdiscursive features.

Fields of application

The dialectical-relational approach addresses the general question: What is the particular significance of semiosis, and of dialectical relations between semiosis and other social elements, in the social processes (issues, problems, changes etc.) which are under investigation? This question is of interest right across the social sciences and humanities, and I would not want to foreclose the range of potentially fruitful fields of application of this approach, nor the range of genres or texts it might be applied to. It is true that certain types of texts would seem to pose particular problems – literary texts, for example – but that is a different matter. In general, I would oppose any view of method that seeks to neatly match methods (methodologies) to fields or text types, or cultivates the view that researchers need to seek the 'right' method for their data and research questions. In short, I would not want to limit in advance the fields of application of the dialectical-relational approach.

The relationship between 'approach' and 'applications' is not a simple one. The dialectical-relational approach in its current form has changed through the process of being 'applied' in various fields. The beginnings of this approach can be seen in my work on discourse and social change in the early 1990s (see especially Fairclough 1992b, 1995a), which itself arose out of earlier work on relations between language, ideology and power (Fairclough 1989/1991). Early applications of that version of CDA included 'marketization' of higher education and the 'enterprise culture' project launched by the Thatcher government, as well as various aspects of political and media discourse (Fairclough 1995b), and 'critical language awareness' in education (Fairclough 1992a). Important theoretical developments arising out of this work were the conceptualization of orders of discourse (a concept used already in Fairclough 1991) as the semiotic dimension of networks of social practices, and development of 'recontextualization' as a CDA category in Chouliaraki's research on classroom discourse (Chouliaraki 1995; Chouliaraki and Fairclough 1999), and the foregrounding of the dialectics of discourse. One application at this stage was to the political discourse of New Labour (Fairclough 2000a). Further theoretical developments arose through exploring neglected semiotic issues in 'critical realism' (Fairclough et al. 2004), and the incorporation of the dialectical-relational approach within 'cultural political economy' (Jessop 2004), which I addressed specifically from a CDA perspective in research on globalization and 'transition' in Central and Eastern Europe[1] (Fairclough 2006).

Methodology

I have referred to a 'methodology' for using a dialectical-relational version of CDA in transdisciplinary social research rather than a 'method' because I see the process as also a theoretical one in which methods are selected according to how the *object of research* (Bourdieu and Wacquant 1992) is theoretically constructed. So it is not just a matter of 'applying methods' in the usual sense; we cannot so sharply separate theory and method. This version of CDA is associated with a *general* method, which I discuss below, but the specific methods used for a particular piece of research arise from the theoretical process of constructing its object.

We can identify 'steps' or 'stages' in the methodology only on condition that these are not interpreted in a mechanical way: these are essential parts of the methodology (a matter of its 'theoretical order'), and while it does make partial sense to proceed from one to the next (a matter of the 'procedural order'), the relationship between them in doing research is not simply that of sequential order. For instance, the 'step' I refer to below of constructing the 'object of research' does need to precede subsequent steps, but it also makes sense to 'loop' back to it in the light of subsequent steps, seeing the formulation of the object of research as a preoccupation throughout. It is also helpful to distinguish 'theoretical' and 'procedural' from the 'presentational' order one chooses to follow in, for instance, writing a paper – other generally rhetorical factors will affect the order in which one presents one's analysis.

The methodology can be seen as a variant of Bhaskar's 'explanatory critique' (Bhaskar 1986; Chouliaraki and Fairclough 1999), which can be formulated in four 'stages', which can be further elaborated as 'steps'.

Stage 1: Focus upon a social wrong, in its semiotic aspects.

Stage 2: Identify obstacles to addressing the social wrong.

Stage 3: Consider whether the social order 'needs' the social wrong.

Stage 4: Identify possible ways past the obstacles.

Stage 1: Focus upon a social wrong, in its semiotic aspect

CDA is a form of critical social science geared to better understanding of the nature and sources of social wrongs, the obstacles to addressing them and possible ways of overcoming those obstacles. 'Social wrongs' can be understood in broad terms as aspects of social systems, forms or orders which are detrimental to human well-being, which could in principle be ameliorated if not eliminated, though perhaps only through major changes in these systems, forms or orders.

Examples might be poverty, forms of inequality, lack of freedom, or racism. Of course, what constitutes a 'social wrong' is a controversial matter, and CDA is inevitably involved in debates and arguments about this which go on all the time.[2]

We can elaborate Stage 1 in two steps:

Step 1: Select a research topic which relates or points to a social wrong and which can productively be approached in a transdisciplinary way with a particular focus on dialectical relations between semiotic and other 'moments'.

We might, for instance, conclude that such an approach is potentially 'productive' because there are significant semiotic features of the topic which have not been sufficiently attended to in existing social research. A topic might attract our interest because it has been prominent in relevant academic literature, or is a focus of practical attention in the domain or field at issue (in political debate or debates over questions of management or 'leadership', in media commentary, and so forth). Topics are often 'given', and they sometimes virtually select themselves – who could doubt for instance that 'immigration', 'terrorism', 'globalization' or 'security' are important contemporary topics, with significant implications for human well-being, which researchers should attend to? Selecting such topics has the advantage of ensuring that research is relevant to the issues, problems and wrongs of the day, but also the danger that their very obviousness can lead us to take them too much at face value. We cannot assume that such topics are coherent research objects; to 'translate' topics into objects, we need to theorize them:

Step 2: Construct objects of research for initially identified research topics by theorizing them in a transdisciplinary way.

Anticipating the example I shall discuss below, let us assume that the selected research topic is the relationship between national strategies and policies and the 'global economy': strategies and policies that are developed for the global economy, or the adaptation of national strategies and policies for the global economy. We might pin this down by focusing for instance on strategies and policies to enhance 'competitiveness' in particular countries (the example I discuss relates to competitiveness policies in the UK). As a topic for critical research, this seems plausible enough: a preoccupation of contemporary governments is indeed adapting to the 'global economy', and this process does indeed have implications for human well-being (it is widely presented as a way towards greater prosperity and opportunity, but as entailing suffering and insecurity for some people). One – controversial – formulation of the social wrong in this case might be that the well-being (material prosperity, security, political freedom, etc.) of some people – arguably the majority – is being unfairly or unjustly sacrificed for interests of others. I shall focus below on one particular, political, aspect of the social wrong: suppression of political differences in favour of national consensus on strategies and policies.

Constructing an object of research for this topic involves drawing upon relevant bodies of theory in various disciplines to go beyond and beneath the obviousness of the topic, and since the focus is on a specifically semiotic 'point of entry' into researching it, these should include theories of semiosis and discourse. There are no 'right answers' to the question of which theoretical perspectives to draw upon: it is a matter of researchers' judgements about which perspectives can provide a rich theorization as a basis for defining coherent objects for critical research that can deepen understanding of the processes at issue, their implications for human well-being, and possibilities for improving well-being. One must work in a transdisciplinary way, either in research teams that bring together specialists in relevant disciplines, or by engaging with literature in such disciplines.

What theoretical perspectives might be drawn upon in this case? These might include (political) economic theories which theorize and analyse the 'global economy' and, for instance, take positions on whether and how it constitutes a 'realm of necessity', a fact of life; State and political theory, which probes the character and functioning of the State and of national and international politics in the era of 'globalization'; theories of 'global ethnography', which address how local groups and individuals seek to adapt to but also sometimes to test and challenge the 'global economy' as a realm of necessity. The importance of discourse theory is indicated by this implicit questioning of the 'global economy': a central issue in both the academic literature and practical responses to the 'global economy' in politics, workplaces and everyday life is the relationship between reality and discourse: the reality and the discourses of the 'global economy' and of its impact, implications and ramifications. We can initially identify analysis of the complex relationship between reality and discourse as a general formulation of the object of research for a semiotic 'point of entry' into this topic, but I shall suggest a more specific formulation, linked to the example I shall discuss, in the section below on political discourse analysis.

Stage 2: Identify obstacles to addressing the social wrong

Stage 2 approaches the social wrong in a rather indirect way by asking what it is about the way in which social life is structured and organized that prevents it from being addressed. This requires bringing in analyses of the social order, and one 'point of entry' into this analysis can be semiotic, which entails selecting and analysing relevant 'texts' and addressing dialectical relations between semiosis and other social elements.

Steps 1–3 can be formulated as follows:

Step 1: Analyse dialectical relations between semiosis and other social elements: between orders of discourse and other elements of social practices, between texts and other elements of events.

Step 2: Select texts, and focuses and categories for their analysis, in the light of and appropriate to the constitution of the object of research.

Step 3: Carry out analysis of texts, both interdiscursive analysis, and linguistic/semiotic analysis.

Taken together, these three steps indicate an important feature of this version of CDA: textual analysis is only a part of semiotic analysis (discourse analysis), and the former must be adequately framed within the latter. The aim is to develop a specifically semiotic 'point of entry' into objects of research that are constituted in a transdisciplinary way, through dialogue between different theories and disciplines. Analysis of texts can effectively contribute to this only in so far as it is located within a wider analysis of the object of research in terms of dialectical relations between semiotic and other elements which comprehends relations between the level of social practices and the level of events (and between orders of discourse and texts).

I shall not elaborate much on the three steps at this stage, because I think they will be clearer when I work through them with the example below.

One point about Step 3, however. I said above that although the particular methods of textual analysis used in a specific case depend upon the object of research, this version of CDA does have a general method of analysis. I alluded to this in the first section: textual analysis includes both linguistic analysis (and, if relevant, analysis of other semiotic forms, such as visual images) and interdiscursive analysis (analysis of which genres, discourses and styles are drawn upon, and how they are articulated together). Moreover, interdiscursive analysis has the crucial effect of constituting a mediating 'interlevel' which connects both linguistic analysis with relevant forms of social analysis, and analysis of the text as part of an event with analysis of social practices – in more general terms, analysis of event (action, strategy) with analysis of structure. Why so? Because interdiscursive analysis compares how genres, discourses and styles are articulated together in a text as part of a specific event and in more stable and durable orders of discourses as part of networks of practices, which (qua *social* practices) are objects of various forms of social analysis.

Stage 3: Consider whether the social order 'needs' the social wrong

It is not all that obvious what this means, and I shall try to clarify it by again anticipating the example. I indicated above that the social wrong I shall focus on when I get to the example is the suppression of political differences over the global economy and national responses to it in favour of seeking to create a national consensus, which is substantively realized in discourse. In what sense might the social order 'need' this? Perhaps in the sense – again anticipating the discussion below – that the internationally dominant strategy for globalizing an economic order based upon neoliberal principles requires that states be able to operate in support of this strategy without being encumbered by the 'old' adversarial politics. Stage 3 leads us to consider whether the social wrong in focus is inherent to the social order, whether it can be addressed within it, or only by changing it. It is a way of linking 'is' to 'ought': if a social order can be shown to inherently give rise to major social wrongs, that is a reason for thinking that perhaps it should be changed. It also connects with questions of ideology: discourse is ideological in so far as it contributes to sustaining particular relations of power and domination.

94

Stage 4: Identify possible ways past the obstacles

Stage 4 moves the analysis from negative to positive critique: identifying, with a focus on dialectical relations between semiosis and other elements, possibilities within the existing social process for overcoming obstacles to addressing the social wrong in question. This includes developing a semiotic 'point of entry' into research on the ways in which these obstacles are actually tested, challenged and resisted, be it within organized political or social groups or movements, or more informally by people in the course of their ordinary working, social and domestic lives. A specifically semiotic focus would include ways in which dominant discourse is reacted to, contested, criticized and opposed (in its argumentation, its construal of the world, its construal of social identities, and so forth).

To conclude this section, let me list core analytical categories of this approach to CDA which I have introduced so far:

Core Analytical Categories

semiosis (and other social elements),

discourse/genre/style, order of discourse (and *social practices*),

text (and *social event*),

interdiscursivity (and *interdiscursive analysis*),

recontextualization,

operationalization (enactment, inculcation, materialization).

An example: Political discourse analysis

The texts I shall discuss below are political texts: the foreword to a government document written by former British Prime Minister Tony Blair, and a critique of Blair's 'New Labour' Government by two former members of the Labour Party. As I have said, how a research topic is constituted as an object of research determines both the selection of texts for analysis and the nature of the analysis. In this section I shall suggest a more specific formulation of the object of research for the research topic anticipated above ('adapting national strategy and policy for the global economy'), which entails some discussion of political theories of the contemporary 'political condition', and the main issues and priorities it suggests for analysis of politics and political discourse. I shall discuss theoretical perspectives on the character of contemporary politics and the State especially in advanced capitalist countries such as the UK, but I should emphasize that this discussion is necessarily partial given the spatial limitations of this chapter. The material in this section will also help with Step 1 of Stage 2 of the methodology when we get to the texts – analysing dialectical relations between semiosis and other elements, especially at the level of social practices and orders of discourse.

Let me begin with a highly condensed summary analysis of the contemporary 'political condition', in the form of four major claims.

- Globalization in its dominant neoliberal form has been associated with changes in the State and national (as well as international) politics (Harvey 2003; Pieterse 2004).
- There is a tendency of the State to become a 'competition state' with the primary objective of securing competitive advantage for capital based within its borders (Jessop 2002).
- There is an associated tendency within mainstream politics for the political division and contestation (e.g. between political parties) characteristic of the previous period to weaken, and for consensus to emerge on the main strategy and policy issues (Rancière 2006).
- This tendency constitutes a fundamental political danger; not only is it a threat to democracy, it also creates a vacuum that can be filled by nationalism and xenophobia (Mouffe 2005; Rancière 1995).

The fourth point is based upon particular views of the general character of (democratic) politics and of politics in modern democracies. I shall refer specifically to Rancière's version. He argues that democracies, both ancient and modern, are mixed forms, as anticipated by Aristotle when he characterized 'a good regime' as a 'mixture of constitutions … there should appear to be elements of both (oligarchy and democracy) yet at the same time of neither … the oligarch sees oligarchy and the democrat democracy' (see Aristotle, *Politics* IV 1294b). This follows from the fact that 'the question of politics begins in every city with the existence of the mass of the *aporoi*, those who have no means, and the small number of the *euporoi*, those who have them' (Rancière 1995: 13). The task of politics is to calm and control the irreducible conflict between rich and poor, which means curbing the excesses of democracy. What we now call 'democracies' are actually oligarchies in which government is exercised by the minority over the majority. What makes them specifically democratic is that the power of oligarchies rests upon the power of the people, most obviously because governments are elected. In democracies, oligarchy and democracy are opposing principles in tension, and any regime is an unstable compromise between them. The public sphere is the sphere of encounters and conflicts between these principles: governments tend to reduce and appropriate the public sphere, relegating non-State actors to the private sphere, democracy is the struggle against this privatization, to enlarge the public sphere and oppose the public/private division imposed by government.

In contemporary democracies, the 'conflictual equilibrium' associated with popular sovereignty is being undermined. The oligarchic system is being combined with a 'consensual vision' on the claim that contemporary reality, the global economy and the prospect of endless 'growth' which it promises, does not leave us with choice. Government is the business of 'managing the local effects of global necessity', which requires consensus and an end to the 'archaic' indulgence of political division. Oligarchies are tempted by the vision of governing without the people, i.e. without the division of the people, which means effectively without politics, rendering popular sovereignty problematic. But the suppressed division inevitably returns, both in the form of mobilization outside the political system (e.g. against the negative effects of neoliberal globalization, or the Iraq war) and in the dangerous form of extreme right nationalism and xenophobia.

A priority for political analysis is consequently contemporary processes of *depoliticization*, which is by no means a new strategy (according to Ranciére [1995], it is 'the oldest task of politics') but is now emerging in a particularly profound and threatening form. Depoliticization is the exclusion of issues and/ or of people from processes of political deliberation and decision – placing them outside politics. But *politicization* is equally a priority if we are to analyse the tension between the principles of oligarchy and democracy, the democratic response to depoliticization, and how responses might develop a momentum capable of contesting the push towards depoliticization. Others have also identified depoliticization and politicization as priorities (Hay 2007; Muntigl 2002b; Palonen 1993; Sondermann 1997), but from different theoretical perspectives.

This prioritization provides a basis for questioning the centrality that has been attributed to other problems and issues. Let me briefly mention two. First, the centrality attributed to 'subpolitics' or 'life politics' by theorists of 'reflexive modernity', which is linked to the recent prominence of 'identity politics'. This accords with the perspective above in giving prominence to 'grassroots' political action, but clashes with it in construing such politics as an alternative to adversarial politics centred around the political system. The 'grassroots' politics of politicization is both defined and limited by the opposing logic of depoliticization, which means that State- and government-focused adversarial politics is by no means outdated. Second, the centrality attributed by for instance those influenced by Habermas (1967) to 'deliberative democracy' also tends to be associated with the assumption that adversarial politics can be superseded and to construe political dialogue as a rational process of consensus-formation, rather than a process that allows divisions, differences and conflicts to be contained within a shared political community without the assumption that these are just 'problems' waiting to be 'solved'. In different theoretical terms, we could say: these are contradictions, and although they can be managed they cannot be solved within the parameters of the existing system (Jessop 2002). This does not diminish or ignore cooperation in politics: conflict in political dialogue requires cooperation (only those who are cooperating at a certain level can stage a conflict), and adversarial politics necessarily includes cooperative moments (e.g. the formation of alliances).

We can fruitfully develop a specifically semiotic 'point of entry' into analysing processes of depoliticization and politicization. I shall illustrate this below in my analysis of the texts. This does not exclude other issues and associated categories which have tended to receive more attention in political discourse analysis, and indeed I shall refer to some (legitimation, manipulation, ideology, cooperation and identity). But it does imply a different 'mapping' of relations between categories which may lead to reconceptualizing or changing some of them.

Politicization and depoliticization are high-level strategies or 'macro-strategies'; so are legitimation and delegitimation. Strategies combine goals and means, and these macro-strategies are both means for achieving oligarchic or democratic goals (e.g. governing with minimal interference from political divisions, or pushing political differences into the public sphere), and goals in their own right associated with further strategies as means. We can identify strategies *for* (de)politicization and (de)legitimation, for instance, 'authorization' and 'rationalization' have been suggested as legitimation strategies (van Leeuwen 2007;

van Leeuwen and Wodak 1999). All of these are *political* strategies, not semiotic (or 'discourse') strategies, though they are generally realized semiotically.

I suggested above that the object of research could be broadly formulated as the complex relationship between discourse and reality in adapting national strategy and policy for the global economy. We can now reformulate it more precisely: semiotic realizations of strategies of depoliticization and politicization in national responses to the 'global economy', focusing on competitiveness policy in the UK.

An illustration: Analysing political texts

I come now to the analysis of two sample texts. The one I shall begin with is the foreword written by the former British Prime Minister Tony Blair to the Department of Trade and Industry's White Paper on Competitiveness (DTI 1998, see Appendix 1). I shall organize my comments according to the stages and steps listed in the methodology section, but I have just been effectively discussing aspects of Stage 1 so I shall keep my comments on it brief.

Stage 1: Focus upon a social wrong, in its semiotic aspect

The social wrong I shall focus upon is the suppression or marginalization of political differences over important issues of strategy and policy – how to respond nationally to radical international economic changes (and the prior question of what the changes actually are) – in favour of creating a consensus, which is as I indicated above a social wrong in that it undermines democracy but also poses the danger that dissent which cannot be politically articulated may emerge in nationalist or xenophobic forms. A semiotic point of entry is possible and fruitful, focusing upon semiotic realizations of the macro-strategy of depoliticization, in accordance with the construction of the object of research which I have discussed above. The second text, an extract from a book (Brown and Coates 1996) written by former members of the Labour Party criticizing Blair's 'New Labour' Government, exemplifies semiotic realizations of the macro-strategy of politicization. (Note that both macro-strategies may, however, be at work in the same text.) Blair's text is representative of the dominant tendency of the times towards depoliticization; but this tendency coexists with politicizing responses such as that of the second text, even if the latter often have a relatively marginal effect on government strategy and policy. I have already discussed steps 1 and 2 above, on the construction of an object of research for the research topic, in anticipation of the illustration, so we can move on to Stage 2.

Stage 2: Identify obstacles to addressing the social wrong

I shall discuss Stage 2 by taking each of the three steps it includes in turn.

> *Step 1:* Analysis of dialectical relations between semiosis and other social elements (orders of discourse and elements of social practices, texts and elements of events)

Step 1 also implicitly includes the dialectic between structures (at the intermediate level of social practices) and events (and strategies). I have already in the previous section given an indication of the social practices and orders of discourse at issue here, but let me fill this out a little with respect to 're-structuring' and 're-scaling' (Jessop 2002) tendencies associated with contemporary capitalism, and a brief note on New Labour in Britain.

Re-structuring is changes in structural relations, notably between economic and non-economic fields, which include extensive 'colonization' of the latter (including politics and the State) by the former; re-scaling is changing relations between global, regional, national and local scales of social life, including changes in government and governance. Analysing these tendencies would help contextualize the UK strategies and policies which are in focus, that is, help determine what they are a part of. National governments are increasingly incorporated within larger networks that include not only other governments but also international agencies (e.g. the European Union, the World Bank, the IMF), business networks, and so forth. Governments, according to Castells (1996), are increasingly coming to function as 'nodes' within a transnational network based upon a business–government complex, whose central 'functions' are focused upon creating the conditions (financial, fiscal, legal, 'human capital' etc.) for successful competition in the 'global economy'. If the government strategies and policies in focus here are locked into this powerful network, this in itself constitutes a substantial obstacle to addressing the social wrong.

But these processes of re-structuring and re-scaling have an important semiotic dimension: the networks of social practices which they entail are also orders of discourse which themselves cut across structural and scalar boundaries. For example, the dominant neoliberal discourse of globalization illustrated in the first text is dominant in education as well as politics, and in the European Union, the World Bank, and many other countries apart from the UK. There are also genres and styles which are disseminated structurally and in scale in a similar way (Fairclough 2006). Moreover, the semiotic dimension is fundamental to re-structuring and re-scaling, in the sense that these processes are 'semiotically driven'. They begin as discourses which constitute 'imaginaries' (Jessop 2004, 2008) – imaginary projections – for new relations of structure and scale in economies, government, education and so forth; these may become hegemonic, or dominant, and may be widely recontextualized; in so far as they do become hegemonic, they are 'operationalized' in new structures, practices, relations and institutions; and the operationalization itself has a partly semiotic aspect in the emergence and dissemination of genres and 'genre networks' (see below), which enable the governance of these complex new networks, as well as styles. The semiotic dimension, deeply embedded within and constitutive of the new structural and scalar relations, is itself a part of the obstacles to addressing the social wrong.

With respect to the dialectic between texts and other elements of social events, the general point is that political texts are not some superficial embroidery upon political events but a fundamental, constitutive, part of them. In this case, for example, the strategies and policies of the Blair government for building British 'competitiveness' in adapting to the 'global economy' have a clearly textual character. They are formed, disseminated and legitimized within complex chains and networks of events (committee meetings, reports, parliamentary debates, press statements and press conferences etc.) which are largely chains and networks of texts – i.e. different types of texts which are regularly and systematically linked together. They are linked for instance in accordance with the 'genre networks' I referred to above – systematically linked genres (e.g. discussion, report, debate) which semiotically constitute procedures, in this case procedures of governance (on 'chains' of events, texts and genres, see Fairclough 2003). These strategy and policy processes thus have a largely textual character, and require textual analysis. The illustrative examples are just two small samples from the complex networks of texts involved.

The analysis would need to go into some detail about politics and social change in Britain. I have no space for such detail here, but let me make a couple of points (see further Fairclough 2000a). First, 'New Labour' abandoned the traditional social democracy of the British Labour Party to embrace the neoliberalism of preceding Conservative governments (those of Margaret Thatcher and John Major). The effect was to produce a neoliberal consensus on major policy issues within mainstream politics and a common political discourse – the associated tendency to exclude opposition is precisely the 'social wrong' I am addressing. Second, the infamous preoccupation of New Labour with media 'spin' (close management and manipulation of the presentation of policies and events in the media) indicates the growing importance of semiotic processes (political 'communication') in government. Thus the form of politics which developed with New Labour poses specifically semiotic obstacles to addressing the social wrong at issue.

Step 2: Selection of texts and categories for analysis

With respect to Step 2, the constitution of the object of research indicates the selection of texts in which the macro-strategies of depoliticization and politicization are semiotically realized. My examples here are both written texts, but one would want also to include, for instance, not only discussions, debates and interviews on TV and radio, and websites, but also material from campaigns, protests and demonstrations centred upon 'the global economy' and government strategy and policy oriented towards it, and material representing how people experience and react to the drive for 'competitiveness' in a variety of situated contexts (e.g. conversations and discussions within workplaces). Appropriate focuses and categories for the analysis include semiotic strategies that realize de-politicization, including argumentation and rhetorical strategies, as well semiotic aspects and realizations of legitimation, manipulation, ideology, cooperation and identity. I shall be more specific about some of these in discussing the texts.

Step 3: Analysis of texts

The first text is structured as an argument whose structure we can schematically reconstruct as follows:

Premises: The modern world is changing.

There are opportunities to succeed and prosper in the modern world.

If we want to succeed and prosper, we must compete effectively.

Implicit premise: (We do want to succeed and prosper.)

Conclusion: Therefore, we must compete (more) effectively.

The argumentation realizes semiotically the macro-strategy of legitimation, and specifically the strategy of rationalization: it is an example of the government's attempt to legitimize its political strategy and the policies associated with it as necessary responses to the situation.

The argument is formally valid, but whether it is sound or not (i.e. whether it is a reasonable argument) depends upon the truth of its premises. We can challenge the argument, argue that it is fallacious, by challenging the truth of its premises (Ieţcu 2006). I want to specifically question the premises on the grounds that they (a) predicate possible success of a problematic identity category as subject ('we'), (b) falsely claim that the change attributed to the modern world is simply an inevitable fact of life which 'we' must accept. Both of these flaws in the premises can be associated with the macro-strategy of depoliticization.

With respect to the first flaw, the identity category 'we' is problematic in that it is based upon a false equation between 'we' = 'Britain' and 'we' = all the citizens of Britain: if Britain achieves 'success' or 'prosperity', it does not follow that all of its citizens do. This is the 'fallacy of division', when a general category has properties that are mistakenly attributed to each of its parts. One sentence clearly implies that this *does* follow: 'That is the route to commercial success and prosperity for all'. This fallacy is a banal feature of governmental discourse, but it is fundamental for the macro-strategy of depoliticization, whose basic strategic goal is to dedifferentiate potentially antagonistic identities, the internal division of the political community, into 'Us' and 'Them'. In this sense, identity and the semiotic construal of identities are a major focus in analysis that prioritizes depoliticization.

The issue in semiotic terms is *personal deixis*. There are two personal 'deictic centres', positionings of the author (Blair), with respect to identity: he positions himself within two group identities, 'we' = the government, and 'we' = the country. It is commonplace in the literature on identity that identity entails difference; 'we' entails 'they' (Connolly 1991). We might say that 'we' = the government is implicitly construed in opposition to 'they'= previous governments which pursued strategies that are rejected because they 'did not and cannot work': 'old-fashioned state intervention' and 'naïve reliance on markets'; whereas 'we' = the country is construed in opposition to 'competitors'. But notice that the construal of personal deixis excludes a 'we/they' division both within the political community ('Britain') and within the contemporary political field (political system), where no contemporaneous political 'opposition' is construed. The implication is that there is consensus within both the political community and the political field. This is depoliticization.

Texts semiotically construe identities and simultaneously seek to make these construals persuasive. The fact that we can show fallacies in Blair's argument does not mean that it will be widely perceived as fallacious, and we must consider what might make the argument and construal of identities persuasive. This brings us to the second flaw, in the construal of world change.

Dominant construals of 'the new global order' have certain predictable linguistic characteristics (on the linguistic categories I mention below, see

Fairclough 2003): processes of change are construed without responsible social agents; they are construed in a timeless, ahistorical present; statements about the new economy (which are often very familiar truisms) are construed categorically and authoritatively as unmodalized truths, and there is a movement from the 'is' of the economic to the 'ought' of the political – from what is categorically the case to what 'we' ought to do in response; the new economic reality is construed as indifferent to place; and series of evidences or appearances in the new economy are construed paratactically as lists. I have shown elsewhere (Fairclough 2000b) that these features are sustained through recontextualization, appearing in economic texts (e.g. texts of the World Bank), political texts, educational texts, and so forth, as well as on different scales.

They are also evident in Blair's text, and they can be seen as aspects of the semiotic realization of depoliticization. In the construal of economic change in the 'modern world' there is an absence of responsible social agents. Agents of material processes are abstract or inanimate. In the first paragraph, 'change' is the agent in the first (passive) sentence, and 'new technologies' and 'new markets' are agents in the second – agents, notice, of intransitive verbs ('emerge', 'open up') which construe change as happenings, processes without agents. The third sentence is existential – 'new competitors' and 'new opportunities' are merely claimed to exist, not located within processes of change. Notice also that in the third paragraph the inanimate 'this new world' is the agent of 'challenges', construing change itself as articulating what responses to it are necessary. By contrast, when it comes to national responses to these implacable and impersonal processes of world change, social agents are fully present – business, the government, the DTI, and especially 'we'.

Turning to time, tense and modality, world change is construed in the ahistorical 'timeless' present tense, as indeed are national responses, and, in terms of modality, through authoritative categorical assertions of truisms (e.g. 'The modern world is swept by change', and indeed all five statements in the first paragraph). The only historical reference is to the 'old-fashioned' strategies in paragraph 4. There is a movement from 'is' to 'ought'. 'Ought' is implicit in paragraphs 2 and 3: 'our success depends on how well we exploit our most valuable assets' implies that we should exploit them, 'this new world challenges business to be innovative' and 'government to create' that business and government should do these things. From paragraph 5 onwards 'ought' is explicit and recurrent – the modal verb 'must' occurs six times. The domain of 'is' is world change; the domain of 'ought' is national responses: a divide is textually constructed between economics and politics (there is an 'industrial policy', but focused on enabling the economic process rather than radically shaping it), fact and value, which excludes the former from the latter. This differs from the social democratic tradition from which New Labour has come; earlier Labour governments used political power to change the economy, e.g. by nationalizing private industries, taking them into state control. In contrast with economic processes, political processes do have responsible social agents: the agent in processes modalized with 'must' is in five cases 'we' and in one case 'the government'. Summing up, world change is a process without a history that 'we' must respond to. Moreover, world change is implicitly construed as indifferent to place – there are no place expressions in the first or third paragraphs.

The syntax is paratactic,[3] in relations between both sentences and phrases within sentences. The first paragraph for instance consists of three paratactically related sentences (the second and third contain paratactically related clauses), listing evidences of world change. The same is true of the second paragraph. Notice that the sequencing of these sentences is not significant and is changeable (with minor rewording) without any substantive meaning change. Indeed, what is included in this list of evidences is somewhat arbitrary; for instance the second sentence of the first paragraph might have been 'Huge amounts of money move across the globe in a fraction of a second, and even our family cat, Socks, has his own homepage on the World Wide Web'. The second clause is fanciful only in that Blair did not have a cat called Socks. It was actually included in a very similar list in a book by Bill Clinton. What is significant, rhetorically, is the relentless accumulation of evidences of change – what Clarke and Newman (1998) call 'the cascade of change' – which persuasively (and manipulatively) establishes the new economy as simple fact, what we must live with and respond to.

Summing up, change is authoritatively construed as lists of known appearances (and truisms) in the present which are indifferent to place and whose social agency is effaced, and which must be responded to in certain ways. These features together construe the new economy as simple fact to which there is no alternative. They locate the 'global economy' within the 'realm of necessity', and therefore outside the 'realm of contingency and deliberation', i.e. outside the realm of politics, semiotically realizing the macro-strategy of depoliticization (Hay 2007). We can say that in so far as this sort of discourse achieves significant public acceptance, which it has, it is part of the obstacles to addressing the social wrong.

Let me briefly comment on interdiscursive analysis. One can see Blair's text as recontextualizing analyses of the 'global economy' more fully elaborated in texts produced, for example, within the World Bank, and their particular discourse (construals of, narratives of and arguments about the 'global economy'). Blair's text is not primarily an analytical text but an advocative text, arguing for 'necessary' policies. But it is interdiscursively complex in grounding this advocative argument in the recontextualized analysis, combining analytical and advocative genres (as well as economic and political discourses). This type of recontextualization and interdiscursive hybridity is common as a semiotic realization of a favoured legitimation strategy: legitimizing by appeal to expert knowledge. Notice that the expert discourse is not the same here as it might be in specialist economic texts. For instance, in the first paragraph the construal of change in the global economy is stripped down to three short sentences which furthermore incorporate characteristic features of political rhetoric (the dramatic metaphor 'swept by change', the antithesis of 'new competitors but also great new opportunities'), and which constitute dramatic and potentially persuasive formulations of premises in the argument. Recontextualization involves transformation to suit the new context, which affects forms of interdiscursive hybridity.

In discussing Stage 2, I have identified a number of obstacles to addressing the social wrong at issue, and shown that they are partly semiotic in nature. Let me summarize them: the national and international networks that government strategies and policies are embedded within; the consensual character of mainstream politics in Britain; an influential political discourse, exemplified in the Blair text, which in various ways contributes to depoliticizing the global economy and national responses to it.

Stage 3: Consider whether the social order 'needs' the social wrong

I anticipated this example in discussing Stage 3 in the methodology section above, where I suggested how the suppression of political differences in favour of consensus might be interpreted as necessary for states to operate effectively within the hegemonic neoliberal strategy. We might add that achieving a broad consensus within the political system depends upon semiotic conditions – achieving semiotic hegemony, broad acceptance of the sort of discourse we have here. And as I noted above, this can be interpreted in terms of ideology as the naturalization of meanings that sustain relations of power and domination. So it seems plausible that the social order does 'need' the social wrong in this case – addressing it might require wider changes in the social order – and that, since the wrong has a partly semiotic character, it also 'needs' certain characteristics of contemporary political discourse.

Stage 4: Identify possible ways past the obstacles

At this point I shall introduce the second text (see Appendix 2), an extract from a book (Brown and Coates 1996) written by two long-standing members of the Labour Party about New Labour's view of what they call 'capitalist globalization'. This will allow some necessarily brief, partial and sketchy comments on the other main macro-strategy, politicization.

I mentioned one adversarial feature in the first text: rejection of the 'old-fashioned state intervention' and 'naïve reliance on markets' of previous governments, while implying there were no contemporaneous divisions on the nature of 'world change' or the national strategies needed to adjust to it. The second text, by contrast, enters into adversarial dialogue with contemporaries, specifically Blairites. The macro-strategy of politicization is semiotically realized in the text's dialogicality. Specifically, there are claims which are denials of claims made 'elsewhere', by New Labour politicians amongst others: 'What has changed is not that capital is more mobile', 'it is not true that national governments – and by extension the European Union – are totally lacking in powers to employ against the arbitrary actions of transnational capital'. In this respect, the strategy is to politicize by construing the nature of 'world change' and government responses as controversial matters, subject to political difference and division.

Text 2 also politicizes by counterposing to the New Labour narrative of collaboration between government and business a narrative of conflict between government and business, capital and labour. Notice that both texts construe the global(ized) economy as a reality that countries need to adjust to, but in radically different ways. In the second but not the first, the construal of the global(ized) economy does include responsible social agents: the companies, whose actions are construed in general and negative terms ('moving internationally from bases...', 'the arbitrary actions of transnational capital', 'divide and conquer'). The text also construes relations between the companies and national governments, contrasting the 'clientelist' relations that tend to exist and which New Labour advocates ('nation-states ... clients of transnational companies') with adversarial relations that could and by implication should exist ('employing' their 'powers ... against the arbitrary actions of transnational capital', 'making or withholding tax concessions', 'bargaining'). The same contrast between what is and what could/should be is construed in relations between the EU and national governments ('reinforcing' the status of nation states as 'clients' of the companies, versus 'offering a lead and challenge to the nation states').

In sum, whereas text 1 depoliticizes by construing a consensus on the global economy as an inevitable fact of life and building national competitiveness as a necessary response, text 2 politicizes by construing the globalized economy as a stake in struggles between governments and transnationals, and capital and labour, and by opposing that construal to the government's consensualist construal. But the mere existence of texts that politicize in this way does not amount to 'ways past the obstacles'. This text offers an imaginary for a different, politicizing strategy in response to a differently conceived global(ized) economy; it shows that different imaginaries are possible and indeed exist, but we would also need to consider how feasible it would be to operationalize this or some other imaginary in a strategy that could actually succeed and be implemented in the face of the sort of obstacles I have begun to indicate. It's not impossible, but it's difficult to see how at present: there are abundant alternative imaginaries, but there is currently no clear counter-hegemonic strategy. A fuller treatment than I have space for would include analysis of attempts to develop oppositional strategies and their semiotic dimensions.

Summary

The theoretical claim that relations between semiosis and other social elements are dialectical in character, and the methodological focus on these relations rather than on semiosis as such, mean that this approach to CDA is particularly attuned to transdisciplinary research, to working with the grain of various bodies of social theory and research, but at the same time bringing to them an enhancement of their capacity to address often neglected semiotic dimensions of their research objects, as well as taking from them perspectives and research logics that can contribute to the further development of the dialectical-relational approach itself.

As with any approach, there are things about which the dialectical-relational approach has little to say. We should distinguish, however, between issues and problems it has not got around to because others seemed more pressing or more interesting or simply because life is short, and issues and problems that fall outside its remit and are thus not issues and problems *for it* (though they may be for other approaches). An example of the former is a relative emphasis on the workings of power rather than the workings of reception, reaction and resistance to power – I stress relative because the latter have not been entirely neglected (see for instance Fairclough 2006). Critics might reasonably say that I have 'done it again' in this paper, spending more time on depoliticization than politicization. This has been a bias in my work, perhaps partly because of the sort of left-wing politics I was involved with in the 1970s, but it is not in my opinion a limitation of the approach as such. An example of the latter is lack of attention to psychological and cognitive matters. I would agree that cognitively oriented research on discourse can complement the dialectical-relational approach, but I would not accept that absence of attention to cognitive issues is a 'blindspot' in the approach, still less that it in some sense invalidates the approach.

Chilton, for example, has suggested that a proper understanding of the cognitive capacities of humans may lead to the conclusion that CDA is trying to teach people what they already know. 'Put bluntly, if people have a natural ability to treat verbal input critically, in what sense can CDA either reveal in discourse what people can ... already detect for themselves or educate them to detect it for themselves?' (Chilton 2005). Yet the closing sentences of Chilton (2004) note that 'if people are indeed political animals ... then they are also in principle *capable* of doing their own political critique. The important question is whether they are free to do so.' I agree. Chilton (2005) argues that although there are various conditions under which people are not free, 'it is doubtful that any of them can be elucidated by purely linguistic or discourse-analytical means. For they would seem to have to do with economic forces or socio-political institutions.' The main problem with this argument is indicated by the contrast between 'purely' linguistic or discourse-analytical factors and economic forces or socio-political institutions. From a dialectical-relational perspective, economic forces and socio-political institutions *are* in part semiotic, and analysis has to be in part semiotic analysis. The fact that people have cognitive capacities which make them in principle capable of seeing through manipulative intentions and even doing their own political critique (which CDA, far from discounting, presupposes) does not mean that they are generally capable in practice of seeing through the complex dialectical relations between semiotic and non-semiotic elements which constitute the social, political and economic conditions of their lives.

Further reading

Chouliaraki, L. and Fairclough, N. (1999) *Discourse in Late Modernity*. Edinburgh: Edinburgh University Press.
This book shows relationships of an earlier version of this approach to various sources and influences in social theory and research.

Fairclough, N. (2000) *New Labour, New Language?* London: Routledge.
A popular introduction to analysis of political discourse, based upon a simplified version of this approach to CDA.

Fairclough, N. (2003) *Analysing Discourse: Textual Analysis for Social Research*. London: Routledge.
This book focuses on using textual analysis in social research within the dialectical-relational approach, with many examples of possible applications.

Fairclough, N. (2006) *Language and Globalization*. London: Routledge.
This text exemplifies the application of the dialectical-relational approach in transdisciplinary research on globalization.

Appendix 1

Building the knowledge-driven economy

Foreword by the Prime Minister

The modern world is swept by change. New technologies emerge constantly; new markets are opening up. There are new competitors but also great new opportunities.

Our success depends on how well we exploit our most valuable assets: our knowledge, skills, and creativity. These are the key to designing high-value goods and services and advanced business practices. They are at the heart of a modern, knowledge driven economy.

This new world challenges business to be innovative and creative, to improve performance continuously, to build new alliances and ventures. But it also challenges government: to create and execute a new approach to industrial policy.

This is the purpose of this White Paper. Old-fashioned state intervention did not and cannot work. But neither does naïve reliance on markets.

The government must promote competition, stimulating enterprise, flexibility and innovation by opening markets. But we must also invest in British capabilities when companies alone cannot: in education, in science, and in the creation of a culture of enterprise. And we must promote creative partnerships which help companies: to collaborate for competitive advantage; to promote a long-term vision in a world of short-term pressures; to benchmark their performance against the best in the world; and to forge alliances with other businesses and employees. All this is the DTI's role.

We will not meet our objectives overnight. The White Paper creates a policy framework for the next ten years. We must compete effectively in today's tough markets if we are to prosper in the markets of tomorrow.

In government, in business, in our universities and throughout society we must do much more to foster an entrepreneurial spirit: equipping ourselves for the long term, prepared to seize opportunities, committed to constant innovation and enhanced performance. That is the route to commercial success and prosperity for all. We must put the future on Britain's side.

The Rt Hon. Tony Blair MP, Prime Minister

Appendix 2

Excerpt from Brown and Coates (1996)

Capital has always been global, moving internationally from bases in the industrialized countries. What has changed is not that capital is more mobile ... but that the national bases are less important as markets and production centres. In other words the big transnational companies are not only bigger but more free-standing ... The European Union, far from offering a lead and a challenge to the nation-states of Europe, reinforces their status as clients of the transnational companies. Indeed, this clientism applies not only to companies based in Europe ... While it is true that a national capitalism is no longer possible in a globalized economy, it is not true that national governments – and by extension the European Union – are totally lacking in powers to employ against the arbitrary actions of transnational capital. There is much that governments can do in bargaining – in making or withholding tax concessions for example ... But such bargaining has to have an international dimension or the transnational companies can simply continue to divide and conquer ... New Labour appears to have abandoned what remained of Labour's internationalist traditions ... Yet the ICTFU, the European TUC and the Geneva trade groups all offer potential allies for strengthening the response of British labour to international capital. (Brown and Coates 1996: 172–4)

Notes

1   *Critical realism* is a realist philosophy of science and social science which has been developed especially in the work of Roy Bhaskar (1986). *Cultural political economy* is a version of political economy which claims that economic processes and systems are culturally and semiotically conditioned and embedded, as well as politically.

2   In the first edition of this book and in other publications, I referred to social 'problems' rather than 'wrongs'. I have changed this because I think that construing all wrongs as 'problems' which need 'solutions' that can in principle be provided even if they have not been so far in practice is part of the self-justifying (and one might say ideological) discourse of contemporary social systems in countries like Britain. The objection to it is that some wrongs are produced by systems and are not resolvable within them.

3   *Paratactic* syntactic relations are relations between sentences, clauses or phrases which are grammatically equal, and are *co-ordinated*; they contrast with *hypotactic* relations, where there is one *main* sentence, clause or phrase, and others are *subordinated*.

5

ANALYSING DISCOURSES AND DISPOSITIVES: A FOUCAULDIAN APPROACH TO THEORY AND METHODOLOGY

SIEGFRIED JÄGER AND FLORENTINE MAIER[1]

CONTENTS

Keywords

discourse analysis, methodology, Foucault, dispositive, media, artefacts, knowledge, reality, critique, subject

---

Introduction

This article aims to give an introduction to the methodology of analysing discourses and dispositives, building on the theoretical insights of Michel Foucault. The chapter is aimed at novices to this approach. Critical discourse and dispositive analysis based on Michel Foucault's discourse theory centres on the following questions:

- What is valid knowledge at a certain place and time?
- How does this knowledge arise and how is it passed on?
- What functions does it have for constituting subjects?
- What consequences does it have for the shaping of society?

> By **knowledge** we understand all elements of thinking and feeling in human minds, or in other words, all contents that make up human consciousness.

Actors derive this knowledge from the discursive surroundings into which they are born and in which they are enmeshed throughout their lives. Knowledge is therefore conditional, i.e. its validity depends on actors' location in history, geography, class relations etc.

Critical discourse analysis and dispositive analysis aim to identify the knowledges contained in discourses and dispositives, and how these knowledges are connected to power relations in power/knowledge complexes. All sorts of knowledge can be analysed, for example: common knowledge transmitted through everyday communication, scientific knowledge, knowledge transmitted by the media, by schools, etc.

To provide an overview of the methodology for critically analysing discourses and dispositives, we first need to establish the foundations of Foucauldian discourse theory on which critical discourse and dispositive analysis build. An outline of this theoretical background is given in the ensuing section.

We will show that the concept of dispositive can be understood as – in the end – identical to the concept of discourse. In the third section, practical methodological guidelines for analysing discourses and dispositives are provided. We conclude with general recommendations on how to use and further develop the proposed methodology.

Theoretical foundations of discourse and dispositive analysis

In this chapter we show the way from discourse analysis to dispositive analysis. We connect both methods, by showing that both aim to illuminate the knowledge that actors need to speak, act and create things.

The concept of discourse

> By **discourse** we understand an 'institutionalized way of talking [and, we may add: non-linguistically performed acting] that regulates and reinforces action and thereby exerts power'. (Link 1983: 60, authors' own translation)

With this understanding we build on the work of literary and cultural scientist Jürgen Link and his team at the University of Dortmund, who have developed an approach, based on Foucauldian theory, to analyse discourses and their power effects, to uncover the linguistic and iconographic means by which discourses work, and to analyse how discourse legitimizes and secures hegemony in bourgeois-capitalist modern society (see Link 1982). We extend their definition by adding non-linguistically performed action, including the creation of material objects, which Foucault refers to in his later works.

This definition can be illustrated by the image of discourses and dispositives as flows of knowledge throughout time and space. Different discourses and dispositives are intimately entangled with each other and together form the giant milling mass of overall societal discourse and dispositives. This milling mass is growing constantly and exuberantly.

Discourses and reality

> Unlike disciplines such as the natural sciences that view material reality as an objective given, discourse and dispositive analysis examine how reality is brought into being by human beings assigning meanings. Only by being assigned a meaning does reality come into existence for actors.

Discourses thus do not merely reflect reality. Rather, discourses shape and enable (social) reality. Without discourses, there would be no (social) reality. Discourses can thus be understood as material reality sui generis. They are not a second-class material reality, not 'less material' than 'real' reality, not passive media into which reality is imprinted. Discourses are fully valid material realities among others (Link 1992).Therefore, discourse cannot be reduced to a notion of 'false consciousness' or 'distorted view of reality', as in some orthodox Marxist approaches to 'ideology critique'. Discourse is a material reality of its own. It is neither 'much ado about nothing', nor a distortion, nor a lie about reality. This characterization of discourse as material reality implies that discourse theory is a materialist theory. Contrary to a common misconception, probably based on the fact that discourse analysis deals with language, discourse theory is not an idealist theory. In other words, discourse theory deals with material realities, not with 'mere' ideas. Discourses may be conceptualized as societal means of production. Discourses are not 'mere ideology'; they produce subjects and reality.

> By **subjects** we mean social constructions of individuals or collectives (e.g. organizations, nations) that feel, think and act in certain ways. An overlapping concept is the one of **actors**.

The two concepts build on somewhat different strands of theorizing, with important works on subject formation for example originating from Althusser (2006) and Foucault (e.g. 1982), and important contributions on the social construction of actorhood, for example coming from Meyer and Jepperson (2000) and Latour (2005). The concept of 'subjects' more strongly emphasizes the double-meaning of subjectivity, with subjects on the one hand being creators of discourse, on the other hand being created by and subjected to discourse. The concept of 'actors', obviously, emphasizes the active side of this relationship. Latour (2005) and Meyer and Jepperson (2000) also bring up the possibility of non-human actors (for example whales as feeling creatures that have their own interests and play an important role in the ecology of oceans; the earth as Gaia; a software as a non-human actor that forces the compliance of humans). This idea opens up interesting new perspectives, and has some interesting connections to Foucauldian thought (e.g. about the panopticon). In what follows, we shall use the terms 'actors' and 'subjects' interchangeably, using the former when we want to emphasize more the active and the latter when we emphasize more the passive side of actorhood and subject creation.

We can therefore say: discourses determine reality, though of course always via intervening active subjects in their social contexts as co-producers and co-agents of discourses. The subjects are able to do this *because* they are entangled into discourse and therefore have knowledge at their disposal. Discourse analysis is therefore not only about the retrospective analysis of allocations of meaning, but also about the analysis of the on-going production of reality through discourse, conveyed by active subjects. We have thus expounded the fundamentals of knowledge, discourse and reality. This leads us to the question of how they are related to materializations and non-linguistically performed action. To answer this question, we introduce the concept of dispositive.

Dispositives

By **dispositive** (building on Foucault 1980a: 194), we mean a constantly evolving synthesis of knowledge that is built into linguistically performed practices (i.e. thinking, speaking, writing), non-linguistically performed practices (vulgo 'doing things') and materializations (i.e. natural and produced things).

The dispositive as a whole comprises the net that is spun between these linguistically and non-linguistically performed elements. Its linguistically and non-linguistically performed elements are interrelated and unable to exist on their own. Together, they constitute reality. Figure 5.1 attempts to give a simplified illustration of such a system.

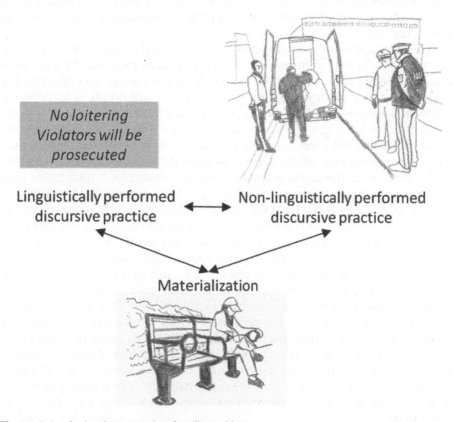

Linguistically performed discursive practice ⟷ Non-linguistically performed discursive practice

Materialization

Figure 5.1 A simple example of a dispositive

Discourse analysis and dispositive analysis have become known as separate approaches, not because of sharp differences in theoretical content or methodological approach, but because they have emerged from different receptions of Foucauldian theory. This is because Foucault has laid a foundation for analysing dispositives in terms of their power/knowledge implications, but has not spelled out a complete and explicit theory on this matter. The obstacle that prevented him from doing so was that in most of his work he saw only linguistically performed practices (and talking and writing more so than thinking) as discursive. Even though on some occasions he crossed that line (for example writing about 'the latent discourse of the painter [...] the murmur of his intentions, which are not transcribed into words, but into lines, surfaces, and colours' (Foucault 1972: 193), most of the time he did not see non-linguistically performed practices and artefacts as discursive. In that, ironically confirming his own theory, he showed himself as a product of his times and origins, where the bourgeoisie valued intellectual activity and saw physical activity as something separate and unintellectual. We shall therefore, for the purpose of this article, leave aside those lines of Foucault's thought that turned out as dead end streets (interested readers can find out more about them for example in Bublitz 1999: 82–115; Jäger and Maier 2009; Waldenfels 1991: 291). Instead, we shall develop the fruitful ones and propose an approach to dispositive analysis that rests on the notion of knowledge as the connecting force. We do so in the spirit of *bricolage*, picking up Foucault's toolbox of theoretical and practical instruments, and developing his ideas further.

The linguistically and non-linguistically performed practices and materializations are connected by knowledge or, to put it more precisely, by a common power/knowledge complex. By knowledge, as stated above, we understand all kinds of elements of thinking and feeling in human minds. Everything in human consciousness is discursive, i.e. constituted by knowledge. Actors derive this knowledge from the discursive surroundings into which they are born: what other people tell them, what they read or hear via the media, what treatments they experience, what material objects they are in contact with, etc. Thereby they learn the conventions of assigned meanings, which helps them to interpret reality in the way it has previously been interpreted by others.

Actors' knowledge is the basis for their thinking, speaking, silent acting and production of things. Thereby knowledge, in human consciousness and transformed into physical action, creates and becomes reality. Foucault explicates this mechanism in the 'Archaeology of Knowledge', where he shows how discourses systematically form the objects (i.e., not just material objects but also topics of thought and speech) of which they speak (Foucault 2002: 54). He also describes how non-linguistically performed practices and materializations ('discursive relations') offer objects of which discourses can speak, and determine the relations that discourse must establish in order to speak of this or that object (2002: 50f.). In doing so, his aim is to define objects 'by relating them to the body of rules that enable them to form as objects of a discourse and thus constitute the conditions of their historical appearance' (2002: 53.). This is also the aim of the approach to critical dispositive analysis that we present here.

For a more precise understanding of knowledge, it is helpful to distinguish between explicit and tacit knowledge. Some of the knowledge that actors have is explicit, for example expressed in words, mathematical formulas or diagrams. (Such as a sign that states: 'Children must be accompanied on lift at all times.') Much knowledge, however, is implicit. It is hardly verbalized (e.g. Do not stare at people when you are inside the lift with them.) or even cannot be adequately verbalized (e.g. What exactly is the borderline between staring at somebody and just looking normally at them?). The tacit knowledge of a particular culture is passed on in non-linguistic practices and materializations. In other words, the knowledge is in the practices and materializations, and actors learn it by watching others and trying it out themselves. Researchers can reconstruct and explicate tacit knowledge by closely analysing non-linguistic practices and materializations, and – as in the case of some ethnographies – also by participating in the practices themselves.

As we have explained above, discourse and dispositive analysis view reality as something that is created by human beings assigning meanings. In dispositive analysis, this process of reality creation is made salient with respect to non-linguistically performed practices and materializations. Of course, this does not mean that human beings are the creators of the raw matter of material reality. But actors shape and use these raw materials. The assignment of meanings includes tangible physical acts. For example, when the Three Gorges Dam was built on the Yangtze River, this happened as part of a dispositive of 'development'. The river was given a new meaning as a major source of hydroelectric power. For the rice farmers who were resettled to make place for the dam, the river lost the meaning of being a source of irrigation for their now flooded paddies. The river lost one meaning and gained another. As the knowledge assigned to a particular part of reality changed, this part of reality turned into a different thing.

An object that is not assigned any meaning is not an object. It is totally nondescript, invisible, even non-existent. I don't see it because I overlook it. We can trace this phenomenon by looking at cases where discourses have withdrawn from the reality that used to be built on them. In such cases, those parts of reality become meaningless in the truest sense of the word. They return to a blank state. For example: after the Second World War, firewood in Vienna was so scarce that people foraged parks for fallen branches. For them, a broken branch was a valuable piece of firewood. Today, when we walk through the park and see a broken branch on the ground, we most likely do not take particular notice of it.

The point is that all meaningful reality exists for us because we make it meaningful for us, or because our ancestors and neighbours assigned meaning to it, and this meaning is still valid for us. Just as for King Midas everything he touched turned into gold, similarly, everything that human beings assign meaning to becomes a particular kind of reality, according to the meaning it was assigned. Ernesto Laclau expressed this connection elegantly:

By 'discursive' I do not mean that which refers to 'text' narrowly defined, but to the ensemble of the phenomena in and through which social production of meaning takes place, an ensemble which constitutes a society as such. The discursive is not, therefore, being conceived as a level nor even as a dimension of the social, but rather as being co-extensive with the social as such. This means that the discursive does not constitute a superstructure (since it is the very condition of all social practice) or, more precisely, that all social practice constitutes itself as such insofar as it produces meaning. Because there is nothing specifically social which is constituted outside the discursive, it is clear that the non-discursive is not opposed to the discursive as if it were a matter of two separate levels. History and society are an infinite text. (Laclau 1980: 87)

We may therefore say that reality is meaningful, that reality exists in the way it does, only insofar as it is assigned meaning by actors, who are themselves entangled into and constituted by discourses. If actors no longer assign the same meaning to an object, the object changes or loses its meaning. This meaning may then at most be reconstructed as a former meaning that has mixed with other meanings or has ceased to be valid. Even if we just watch the night sky and see constellations of stars there, we see them as a result of a discourse. We see the constellations because we have learnt to see them. To assign meaning is not a noncommittal, 'merely symbolic' act. To assign meaning is to animate whatever one comes across, to re-shape and change. For example, from the collective symbolism used with regard to immigrants, it is apparent that many people have learnt to assign negative meanings to immigrants, and now actually perceive them as floods that need to be held back.

The elements of a dispositive are connected not just by a certain kind of knowledge, but also by a common purpose they serve, namely the purpose of dealing with an urgent need. In fact, Foucault saw this as the major inner bond that holds a dispositive together. He defined a dispositive as:

[...] a sort of – shall we say – formation which has as its major function at a given historical moment that of responding to an *urgent need [urgence]*. The [dispositive] thus has a dominant strategic function. (Foucault 1980b: 195)

If a society – or rather: its hegemonic forces – are confronted with an urgent need that has arisen due to some shift in power/knowledge relations (for example a state has become insolvent, or an airplane has crashed into the World Trade Center), they will gather all the elements they can get hold of to deal with it. These may be speeches, full-body scanners and biometric passports, new laws, a new committee such as the Troika, and so on. By these means, they mend the 'leak', the urgent need that has arisen (see Balke 1998; Deleuze 1988). The dispositive then stays in place until a new shift occurs.

Discourses and dispositives are therefore specific to particular times and places. Different cultures have different discursive objects, which can make it difficult to translate texts from one language into another, or to understand texts and other symbolic practices from other cultures and historical periods. Changes of discourse do not happen out of the blue. Often discursive changes take place in long processes that impalpably but thoroughly change everything. But also abrupt changes can happen, when a discourse that previously seemed like a quiet little brook turns into a torrent (for example when the self-incineration of a Tunisian street vendor sparked off the Arab spring). In other words, the contents of discourses and dispositives are malleable to change.

Discourses and power

As we have noted above, discourses are not only expressions of social practice but also serve particular ends, namely the exercise of power. It is therefore necessary to discuss the Foucauldian concept of power. The question of how the production of discourses and the temporarily and spatially contingent knowledge they contain are connected to mechanisms and institutions of power has been central for Foucault (as he states in the introduction to the German version of *The History of Sexuality* – see Foucault 1983: 8).

> **Power**, in a Foucauldian sense, refers to 'a whole series of particular mechanisms, definable and defined, that seem capable of inducing behaviours or discourses'. (Foucault 1996: 394)

Discourses exercise power because they institutionalize and regulate ways of talking, thinking and acting. Based on the above outline of the connection between discourses and reality, we can distinguish two kinds of connections between discourses and power: On the one hand, there is the power of discourse. On the other hand, there is something like the power over discourse.

The *power of discourse* lies in the fact that discourses delineate a range of elements of knowledge, which are sayable, makeable and seeable. This means that they simultaneously inhibit other elements of knowledge that are not sayable, not makeable and not seeable (cf. Jäger 2012; Link and Link-Heer 1990). As flows of knowledge through time and space, discourses determine the way in which a society interprets reality and organizes further linguistically and non-linguistically performed discursive practices (i.e. further talking, thinking, acting and seeing). To put it more precisely, we can distinguish two effects of discourse: Firstly, discourses form individual and mass consciousness and thereby constitute individual and collective subjects. Secondly, since consciousness determines action, discourses determine action, and action creates materializations. Discourses thus guide the individual and collective creation of reality.

From a discourse-theoretical point of view, it is thus not the subject who makes the discourses, but the discourses that make the subject (which may be irritating for those attached to the idea of the uniqueness of the individual). The subject is of interest not as an actor, but as a product of discourses. As Foucault argues:

> One has to dispense with the constituent subject, to get rid of the subject itself, that's to say, to arrive at an analysis which can account for the constitution of the subject within a historical framework. And this is what I would call genealogy, that is, a form of history which can account for the constitution of knowledges, discourses, domains of objects etc. without having to make reference to a subject which is either transcendental in relation to the field of events or runs in its empty sameness throughout the course of history. (Foucault 1980b: 117)

Foucauldian discourse theory, though often wrongly accused of so doing, does not deny the subject and actorhood. It aims to analyse the constitution of the subject in its historical and social context from a diachronic (i.e. longitudinal) and synchronic (i.e. cross-sectional) perspective: who was conceived of as a subject at a particular point in time? How, and how come? For example, unlike in the past, women and children in Western society usually have subject status today (see, for example, Aries 1962; Meyer and Jepperson 2000). In modern management, in contrast to traditional bureaucracy, employees are depicted as subjects. They are 'empowered', with all the responsibilities that involves. The subject status of fetuses and apes is hotly debated. Asylum seekers and criminals are denied subject status when they are portrayed as maniacs, dogs or viruses (these are collective symbols – see the section below on collective symbols). In a nutshell, Foucauldian discourse theory contests the existence of an autonomous subject, but that does not mean that it is against the subject. The active individual is fully involved when it comes to realizing power relations in practice. The individual thinks, plans, constructs, interacts and fabricates. Individuals also face the problem of having to prevail, to assert themselves, to find their place in society.

When analysing the power effects of discourse, it is important to distinguish between the effects of a text and the effects of a discourse. A single text has minimal effects that are hardly noticeable and almost impossible to prove. In contrast, a discourse, with its recurring contents, symbols and strategies, leads to the emergence and solidification of knowledge and therefore has sustained effects. What is important is not the single text, the single film, the single photograph, etc. but the constant repetition of statements. The philologist Victor Klemperer recognized this mechanism as early as the 1930s, when he observed the language of the Nazis. In his analysis of the language of the Third Reich (Klemperer 2001, 2006), he contends that fascist language works like the continuous administration of small doses of arsenic, which unfold their effect only over the long term.

With regard to *power over discourse*, different individuals and groups have different chances of influence. However, none of them can simply defy hegemonic discourse, and none of them alone has full control over discourse. Discourses are supra-individual. Everybody is co-producing discourse, but no single individual or group controls discourse or has precisely intended its final result. Discourses take on a life of their own as they evolve. They transport more knowledge than the single actor is aware of. In Foucault's words, '[p]eople know what they do; they frequently know why they do what they do; but what they don't know is what what they do does' (*sic*, personal communication, quoted in Dreyfus and Rabinow 1982: 187). The power effects of discourses should therefore not necessarily be interpreted as the conscious and manipulative intent of some individual or group. There may be a difference between a speaker's reasons for using a particular discourse, and the social consequences of doing so (Burr 2003: 61). Yet, in the long run actors can accomplish changes in discourse. This – by definition – qualifies them as powerful actors. They may be members of political and economic elites who have greater financial resources or privileged access to the media. For example, the Basic Constitutional Law that governs the right of asylum in Germany was tightened after more than 10 years of intensive political and media lobbying. Exclusions inherent to the structure of discourse can thus be amplified by institutional conditions. But also less elite actors are able to shift discourses, if they are skilful communicators (which to no small degree requires education). For example, the Occupy movement, with its slogan 'We are the 99%', has put the issue of economic inequality back into daily political discourse in the Global North, and Arab Spring uprisings have brought the issue of democracy to the table in countries that previously seemed like unshakable authoritarian regimes. It is probably no coincidence that both of those movements were driven by groups of rather well-educated people.

Critique and the aims of critical discourse analysis

After having shed some light on the issue of power, we can further clarify the notion of critique and the aims that underlie critical discourse analysis. As stated in the introduction, critical discourse and dispositive analysis aim to identify the knowledges contained in discourses and dispositives, and how these knowledges are connected to power relations in power/knowledge complexes. This comprises two aspects: Firstly, it entails disentangling the giant milling mass of discourse, charting what is said in a given society, in a particular time and place, with regard to its qualitative spectrum (What is said? How is it said?), and uncovering the techniques through which discursive limits are extended or narrowed down. Secondly, it entails subjecting these workings of power/knowledge to critique.

> **Critique** does not mean to bluntly evaluate whether a particular discourse is good or bad. It means to expose the evaluations that are inherent in a discourse, to reveal the contradictions within and between discourses, the limits of what can be said, done and shown, and the means by which a discourse makes particular statements, actions and things seem rational and beyond all doubt, even though they are only valid at a certain time and place.

In doing so, critical analysts orient themselves towards ethical principles (for example that all human beings are of equal value and that their physical and mental integrity should not be violated). Obviously, since all knowledges are valid only in particular times and places, these ethical principles also cannot claim the status of objective truths. They have emerged out of a long discursive process of debate and struggle, and their validity is ever precarious. Nonetheless – or rather, as a result of this process – the analyst has come to understand them as valid.

Critical discourse analysts need to be clear about the fact that their critique is not situated outside discourse. They participate in discourse as parrhesiasts: They make clear that they are expressing their *own* opinion which they understand to be true. They express it in the most direct words they can find. And they do so even at personal risk, for example when they say something inconvenient to the audience and contradict mainstream opinions (Foucault 2001). This kind of critique is not ideological, because unlike ideology it does not make claims to absolute truth. Critical discourse analysts should, in our opinion, adopt a democratic attitude, meaning that researchers, audiences, and other actors exchange ideas on equal footing, try to understand each other and are open to modifying their position based on sound arguments.

The following section provides some ideas on how discourses and dispositives can be analysed systematically. For this purpose, we first introduce concepts to analyse the structure of discourses and dispositives. After that, we discuss under what conditions discourse analyses can be considered as complete. We proceed by going through a 'little toolbox' of discourse analytic methods, giving step-by-step guidelines for matters ranging from the choice of a subject, to analysis proper. We close with thoughts on the peculiarities of dispositive analysis.

Methods for analysing discourses and dispositives

The theoretical considerations introduced in the previous section of this chapter are the basis for the development of concepts and methods that facilitate analysis. A range of these concepts and methods is outlined in this section. The scope of this chapter does not allow for detailed methodological justifications of each of these concepts and methods, but such explanations can be found in the book on methods of critical discourse analysis by Jäger (2004, 2012).

Methods of critical discourse analysis also include linguistic concepts (e.g. figurativeness, vocabulary, pronominal structure, argumentation) which can be used to examine the more subtle workings of texts. However, these linguistic instruments are not described in detail here, as explanations can be found in works on style and grammar. Linguistic concepts fill only one slot in the 'toolbox' of discourse analysis. Depending on the research question and subject matter, various other tools can be added to the toolbox. In any case, certain methods are part of a standard repertoire. These are described in the remainder of this section, putting the emphasis on the analysis of linguistically performed discursive practices – what is usually known as discourse analysis – and shining a more cursory light on the analysis of non-linguistically performed discursive practices and materializations in an extended form of discourse and dispositive analysis.

The structure of discourses and dispositives

The following suggestions on terminology, in a first step, aim to provide some help in making the structure of linguistically performed discourses more transparent and amenable to analysis.

Special discourses and interdiscourse

A basic distinction can be drawn between special discourses and interdiscourse. Special discourses are located on discourse planes that have special and explicit rules for regulating knowledge production, for example the natural and social sciences, the humanities, engineering, business management, etc. (Link 1988). Interdiscourse does not have such rules. Elements of special discourses continuously feed into interdiscourse and vice versa.

Discourse strands

In general societal discourse, a great variety of topics arise. Flows of discourse that centre on a common topic are called discourse strands. Each discourse strand comprises several subtopics, which can be summarized into groups of subtopics.

The concept of discourse strands is similar to the one of discourses. The difference is that discourse is the more abstract concept, located at the level of statements (*enoncés*, i.e. all the kernels of meaning that constitute the 'atoms' of a particular discourse). Discourse strands, in contrast, are conceived of at the level of concrete utterances (*énonciations*) or performances located on the surface of texts (cf. Foucault 2002).

Every discourse strand has a diachronic and a synchronic dimension. A synchronic analysis of a discourse strand examines the finite spectrum of what is said and sayable at a particular point in time and place. For example, researchers can analyse the discourse of legitimation in the annual reports of nonprofit organizations in one given year (Meyer et al. 2013). A diachronic analysis cuts through a discourse strand at various points in time and place, for example at particular discursive events. By comparing these synchronic cuts, the analysis provides insights into the changes and continuities of discourse strands over time. For example, by examining a nonprofit organization's discourse of legitimation in annual reports over a period of more than a decade, researchers can identify ebbs and flows in the salience of particular accounts for legitimation. For example notions of efficiency and effectiveness may become increasingly taken for granted and hence less emphasized in annual reports, and notions of stakeholder needs and innovation may become more prominent, because they are seen as interesting new aspects (Meyer et al. 2013).

In a way, a synchronic cut through a discourse strand is always also a diachronic one. This is because each topic has a genesis, a historical a priori. When analysing a topic, the analyst has to keep an eye on its history. To identify the knowledge of a society on a topic, the analyst has to reconstruct the genesis of this topic. Foucault has undertaken several attempts to do so, not only with regard to the sciences, but also with regard to everyday life and institutions (e.g. the hospital and prison in France).

Discursive limits and techniques for extending them or narrowing them down

Each discourse delineates a range of statements that are sayable and thereby inhibits a range of other statements, which are not sayable (cf. Link and Link-Heer 1990). The borders to what is not sayable are called discursive limits.

Through the use of certain rhetorical strategies, discursive limits can be extended or narrowed down. Such strategies, for example, include direct prescriptions, relativizations, defamations, allusions and implicatures. Discourse analysis examines these strategies in their own right, and also uses them as analytic clues to identify discursive limits: if 'tricks' are used, this is an indicator that certain statements cannot be said directly without risking negative sanctions. For example, in modern day racism, statements are often introduced with the clause 'I am not racist, but…', which extends the limit of what can be said without being accused as racist. When politicians say that 'there is no alternative' to a particular course of action, this narrows down discursive limits, because it suggests that there is no possibility to call this action into question and publicly debate it.

Discourse fragments

Each discourse strand consists of a multitude of elements that are traditionally called texts. We prefer the term 'discourse fragment', because one text may touch on various topics and thus contain various discourse fragments. A discourse fragment therefore refers to a text or part of a text that deals with a particular topic. For example, if we are interested in the discourse of immigration, we may find relevant discourse fragments in immigration laws and news articles that focus on immigration, but also in news articles that focus on other topics and mention immigration only in passing. For example in an article with the title 'Man cuts his ex-girlfriend's throat: 20 years of prison' we may read: '"I could not live without her", said the accused, a Romanian who has been living in Austria since 2006.' Or in a shop we may find a Halloween costume, consisting of an orange prison jumpsuit and a space alien mask, sold as 'Illegal Alien' costume (which is a splendid example of a dehumanizing collective symbol). All such discourse fragments on the same topic form a discourse strand.

Entanglements of discourse strands

A text usually refers to various topics and therefore to various discourse strands. In other words, it usually contains fragments from various discourse strands. These discourse strands are usually entangled with each other. An entanglement of discourse strands can take the form of one text addressing various topics to equal degrees, or of one text addressing mainly one topic and referring to other topics only in passing.

A statement where several discourses are entangled is called a **discursive knot**. For example, in the statement 'integrating immigrants into our society costs a lot of money', the discourse strand of immigration is entangled with the discourse strand of the economy. In the statement 'in [insert any Islamic country here], they still live in a patriarchal society', the discourse strand of immigration is entangled with the discourse strand of gender.

Two discourse strands can be entangled more or less intensively. For example, in everyday discourse in Germany, the discourse strand of immigration is intensively entangled with the discourse strand of gender, as sexist attitudes and behaviours are attributed to immigrants (see Jäger 1996).

Collective symbols

An important means of linking up discourse strands is the use of collective symbols. Collective symbols are 'cultural stereotypes', also called 'topoi', which are handed down and used collectively (Drews et al. 1985: 265). They are known to all members of a society. They provide the repertoire of images from which we construct a picture of reality for ourselves. Through collective symbols we interpret reality, and have reality interpreted for us, especially by the media.

An important technique for connecting collective symbols is **catachresis** (also called image fractures). Catachreses establish connections between statements, link up spheres of experience, bridge contradictions and increase plausibility. Thereby, catachreses amplify the power of discourse. An example of a catachresis is the statement 'the locomotive of progress can be slowed down by floods of immigrants'. Here, the symbols of the locomotive (meaning progress) and floods (meaning a threat from the outside) are derived from different sources of images. The first one is taken from traffic and the second from nature. With a catachresis, the images are connected.

As a special form of collective symbols, pragma-symbols deserve mention. These are terms that refer to material objects while at the same time pointing to a meaning beyond that. For example: 'In this civil war, it is tanks against stones.' This refers not just to the concrete fighting situation, but also to the unequal strength of conflict parties.

Discourse planes and sectors

Different discourse strands operate on different discourse planes. By discourse planes we mean various social locations from which speaking takes place. In other words we may call them genres: forms of expression that take place in distinct settings and share particular stylistic features. For example we may distinguish between the discourse planes of the sciences, politics, the mass media, education, everyday life, business, administration, etc.

Discourse planes evolve in time, influence each other and relate to each other. For example, on the mass media plane, discourse fragments from scientific specialist discourse or political discourse are taken up. The mass media also take up everyday discourse, bundle it, bring it to the point, or – especially in the case of the yellow press – spice it up with sensational and populist claims. In this way, mass media regulate everyday thinking and exert a considerable influence on what is and what can be done in politics and everyday life. For example, the larger-than-life image of the now defunct Austrian populist Jörg Haider would hardly have come about without the help of pervasive media reports that lumped all immigrants together with criminals, and that celebrated Jörg Haider's can-do image by covering his athletic achievements in running city marathons.

A discourse plane consists of various sectors. For example, TV, newspapers and the internet are different sectors of mass media. When analysing discourse planes, it is important to consider the relative importance of various sectors for the research question at hand. For example, social media and Web 2.0 are gaining importance as forms of mass media that open up unprecedented opportunities for two-way communication and – at the same time – for surveillance.

A discourse plane is tightly interwoven in itself. For example, on the discourse plane of the mass media, a TV broadcast may repeat and build on contents that have been brought up in social media, and vice versa. It is therefore all the more justified to talk about *the* mass media discourse plane, which – especially with regard to traditional mainstream media in a society – can be considered as integrated in its major aspects.

Discursive events and discursive context

All events are rooted in discourse, and in this sense, could be called discursive events. The theoretical concept of 'discursive events', however, refers specifically to events that appear on the discourse planes of politics and the mass media intensively, extensively and for a prolonged period of time.

Discursive events are important because they influence the future development of discourse. For example, the Three Mile Island nuclear accident near Harrisburg was comparable to the one in Chernobyl. But while the Three Mile Island accident was covered up for years, the Chernobyl accident was a major media event and influenced global politics. The nuclear accident of Fukushima again changed the discourse of nuclear power worldwide. Whether an event, such as a nuclear accident, becomes a discursive event or not depends on the power constellations at work in politics and the media. Discourse analysis can examine whether an event becomes a discursive event or not. If it becomes a discursive event, it influences the further development of discourse.

Another example for a discursive event is the Eurozone crisis. It is a combined crisis, or series of crises, in several dimensions such as sovereign debt, banking, unemployment, etc. It is roughly agreed that it started in 2008 or 2009, but there is no consensus about its duration and precise nature. Repeatedly, politicians, scholars and journalists have declared the end or near end of the crisis. We see here a discursive struggle, whether or not a discursive event is still going on. If the crisis is still going on, further measures need to be taken, probably more far-reaching ones than the ones taken so far. If the crisis is over, there is no such need. The attempts at crisis management can be understood as attempts to get the urgencies of various interest groups (nations, different groups of the population, corporations, ...) under control.

Another reason why the identification of discursive events is important is that they outline the discursive context that a discourse strand relates to. For example, a synchronic (i.e. cross-sectional) analysis of a discourse strand can be enriched with diachronic (i.e. longitudinal) elements by adding a chronicle of the discursive events belonging to it. Such historic references can be helpful for synchronic analyses of discourse strands (as, for example, demonstrated by Caborn 1999).

Discourse positions

A discourse position describes the ideological position from which subjects, including individuals, groups and institutions, participate in and evaluate discourse. Also, the media take up discourse positions, which become evident in their reporting. (As noted above, subject status is nothing natural and obvious, but something that in itself needs to be established through discourse.)

Subjects develop a discourse position because they are enmeshed in various discourses. They are exposed to discourses and work them into a specific ideological position or worldview in the course of their life. This relationship also works the other way around. Discursive positions contribute to and reproduce the discursive enmeshments of subjects (Jäger 1996: 47).

Discourse positions can be identified through discourse analysis. But a rough outline of discourse positions is also part of actors' everyday knowledge. People know roughly which politicians and newspapers tend towards the left, the right or the centre. Everyday self-descriptions of one's discourse position, however, should be taken with a pinch of salt. For example, newspapers often describe themselves as 'independent' and 'impartial', which from a discourse-theoretical perspective is impossible.

Subjects can take up widely diverging positions. For example, with regard to the discourse strand of the economy, some subjects take up a neoliberal discourse position (e.g. favouring privatization, free trade, low taxes, fiscal policy discipline). Others, in contrast, reject neoliberalism and take up a neo-Keynesian position (e.g. favouring fiscal stimulus packages and stronger government regulation of markets) or something even more unorthodox.

Discourse positions are homogeneous only in their core and become diffuse with regard to less central issues. For example, subjects who embrace the discourse position of neoliberalism agree that it is in principle right and important to reduce the nation's budget deficit. They do not question the current economic system. However, they may have differing views on the best way to reduce the budget deficit.

Within a hegemonic discourse, discourse positions are fairly homogeneous, which itself is already an effect of hegemonic discourse. Dissenting discourse positions often belong to remote counter-discourses (e.g. a fundamental questioning of the current economic system may not arise from economic discourse, but from ecology or ethics). However, these counter-discourses can pick up arguments from hegemonic discourse and subvert their meaning (for example an Occupy Wall Street protester who defied the rain, holding up a sign saying 'Do you feel it trickle down?').

Overall societal discourse and global discourse

All the entangled discourse strands in a society together form the overall societal discourse. A society is never totally homogeneous but consists of different subcultures. In Germany, since reunification in 1989, overall societal discourse has become ideologically more homogeneous, and it seems unlikely that this is going to change easily (Teubert 1999). The overall societal discourse of a society, in turn, is part of global discourse. Even though global discourse is very heterogeneous, there is evidence of homogenizing tendencies (see, for example, Meyer 2009).

Overall, societal discourse is a complex network. Discourse analysis aims to disentangle this net. The usual procedure is to first identify single discourse strands on single discourse planes or sectors (for example, the discourse strand of immigration on discourse sectors of traditional mass media). Subsequently, analyses of this discourse strand on further discourse planes, such as politics or everyday communication, can be added. At the end of such analyses, the question is usually how the different discourse planes and sectors of a discourse strand relate to each other. For example, one may examine whether and how the political discourse plane is linked to discourse sectors of traditional mass media or to the discourse plane of everyday communication, whether and how traditional mass media influence everyday communication, and so on.

The history, present and future of discourse strands

Discourse strands have a history, a present and a future. In order to identify the changes, ruptures, ebbings and recurrences of a discourse strand, it is necessary to analyse longer periods of time. To put it into Foucault's words, an 'archaeology of knowledge' or a 'genealogy' is needed. On the basis of such an analysis, even prognoses about discourse can be undertaken. These can take the form of scenarios based on different future discursive events. Discourses may change, but normally they do not vanish totally and suddenly. Therefore discourse analysis allows prognoses.

Of course, an analysis of the history, present and future of overall societal or even global discourse is an enormous endeavour and can only be tackled in the form of many single projects. Such single projects create reliable knowledge about certain subzones of overall societal discourse. This scientific knowledge can be the basis for a change of everyday, political and media knowledge, and can change behaviours and policies. Work on the discursive plane of science can thus influence the further development of a particular discourse strand.

On the completeness of discourse analyses

A discourse analysis fully captures the qualitative range of what can be said and how it is said in one or more discourse strands. It is complete if further analysis leads to no further new findings. Social scientists who mainly work with large amounts of quantitative data will be surprised to learn that in discourse analysis, a relatively small amount of qualitative data suffices to reach this point. The arguments and contents that can be read or heard about a particular topic (e.g. immigration) at a particular time in a particular social location are amazingly limited (often in both senses of the word). With regard to methodology, this means that analysts continue to analyse new materials until they notice that arguments begin to repeat themselves. If this is the case, completeness (in the sense of theoretical saturation) has been achieved.

While qualitative analysis is the bedrock of discourse analysis, quantitative analyses can also be interesting. The analyst can examine with what frequency particular statements occur. In this way, focal issues in discourse strands, or statements that have the character of slogans and are therefore accompanied by a bulk of judgements and prejudices, can be identified. If a statement occurs frequently, it has sustained effects and strongly solidifies a particular knowledge. In diachronic analysis, frequencies can be used to identify trends (e.g. Meyer et al. 2013). However, for the explanatory power of a discourse analysis, the qualitative aspect is of greater importance than the quantitative.

A little toolbox for discourse analysis

In this section, a brief summary of our toolbox for discourse analysis is presented. Detailed methodological justifications for each of the tools can be found in the volumes by Jäger (2004, 2012). In our own research projects, we use short hand-outs like the following as memory aids or checklists when first dealing with materials.

Choosing a subject matter

Formulating an initial research question should be the foundation of a discourse analysis project. As the project evolves, this research question may be fine-tuned. Based on the research question, the next step is usually to choose a subject matter. Alternatively, the project can start out from a subject matter that researchers find interesting, and then formulate the research question.

In the project report (usually in the introduction), a rationale for the project and its subject matter has to be given. It needs to be kept in mind that the relationship between a phenomenon of interest and particular discourse strands is often not straightforward because a phenomenon may permeate many discourse strands. For example, in a research project that aims to examine how racism permeates the media, the researcher has to decide which discourse strand(s) to focus on. To make the choice, the researcher has to have an initial concept of racism in mind. This concept may be developed further in the course of the analysis. Theoretical concepts are always debatable, and the researcher needs to clarify and justify which concept he is working with.[2] Equipped with this concept, the researcher can think about promising discourse strands where racism may be found. In the case of racism, it is, for example, the discourse strand of immigration, refugees and asylum seeking. Of course, the discourse strand of immigration could also be interpreted in the light of other research interests. To choose a subject matter means to choose a phenomenon of interest and a discourse strand that will be examined. This discourse strand delineates the scope of materials for analysis.

Choosing a discourse plane and a sector and characterizing them

Typically, it will be necessary, at least initially, to confine the analysis to one discourse plane (for example mass media) and one place (for instance Cairo, or international airports). When examining a discourse plane, analysis may cover one or several sectors of this plane (for example, the sector of newspapers) and some important place. The choice of sector needs to be justified. For example, a sector may be exemplary for how an issue is dealt with in the mass media, or a sector may not have previously been examined in any research project. In the latter case, of course, a review of previous research should summarize the findings from an analysis of other sectors.

In some cases, it may be possible to examine several discourse planes at once. The analysis of interactions of several discourse planes in the regulation of mass consciousness is extremely interesting, but also time-consuming. To achieve this task, it is necessary to base the analysis on well-justified examples of sectors of these discourse planes and instances of their interaction. The task becomes even more complex if entanglements of discourse strands are also considered.

Accessing and preparing the materials

As a next step, the concrete corpus for analysis needs to be delineated. For example, when analysing newspapers, the particular newspapers and the time periods under consideration need to be selected. Often it will be advisable to select several important newspapers from a particular country, or from several countries, covering an extended period of time. In contrast, a project that examines the portrayal of women in pop songs could probably rely on a few exemplary songs (though this would have to be demonstrated in the particular project). In any case, the selections have to be justified.

As a preparation for analysis, a general characterization of data sources needs to be provided. For example, in the case of newspapers: What is their political orientation, who are their readers, what is their circulation, and so on?

Analysis

Analysis typically takes place in three steps: structural analysis of the discourse strand, detailed analysis of discourse fragments, and synoptic analysis. Usually, these steps have to be gone through several times. Their sequence can be modified. In the cycles of analysis, connections between different levels of analysis are discovered, interpretations are developed and weak arguments are discarded.

A structural analysis of the discourse strand

The first typical step is the structural analysis of discourse strands. Its detailed steps are as follows:

1. A list of all articles of relevance for the discourse strand is compiled. This list should include bibliographical information, notes about topics covered in the article, the literary genre, any special characteristics and the section in which the article appears.
2. Structural analysis should roughly capture the characteristics of articles on particular aspects of interest, such as any illustrations, the layout, the use of collective symbols, the argumentation, the vocabulary and so on, and identify which forms are typical for the newspaper. This outline will be needed later to identify typical articles for the detailed analysis of typical discourse fragments.

3. A discourse strand encompasses various subtopics. These are first identified and then summarized into groups. For example, in the case of the discourse strand of stem cell research, subtopics may be summarized into groups such as the 'legal implications of stem cell research', the 'benefits of stem cell research', the 'technical procedures of stem cell research', the 'ethical problems of stem cell research', the 'costs of stem cell research' and so on. The development of groups of subtopics is an iterative process, which should lead to a good compromise between parsimony and discriminatory power.
4. The next step is to examine with what frequency particular groups of subtopics appear. Which ones are focused on and which ones are neglected? Are there any subtopics that are conspicuous by their absence?
5. If the analysis is diachronic, it will also examine how subtopics are distributed over the course of time. Are some subtopics particularly frequent at particular times or places? How does this relate to discursive events?
6. Discursive entanglements are then identified. For example, the discourse strand of stem cell research is entangled with the discourse strands of ethics, business and medicine.

The findings from these steps of analysis are combined and interpreted together. Thereby, a characterization of the newspaper's discourse position begins to emerge. For example, does the newspaper perceive stem cell research positively or negatively?

The structural analysis of a discourse strand can and should already yield ideas for the ensuing detailed analysis of typical discourse fragments (see the next subsection) and for the final synoptic analysis (see the subsection on synoptic analysis). These ideas should be written down immediately and marked accordingly.

Detailed analysis of typical discourse fragments

To identify the fine detail within the newspaper's discourse position and to assess the effects of this discourse on readers, certain discourse fragments are subjected to detailed analysis. Discourse fragments that are typical of the particular newspaper are selected for this purpose. Criteria for typicality are, for example, typical illustrations, typical use of collective symbols, typical argumentation, typical vocabulary and so on. The typical forms of these aspects have been identified in the preceding structural analysis.

To select typical discourse fragments, the researcher can proceed in several steps and rate the articles according to defined criteria. To ensure that the selection is intersubjectively plausible, several researchers can engage in this rating. The articles that score highest on typicality are then subjected to detailed analysis. If time restraints require it, or if one article exhibits all typical characteristics of the discourse strand, detailed analysis may be confined to one article only. If structural analysis has shown that the discourse strand is very heterogeneous, and if no single homogeneous discourse position can be discerned, the researcher can address several typicalities, i.e. several kinds of 'typical' articles.

129

The procedures for selecting typical articles should be systematic and transparent, but not mechanical. What is an appropriate procedure depends on the concrete research project and the discourse strand in question. The aspects that should be covered by a detailed analysis of typical discourse fragments are summarized in Table 5.1.

Table 5.1 Aspects for consideration in the analysis of discourse fragments

Aspect	Questions
Context	• Why was this article selected? Why is this article typical? • What is the general topic of this article? • Who is the author? What is her position and status within the newspaper? What are her special areas of coverage, and so on? • What was the occasion for the article? • In which section of the newspaper does the article appear?
Surface of the text	• What is the layout like? What kinds of pictures or graphs accompany the text? • What are the headings and subheadings? • How is the article structured into units of meaning? • What topics are touched upon in the article? (In other words, what discourse strands is the article a fragment of?) • How do these topics relate to each other and overlap (entanglements of discourse strands)?
Rhetorical means	• What kind and form of argumentation does the article follow? What argumentation strategy is used? • What logic underlies the composition of the article? • What implications and allusions does the article contain? • What collective symbolism is used (linguistic and graphic, involving, for example, statistics, photographs, pictures, caricatures, etc.)? • What idioms, sayings and clichés are used? • What are the vocabulary and style? • What subjects are mentioned, and how are they portrayed (persons, pronouns used)? • What references are made (e.g. references to science, information about the sources of knowledge used)?
Content and ideological statements	• What concept of humankind does the article presuppose and convey? • What concept of society does the article presuppose and convey? • What concept of (for example) technology does the article presuppose and convey? • What perspective regarding the future does the article give?
Other peculiarities of the article	
Discourse position and overall message of the article	

In analysing each of these aspects, the researcher has to ask herself what this peculiarity of the article means, what it implies. For example, what does it mean that a particular image accompanies this text? What effect does this image create? Each of these interpretations remains open to revisions. At the end of the detailed analysis, the interpretations of single aspects are combined into a total interpretation of the article. Usually, the interpretations of the single aspects fit together like the pieces of a jigsaw puzzle and form a unitary picture. If one aspect stands out, it is often due to special circumstances, such as when a photo or a headline has not been provided by the author but by the editor, who had other purposes in mind, such as spicing up the article. Such discrepancies also provide important insights into the newspaper's discourse position. Together with the findings from structural analysis, the findings from detailed analysis form the basis for synoptic analysis.

Synoptic analysis

In synoptic analysis, a final assessment of the newspaper's discourse position is made. For this purpose, the findings from structural analysis and detailed analysis are interpreted in relation and comparison to each other.

Some thoughts on analysing dispositives

Although a dispositive has certain durability, it is subject to historical changes **and** constant influence by other dispositives. A synchronic analysis serves to identify the current state of a dispositive. A particular materialization, linguistically or non-linguistically performed discursive practices can be relevant for various dispositives. For example, the dispositive of 'traffic' encompasses streets, cars, traffic jams, drivers, traffic signs and so on. But 'traffic' is also an economic problem that creates costs and affects business. 'Traffic' is therefore embedded into the economic dispositive. The economic dispositive, in turn, is embedded into the political dispositive. In a society, dispositives overlap and are entangled with each other. These entanglements may be what unifies a society.

A dispositive analysis has to include the following steps:

1. Reconstructing the knowledge that is built into linguistically performed practices (through discourse analysis, as described above). This analysis is the basis for the further steps in a dispositive analysis. It already creates an awareness of important aspects of the dispositive, such as uncharted territories in discourse, significant materializations and so on.
2. Reconstructing the knowledge that is built into non-linguistically performed discursive practices.
3. Identifying the knowledge that is built into materialization.

Reconstructing this knowledge usually results in texts. A dispositive analysis thus translates knowledge about non-linguistically performed practices and materializations into linguistically expressed knowledge.

A dispositive analysis should consider the form in which the examined knowledge occurs. Is the knowledge manifestly apparent? Or is it implicit, for example hidden in implicatures? Into what arguments is the knowledge packed? And so on. It should be noted again that the concept of knowledge is here a broad one, including not only cognitions but also emotions.

Since the analysis of discursive elements of a dispositive has already been discussed extensively above, the remainder of this section will focus on reconstructing the knowledge that is built into non-linguistically performed discursive practices.

Knowledge about non-linguistically performed practices

Non-linguistically performed discursive practices can be observed and described. The task is to identify the knowledge that enables and accompanies these practices.

For example, the analyst can observe a man who crosses a street and walks into a bakery, where he buys a loaf of bread. The analyst's task is now to find out what this man knows and wants. The man knows that he has to go to a certain place to be able to buy bread. He knows that for this purpose he has to dress in a certain way (e.g. put on shoes and a coat). He knows that when crossing a road, he has to pay attention to the traffic and observe the traffic rules. Moreover, he knows that the bakery is located in a particular place, or how to look for a bakery. He knows that in a bakery he can buy bread, and that he needs money for that. The simple act of buying bread is thus already based on a considerable amount of knowledge, and this analysis only gives a small hint of it.

The following is a more complex example. Suppose the analyst observes a man who has dug a hole at the side of a road, and is now standing in this hole and manipulating a large pipe. To reconstruct the knowledge built into this practice, the analyst has to share in this knowledge and understand what the man is doing. Suppose that to a large extent she is lacking this knowledge. There are basically three things she can do to gain an understanding of what the man is doing.

Firstly, the researcher can draw on existing texts. For example, she can consult previous research, but also more mundane documents such as practitioners' literature, instruction sheets, or field manuals.

Secondly, the analyst can ask the man what he is doing. In ethnographic methodology, this is called an ethnographic interview (see, for example, Spradley 1979)[3]. When the researcher asks the man what he is doing, the man may answer: 'I am repairing a burst pipe.' With this information, she already understands better what he is doing. Next, she may ask him: 'Why are you doing that?' He may answer something like: 'Because the pipe has burst', or 'That's my job', or 'I need to earn money somehow', and so on. The knowledge built into his activity is thus fairly complex and can be followed up to the economic practice of dependent wage labour.

A large part of knowledge is available only to actors in their practices (tacit knowledge), and actors cannot easily explicate it in talk. In other words, people will know more than they can tell. As a third option, the researcher can therefore rely on participant observation (see, for example, Agar 2002; Emerson et al. 1995; Hammersley and Atkinson 2007; Spradley 1980) to learn about this implicit knowledge and make it explicit in her research. In the extreme case, the researcher may herself learn to dig holes and mend burst pipes. A fascinating example of such work is Wacquant's (2004) study of boxing.

Knowledge with regard to materializations

Knowledge in general is not resting *within* actions or things. It is assembled in the minds of actors only. When an analyst observes an object, such as a house, a church or a bicycle, obviously he cannot ask this object about its meaning. However, there are indirect ways of reconstructing knowledge about materializations. Methodological guidelines for doing so can, for example, be found in multimodal discourse analysis (van Leeuwen 2005) and artefact analysis (Froschauer 2002; Lueger 2004); for an example of empirical work that combines multimodal discourse analysis and artefact analysis, see Maier (2009).

To analyse materializations, the researcher has to rely on his own and his fellow researchers' background knowledge. In addition, he should extend this knowledge by drawing on the pertinent literature, and by asking users, producers and other persons who are experts on the activities and materialization in question.

Artefact analysis, as developed by Lueger (2004) and Froschauer (2002), suggests that one of the first steps in analysing a materialization is to deconstruct the materialization by dividing it into its constituent parts and transcribing it into a field protocol. The material object is thus transformed into a text. Here, another problem arises, which incidentally also applies to the field notes and observation protocols produced in the participant observation of non-linguistic practices. The field protocols written by the researcher are not neutral. Like any text, they pursue particular interests, and in the ideal case, this interest should be to answer the research question.

In some cases, the researcher may even be able to draw on previous research that has already discursified the materialization in question as, for example, Caborn (1999, 2006) has done with regard to state architecture in Berlin after the reunification.

It should be emphasized again that the meaning of materializations is not fixed. The knowledge one imputes into a materialization today may be different from the knowledge that it conveyed in the past. 'Legends' might have formed around it, and meanings may have changed. Moreover, a materialization may have different meanings for members of different cultures (as well as cultures understood in the broad sense of the term) and inhabitants of different places. A good case in point is the Aztec crown of feathers, which is exhibited in the Anthropological Museum in Vienna. In pre-Columbian times, it was a ritual headdress, worn by priests or even by the Aztec emperor Montezuma. For the Spanish conquistador Hernán Cortes, it was a treasure which he stole. The Habsburg emperors bought it as an exotic curiosity. In today's Anthropological Museum, it is an exhibit of scientific value. For today's descendants of the Aztecs, the crown is a symbol of their cultural identity and stands for the blossoming and ensuing destruction of their culture. They argue that the crown was stolen from them, and that the Museum should return it. For Austrian politicians and diplomats, the crown has thus become a cause for political dissonance with Mexico. (For an in-depth analysis of the transformations of exhibits in anthropological museums, see Döring and Hirschauer 1997.)

As the example of the feather crown shows, each of the meanings assigned to a materialization is tightly related to power relations (e.g. whether the crown is a ritual item, a scientific exhibit, or a symbol of collective identity).

The object itself does not change, but its meanings change, as actors apply to it new kinds of knowledge. In the materialization as such, these power relations are invisible, and the task of the analyst is to bring them out into the open. The analyst can do this only if he considers historical contexts.

As these initial thoughts on methods for analysing dispositives indicate, the task of a dispositive analysis is complex. It encompasses the analysis of knowledge about linguistically and non-linguistically performed discourses. An example of such an analysis is Michel Foucault's (1979) book *Discipline and Punish*. Also, Victor Klemperer's (2001) *Diary of the Nazi Years* can be read as a dispositive analysis. Both authors provided little explicit information on their methodology. They apply their methodology implicitly, or as Foucault calls it, in the form of *bricolage*. They analyse discourse, assemble knowledge, consult statistics, deconstruct them, draw conclusions, add their own opinions, and so on.

The thoughts on dispositive analysis presented in this chapter do not provide a recipe or schema. However, they do give some ideas on how to approach dispositive analysis. A central part of dispositive analysis is the discourse analysis of texts. Moreover, dispositive analysis comprises the analysis of non-linguistic practices, for which methods developed in ethnography, such as ethnographic interviews and participant observation, provide important means. A final component is the analysis of materializations, which can draw on methods such as multimodal discourse analysis and artefact analysis. An explicit methodology for combining these approaches has yet to be developed. Such an endeavour can only be achieved by means of concrete research projects that devote space and time to explicit reasoning about methodology. This promotes the development of dispositive analysis, and contributes to bridging the gaps between discourse analysis and other methods of empirical social research.

Summary

The methodology we have presented here has been continuously developed since the mid-1980s, and has been applied in a wide range of studies.[4] It is not a rigid formula that can be followed mechanically. It is a flexible approach and a systematic incitement for researchers to develop their own analytic strategies, depending on the research question and type of materials at hand. An article like this one can provide initial insights, but – since every study needs a customized approach – it cannot anticipate the full range of possibilities. This is in accordance with Foucault's understanding of methodology:

> If you want an image, think of a network of scaffolding that functions as a point of relay between a project being concluded and a new one. Thus I don't construct a general method of definitive value for myself or for others. What I write does not prescribe anything, neither to myself nor to others. At most, its character is instrumental and visionary or dream-like. (Foucault 1991: 29)

However, Foucault by no means implies that 'anything goes'. As he emphasizes, he is very much interested in discovering truths, albeit truths that are valid in a certain time and place:

In the course of my works, I utilize methods that are part of the classic repertory: demonstration, proof by means of historical documentation, quoting other texts, referral to authoritative comments, the relationship between ideas and facts, the proposal of explanatory patterns, etc. There's nothing original in that. From this point of view, whatever I assert in my writing can be verified or refuted as in any other history book. (Foucault 1991: 32f.)

In this spirit, we encourage researchers to develop a thorough theoretical understanding that underlies their methodology and – on this basis – to innovate, adapt, mix and match the methods as it fits their research purpose. The best way to learn critical discourse analysis is to do it.

Further reading

Dreyfus, H. L. and Rabinow, P. (1982) *Michel Foucault: Beyond Structuralism and Hermeneutics*. Sussex: The Harvester Press.
A classical exposition of Foucault's work as a whole, judged accurate by Foucault himself.

Foucault, M. (1990) *The History of Sexuality. Volume 1: An Introduction*. New York: Vintage.
One of the thinner and more accessible works by Foucault, this gripping little book can be recommended as a starting point for reading Foucault in the original. It is actually more about the general workings of power/knowledge than about the specific issue of sexuality.

Jäger, S. (2012) *Kritische Diskursanalse. Eine Einführung*, 6th rev. edn. Münster: Unrast.
A thorough and comprehensive outline of discourse theory and the method of critical discourse analysis developed by Siegfried Jäger (in German).

Jäger, S. and Zimmermann, J. (eds) (2010) *Lexikon kritische Diskursanalyse: Eine Werkzeugkiste*. Münster: Unrast.
A dictionary of key concepts of critical discourse analysis (in German).

Wetherell, M., Taylor, S. and Yates, S. J. (2001) *Discourse Theory and Practice: A Reader*. London: Sage.
This reader is a good starting point for reading primary literature on discourse theory and discourse analysis. It covers major authors, various strands of theorizing and key epistemological and methodological issues.

Tasks

1. Explore your surroundings (for example: the street where you live, or your classroom), applying the concept of dispositives. What materializations and non-linguistically performed discursive practices do you see? How do they support (or contradict) the linguistically performed practices taking place in those surroundings? How do the materializations shape human action? Why were those materializations created this way?
2. Go to a social media website of your choice and examine how personal profiles are created there. What sort of information is required or invited? When users fill out these forms, what sort of subject is created? Who creates this subject?
3. Work through the 'little toolbox'.

   • To choose a subject matter, you may think about the conditions in today's world. What issues do you find unacceptable? Choose one of them as your subject matter.

- Choose and define a discourse plane, discourse sector and temporal scope for examining this issue.
- Formulate your research question(s). As explained in the introduction, these could include questions such as:

  o What is valid knowledge about [issue X] in [discourse sector Y] at [time Z]?
  o How does this knowledge arise and how is it passed on?
  o What functions does it have for constituting subjects?
  o What consequences does it have for the shaping of society?

- Prepare your data set.
- Analyse the data, developing the answers to your research questions.

Notes

1 The author order is alphabetical, reflecting the closely entwined and equally important contributions of both authors.
2 For example, a definition of racism that is generally justifiable and well accepted in the sciences encompasses the following three elements. (1) One or several people are for biological or cultural reasons constructed as an ethnic group or even a race. (2) This group is evaluated (negatively or positively, e.g. when blacks are assumed to be superior jazz musicians). (3) The construction and evaluation takes place from a position of power (which in discourse analysis is obvious, since discourse is *per se* 'powerful').
3 Ethnographic interviews take place in the course of participant observation, i.e., while research subjects engage in the action of interest. Such an interview can be long, or short, when the researcher asks just a quick question and then continues with silent observation and note-taking.
4 See for example the project summaries in Margarete Jäger and Siegfried Jäger (2007).

6

DISCOURSE AS THE RECONTEXTUALIZATION OF SOCIAL PRACTICE – A GUIDE

THEO VAN LEEUWEN

CONTENTS

Keywords

social practice, recontextualization, discourse, social action, leadership

---

Introduction

The term 'discourse' is often used to mean an extended stretch of connected speech or writing, a 'text'. 'Discourse analysis' then means 'the analysis of a text, or type of text'. Here I use it in a different sense, building on the work of Michel Foucault (e.g. 1977) and defining discourses (note the plural) as *socially constructed ways of knowing some aspect of reality* which can be drawn upon when that aspect of reality has to be represented, or, to put it another way, *context-specific frameworks for making sense of things*. In this chapter I will use discourses of 'leadership' as an example. Clearly there are different conceptions of what a 'leader' is and does. The discourse of the 'opinion leader', for instance, which was developed in the context of US public communication research (Katz and Lazarsfeld 1955) is one in which leaders are 'first among equals', role models who provide examples for others to follow. Such leaders may never be formally recognized as leaders, but they will influence what their peers think, say and do. In other discourses, leaders are constructed as fundamentally different from ordinary mortals, and said to rule by 'divine right'. In his book on Nazi language, Klemperer (2000 [1957]: 111ff.) documents how the Nazi ideology 'again and again underlined [Hitler's] uniquely close relationship with the Godhead, his special status as the chosen one, his special sonship, his religious mission' (p. 111), but in more recent times, too, we have seen leaders such as Bush and Blair claim divine approval for their actions. Clearly, discourses of leadership have a long history. The New Testament introduced the discourse of the leader as 'shepherd', Plato's *Republic* the discourse of the 'philosopher king', the leader as expert. And ever since then, political thinkers, philosophers and others have struggled to balance people's need for freedom and persuasion with society's need for guidance and some form of coercion.

In this chapter I argue that discourses are ultimately modelled on social practices, so that, for instance, knowledge of what 'leadership' *is*, is ultimately based on what leaders *do*. However, discourses will *transform* these doings, for instance by leaving out some of the less palatable things leaders may do, or by representing, not just what leaders do, but also why they do it, and, therefore, why their actions are to be seen as legitimate (cf. van Leeuwen 2007). And different discourses, different ways of making sense of the same aspect of reality, will do all this in different ways, including and excluding different things, and doing so in the service of different interests.

As I have said, in this chapter the term 'discourse' will not be synonymous with the term 'text'. Yet, evidence for the existence of discourses will inevitably have to come from texts, from what is said or written about 'leadership', for instance. More specifically it will have to come from the similarity between what is said and written about a given aspect of reality in *different* texts that circulate in the same context. It is on the basis of such similar statements, repeated or paraphrased in different texts, and dispersed among these texts in different ways, that we can put the puzzle back together and reconstruct the discourses texts draw on. This chapter introduces methods for just this kind of reconstruction. After discussing the theoretical background of my approach to discourse, I will show (1) how to use text analysis to piece together a discourse, and to connect it to the practice from which it ultimately derives its meaning, and (2) how to analyse the processes of transformation, or *recontextualization* (Bernstein 1981, 1986), that occur as practices are turned into discourses.

I will use a single example, an online leadership questionnaire for assessing the performance of managers and executives. Called 'Voices', it was designed by the US company Lominger-International, and is used by companies and other organizations the world over. The person to be assessed, referred to by Lominger as the 'learner', nominates five people to assess him or her in each of four categories: 'direct reports' (i.e. people he or she is supervising), 'peers', 'customers' and 'others'. In addition the 'learner' is assessed by his or her boss and by the 'learner' him- or herself. The selected 'raters' complete the 'tool' online, rating the 'learner' in terms of 30 'competencies', such as 'hiring and staffing', 'interpersonal savvy', 'sizing up people', 'problem solving', 'confronting direct reports', 'drive for results', 'customer focus', 'integrity and trust', etc., and also in terms of 30 'career stoppers and stallers' which are formulated in terms of 'overuse' of these same competencies. Each 'competency' and each 'stopper and staller' is glossed by a paragraph of description, e.g.:

Conflict Management – Steps up to conflicts, seeing them as opportunities; reads situations quickly; good at focused listening; can hammer out tough agreements and settle disputes equitably; can find common ground and get cooperation with minimum noise.

This contrasts then to the following 'stopper and staller':

Overuse of **Conflict Management** – May be seen as overly aggressive and assertive; may get in the middle of everyone else's problems; may drive for a solution before others are ready; may have a chilling effect on open debate; may spend too much time with obstinate people and unsolvable problems.

Both competencies and their 'overuse' are then rated on a 5-point scale. 'Competencies' are rated as (a) 'a towering strength', (b) 'talented', (c) 'skilled/OK' (d) 'weakness' or (e) 'serious issue'. 'Overuse' is rated as happening (a) 'constantly', (b) 'much of the time', (c) 'some of the time', (d) 'every so often', or (e) 'not at all'. Competencies are also rated in terms of their perceived importance for the job of the 'learner': (a) 'mission critical', (b) 'very important', (c) 'useful/nice to have', (d) 'less important' and (e) 'not important'.

As I have said, a single text does not provide enough evidence for reconstructing a discourse, although it can of course be used for methodological demonstration, as I do in this chapter. I would nevertheless argue for the special importance of texts such as 'Voices'. 'Voices' is used very widely and is therefore not only a discourse *about* leadership, but also constitutive of actual leadership practices and actual ways of talking about these practices. When introduced in universities, as it was in the university where I work, 'Voices' plays a key part in the move from the old elected 'first among equals' style of leadership to new, corporate leadership discourses and practices (cf. Fairclough 1993). And as 'learners' are obliged to discuss their 'weaknesses' with an 'executive coach', they will more or less be forced to introduce the discourse of 'Voices' into their thinking and talking about their own role and identity as 'leaders'. For all these reasons, it is important to critically analyse texts such as 'Voices', so as to reveal how they construct 'leadership'.

Theoretical background

Anthropologists and sociologists have always realized that representation is ultimately based on practice, on what people *do*. The primacy of practice runs like a thread through the classics of European as well as American sociology. It is true that sociologists sometimes derive concrete actions from abstract concepts and processes from systems – Durkheim's 'collective consciousness' (Durkheim 1933), Bourdieu's 'habitus' (Bourdieu 1977), Talcott Parsons' systems theory (1977) and Lévi-Strauss's structuralist anthropology (1964) are examples. Yet the primacy of practice keeps asserting itself also in the work of these writers, sometimes against the grain of their methodology, at other times as a fundamental cornerstone of their theory (e.g. Berger and Luckmann 1966). Bourdieu elaborated the primacy of practice and the fundamental difference between participant knowledge and 'outsider' knowledge in his *Outline of a Theory of Practice* (1977) and elsewhere. Talcott Parsons, even in his systems theory, can still say that 'the subject of social interaction is in a fundamental sense logically prior to that of social system' (1977: 145), and even Lévi-Strauss (1964) at times derives the meaning of myths from social practices rather than from abstract schemata. Durkheim leaves no doubt about it, especially in *The Elementary Forms of Religious Life* (1976) and *Primitive Classification* (Durkheim and Mauss 1963): myths are modelled after rites, conceptual life after social life, representations of the world after social organization. And Malinowski (1923, 1935), shows how representation originates in action and in uses of language that are inextricably interwoven with action, and how action is then twice recontextualized, first as representation, in 'narrative speech', and then in the construction of new realities, in 'the language of ritual and magic', as Malinowski calls it. Later, Bernstein's theory of recontextualization applied a similar idea to educational practices, describing how knowledge is actively produced 'in the upper reaches of the education system' (1986: 5) and then embedded into a pedagogic content in the 'lower reaches', where it is objectified and made to serve the contextually defined purpose of a 'discourse of order', a form of 'moral education', in the Durkheimian sense. In the approach to critical discourse analysis I present in this chapter I connect this idea to the term 'discourse', used in Foucault's sense (e.g. 1977). This definition of discourse has also been introduced into critical discourse analysis by Fairclough (e.g. 2000a) and the emphasis on discourse as 'social cognition' has been inspired by the work of van Dijk (e.g. 1998).

Linguists have generally differed from sociologists in deriving processes (syntagms) from systems (grammars, paradigms), rather than processes (practices) from systems (institutions and objectified forms of knowledge). But when linguists began to study texts, in the 1970s, many found it hard to conceptualize the production and interpretation of texts without recourse to experience, to 'world knowledge' (e.g. Schank and Abelson 1977), or 'background knowledge' (e.g. Brown and Yule 1983; Levinson 1983). Martin (1984, 1992) reintroduced the 'field' of discourse, using lexical cohesion analysis to construct 'activity sequences' – sequences of represented activities. Together with the work of Gleason (1973) and Grimes (1975), who paid attention, not just to represented activities, but also to represented 'roles', 'settings' etc., this work has been of fundamental influence on the ideas I present in this chapter. The main difference is that I have extended it beyond procedural and narrative texts, in which there tends to be a close relation between the represented and representing activity sequences, and applied it also to other kinds of text, in which there is a greater difference between the structure of the text, which may be some rhetorical, argumentative structure, and the underlying discourse, i.e. the representation/transformation of a practice together with the purposes, legitimations and evaluations of that practice.

Finally, the study of the way discourses transform social practices, which in this chapter is represented especially by my theory of social action, derives to a large degree from the work of Halliday (1978, 1994), whose theory of transitivity made it possible to interpret differently worded representations of the same reality as different social constructions of that reality, and from the work of Kress, Hodge, Fowler, Trew and others (Fowler et al. 1979; Kress and Hodge 1979) who demonstrated how Halliday's work can be used and extended for the purpose of critical discourse analysis, or, as they said, quoting Whorf (1956), how linguistics can become 'an instrument of discovery, clarification and insight' for the analysis of the social world (Kress and Hodge 1979: 14).

Discourse and social practice

As I have said, the approach to discourse I introduce in this chapter is based on the idea that discourses are recontextualizations of social practices. To bring this out, I start with a simple schema of the crucial elements of social practices. Actual social practices will always contain all these elements. Specific discourses about social practices will select from them, transform them and add further elements.

Actions

The core of a social practice is formed by a set of actions, which may or may not have to be performed in a specific order. The 'conflict management' text above, for instance, contains the following actions (I ignore for the moment that they have been transformed in different ways, for instance by being generalized or represented in a relatively abstract way):

Stepping up to conflict
Reading situations

Listening
Hammering out agreements
Settling disputes
Finding common ground
Getting cooperation

Performance modes

These actions may have to be performed in specific ways. In the 'conflict management' text, listening has to be *focused*, agreements have to be *tough*, and cooperation has to be achieved *with minimum noise*. Clearly it is not just important what leaders do, but also how they do it – or how they should *not* do it, as can be seen in the '*Overuse* of Conflict Management' text, where 'overly aggressive and assertive' actions are disapproved of.

Actors

Social actors participate in practices in one of a number of roles – as 'agents' (doers of action), 'patients' (participants to whom actions are done), or 'beneficiaries' (participants who benefit from an action, whether in a positive or negative sense). In the 'conflict management' text the key participant is the 'learner' whose performance is being assessed. Although the actions in the text would in reality require further participants (the people who are in conflict, the people who are being listened to, etc.), they have been deleted in this particular discourse. Only the actions of the 'learner' seem to matter – as 'behaviour', rather than as what they really are, *inter*actions, actions undertaken for and with other people. In the 'Overuse of Conflict Management' text, on the other hand, other people are mentioned, though for the most part vaguely ('everyone else', 'others', 'obstinate people').

Presentation styles

The way in which actors present themselves (their dress, grooming, etc.) is an important aspect of all social practices, even if it may be taken for granted in some representations, as is the case in 'Voices'. In my experience, senior managers constantly evaluate each other's presentation style, but this is done informally, rather than as part of formal performance assessment procedures.

Times

Social practices (or parts of them) will take place at more or less specific times. 'Focused listening', for instance, will happen in regular, scheduled, face-to-face meetings with 'direct reports'. I have italicized some examples in the text below:

Timely Decision Making – Makes decisions in a *timely* manner, sometimes with incomplete information and under *tight deadlines* and pressure; able to make a *quick* decision.

Confronting Direct Reports – Deals with problem direct reports firmly and *in a timely manner*; doesn't allow problems to fester; *regularly* reviews performance and holds *timely* discussions; can make negative decisions when all efforts fail; deals effectively with troublemakers.

Spaces

Social practices (or parts of them) also take place in specific spaces, chosen or arranged as a suitable environment for the practice. The discourse of 'Voices', however, steers away from such concrete specifics, perhaps because it is designed to apply to many different institutional contexts.

Resources

Social practices also require specific resources, specific tools and materials. 'Providing information', for instance, may require computers, an intranet, and so on. But these too have been left out of the 'Voices' text as somehow not relevant to leadership practices.

Eligibility

Specific qualities of the concrete elements of social practices (the actors, settings and resources) make them eligible to function as actors, settings or resources in those practices. In fact, the whole of the 'Voices' leadership questionnaire can be seen as a discourse focusing specifically on 'eligibility', on the characteristics an actor needs to have to be eligible to play the role of 'leader' in an organization. I will return to this point below.

As I have already said, discourses are transformations, or recontextualizations of social practices. Three types of transformation are particularly important:

Deletion

Some elements of a social practice may not be represented in a particular discourse. As we have seen, in the 'Conflict management' text all actors other than the 'learner' are deleted, and so are times, spaces and resources. Such deletions happen for context-specific reasons. First of all, 'Voices' centres on assessing 'learners', focusing on their behavioural patterns, often in abstraction from the specific situations in which these behaviours occur. 'Voices' also has to be applicable to many different contexts and therefore tends towards decontextualization, towards leaving out concrete specifics.

Substitution

The key transformation is of course the transformation from an actual element of an actual social practice into an element of discourse, and this can be done in many different ways. Actors, for instance, can be represented as specific individuals or as *types* of people, they can be referred to in abstract or specific terms, and so on. In the next section I will deal in detail with the transformation of social action in discourse. van Leeuwen (2008) provides an account of the ways in which actors, times and spaces can be transformed in discourse.

Addition

Discourses can also add *reactions* and *motives* to the representation of social practices. Reactions are the mental processes which, according to a given discourse, will accompany specific actions of specific actors, for instance the way the actors *feel* about specific actions, or the way they *interpret* specific actions. Needless to say, in different discourses different reactions may accompany the same actions of the same actors. In the 'Voices' text, as in many other discourses, the focus is on the reactions of the 'patients', the people on the receiving end of the leader's actions. In the example below, for instance, I interpret 'being direct' as a 'performance mode', and 'being uncomfortable' and 'being off-guard' as reactions:

> *Overuse of* **Integrity and Trust** – May be too direct at times, which may catch people off guard and make them uncomfortable; may push openness and honesty to the point of being disruptive ...

The most important motives are *purposes* and *legitimations*. Different discourses may ascribe different purposes to the same actions. In the following example the purpose of 'getting first-hand customer information' is 'to improve products and services', because the relevant 'competency' is 'customer focus'. If the competency had been 'profit focus' the same action might be given another purpose, for instance 'meeting demand' or 'increasing sales':

> **Customer Focus** – Is dedicated to meeting the expectations and requirements of internal and external customers; gets first-hand customer information and uses it for improvements in products and services ...

Legitimations provide *reasons* for why practices (or parts of practices) are performed, or for why they are performed the way they are. These reasons may be spelled out in explicit detail or be communicated through what, elsewhere (van Leeuwen 2007), I have called 'moral evaluation'. 'Moral evaluation' is an abstract way of referring to specific actions which serves to highlight qualities of that action that carry positive connotations (or, in the case of de-legitimation, negative connotations). In the 'conflict management' text, for instance, a particular action is referred to as 'getting cooperation'. This formulation does not reveal much about what the leader is actually, concretely, doing here. Persuading? Giving directives? Bribing? But it does legitimize the action, because it suggests that it is based on voluntary 'cooperation', rather than as 'compliance' with top down orders, and it also reveals the purpose of the action ('getting cooperation').

To reconstruct a discourse (or rather, that part of it that is realized in a specific text), I enter a text's representations of the concrete elements of the social practice (actors, actions, times, places and so on), as well as the reactions and motives that have been added, in the different columns of a table, using the following principles:

1. Actions that are referred to several times in different wordings are combined, but where an alternative wording adds a purpose or legitimation it is entered separately in the relevant column.
2. Where possible, actions are ordered chronologically, e.g.:

Find common ground

↓

Hammer out agreement

Where actions are simultaneous rather than sequential, I use a ' ≈' sign. Where there is a choice of two (or more) possible actions, I use a flowchart notation. Where it is not possible to decide on any chronological connection, I use a '+' sign, e.g.:

Monitors process

+

Monitors progress

3. Elements other than actions are horizontally aligned with the actions to which they pertain, e.g. timings with the actions they are timings of, spaces with the actions that take place in that space, legitimations with the actions they legitimize, and so on.

The example below (Table 6.1) analyses the 'conflict management' text. For the sake of convenience, I first show this text again.

Table 6.1 Analysis of the 'conflict management' text

Action	Actor	Performance mode	Timing	Reaction	Motive
Conflict management	*(leader)*	*'stepping up' (decisive)*		*see as opportunity*	
read situation ↓	(leader)		quickly		
listen ↓	" "	focused			
find common ground ↓	" "				
hammer out agreement/ settle disputes ↓	" "	tough; hammer			equitably
get cooperation	" "				cooperation

Conflict Management – Steps up to conflicts, seeing them as opportunities; reads situations quickly; good at focused listening; can hammer out tough agreements and settle disputes equitably; can find common ground and get cooperation with minimum noise.

The text contains two *overall labels* for this particular episode of leadership practice, a more neutral, technical one ('conflict management') and a more connotative one ('stepping up to conflict') which adds a hint of 'decisiveness' or 'boldness', hence a 'performance mode' that pertains to the whole of the practice. I have bolded and italicized such overall labels in the analysis.

Even this brief example reveals some aspects of the way the 'Voices' discourse defines leadership. Two motives intermingle: 'decisiveness' and 'toughness' on the one hand, and 'fairness' and 'attentiveness' on the other hand. It is also clear that the discourse focuses entirely on the leader and the way in which s/he performs the actions that define his/her leadership. The other participants are, so to speak, kept out of the frame.

Three further aspects of discourse need to be mentioned at this point.

- *Some discourses provide discursive resources for other discourses.*

In Van Leeuwen (2008) I look at how the practice of 'the first day at school' is recontextualized in different discourses and note that parent- and teacher-oriented 'first day' discourses rely a great deal on a lay version of child psychology for legitimation. Parents are advised to take their time 'because children don't like to be rushed', and to 'establish the same routine going to and from school' because that 'will make your child feel secure'. Psychologists are quoted to lend authority to such pronouncements. Clearly, certain discourses elaborate forms of knowledge (for instance about what children are like) or systems of moral values (e.g. religions), that can be used in a wide range of discourses to legitimize a wide range of different practices (cf. Berger and Luckmann 1966). In my view 'Voices' is such an expert discourse, supplying legitimate eligibility criteria for leaders and leadership that can be used in a wide range of settings, as borne out by this quote from the website of Lominger-International:

> Lominger's LEADERSHIP ARCHITECT Competencies drive our research-based, experience-tested and integrated talent management solutions. Flexible, useable, and customizable, the suites can be deployed together as a fully integrated system or individually to meet your immediate business needs. No matter where you start, the LEADERSHIP ARCHITECT Competency Library allows you to maintain a common language for leadership …

- *Discourses may be modalized*

'Voices' uses a great deal of *ability modality*. The leader '*can* hammer out tough agreements', '*can* find common ground' and so on. In other words, the 'Voices' discourse is not so much about what leaders actually do as about what they are *able* to do, and this is probably true for all discourses that construct eligibility criteria for specific roles, and for all discursive practices that test and certify what 'learners' *can* do.

'Ability' modality is not the only way in which discourses can be modalized. Practices may be recontextualized as *past* or *future* practices, for instance, as *actual* or *possible* practices, or as *right* or *wrong* practices. Such modalizations should be indicated in the analysis, for instance by using superscripts:

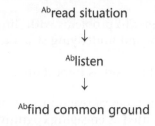

[Ab]read situation

↓

[Ab]listen

↓

[Ab]find common ground

• *Discourses combine in specific ways*

A given text may include several discourses. Nevertheless, one discourse is usually central and other, 'secondary' discourses relate to it in specific ways. Texts may, for instance, contrast past and present discourses about a given practice, usually to position the present discourse as an improvement on the past, or 'right' and 'wrong' discourses, as in the case of Voices' juxtaposition of competencies and 'overuses' of those competencies. Other discourses may play the role of 'preparatory' discourses, dealing, for instance, with practices or arranging spaces for the central practice, or with acquiring the qualifications needed to participate in the central practice. 'Secondary' discourses may also be legitimatory. In an interview with the CEO of a large company, conducted as part of a research project on leadership in which I am currently involved, the CEO interrupted his description of his company's corporate responsibility practices with a lengthy account of how he built his own house and included a rainwater tank and low energy lightbulbs. He did this to show that he was personally engaged in sustainability practices, and really believed in them, so positioning himself as a charismatic leader who leads by example and inspires rather than imposes.

Needless to say, what in one context is a 'central' discourse may in another be 'secondary', and vice versa.

Social action

In this section I deal with the ways social actions can be, and are, transformed in discourse, again using 'Voices' as my main example. I will begin by explaining the main ways in which social actions can be transformed.

Actions and reactions

I have already touched on the way discourses may infuse a version of a social practice with representations of the actors' reactions to the actions that constitute the practice. As Berger has said (Berger and Luckmann 1966: 113), social practices involve not only 'a regulatory pattern for externally visible actions, but also the emotions and attitudes that belong to these actions', and these may be differently construed in different discourses about these practices.

Reactions can be formulated in a number of ways. They can be *unspecified* (through verbs such as 'react', or 'respond') or *specified* as *cognitive* (e.g. 'grasp'), *perceptive* (e.g. 'has a nose for') or *affective* (e.g. 'feel'):

> *responds* in a timely manner to problems with direct reports
> quickly *grasps* the essence and underlying structure of anything
> *has a nose for* talent
> makes people *feel* his or her work is important

In many discourses different types of reactions are attributed to different social actors. Some may be represented as engaging cognitively with social actions, for instance, others as reacting at a more emotional level.

Material and semiotic action

Actions can be interpreted as *material*, as 'doings' (e.g. 'act'), or as *semiotic*, as 'meanings' (e.g. 'articulate'). Most of a leader's actions are in fact speech acts, hence semiotic actions, but they may be represented as material actions, to make them seem more active and dynamic, as in the last two examples below:

> *acts* with customers in mind
> can *articulate* the strengths and limitations of people inside and outside the organization
> *provides the information* people need to know to do their job
> *creates mileposts and symbols* to rally support behind the vision

Material actions can be *transactive*, involving two participants, so that the action is represented as actually having an effect on people or things (e.g. 'hire' and 'assemble') , or *non-transactive*, involving only one participant, which represents the action as 'display', as 'behaviour' that does not affect anyone or anything other than the actor him- or herself (e.g. 'perform'):

> *hires* the best people available
> *assembles* talented staff
> tends to trust people to *perform*

Transactive material actions are *interactive* if they are realized by a verb that can only take a human object (e.g. 'be candid with') and *instrumental* if they can (also) take a non-human object (e.g. 'deal with', 'manage'). If the latter dominates in a given discourse, there is clearly more of a sense of the actor 'using' people 'instrumentally', to achieve goals, rather than thinking of them as people with their own goals and interests:

> *manages* all kinds and classes of people equitably
> *deals* effectively *with* troublemakers
> can *be candid with* peers

The same distinction applies to semiotic actions. They can be behaviouralized, in which case the meanings conveyed by the speech acts are not included in the representation, e.g.:

> *communicates* effectively
> can *motivate* many kinds of direct reports

Or they can include those meanings, whether through *quotation*, *'rendition'* (reported speech) or by specifying the nature of the signified (*topic specification*), or the signifier (*form specification*) as in:

> *talks about possibilities*
> can accurately *restate the opinions of others*
> can easily *pose future scenarios...*

Objectivation and descriptivization

Actions and reactions can be *activated*, that is represented dynamically, *as* actions (e.g. 'analyse') or *de-activated*, represented in a static way, as though they are entities or qualities rather than actions (e.g. 'analysis'):

> *analyses* both successes and failures for clues to improvement
> is excellent at honest *analysis*

Deactivated representations of social actions may be *objectivated* or *descriptivized*. In the case of objectivation, actions or reactions are represented as though they were things, for instance by means of nominalization or process nouns, or by various metonyms, such as substituting the time of the action (*'temporalization'*) or the space of the action (*'spatialization'*) for the action itself:

> can diffuse even *high tension situations* comfortably
> fosters open *dialogue*
> may have a chilling effect on getting everyone's *input*

In the case of descriptivization, actions and reactions are represented as more or less permanent qualities of social actors, that is, usually, either as 'epithets' or as 'attributes':

> can *be candid with* peers
> may *be* overly *optimistic about* how much people can grow

De-agentialization

Actions and reactions can be *agentialized*, represented as brought about by human agency, or *de-agentialized*, represented as brought about in ways that are impermeable to human agency – through natural forces, unconscious processes and so on.

To mention three types of de-agentialization: In the case of *eventuation*, the action or reaction is represented as an event, as something that 'just happens', without anybody doing it. This may be done in a number of ways, for instance through verbs of involuntary action, such as 'happen' or 'occur'. I have not found an example of this in the 'Voices' text.

In the case of *existentialization*, an action or reaction is represented as something that simply 'exists', usually through an 'existential process', as in *high tension situations*.

In the case of *naturalization*, an action or reaction is represented as a natural process through abstract verbs such as 'vary', 'expand', 'develop', which link actions and reactions to specific interpretations of material processes – to discourses of rise and fall or ebb and flood; of birth and death; of growth and decay; of change and development and evolution; of fusion and disintegration; of expansion and contraction, and so on. This will often have a legitimatory function. Examples in 'Voices' include terms such as *growth*, *development*, *workflow*, *turnaround*, and *breakthrough*.

Generalization and abstraction

Actions and reactions may be *generalized* to different degrees. Generalizations abstract away from the specific actions that make up a practice or some episode that forms part of it, and label the practice or episode as a whole, as in our earlier example of 'conflict management', and as also in the following examples:

> *distributes the workload* appropriately
> regularly *reviews performance*
> *provides* challenging and stretching *tasks and assignment*

Actions and reactions may also be represented abstractly, in which case a quality, often apparently peripheral, is used to name the whole. This I refer to as *distillation* – a quality is distilled from the whole that has particular relevance in the given context, usually for purposes of legitimation, as in our earlier example of 'getting cooperation', and also in:

> *builds* appropriate *rapport*
> *uses diplomacy and tact*
> *eliminates roadblocks*

Overdetermination

I use the term *overdetermination* to refer to two specific types of representation where a given social practice stands for more than itself. I have not found an example of this in the 'Voices' text.

In the case of *symbolization*, an – often fictional – social practice stands for a number of social practices. This is the case in myths, and it is the reason why myths have such an important function in society: 'Myths are a model of social action based on a mythical interpretation of the past' (Wright 1975: 188). The killing of the dragon in the myth can stand for passing the entrance examination, winning the election, in short for any trial in which the hero overcomes an obstacle towards achieving his or her goal. This accounts for its enduring quality as a 'model' for many different practices.

In the case of *inversion*, one or more elements of the social practice are changed into its opposite. In comic strips such as *The Flintstones* and *Hagar the Horrible*, the characters and settings and objects are set in the past, but the way they interact and live are more or less contemporary – the ways of contemporary suburban families. This gives a kind of universality to these practices that helps legitimate it as natural and unavoidable rather than culturally and historically specific.

The system network in Table 6.2 provides an overview of the categories I have discussed and also indicates which transformations can and which cannot co-occur. Square brackets are 'either–or' choices and curly brackets simultaneous choices. It is therefore possible, for instance, for an action to be semiotic (behavioural) and objectivated and de-agentialized and generalized (but not overdetermined), e.g. 'workplace communication' in a sentence such as 'good workplace communication improves productivity'. However, it is not possible for an action to be both interactive and instrumental.

Table 6.2 Social action network

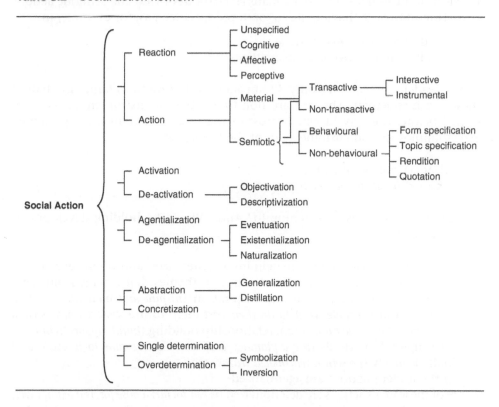

A text analysis using this network will allow two kinds of question to be asked:

1. What kinds of actions are attributed to what kinds of participants?
2. What kinds of actions tend to be objectivated, de-agentialized and so on?

Here are some observations resulting from my analysis of the 'Voices' text:

- Most actions and reactions in the text are attributed to the leader (199), rather than to employees (28) or customers (4).
- About one-third (9 out of 25) of the reactions attributed to employees, and all reactions attributed to customers, are affective reactions such as *like*, *respect, trust, feel*, for instance. Only 2 of the reactions attributed to employees are cognitive:

  (employees) *like* working for (the leader)
  (employees) *feel* their work is important
  (employees) *need* further development
  (the leader) gains (customers') *trust* and *respect*

On the other hand, out of a total of 64 reactions of the leader, only 7 are affective, and 42 cognitive. The leader *is aware of, assesses, plans, judges, projects, learns, reads the situation* and so on.

- Most of the leader's actions are material (101 out of 199) and semiotic actions (34) tend to be 'behaviouralized' or 'topic-specified', as, for example, in:

  (leader) *represents his interests*
  (leader) *diffuses high tension situations*

Of the leader's 199 actions, only 32 impact on other humans (and only half of these are interactive). The rest are non-transactive or instrumental. As mentioned before, the way in which most of the leaders' actions are represented leaves employees and customers out of the frame, e.g.:

  (leader) *practises listening*
  (leader) *holds development discussions*

We might ask: Who is he listening to? And: Who is he holding development discussions with?

- The leader's actions are overwhelmingly generalized and often represented in terms of distillations. The most common themes that emerge from these distillations are: motivation and inspiration (*inspire and motivate, create a climate in which people want to do their best* etc.), future vision (*look beyond today, project into the future* etc.), relationship building (*build rapport, relate to*), 'instrumental' methods (*use diplomacy and tact, use rigorous logic* etc.), and finally honesty (*present unvarnished truths*, etc.).
- All the leader's actions are agentialized.
- 29 of the leader's actions are descriptivized (*is fair to, has a nose for, is a teamplayer, is cooperative, is good at figuring out*, etc.), whereas this is the case for only 2 of the employees' actions. Only 8 of the leader's actions are objectivated, while the employees' actions, on the other hand, are always objectivated (*career goal, trust, input, work*) – only their reactions are activated.

Summary

What can we conclude from this? First of all, that in this discourse leaders are constructed as knowledgeable doers, who act at a broad, general level and whose actions are imbued with specific purposes and motives. They are at once tough, decisive, quick to act and patient, understanding and fair, at once practical and down to earth and visionary. That sounds good, but it is as if they act all this out in front of a mirror. Mirror, mirror on the wall, who is the toughest of them all? And the employees for and with whom they do their work are under-represented, their work conveyed by nouns and nominalizations which deprive it of its dynamic and productive character. Customers, finally, are almost entirely absent. Not to put too fine a point on it, this is not a form of leadership which is focused on *doing*, on service, facilitation, enablement, but a self-obsessed form of leadership which is focused on being a leader, and on glorifying the characteristic attributes of leaders, rather than their deeds.

Further reading

Bernstein, B. (1990) *The Structuring of Pedagogic Discourse*. London: Routledge.
Chapter 5 presents the theory of recontextualization which has inspired especially the earlier part of this present chapter. Difficult to read, but rewarding.

Fairclough, N. (1995) *Critical Discourse Analysis*. London: Longman.
Norman Fairclough was the first critical discourse analyst to turn his attention to corporate discourses, as exemplified in this work by chapters 5 and 6.

Malinowski, B. (1923) The problem of meaning in primitive languages. In: C. K. Ogden and I. A. Richards, *The Meaning of Meaning*. London: Routledge and Kegan Paul.
Written in the 1920s, this is the classic account of how practice gets to be transformed, or 'recontextualized', into discourse.

van Leeuwen, T. and Wodak, R. (1999) Legitimizing immigration control: A discourse-historical analysis. *Discourse Studies* 1 (1): 83–119.
This was the first published version of the theory of discourse as recontextualized social practice.

van Leeuwen, T. (2006) Critical discourse analysis. In: K. Brown (ed.), *Encyclopedia of Language and Linguistics*, 2nd edn. Vol. 3, pp. 290–4.
In this encyclopedia article I have attempted a general overview of critical discourse analysis.

van Leeuwen, T. (2008) *Discourse and Practice – New Tools for Critical Discourse Analysis*. New York: Oxford University Press.

7

CHECKS AND BALANCES:
HOW CORPUS LINGUISTICS CAN
CONTRIBUTE TO CDA

GERLINDE MAUTNER

CONTENTS

> ## Keywords
>
> corpus linguistics, mixed methods, triangulation, collocation, interpretation

Introduction

This chapter focuses on the role that corpus linguistics can play in CDA projects. It will introduce readers to previous work in this area, explain basic concepts and techniques, present two worked examples, and encourage critical engagement with the methodology.

Those with previous experience of corpus linguistics (CL) will be aware that it is a methodology that uses computer support – in particular, software called 'concordance programs' – to analyse authentic, and usually very large, volumes of textual data. Its potential usefulness in CDA, rather than purely for lexicographers and grammarians, may be less familiar, though. Reflections on the potential of combining CL and CDA go back quite a long way now (e.g. Hardt-Mautner 1995), and in the 1997 edited volume on discourse studies (van Dijk, ed. 1997) de Beaugrande argued that 'large corpuses offer valuable support for the project of discourse analysis to return to authentic data' (de Beaugrande 1997: 42). Still, none of the other contributors to that edition actually used the method. Awareness of its potential does seem to be growing, however, and there has been a spate of more recent CDA work using corpus linguistics (e.g. Bednarek and Caple 2014; Baker et al. 2008; Baker and McEnery 2005; Baker et al. 2007; Cotterill 2001; Fairclough 2000a; Mautner 2007; Nelson 2005; Orpin 2005; Potts 2013), including exciting new departures. Partington (2014), for example, deals specifically with the role of CL in evaluating the significance of items being absent from corpora, while O'Halloran (2012 and 2014) draws on Derrida's idea of deconstructive reading to introduce a corpus-based procedure for revealing tensions in persuasive texts.

In spite of these fruitful new developments, however, it seems fair to say that corpus linguistic techniques are not yet generally regarded as being at the core of CDA's methodological canon. That the previous edition of this present volume, published in 2009, included this chapter for the first time could thus be said to reflect a change in trend.

What, then, can one expect corpus linguistics to contribute to CDA? In a nutshell, the potential of this methodology rests on five pillars:

- Corpus linguistics is based on the belief 'that language variation is both systematic and functional' (Gray and Biber 2011: 141). Furthermore, from its early roots in the 1930s, corpus linguistics has been aware of its potential application as a 'contextual and sociological technique' (Firth 1935 [1957]: 13). On both counts, CL makes a good ally for CDA.

- Corpus linguistics allows critical discourse analysts to work with much larger data volumes than they can when using purely manual techniques.
- It also allows different perspectives on the data, thus contributing to methodological triangulation (McEnery and Hardie 2012: 233), that is, the use of several methods to study the same phenomenon (Creswell and Miller 2010).
- In enabling critical discourse analysts to significantly broaden their empirical base, corpus linguistics can help reduce researcher bias, thus coping with a problem to which CDA is hardly more prone than other social sciences but for which it has come in for harsh and persistent criticism (e.g. Widdowson 1995, 2004b).[1]
- Corpus linguistics software offers both quantitative and qualitative perspectives on textual data, computing frequencies and measures of statistical significance, as well as presenting data extracts in such a way that the researcher can assess individual occurrences of search words, qualitatively examine their collocational environments, describe salient semantic patterns and identify discourse functions.

This chapter cannot offer detailed step-by-step guidance on project design and execution. For that, there are other, and arguably more suitable, sources that readers may want to turn to, notably Baker (2006) and McEnery et al. (2006). However, a few basics will be covered in the following section, using original sample analyses as well as cross-referencing existing work in this area. Throughout, the emphasis will be less on technical detail than on enabling readers to make their own informed judgements on whether the method is right for them. There are two worked examples: the first shows how a large reference corpus – i.e., a large corpus used as a standard of comparison (Teubert and Cermakova 2004: 65–8) – can be mined for socially relevant information in order to establish a collocational profile of a key expression from the lexis of work, namely *unemployed*. The second takes a single newspaper article as its starting point and uses large-corpus data as an aid in interpreting what appears to be a particularly 'loaded' expression from the article, the adjective *hard-working*.

Both case studies are based on the assumption that language and the social are inextricably, and dialectically, linked. In other words, the way in which labels, in this case *unemployed*, and *hard-working*, are used reflects social attitudes, perspectives and categorizations. And the labels, in turn, shape the way in which social structures and relationships are perceived. By referring to a person or group as *unemployed*, one cannot help implying that being employed is the desired default, just as *hard-working* comes with a host of positive connotations directly related to an essentially capitalist work ethos.

Different approaches to discourse, and concomitant definitions of the term, exist in abundance, as do various notions of what it means to carry out 'critical analysis' (see Wodak 2004: 198–9 and Wodak 2006b for comprehensive overviews). The perspective adopted in this chapter is functional and constructivist (as well as unabashedly simple). *Discourse* is taken to refer to authentic texts used in multi-layered environments to perform social functions.

Analysing discourse is understood as the systematic attempt to identify patterns in text, link them to patterns in the context, and vice versa. Doing so *critically* means unveiling and challenging taken-for-granted assumptions about language and the social, as well as recognizing discourse as a potentially powerful agent in social change.

It will not have escaped readers' attention that the title of this chapter contains two hedging devices, one modal (*can*) and another lexical (*contribute*). These correspond to two caveats which are worth spelling out right at the beginning. One is that the usefulness or otherwise of this method, as of any other, depends crucially on recognizing what kinds of research questions it is suitable for tackling. With corpus linguistics, the key limiting factors are the capabilities of the software, as well as the features – mainly in terms of composition and annotation – of the electronically held corpora that are used. At the current state of play, and considering the limitations of those tools that are sufficiently widely available, there is a very strong bias in favour of the individual lexical item and clusters thereof. Put simply, 'the word' is the peg that everything else is hung on. It follows that if the linguistic phenomenon you are interested in is in fact tied to, or at least crystallizes around, discrete lexical items, then you are likely to find this method a boon both as a practical and efficient time-saver, and as a powerful heuristical tool helping to clear pathways to discovery. If, on the other hand, the phenomenon to be focused on is one that is played out on a larger textual stage, and with varying and unpredictable lexical realizations, then corpus linguistic methods will be of little or no help. However, at some point or other, as soon as questions of micro-level linguistic realization are addressed, even projects located very much at the macro end of the CDA spectrum will have occasion to benefit from a corpus linguistic approach.

The second caveat, related to corpus linguistics' 'contributing' role, is that we need to recall one of the principal tenets of what might be termed 'mainstream' CDA (broadly, the traditions shaped by Fairclough, Wodak and van Dijk[2]), namely that the analyst must, precisely, look *beyond* the text proper in order to unearth socially meaningful interpretations that can then be enlisted to do socially transformative work. We need our much-famed 'context', history and as firm a grasp as possible of the politics, in the widest sense, that has a bearing on the production and reception of the text. This social hinterland and the textual evidence before us are intricately linked, but rarely in a fully transparent, one-to-one type of relationship; hence the idea of making corpus linguistics 'contribute' to CDA rather than it 'doing CDA' of its own accord. All the same, at an Oscar night of methods, my vote would be on corpus linguistics as Best Supporting Actor, and the present chapter sets out to make the case for that award.

Also, there is the added benefit that if you decide to include corpus linguistic methods in your CDA project design, you need not in fact discard, 'unlearn' or in any other way throw overboard whatever more traditional methods you have grown accustomed to using. As an ancillary method, corpus linguistics is flexible and unobtrusive, and if handled appropriately, will enrich but not prejudice the rest of the research design or the interpretation of the results.

Key concepts and a worked example

As with any method, researchers will want to know, first and foremost, what it can do, what kind of data and research questions it is suitable for, and what obstacles may be encountered when applying it. These are the concerns of the present section.

Concordancing software

Programs known as concordancers do not, by themselves, 'produce' analyses, but perform operations on text that make it easier for humans to analyse it. Some of the information that concordancers provide is quantitative, such as absolute and relative word frequencies. Programs also compute measures that indicate the relative statistical significance of the co-occurrence of items. Examples are t-scores, which capture certainty of collocation, and MI ('mutual information') scores, which tell us about the strength of the bond between two items, that is, whether there is a higher-than-random probability of the two items occurring together (Church and Hanks 1990; Clear 1993: 281; Hunston 2002: 73; McEnery and Wilson 2001: 86;).[3]

To see how this works in practice, let us have a look at the first worked example of this chapter: building a collocational profile of the adjective *unemployed*. Although this serves as a stand-alone case study here, with a focus on method rather than content, it could also form the nucleus of a substantive contribution to the existing body of discourse-analytic research on unemployment (see Muntigl et al. 2000 and the 2002 special issue of *Text*[4]). As we shall see, the corpus linguistic approach allows the researcher to work with enormous amounts of data and yet get a close-up on linguistic detail: a 'best-of-both-worlds' scenario hardly achievable through the use of purely qualitative CDA, pragmatics, ethnography, or systemic functional analysis.

Table 7.1 t-scores and MI scores for collocates of *unemployed* in the *Times* corpus of Wordbanks Online

Collocate	t-score	Collocate	MI score
1. *an*	6.648362	1. *steelmen*	13.465279
2. *are*	6.227450	2. *househusband*	11.780613
3. *people*	5.779392	3. *unemployable*	11.228017
4. *who*	5.725799	4. *housewives*	8.733004
5. *and*	4.842066	5. *4m*	8.066547
6. *term*	4.212151	6. *youths*	7.898282
7. *long*	3.749890	7. *disadvantaged*	7.547531
8. *million*	3.623313	8. *homeless*	7.213343
9. *for*	3.605234	9. *pensioners*	6.965925
10. *workers*	3.516933	10. *claimants*	6.889355

Given the key role that the mass media play in constructing social reality, a corpus of newspaper articles would appear a suitable starting point. Wordbanks Online,[5] a multi-genre corpus of more than 500 million words of mainly British and American text, includes a nearly 60-million-word corpus of articles from the British daily paper *The Times*. This is the subcorpus we will turn to first. The search reveals that the *Times* corpus contains 567 instances of *unemployed*. Table 7.1 gives the 10 collocates with the highest t-scores and MI scores respectively:[6]

The t-score part of the table is headed, as is invariably the case, by high-frequency grammatical items. Here, these are *an* and *are*, with *who*, *and* and *for* not far behind. Such 'function' words, devoid of separate meaning as they are, tend not to be as interesting to discourse analysts as to grammarians, and it is generally safe in a CDA setting to ignore them and indeed the whole t-score rank scale. Somewhat unusually though, the top 10 by t-score here include five content words (*people*, *term*, *long*, *million* and *workers*), with the presence of both *long* and *term* probably being due to the phrase *long-term unemployed*. Comparing this with the collocation list of two other, randomly picked adjectives, *happy* and *sad*,[7] we can see how unusual it is for content words to appear so high up in the t-score rank scale: the group of top 10 in the t-score list for *happy*, for example, contains no content word at all, and the one for *sad* includes only one (the intensifier *very*). For lexical items to be in the same t-score league as grammatical ones points to a high degree of what one might call patterned bonding; that is, of a lexical connection so formulaic that the degree of certainty with which it occurs equals that of patterns involving grammatical items. Translated into CDA terms, the 'phrase-ness' of a noun group referring to people could point to the solidified discursive construction of a social group (a necessary first step towards stereotyping).

Turning now to the right half of Table 7.1, which lists the top 10 collocates according to 'Mutual Information' scores, we can see which social attributes being unemployed is associated with: *unemployable*, *disadvantaged* and *homeless*. Frequent nominal collocates include several labels for marginalized, dependent and economically inactive social groups: *househusband*, *housewives*, *youths*, *pensioners*, *claimants*.[8] In a full-blown study, rather than one done for demo purposes only, each of these high-frequency collocates would be interesting entry points to the corpus. For example, it would be worth looking at what kind of activities 'unemployed youths' are seen to engage in (by running a search of *unemployed youths* followed by a verb form), how the usage of *househusband* and *housewives* compares, how *unemployed* is linked syntactically to the negative adjectives it frequently collocates with, how quantification (cf. the collocate *4m*) contributes to establishing the unemployed as a problem group, and so on.

These sorts of questions lead us to another feature of concordance programs, one that a discourse analyst with a predominantly qualitative mindset might get more mileage out of than frequencies and statistics: their eponymous capacity to produce concordances. These are extracts from the corpus, displayed in such a way that the search word or phrase (also referred to as the 'node') appears in the middle of a line. The text that the extract comes from can be accessed at all times and with a simple operation such as a double mouse click or selecting an option from a menu bar. Accessible co-texts vary from just over 500 characters (e.g. with Wordbanks Online) to full texts (e.g. with Wordsmith Tools[9]).

Lines can be sorted alphabetically: for example, according to the word immediately preceding or following the search word. When sorted like this, the collocational environment of the search word can be assessed rapidly, with frequent patterns standing out clearly. For example, the concordance of *unemployed* followed by *and* and another adjective shows up a preponderance of items (six out of a total of nine) with a negative semantic load: *desperate, disadvantaged, divorced, homeless* and *unemployable* (which occurs twice):

Table 7.2 Occurrences of *unemployed*, followed by *and* and another adjective, in the *Times* corpus of Wordbanks Online

```
        mince. Tony Shalhoub is broke, unemployed and desperate. His fortune went
           <p> Liam Parker, services to unemployed and disadvantaged people. Alison
        near Consett, Co Durham, Sheila, unemployed and divorced, lives in a council
        about 12,000 former teachers are unemployed and free to work." <p> He added
        new law had effectively made him unemployed and homeless. He is married with
               <p> Ronnie (Ben Miles), 35, unemployed and Jewish, is back from Israel,
        full-time mothers, selfemployed, unemployed and retired people across the
                needed to keep the largely unemployed and unemployable Saudi young from
        the welfare state that bribes the unemployed and unemployable middle-class
```

To make sure that this semantic pattern is not just confined to newspaper discourse, it is worth checking the corresponding data from the British spoken corpus. The picture is in fact very similar.

Table 7.3 Occurrences of *unemployed*, followed by *and* and another adjective, in the British spoken corpus of Wordbanks Online

```
        to say hello to everybody who's unemployed and bored at the moment and hasn'
        to town looking for work. He was unemployed and homeless when he turned up at
        say he is thirty-two years old, unemployed and single, and will appear in
        apprenticeship's over he becomes unemployed and unemployable himself. It's
```

These results are further confirmed if we extend the search to the complete 500+ million word corpus of Wordbanks Online. The adjectives joined to *unemployed* include more occurrences of the items already identified in the two subcorpora (see Tables 7.2 and 7.3) as well as new and similarly negative collocates such as *angry, demoralised, destitute, disabled, dreary, drunk, excluded, poor, struggling* and *underprivileged*. By examining concordances, therefore, we can see more or less at a glance that the search word, *unemployed*, has a so-called negative 'semantic aura', or 'semantic prosody' (Hunston 2004: 157; Louw 1993; Partington 2004). Alternatively, readers of this volume will be interested to note, this concept has been referred to as '*discourse* prosody', for example by Stubbs (2001: 65), in order to emphasise its role in expressing attitudes and in establishing coherence.

Detractors of corpus-based methods could argue, of course, that one hardly needs a huge database of text and sophisticated software to 'prove' that being unemployed is not a pleasant thing to be. On the other hand, we should not forget the following considerations. Firstly, a fair proportion of any empirical work is devoted, precisely, to finding evidence for the intuitively obvious. Secondly – and here we are heading into the epistemological territory that will be discussed in more detail in the section headed Critique – there is a crucial difference between something *being* unpleasant and it being *constructed* as such by the discourse. Thirdly, some insights may appear 'obvious' *after* having emerged from data but were nothing of the kind before. Supposedly neutral words such as *cause* or *provide*, to use one of Stubbs's examples, can in fact be heavily skewed in terms of their evaluative content when concordance evidence is examined. Patterns are revealed that are not easily accessible even to native speakers' intuition: *cause*, it turns out, collocates predominantly with unpleasant events, such as *damage, death, disease* or *trouble*, whereas *provide* occurs with desirable things, such as *care, help, money* or *service* (Stubbs 2001: 65). Thus, if a speaker or writer uses *provide*, that choice in itself implies that what is provided is being presented as good rather than bad.

Fourth, and finally, the concordancer does more than highlighting the evaluative polarity, be it good or bad, of an item's collocational environment. Collocates may also turn out to belong to a class of words that share a semantic feature, that is, the search word may have a particular 'semantic preference' (Stubbs 2001: 88). For example, Baker (2006: 79, 87) concludes from corpus evidence that *refugees* has a semantic preference for quantification, collocating frequently with numbers and phrases such as *more and more* (see also Baker and McEnery 2005). In a study using a similar approach, Mautner (2007) shows that *elderly* often co-occurs with items from the domains of care, disability and vulnerability. By the same token, if we return to our concordance output related to *unemployed* and its co-ordinated adjectives, we can see that, broadly speaking, these denote either social states (e.g. *available for work, excluded, immigrant, nomadic, unemployable, unpaid*), negative emotions (e.g. *angry, bored, depressed*), or indeed a condition at the interface of both (*unloved*). The collocational profile thus points to the twin nature of unemployment as a social phenomenon with a manifestly psychological impact on individuals.

Taken together, then, semantic preference and discourse prosody show us what kinds of social issues a particular lexical item is bound up in, and what attitudes are commonly associated with it. Importantly, collocational patterns are not merely instantiated in text, but also cling to the lexical items themselves. 'Words which are co-selected', Tognini-Bonelli (2001: 111) reminds us, 'do not maintain their independence. If a word is regularly used in contexts of good news or bad news or judgement, for example, it carries this kind of meaning around with it'.

Finally, some software packages, such as Wordsmith Tools, allow the analyst to compare wordlists compiled from different corpora and to determine which words are significantly frequent (i.e., so-called 'positive keywords') or significantly infrequent (i.e., 'negative keywords') (Baker 2006: 125; Baker et al. 2008: 278; Evison 2010: 127; Mulderrig 2006: 123; Scott 2010: 149). Fairclough's (2000a) study, for example, focuses on the keywords of New Labour – words, that is, that are more frequent in New Labour material than in earlier Labour texts, and more frequent, too, than in general corpora (Fairclough 2000a: 17).

To sum up, Table 7.4 shows the features concordancing software offers that are useful for CDA applications.

Table 7.4   Tools and types of linguistic evidence provided by concordance software

Quantitative evidence	Frequency lists
	Comparisons of wordlists, giving information on relative frequency ('keyness')
	Measures of statistical significance:
	• t-score
	• 'Mutual Information' (MI) score
Qualitative evidence	Concordance lines sorted alphabetically, enabling the researcher to identify
	• semantic preference
	• semantic prosody

Corpus design issues

These days, when linguists talk about *a corpus* they generally refer to 'a collection of (1) *machine-readable* (2) *authentic* texts [...] which is (3) *sampled* to be (4) *representative* of a particular language or language variety' (McEnery et al. 2006: 5, original emphasis). Let us look at each of these four characteristics in turn, with an eye to whatever specific implications they may have for applications in CDA.

Machine readability is the obvious prerequisite for analysing language with the concordancing software described in the previous section. This sounds straightforward enough, but when it is coupled with the second feature, authenticity, issues of data quality arise that critical discourse analysts will want to address. Standard concordancers need 'plain text' files, stripped of formatting, layout and accompanying visuals. While traditional lexico-syntactic research won't see this as a loss, critical discourse analysts will (or should). After all, it is one of the foundational assumptions of discourse analysis, whether of the critical persuasion or not, that meaning-making works simultaneously on several levels, including the non-verbal. Elements of textual design, including typography, colour and text-image relationships, are not merely embellishments, but play an integral role in making text function as socially situated discourse (see van Leeuwen in this volume). The semiotic reduction that concordancing inevitably entails (Koller and Mautner 2004) need not jeopardize the validity of one's analyses, but there ought to be adequate safeguards ensuring that whatever is lost along the way can be salvaged at a later stage. In mundanely practical terms, this means collecting and storing hard-copy or scanned originals for future reference, to be drawn upon should multimodality become an issue. Likewise, audio or video recordings of spoken data ought to be preserved, so that contextual clues lost through transcription and conversion into machine-readable format can be retrieved if and when necessary.

As far as criteria (3) and (4) are concerned, sampling and representativeness, the requirements for ensuring methodological rigour are basically no different here than they are for other approaches (see Mautner 2008).

The first step is to identify the 'universe of possible texts' (Titscher et al. 2000: 33), while the second involves sampling. This can be random (i.e., done by first numbering the texts in the 'universe' and then selecting those with the numbers that a random number generator has picked out). Alternatively, it may be guided by criteria that are applied systematically and, in a top-down selection process, narrow down the corpus to a manageable size (e.g. 'take one article about Topic A from newspapers B and C published each week between dates X and Y'). There is a third sampling method, common in qualitative research but unlikely to be suitable for corpus linguistic work, which uses a cyclical process, building a small and homogeneous corpus, then analysing it and adding to it on the basis of the first results (Bauer and Aarts 2000: 31). The process is repeated until 'saturation' has been reached – a situation, that is, where adding new data does not yield any new representations (Bauer and Aarts 2000: 34).

The problem with this procedure from a corpus linguist's point of view is the flip side of what makes it appealing to the purely qualitative researcher: that you stop collecting data as soon as what you find is simply more of the same. In corpus linguistics, the frequency of an item or structure is taken to be a key indicator of its significance. If you stop adding text to your corpus as soon as repetition becomes apparent, you are effectively closing off any frequency-based line of inquiry. This may well be an acceptable decision to take in a particular project; after all, the qualitative analysis of concordance lines is as important and valuable as the quantitative inquiry that concordancing software allows. But it would have to be a decision taken with full awareness of the loss involved. Certainly, care must be taken not to indulge in hasty judgements about what can be excluded from the corpus on the grounds that it is 'similar' to what is already there. Such rashness can easily defeat the whole purpose of the corpus building exercise, the point of which is, in a sense, to outwit the analyst who may be tempted to know the data *before* rather than *after* the analysis.

Summing up, corpus design involves the following issues, as shown in Figure 7.1.

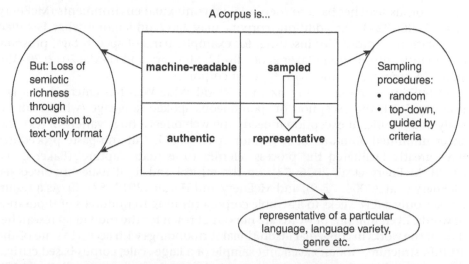

Figure 7.1 Corpus characteristics and issues of corpus design

Types of corpora and data capture

Corpora come in many shapes and sizes. There are huge, multi-million-word corpora such as the British National Corpus[10] (BNC), the Corpus of Contemporary American English[11] (COCA) and Wordbanks Online, from which the *unemployed* example in the previous section was taken. These are ready-made, commercially available and each comes with bespoke software unique to it (usually a source of frustration if you want to use both corpora simultaneously). Both were the results of large-scale projects spanning many years and involving teams of linguists and computer experts. In CDA, such corpora are ideal for painting on a very large canvas, investigating how broader social issues are reflected in the genres and discourses represented in the corpus (such as fiction, newspapers and spoken dialogue). This approach is used in studies such as Krishnamurthy's (1996) on racism and Mautner's (2007) on ageism.

At the other end of the spectrum, there are much smaller, 'do-it-yourself' (DIY) corpora (Koester 2010; McEnery et al. 2006: 71), purpose-built by individual researchers or small teams to investigate specific research questions. Issues of size apart, corpora may also be classified according to whether they are synchronic, reflecting a language variety at any given point in time, or diachronic, reflecting historical development. They can be general, including a wide variety of genres and media, or specialized, focusing on a particular genre (e.g. corporate mission statements), a particular medium and topic (e.g. web-based texts on disability rights), a particular genre and topic (e.g. parliamentary speeches on global warming), or a particular topic in various genres and media (e.g. the 'Evolution vs Creationism' debate in sermons, newspaper articles and web logs). Corpora may also differ in terms of which meta-linguistic information is encoded with the text. Critical discourse analysts will be particularly keen to insert codes describing extratextual information (a procedure known as 'corpus mark-up'), such as text type, speakers' or writers' sociolinguistic characteristics, or indeed any feature that is relevant for a particular research question. Mark-up plays a key role in allowing the analyst to relate the examples shown up by corpus searches back to their original contextual environments (McEnery et al. 2006: 22–3). In addition, corpora may have undergone what is called 'annotation', a process of inserting, for example, parts-of-speech tags, prosodic or semantic information (Baker 2006: 38–42; McEnery and Hardie 2012: 29–35). Table 7.5 summarizes the main types of corpora.

In building corpora of any size, the World Wide Web has emerged as a key resource. With the exception of spontaneous spoken language (which, admittedly, is a significant exception indeed), the web offers a huge variety of text and sheer unlimited amounts of it (Hundt et al. 2007). Cut-and-paste procedures have greatly facilitated the process referred to as 'data capture' (Baker 2006: 31–38; McEnery et al. 2006: 73); on the ethical and legal issues involved see McEnery et al. (2006: 77–9), and McEnery and Hardie (2012: 57–70). As a result, it takes only a few weeks to assemble corpora running to hundreds of thousands of words. Even millions of words are not out of reach for the individual researcher if he or she works in congenial institutional surroundings with access to state-of-the art infrastructure – for an excellent example of a large-scale, corpus-based critical discourse analysis of social actor construal in US media discourse, see Potts (2013).

Thus, by and large, you do not need a position high up in the institutional pecking order to do corpus-assisted research. Seen from this angle, enlisting corpus methods also has a democratizing effect on critical research.

Table 7.5 Main types of corpora

Reference corpora	'Do-it-yourself' (DIY) corpora
Ready-made, 'off the peg', including a wide variety of genres (written, spoken, newspapers, fiction etc.) and millions of words per genre e.g. BNC (100 million words), Wordbanks Online (approx. 500 million words), COCA (approx. 450 million words) Other criteria: - synchronic vs. diachronic - general vs. specialized - types of mark-up and annotation	Purpose-built by individual researchers, designed to tackle smaller-scale research questions, processed with the help of concordancing software such as Wordsmith Tools

Thus, in terms of sheer corpus availability, most critical discourse analysts' interests will be catered for by the web (which makes it all the more surprising that until relatively recently, only comparatively few CDA projects were actually based on online material (Mautner 2005). Digital databases such as LexisNexis and Factiva are also treasure troves. Yet, in spite of this new abundance, many of the old questions remain – which brings us back to the design issues raised in the previous section. Modern technology may have reduced the manual drudgery of corpus-building, but not the need for brainpower to make the *right* choices. To recap briefly, the key issues involved, all of them well known from traditional corpus gathering, are: first, ensuring adequate fit between the corpus and the research question(s) to be tackled, and, second, the triangle of issues concerning corpus size, homogeneity and representativeness.

Using a reference corpus to support interpretation: a second worked example

It is true, as the previous section explained, that corpus linguistic methods can be applied either to smaller, purpose-built corpora or to large reference corpora. Nonetheless, critical discourse analysts are likely to get most mileage out of a combination of the two approaches. Arguably, the smaller your own corpus, the more important it becomes to validate interpretations by checking them against evidence from larger corpora. We might feel, for example, that a certain word or phrase is used in a particular text because it carries a particular evaluative load, but is this borne out by data from a reference corpus reflecting general language use? What kind of collocational 'baggage' do words occurring in the text carry in wider universes of discourse? It is through comparative evidence from large corpora that suspicions can be confirmed or rejected, thus safeguarding against 'overinterpretation and underinterpretation' (O'Halloran and Coffin 2004). It has to be conceded, of course, that making sense of this comparative evidence still involves acts of interpretation on the part of the analyst. Neither the quantitative nor the qualitative evidence that large corpora lay before us speaks for itself, and to claim that it does so would be seriously misguided or, at the very least, naïve. On the other hand, surely, any improvement in CDA's empirical credentials ought to be welcome, tempered though it may be by the sobering realization that completely mechanized discourse analysis is impossible. Or, were it possible, it would cease to be critical.

The idea of comparative evidence is illustrated by the second worked example. It relates to a column in the British popular daily *The Sun*, published in July 2007, at a time when major floods were devastating large areas in central England. The headline reads *It's time to turn off the spongers' money tap* (with *spongers*, or *scroungers*, referring to people who are perceived to be abusing the social benefits system). The article is built around the contrast between the lives of 'hard-working people' whose homes have been destroyed by the flood in Gloucestershire, and a family with twelve children from Berkshire (*the scrounging Gillespies*) who have been given a new council house paid for by *the hard-working taxpayer*. The father of the family is quoted as saying, 'if it was economical for me to work then I would do'. A benefits system producing such attitudes, the article demands, ought to be changed; also, foreign aid should be put on hold 'until *our* national crisis is sorted out' (original emphasis). There are two large pictures, one of a flooded house in Gloucester and a second of the Gillespies' £500,000 *council home*, which has a small inset showing the couple surrounded by their twelve children. Addressing politicians from both government and opposition, the columnist pleads: *The hard-working people of Britain should come first.*

Like many opinion pieces in the popular press, this column develops a stark black-and-white dichotomy, pitting 'us' against 'them'. 'Us' refers to the *grafting taxpayer* (with *grafting* being a colloquial British expression meaning 'hard-working'), whose *hard-earned home* has been flooded, whereas 'they' are *the blatantly idle Gillespies of this world* and, less prominently, recipients of development aid in Africa. In establishing the 'we' group, the adjective *hard-working* clearly plays a central role. In an article of around 1,300 words, it occurs five times. In four of these instances, *hard-working* is part of a noun group that includes at least one other in-group marker (*people of Britain, British taxpayers, our own people, the communities*). The occurrences, quoted below, are spread fairly evenly throughout the text, contributing to its cohesion:

[1] ... there's only one basic rule to remember: The **hard-working** people of Britain should come first.
[2] Yet frankly, when the **hard-working** British taxpayers need them most, our politicians look as washed up as the million-plus doormats floating around the streets.
[3] ... not to mention the indirect £8 billion of our taxes the PM [Prime Minister] has recently pledged to Africa. But when our own **hard-working** people are in trouble, there should be an instant amnesty on all other benevolent activity until *our* national crisis is sorted out [original emphasis].

[4] There's more rain on the way, so I suggest Brown [= the Prime Minister], Cameron [= the Leader of the Opposition] et al get their galoshes on and *show* they care about the blighted, **hard-working** communities (...) [original emphasis].

[5] ... the skewed thinking that the **hard-working** taxpayer is a cash cow only to be milked and never fed.

On this evidence, it would be fair to claim that in this text *hard-working* does ideological work, establishing a 'we' group and attributing a positive quality to it. But then, what is it about *hard-working*, exactly, that makes it such a powerfully positive label? And is this evaluative load true of general language use, or specific to certain discourses? In other words, is there a specifically 'tabloid' attitude towards 'hard-working' people?

Let us see what the Wordbanks reference corpus has to say. First of all, the collocation list for *hard-working* from the total 500+ million word corpus, ordered by MI score, reveals a long list of other positive adjectives. Picking out those that also have double-digit joint frequencies (that is, not only exhibit a strong collocational bond with *hard-working*, evident through an MI score of 5 or above, but also occur at least 10 times), we arrive at the list in Table 7.6.

Table 7.6 Collocates of *hard-working* in the total 500+ million word Wordbanks corpus, with joint frequencies of at least 10 and MI scores of at least 5

Word	Joint frequency	MI score
industrious	11	9.531038
conscientious	19	9.158034
abiding	19	8.612447
honest	75	7.322699
dedicated	46	7.307235
disciplined	11	7.087851
loyal	28	7.047991
sincere	12	7.001116
competent	12	6.847253
ambitious	28	6.793461
decent	38	6.724341
intelligent	27	6.611245
enthusiastic	14	6.242391
caring	17	6.127628
talented	15	6.044615
skilled	10	6.039344

Some of these are fairly closely related to the idea of working hard or in a particularly focused manner (*industrious, conscientious, dedicated, disciplined, ambitious, skilled*), but others refer to very general attributes that are quite independent of the domain of employment: *honest, loyal, sincere, decent* and *caring*.

There is a semantic preference for character traits, and the semantic prosody is unequivocally positive. To find that there is a statistically significant collocational bond between these adjectives and *hard-working* means that when someone is described as 'hard-working' there is a higher than random possibility that one of these other, non-work-related qualities will appear in close proximity. For each of these collocates, of course, we need to check what the syntactic relationship with *hard-working* is, because 'being close' could also mean 'close and linked through *but*', in which case the other adjective would be expressing a contrast, not confirmation, of the virtues implied in hard work (cf. the hypothetical, not attested, phrase *hard-working but caring*). However, it can be established easily by examining the relevant concordances – such as the one for *decent*, which is given in Table 7.7 – that the 'virtuous' adjectives are linked to *hard-working* through *and* or a comma and do in fact refer to the same individuals or groups of people. In addition to showing how *hard-working* and *decent* (highlighted in bold capitals) are related syntactically and semantically when they appear together, the concordance in Table 7.7 also reveals a number of other positive attributes in close proximity (highlighted in bold), some with distinctly moralizing overtones (e.g. *honest family man*, *genuine and Christian*, *self-sacrificing*).

Table 7.7 Co-occurrence of *hard-working* and *decent* in the 500+ million Wordbanks Online corpus

```
      to denigrate Kilbane, who is a hard-working and DECENT professional. Yet on
      a more responsible, DECENT and hard-working British citizen. He is a credit to
       is that they are DECENT and hard working people," he said. Mr Xynias said
         the barrel, most fathers are hard working DECENT family types trying to do
          thousands of DECENT, brave, hard-working coppers. It's hardly surprising
                that Hart was a DECENT, hard-working and honest family man, but added
     lost on Saturday night. DECENT, hard-working people, people who are prepared to
        things are bad when a DECENT, hard-working father resorts to taking surgeons
           just as you see him. DECENT, hard-working, genuine and Christian. He's the
              The bishops are DECENT, hard-working men in thankless roles, but the
         Paul Duckworth was a DECENT, hard-working and loving father. <p> "The
       The former teacher is DECENT, hard-working and dutiful. But as my colleague
          of him is that he is a DECENT, hard-working bloke who was caught up in
      TV. <p> Meanwhile most DECENT, hard working citizens will be lucky to see any
         great to her family -a DECENT hard-working girl." <hl> Open house contest
      town I grew up in was a DECENT, hard-working, hard-drinking, cloth-cap- and-
      Erfurt, Germany, as "a DECENT, hard-working man". <p> But Judge Gareth
      he said: "They were all DECENT, hard-working men - great lads and great mates. I
       make life a misery for DECENT, hard-working people. <p> The phone number to
         badly on thousands of DECENT, hard-working taxi men and women who want these
```

```
      employer as "good, DECENT, hard-working men" who were mown down in a hail
      with admiration as DECENT, hard-working people, who despite having very
      but my parents were DECENT hard-working people. We used to go to church
      of the game - the DECENT, hard-working people who work in and around
              When I see a DECENT, hard-working man like you, with a responsible
      admired his wife, a DECENT, hard-working, self-sacrificing woman; he couldn'
        coal miners, each DECENT, hard-working union men with large families,
      Slick Willy" into a DECENT, hard-working child of the middle class. He told
      with New York: the DECENT, hard-working people who live here. And here's
              he said, "a generally hard-working and DECENT people prepared to put
          found them DECENT, kindly, hard-working, and knowledgeable within their
   they will effectively stop many hard working DECENT Sikhs from earning a
     of humanity; there's a lot of hard-working, DECENT people, a lot of children
          level-headed, reliable, hard-working, DECENT, orderly" - are
   and more time listening to the hard-working, DECENT majority that elected New
   character who came from a "very hard-working and DECENT family". <p> The judge
      <p> The puzzling aspect is why hard-working, DECENT people can see what is
```

Such instances of collocation – repeated, statistically significant and attested across a multi-million word corpus – 'provide objective, empirical evidence for evaluative meanings', and these meanings 'are not merely personal and idiosyncratic, but widely shared in a discourse community' (Stubbs 2001: 215). Effectively, the frequent collocates of a word *become* part of its meaning. Thus, by drawing on corpus-based collocational information a discourse analyst can replace his or her *individual*, intuitive judgement on evaluative meaning with *shared* assumptions and judgements.

In further attempting to put the use of *hard-working* in this *Sun* article into perspective, another angle worth looking at is to see how it is used in a newspaper catering for a different readership. The relevant subcorpus that Wordbanks Online offers is the nearly 60-million words from the British daily *The Times*. Whereas more than 60% of *Sun* readers are in the C2, D and E social grades, 89% of *Times* readers belong to the A/B/C1 socio-economic group.[12] The results (see Table 7.8) show that *hard-working* occurs more than twice as often in *The Sun* (in relative terms, that is, per million words) than it does in *The Times*:

Table 7.8 Frequency of *hard-working* in the *Sun* and *Times* subcorpora of Wordbanks Online

	absolute frequency	relative frequency, per one million words
The Sun	393	8.69
The Times	243	4.06

Furthermore, although the lists of high-frequency collocates appear to be rather similar in the two subcorpora, containing many of the items that showed up when we examined the whole 500-million word corpus (see Table 7.6), two differences between the collocation lists for *The Sun* and *The Times* do stand out. One is that *honest* and *decent*, though present in both lists, are relatively more frequent in the *Sun* corpus.[13] The other is that the collocation list for *hard-working* in *The Sun* includes a collocate – the one with the highest MI-score, in fact – that is not present in the *Times* list at all: *abiding*. Switching from the collocation list to concordance mode, we can see that all six occurrences of *abiding* are due to *law-abiding* being one of the positive attributes closely associated with *hard-working* (Table 7.9).

Table 7.9 Co-occurrence of *hard-working* and *law-abiding* in the *Sun* corpus of Wordbanks Online

```
        against the respectable, hard-working, LAW-ABIDING majority. No wonder
   redit to their LAW-ABIDING and hard-working community. <p> A V DAVAR, East
    > Then hopefully LAW-ABIDING, hard-working parents like the Gells need neve
    t better meals than a lot of hard-working LAW-ABIDING people, better medic
    time all decent, LAW ABIDING, hard-working people were given some
        even exists. <p> How many hard-working, honest, LAW-ABIDING people can
```

The social construction involved in this collocational link, rather than any 'objective' semantic association, could hardly be more obvious. After all, it is perfectly possible to be 'lazy' and abide by the law, or work a very busy 70-hour week dedicated to breaking it. Incidentally, taken by itself, *law-abiding* is also considerably more frequent in *The Sun* (145 instances, or 3.2 occurrences per million words) than in *The Times* (111 instances, or 1.86 per million).

Summing up, and relating the evidence back to the article that made us turn to the reference corpus for support, we can draw the following conclusions:

- *Hard-working* is much more than a descriptive label. Its semantic preference and prosody, evident in the concordance lines, indicate that it is part and parcel of a moralizing discourse, linking hard work with positive attributes such as decency, honesty, loyalty, family values and the like.
- These patterns are relatively more prominent in the popular, working-class tabloid *The Sun* than they are in *The Times*, which caters for a predominantly middle-class readership.
- In a critical discourse analysis of a text using *hard-working*, a good case can therefore be made for arguing that the contribution of *hard-working* to the overall meaning of the text is based partly on the ideological baggage that the word carries, and that this, in turn, is derived from attested patterns of usage in larger universes of discourse. Large-corpus evidence thus provides 'checks and balances' by opening a window on values and attitudes present throughout a discourse community rather than held only by individual researchers.

Critique

This chapter has made a case for combining CDA with CL. The main argument was that CL allows researchers to closely examine much larger, and hence potentially more representative, data volumes than without CL support. Furthermore, from a broader perspective, the integration of CDA and CL is a significant move towards methodological pluralism (McEnery and Hardie 2012: 233).

In spite of the clear benefits involved, there are six areas of potential concern, which I will deal with in turn under the following headings:

1. Skills gap and lack of standardization
2. Institutional barriers
3. Resisting temptation in data collection
4. Decontextualized data
5. Language innovation
6. Epistemological issues

1. Skills gap and lack of standardization

This is a practical rather than substantive issue, and may well disappear over time. At the time of writing, though, it still looms rather large. To anyone advocating the integration of corpus linguistics into mainstream CDA it is quite tempting to downplay the effort involved and make reassuring noises along the lines of 'it's not rocket science'. Indeed it isn't, but there is no denying the fact that becoming a confident user takes time and effort. Not much, perhaps, for the mundane task of learning to master the tools; but certainly a significant amount in order to develop the type of mindset that can appreciate the potential of the method, recognize its limitations, hone your analytical skills and refine your discovery procedures, so that ultimately you are able to fashion your research designs accordingly.

The reluctance, still, of many discourse analysts to become involved may well be due in part to the deplorable lack of standardization within corpus linguistics. The British National Corpus and Wordbanks Online, to use just two examples of multi-million word corpora, do not use the same software. The same is true of the various concordancing packages available for analysing DIY corpora (such as Wordsmith Tools, Monoconc Pro, Sketchengine or AntConc[14]). Search commands differ, screens differ, analytical tools differ: not a happy state of affairs if all you want to do is get on with the job.

2. Institutional barriers

The second point is related to the first, but located on the institutional rather than the individual level. Critical discourse analysts and computer linguists do not necessarily work in the same departments and, if they do, may not communicate well with each other. They often go to different conferences and publish in different journals. As a junior researcher, you are likely to be socialized into either the one methodology or the other, but rarely into both.

As most linguists know, but not all care to admit, it is often early exposure to a particular methodology, rather than any inherent merits this may have, that tends to bias one's methodological choices for a long time.

At the risk of launching into after-dinner-speech mode, this is the moment to call for more communication between critical discourse analysts and computer linguists. This should not, I hasten to add, stop at CDA people begging for IT support, realistic though this image may be, but should also lead to corpus linguists picking their CDA colleagues' brains on how best to sharpen their computing tools so that they deliver optimum value for applications in socially relevant, applied discourse studies. Existing reference corpora, too, could do with some overhaul in that respect. In Wordbanks, for example, source referencing – such a key factor in determining context – is notoriously deficient.

3. Resisting temptation in data collection

Whereas the first and second issues relate to potential hurdles encountered by those new to the method, the third centres on the need to curb the enthusiasm of the newly converted. We saw earlier that the World Wide Web and electronic processing have made for temptingly laden data tables. And indeed, being able to assemble and analyse large corpora is a key element in defusing the 'cherry-picking' charges frequently levelled at CDA. Generally speaking, corpus size undoubtedly boosts representativeness, and this, in turn, enhances the validity of analysts' claims. On the other hand, as is so often the case, a technological advance comes with strings attached. Somewhat paradoxically, the ease with which corpora can be assembled can prove to be at once overwhelming and tempting for the analyst, novice and seasoned researcher alike. They may well react like a glutton at an all-you-can-eat diner, guzzling data 'food' indiscriminately without due regard for the principles of discerning composition, be it of a menu or of a corpus. In our case, these will revolve, as ever, around questions such as: What kind of texts are most likely to allow me to answer my research questions? Is the selection of texts which make up my corpus reasonably representative of the 'universe of discourse' that is 'out there'? None of these questions, and the principles underlying them, have ceased to be relevant. If anything, they have become more pressing, precisely because of the *embarras de richesses* surrounding the analyst engaged in corpus building. Amid the bewildering surplus of easily storable text, it has become easier to lose sight of the need for constant reflexivity, even in the early stages of a project, and particularly with regard to what should go into the corpus. This is not a plea for allowing too much biased selectivity too soon; if it were, it would amount to reverting to the very 'cherry-picking' procedure that a corpus-based approach wishes to counteract (and which is why cyclical corpus building up to saturation was rejected in our discussion of sampling). The point is, rather, that critical discourse analysts putting together corpora should, quite simply, not get carried away.

4. Decontextualized data

The fourth area of concern, mentioned earlier but worth restating here, relates to the fact that both the input to and output from concordancing software is decontextualized, semiotically reduced language. Although programs allow instant access to wider co-texts or even the full texts that the concordance lines come from, a considerable amount of non-verbal information is lost when text is transferred to machine-readable form. Corpus mark-up can help compensate up to a point but, at the current state of technological development and commercial availability, it is impossible to run concordancing software while preserving the full textual integrity of the original. This is an area, therefore, where the idea of 'checks and balances' needs to work the other way round, with the analyst having to make sure that whatever information concordancers cannot deal with, such as typography and pictures, remains accessible somewhere and is not entirely and irretrievably lost to the analysis.

In this context, we should also remind ourselves that concordancing software is biased towards the discrete lexical unit. Larger-scale discursive phenomena, such as argumentative patterns, may be captured through corpus linguistic techniques, but only if they crystallize systematically around certain words, phrases or lexico-semantic patterns.

Finally, and precisely because corpus linguistics has this fantastic potential for focusing on linguistic detail, there is a need to guard against becoming so engrossed in building collocational profiles of ideologically loaded individual words that the bigger picture is lost. There is a fine line between an eye for detail and myopia. Returning briefly to the *hard-working* example in the previous section: were this part of a full-blown study, it would of course be insufficient merely to look at *hard-working* (central though it is to this newspaper article). In addition, one would not only have to explore the full range of synonyms and related expressions that the article uses, but also to delve deeper into the history, politics and social psychology of wage labour and the work ethic.

5. Language innovation

The fifth issue to be borne in mind is that large and static reference corpora, such as the BNC and Wordbanks Online, are useless for investigating developments at the sharp end of language. Where social change is at its fastest – and arguably of keenest interest to CDA – these corpora fall silent. Youth culture, advertising and code-switching varieties emerging among new immigrant populations would be cases in point. For such applications, building ad-hoc DIY corpora is the only solution.

6. Epistemological issues

In CDA projects, computer support provides empirical backing, so that you can feel more confident about the claims you make. Yet a word of warning is in order.

There is always a danger that the use of computers alone lulls us into feeling *too* confident about our findings, and into forgetting that no matter what method is involved, fundamental epistemological issues must be addressed. If they are not, they will come back to haunt us anyway – in the form of shaky interpretations of the data, less than convincing written-up accounts and rejected papers.

Lofty though it may sound, epistemology – the theory of knowledge – can be broken down into rather mundane, if complex, questions: How do we know what we know? What do we accept as evidence? And more specifically, in the context of CDA research, how do we relate *textual* data to *social* reality? What does the use of a word or phrase actually tell us? What kind of conclusions can we legitimately draw from the presence, absence or frequency of a given linguistic item?

There are no straightforward answers to these questions, and certainly none that would be relevant across the board, for every project, corpus and research design. Still, the very act of asking such questions is crucial because it prevents us from rushing headlong into assuming that the social and political import of a text can be directly and definitively 'read off' individual linguistic choices made by the speakers or writers of the texts we investigate. To guard against such naïve assumptions, the following points ought to be borne in mind:

a. The evidence that corpus software lays before us never speaks for itself. Knowledge is not generated by the mere act of data processing, but as a result of what the analyst makes of the evidence – identifying patterns, spotting interesting outliers, and relating both of these to the context in which the texts concerned were produced and received. If we compare research with a join-up-the-dots puzzle, then the computer's help is invaluable in showing where the dots are, and how many of them, but it takes humans to join them up if a recognizable picture is to emerge.

b. There is no one-to-one relationship between linguistic forms and their social functions (Stubbs 1997: 6). Although this is a truism that should not need pointing out, it is easily forgotten in the face of readily available, copious and spuriously 'objective' computer-generated data. In working out an item's social significance, (re)contextualization is of the essence: from lexical item to phrase, from phrase to concordance line, from concordance line to text, from text to other texts (and thus the intertextual chains formed by them), and finally from texts to context.

c. Computer-held corpora are no doubt extremely useful in strengthening CDA's empirical base. Yet any corpus, however large and varied, is only a fragment of the universe of texts that might have been chosen. Hence, any conclusions we draw from a corpus must be tentative, commensurate with the representativeness of the corpus, and open to review should new evidence come to light.

d. A corpus is inevitably an artefact in its own right. (See also the comments above under the headings of Corpus Design Issues and Decontextualized Data). 'We must not confuse corpus data with language itself', McEnery and Hardie remind us (2012: 26), and they continue:

Corpora allow us to *observe* language, but they are not language itself. Furthermore, we do not claim that corpora are the only tool that linguists should use to explore language – introspection and other data collection methods do have their role to play in linguistics. Indeed, without some ability to introspect, it is doubtful whether a linguist could ever formulate a question to ask of a corpus (original emphasis).

e. There is no hard-and-fast rule about where exactly in the analytical process CL methods ought to be brought in, or how much space they should take up in the research design overall. The CDA community's reluctance to come clean on 'how to do discourse analysis' extends to CL applications. Critical discourse analysts' wariness of neat analytical algorithms emerged in the debate following Leitch and Palmer's (2010) paper on 'protocols' for dealing with context. In their response, Chouliaraki and Fairclough (2010: 1218) remarked that CDA should not be reduced to 'a series of instrumental choices of operations'. Instead, they argued in favour of 'a purposefully porous and integrationist orientation to research methodology that privileges transdisciplinarity over rigour'.

f. When you bring CL on board, you should do so on the understanding that the evidence it generates is not inherently superior to what manual and qualitative procedures can reveal. Corpus tools offer different and complementary insights, and have, quite rightly, been called 'a substantial and transformative source of support' (McEnery and Hardie 2012: 233). Yet their merits do not, as such, eclipse those of other approaches. The spirit in which triangulation is undertaken should therefore be collaborative, not competitive. As McEnery and Hardie (2012: 233) further explain:

> This is a key point of a methodologically pluralist approach: one type of data does not necessarily trump another, rather different types of data may be used to complement one another – either confirming some finding, or conflicting with it.

g. When you evaluate corpus evidence, remember that statements on the presence, absence or frequency of an item in one data set only make sense in comparison with another. A suitable point of reference is particularly important where 'claims of malign intent' (Partington 2014: 135) are made and need to be supported with evidence.

h. Concordancing software offers tools for both quantitative and qualitative analysis, and we should always remain clear about which is which. Frequency lists and MI scores, for example, are indeed automated, quantitative measures. KWIC concordances, on the other hand, merely prepare the ground for qualitative analyses. These, in turn, may include a quantitative component – for example, if you classify each occurrence of the item in question and then tot up how many occurrences exhibit a particular type of semantic preference. However, unless you use a sophisticated automatic semantic annotation system (such as those developed at Lancaster University (cf. Potts 2013: 71–3), such line-by-line classification is an interpretive act that is as prone to researcher bias as methods that do not involve computers.

The only difference, albeit an important one, is that the concordance enables one to plough through significantly larger amounts of data.

i. When you present your findings, beware of making pseudo-quantitative statements. For novice researchers especially, it is not uncommon to be in thrall to quantifiable data, but then to shy away from actual quantification. Instead, in writing up their results, they often resort to impressionistic pseudo-quantifiers such as *the majority*, *some*, *relatively few*, *almost all* or *hardly any*. When you analyse data, you either count or you don't; there is no legitimate halfway house.

j. Finally, remember that computer-based methods cannot work miracles. Specifically, they cannot make up for flaws elsewhere in the research design. If your sampling technique is faulty and your sample skewed, it will remain so even when computerized, concordanced and subjected to every statistical procedure under the sun. Similarly, if your choice of statistical techniques is such that the data are, as Baker (2006: 179) graphically puts it, 'subtly massaged' in order to produce the desired results; if results are reported selectively, or inconvenient concordance lines ignored, then the fault lies not with the methodology but with the analyst's integrity. To put it bluntly, incorporating CL into your CDA research design isn't about window-dressing, throwing in a few frequency tables here and some corpus statistics there, for good measure. Nor can we expect CDA's critics to be silenced by a few showy paraphernalia of 'objectivity'. What the discerning reader, of any disciplinary and ideological background, will be looking for is increased validity and reliability, and hence a boost in the overall plausibility of our results and how we interpret them.

Essentially, most of these areas of concern relate to the same issue; the need for a realistic assessment of a method's potential. Our metaphorical tools for setting to work on text are subject to very much the same limitations as tools in a literal sense. It makes as much, or as little, sense to criticise corpus linguistic methods for not permitting more contextually embedded analysis, or a static, 10-year-old corpus for being silent on the latest neologisms, as it does to criticize a screwdriver for being no good at hammering in nails.

Summary

Corpus linguistics has a lot to offer to CDA. It helps researchers cope with large amounts of textual data, thus bolstering CDA's empirical foundations, reducing researchers' bias and enhancing the credibility of analyses. On the other hand, critical discourse analysts ought to be self-confident enough to assert that, conversely, corpus linguistics is enriched by being applied to research questions inspired by social concerns, such as power, inequality and change. Ultimately, through their 'theoretical and methodological cross-pollination' (Baker et al. 2008: 297), both CDA and corpus linguistics ought to benefit.

Combining the two approaches typically involves the following steps:

- Compiling an electronically held corpus that allows the investigation of research questions arising from social issues
- Running the corpus through concordancing software that compiles frequency lists, identifies keywords and reveals statistically significant collocations
- Analysing concordances qualitatively in order to establish the dominant semantic preferences and prosodies of lexical items relevant to the social issues under investigation
- Putting the results from the purpose-built corpus into perspective by comparing them with evidence gleaned from large reference corpora.

Alternatively, a multi-million word reference corpus may itself serve as the starting point, allowing researchers to build collocational profiles of socially contested lexical items across a wide range of genres, media and geographical areas.

The undoubted appeal of corpus assistance should not blind us to the fact that there is no such thing as fully automated CDA (or indeed any other kind of linguistic analysis). Concordancing software is good at processing large amounts of data, but it still falls to the researcher to produce meaningful, contextualized analyses. However, whatever the limitations of corpus linguistics, the complexity of discourse is such that any change in perspective and any insight not otherwise available ought surely to be welcomed as an addition to the methodological toolbox.

On the other hand, we should not forget that, in choosing methods, there is a rather thin dividing line between eclecticism that is imaginative and productive, and aimless patchworking, which is neither. Whether your research design ends up on the right side of this divide depends crucially on (i) a clear statement of the aims of your project, (ii) a rigorous assessment of what each method can and cannot do, and (iii) robust theoretical foundations capturing core assumptions about language and the social. If deployed wisely, corpus linguistics provides an enriching complement to qualitative CDA, aiding discovery and adding analytical rigour. To return to the metaphor introduced earlier: even an Oscar-winning supporting actor cannot rescue a bad film, but they can make a good film great.

Acknowledgement

Material from the Bank of English® is reproduced with the kind permission of HarperCollins Publishers Ltd.

Further reading

Baker, P. (2006) *Using Corpora in Discourse Analysis*. London and New York: Continuum.
This book is ideally suited for critical discourse analysts who are first-time users of corpus linguistic methods. It combines theoretical background with hands-on advice and several worked examples.

McEnery, T., Xiao, R. and Tono, Y. (2006) *Corpus-Based Language Studies: An Advanced Resource Book*. London and New York: Routledge.
This book caters for both novice and more experienced researchers, proceeding from the basics to a section with key readings from corpus-based language studies. In a third section, six extended case studies are presented, covering areas as diverse as pedagogical lexicography, L2 acquisition, sociolinguistics, and contrastive and translation studies.

O'Keefe, A. and McCarthy, M. (eds) (2010) *The Routledge Handbook of Corpus Linguistics*. Abingdon and New York: Routledge.
An excellent entry point to the field, as well as a good primer if you have done some corpus-assisted work before but need to brush up on recent developments, or wish to branch out into new applications. The 45 chapters include several on each of the following: corpus building and design, key analytical procedures, and ways in which CL can be applied to other areas of research.

Stubbs M. (1996) *Text and Corpus Analysis: Computer-Assisted Studies of Language and Culture*. Oxford and Cambridge, MA: Blackwell.
Stubbs, M. (2001) *Words and Phrases: Corpus Studies of Lexical Semantics*. Oxford and Cambridge, MA.: Blackwell.
Both volumes are seminal classics. Although the author positions them, as their respective subtitles reveal, as 'Computer-Assisted Studies of Language and Culture' and 'Corpus Studies of Lexical Semantics', rather than CDA, they make essential reading for critical discourse analysts, especially those that may be 'challenged' in terms of empirical rigour.

Tasks

1. Scan two years' worth of recent articles – on the one hand, from a journal typically associated with CDA, such as *Discourse & Society*; on the other, from one that specializes in CL, such as the *International Journal of Corpus Linguistics*. What proportion of the CDA articles employ CL methods, and, conversely, what proportion of the CL articles tackle socio-political issues (rather than, say, grammatical or lexicographic ones)? What does the result of your count suggest about the degree of 'cross-fertilization' between the two approaches?

2. In contemporary post-industrial societies, employees are expected to engage in self-marketing, develop 'personal brands' and consciously construct their identities so that they are aligned with the prevailing – indeed increasingly hegemonic – market ideologies. As a result, the self is being commodified, (i.e., treated like a product that can be bought and sold). These trends are reflected in discourse, and, following the dialectic between language and society, 'marketized' discourse in turn promotes commodification. One of the tell-tale signs on the level of lexis is the widespread use of the verbs *sell*, *market* and *brand* followed by reflexive pronouns such as *yourself* and *yourselves* (Mautner 2010: 126–7). Search for these expressions (i) on the web, (ii) in a multi-million static corpus, such as the BNC (British National Corpus), (iii) in a large dynamic corpus, such as COCA (Corpus of Contemporary American English) and (iv) in a small, purpose-built corpus of texts where the expressions are likely to occur (e.g. career advice websites). Looking at the quantitative evidence first, how do the results of these searches differ, and why? Can frequencies be compared across corpora? Next, turning to a qualitative interpretation of keyword-in-context results, try to ascertain which social domains these occurrences come from

(e.g. business consulting, human resources, recruiting, education). Are there any domains that appear to be underrepresented, or even downright rare? Could these outliers be all the more interesting for that very reason?

3. In academic contexts, it has become common to refer to publications as *research output*. While there is little doubt that academia is increasingly subject to market principles, care must be taken not to jump to conclusions about which lexical choices are or aren't evidence of that development. What corpus-based evidence, if any, is there for claiming that *output* is indeed a word imported from the business domain? Access a large corpus and build a collocational profile of *output* by examining frequency tables, MI scores and a selection of 500 KWIC concordances.

Notes

1   This criticism, in turn, has been refuted strongly by, for example, Fairclough (1996) and Wodak (2006a: 606–9).
2   See Fairclough (1992b, 1995b); Fairclough and Wodak (1997); Toolan (ed.) (2002); van Dijk (ed.) (2007); Wodak (2006b); Wodak and Chilton (eds) (2005).
3   The MI score relates the *observed* frequency of a given co-occurring item within a certain collocational span to the left and right of the search word with the *expected* frequency of the co-occurring item in that span (McEnery et al. 2006: 56). For details of the statistical computation involved, see Matsumoto (2003: 398–9).
4   The issue in question is *Text* 22 (3). See, in particular, Graham and Paulsen (2002); Muntigl (2002a); Wodak and van Leeuwen (2002).
5   See www.collinsdictionary.com/wordbanks, accessed 24 August 2015.
6   The cut-off point above which results are considered statistically significant is 2 for t-scores and 3 for MI scores (Hunston 2002: 71–2).
7   On the basis of the same number of occurrences, 567, as in the *unemployed* example.
8   In this particular corpus, *steelmen* is not as promising a collocate to follow up as it looks, because all nine occurrences refer to the film *The Full Monty*.
9   www.lexically.net/wordsmith/, accessed 12 May 2014.
10 www.natcorp.ox.ac.uk/, accessed 12 May 2014.
11 http://corpus.byu.edu/coca/, accessed 12 May 2014.
12 According to figures from the National Readership Survey, available at www.nrs.co.uk, accessed 9 August 2007.
13 In *The Sun*, there are 0.3 occurrences of *honest* per one million words (15 instances in total), and 0.1 in *The Times* (7 instances). The figures for *decent* are 0.26 per million for *The Sun* (12 instances) and 0.06 for *The Times* (4 instances).
14 www.laurenceanthony.net/software/antconc, accessed 24 August 2015.

8

CRITICAL ANALYSIS OF VISUAL AND MULTIMODAL TEXTS

DENNIS JANCSARY, MARKUS A. HÖLLERER AND RENATE E. MEYER

CONTENTS

Keywords

multimodality, critical discourse analysis (CDA), semiotics, visuals, visuality, visual discourse, visual analysis, sociology of knowledge, meaning reconstruction, qualitative research methods

---

Introduction

This chapter is dedicated to the critical analysis of multimodal texts – i.e., texts that incorporate semiotic resources beyond verbal language. Our focus here is, in particular, on the relationship between the verbal and the visual mode of communication. In a first section, we touch briefly on the ubiquity of multimodality in contemporary society and provide definitions of core concepts. We then continue, in a second section, to systematically develop an argument for the relevance of multimodality within critical discourse analysis (CDA). The third section summarizes a number of exemplary studies that have adopted a critical approach in multimodal discourse analysis. These studies cover a variety of issues and areas of scholarly inquiry, and therefore aptly demonstrate that multimodal CDA can be applied in various forms. In the fourth section, we introduce – as a practical example – one particular methodological approach in more detail, and illustrate its various analytical steps on the basis of two selected multimodal texts. We close with a brief reflection and some concluding remarks.

What is multimodal discourse?

Imagine yourself sitting in a Sydney beachside café on a Sunday morning in 2012, browsing through a pile of newspapers. You grab the weekend edition of the *Australian Financial Review*. What you see on the front page is an article that explores how the Euro crisis has started to show repercussions in Australia. The article further expands on how the fear of the Chinese economy taking a hit has led to plummeting shares in Australia, and then continues to discuss related events in more detail, also providing concrete figures. But those facts – even if substantial – might not be what caught your attention in the first place. Indeed, the very first thing you most probably noticed was a large photograph of an experienced businessman, staring at a screen with utter bewilderment, one hand pressed close to his temple in a gesture of disbelief; this striking picture is complemented by a series of abstract graphs showing decreasing trends in different economic variables. If you had to tell a friend later what the article was about, would you still provide the same overall narrative, even if it did not contain such imagery?

Discourse studies display, by their nature, a strong affinity to language. Language, after all, is the most prominent resource for the social construction of reality and the storage of social knowledge (Berger and Luckmann 1967). Unfortunately, this also means that in actual analysis, researchers often focus on written and spoken verbal text, and ignore, or at least downplay, the importance of other information. Multimodal analysis (e.g. Kress and van Leeuwen 2001; Kress 2010) aims at addressing this shortcoming in existing research, and acknowledges the multitude of different materials and 'meaning resources' that people use to create and distribute meaningful signs. Over the last decade, multimodal discourse analysis has gained considerable momentum, resulting in a number of edited volumes on the subject (e.g. Jewitt 2009; LeVine and Scollon 2004; O'Halloran 2004; Royce and Bowcher 2007). According to Kress (2010: 79 [original emphasis]), *'mode* is a socially shaped and culturally given semiotic resource for making meaning. *Image, writing, layout, music, gesture, speech, moving image, soundtrack and 3D objects* are examples of modes used in representation and communication'. Note that Kress uses the term 'mode' in the sense of a 'resource', something to be employed in order to create meaning. How a particular act of communication is created, then, depends on which resources are available and regarded as appropriate in a specific social situation. Within a particular cultural domain, similar meanings can be expressed in different modes (e.g. Kress and van Leeuwen 2001). But not everything is possible, or appropriate, all of the time – the 'pool' of available resources as well as their meaning potential are culturally restricted. Imagine, for instance, 'modal taboos': some religions explicitly prohibit the depiction of particular subjects. History has seen quite a few instances of *iconoclasm*, the intentional destruction of visual references to particular people, events, values, or beliefs. But we do not even have to go that far. Think of different genres of books. Children's books are usually heavily illustrated, to the point where visuality is the dominant mode, and written text becomes secondary (e.g. Kress and van Leeuwen 2006). In contrast, legal codices are mostly verbal, and even use a particular language quite different from everyday speech and writing, as well as typography in the form of clauses and articles. The reverse – photographs in legal codices or clauses in a children's book – is unlikely to be seen.

We may therefore conclude that multimodality is governed by cultural and institutional rules – norms, conventions, and guidelines that tell us what is adequate, and what is not. Within these boundaries, people have considerable leeway with regard to the presentation of their messages. For instance, if I wish to describe to a friend the new car I have just bought, I can give her a description including more general details (e.g. type, brand, colour, or interior design features) and technical specifications (e.g. engine performance, fuel consumption, hybrid drive, or exhaust system). Of course, I can also show her a picture so that she can actually *see* it, which might give her a more immediate and holistic impression, but at the same time omits information that is not visible as such (e.g. fuel consumption). Maybe, however, a verbal or visual description is not at all what I had in mind. If I am, for instance, particularly enthusiastic about the noiseless electric power unit (or, alternatively, the sound of its sporty engine), I might want my friend to *hear* it, and invite her to join me for a ride in my new car. Still more intimate is the desire to communicate how driving my new car *feels* ('I can't describe it – you have to experience it yourself'), which would involve the experience of touching it and actually sitting behind the steering wheel. All these modes communicate different aspects of the idea of what 'my new car' is about. I can combine some of them in my presentation to harness their particular strengths and give my friend a more 'complete' impression; or I focus on one mode that is, in this particular communicative situation, of singular importance for me. In any case, I make a decision, and this decision is guided by the cultural and institutional rules in place (for instance, it would be quite extravagant to send a piece of the leather seat cover to someone so that he or she could smell it) and my particular interest at the moment (for instance, the sound of the engine as a synecdoche for the power of the car). Multimodal discourse analysis pays particular attention to the different functions of each of these modes, and also to their inter-relationships (e.g. Machin and Mayr 2012; Unsworth and Cléirigh 2009).

The meaning potential of individual modes is not the same everywhere and changes over time. Put differently, it is culturally and historically contingent, and individual actors are born into a 'socio-historical a priori' (Luckmann 1983) that delineates the boundaries within which different modes can be used and made sense of. In the modern Western world, we have witnessed an incredible rise, for instance, in the amount and quality of visual information that we experience in our everyday lives (e.g. Kress and van Leeuwen 2006; Meyer et al. 2013; Mitchell 1994). The possibility of digitalizing visual information and the opportunity to globally diffuse it within seconds have brought about an enormous change in the way we communicate with each other. One might be tempted to speak of some sort of 'democratization' of communication (e.g. Kress 2010) – with all its positive, and negative, implications. In other societies and cultures, the verbal was never as strictly differentiated from the visual, meaning that multimodality might take other shapes and fulfil different functions. The particular 'division of labour' between the modes is a cultural construction and matches the respective social arrangements. Critical analysis has to be aware of this and must have a clear concept of what the predominance of one mode over the other means in a particular cultural and institutional setting.

Relevance of multimodality for critical discourse analysis

A note on the meaning of 'critical'

There are a number of aspects that we consider vital for our understanding of 'critical' multimodal discourse analysis. First, critical discourse analysis (CDA) is not a method, but rather a research program that encompasses a variety of approaches, theoretical models, and research methods (e.g. Wodak 2011a; see also Wodak and Meyer in this volume). Similarly, 'multimodal' CDA is not a particular analytical approach, but, on a very basic level, constitutes the acknowledgement that discourse is not just verbal, but combines a variety of modes. Second, 'critical' is related to questions of how things are, why they are like that, and how they could be different (e.g. Fairclough 2010; Wodak 2011a). Such questions only prove meaningful against the backdrop of a broadly constructionist epistemology, postulating that discourse is performative and constitutive, rather than representative. This means that social reality is a human achievement and could be – at least in theory – constructed differently. However, social reality also acts back on its producers, constituting them as actors, as well as their interests and potential for further meaning-making (Berger and Luckmann 1967). We have already argued that language, in such a perspective, is the most prominent resource for meaning construction. Third, what is central to multimodal CDA is a focus on how power and interest underlie particular constructions of social reality; analysis is therefore centred on the role of discourse in the (re-)production and contestation of dominant 'truths' (e.g. van Dijk 1993). By purposefully 'alienating' the researcher from the object of study, and through the extensive interpretation of texts, critical analysis facilitates the 'unearthing' of such structures of dominance in particular discourses, and the identification of alternative realities.

A variety of specific approaches to CDA with divergent foci, conceptual backgrounds, and analytical approaches exist; however what they all share is the view that discourse shapes, and is simultaneously shaped by, society.

The contribution of multimodality to critical discourse analysis

Following our discussion so far, it is easy to acknowledge how multimodality is a crucial topic for CDA. As Machin and Mayr (2012: 6) summarize, 'meaning is generally communicated not only through language but also through other semiotic modes'. Power, truth and interest are, then, also represented in these other modes. Research on visual communication, for instance, has argued that visualization, due to its fact-like character, is particularly suited to supporting the truth-claims of its authors (e.g. Graves et al. 1996). Visuals are often able to 'disguise' power structures and hegemony as 'objective' representations. At the same time, power relations are inherent in practices of looking at things, and the 'gaze' has been identified as a disciplinary technique, disciplining both the viewer and the viewed (e.g. Foucault 1979; Kress and van Leeuwen 2006; Styhre 2010). One important point for multimodal CDA is that modes constitute conscious and unconscious *choices* made by the author that reflect her particular social and cultural positioning as well as interests at the moment of creation (e.g. Kress 2010; Machin and Mayr 2012).

There are several ways in which multimodal CDA should assess the relationships between modes and power: First, issues of power and dominance are related to the question of *how* multimodal discourse is created. Kress argues that 'powerful' sign makers do not have to take into account the interests and capabilities of their audiences (Kress 2010; Kress and van Leeuwen 2001, 2006). Their sign making is strictly oriented towards their own needs, while the interpretive work is left for the audience. This, for instance, has traditionally been true in state bureaucracies, where citizens simply have to 'learn' the particular language of 'officialese' (in German, the word 'Beamtendeutsch' was coined for this; see, for example, the study of van Leeuwen and Wodak 1999). Conversely, if audiences possess more power than sign makers, communication and design will be more strongly oriented towards their needs and interests – although it might still try to 'hide' information that is detrimental to the interest of the sign maker. Contemporary corporate reporting practices, where corporations have to convince stakeholders of proper conduct and practices, are an excellent example. In such situations (multimodal) communication has to anticipate the expectations of these stakeholders (e.g. Höllerer 2013); it thus employs multiple modes to exploit their maximum persuasive potential. We could hold that this kind of power is embodied in the *form* and *design* of communication.

Second, power and power structures are, of course, created, challenged and re-negotiated in *content* – the *what* of communication. Corporate communication will usually present the board of directors in a confident stance and in a way that communicates competence and professionalism and engenders trust. Newspapers construct particular actors or actor groups in both positive and negative ways, and regularly use multimodal designs to do so. For instance, Hardy and Phillips (1999: 19) found that in editorial cartoons, immigration discourses 'portrayed refugees as frauds, the immigration system as inadequate and the public as requiring protection'. Multimodal discourse is also used by social movements in their protest material (e.g. Philipps 2012), where visuals convey central messages and create strong emotional responses much more immediately than verbal descriptions. In all these examples, multimodal CDA provides a unique perspective that acknowledges that each mode constitutes a particular contribution to the overall signification work. It is, therefore, the central task of a student of multimodal discourse to reconstruct the ways in which the combination (or 'ensemble'; see Kress 2010) of modes suggests particular versions of social reality that are not neutral with regard to power: they serve some interests while marginalizing others.

Finally, multimodality is linked to power in society by asking who is empowered to 'speak', i.e., who is granted *'voice'* by a particular mode. Given that in modern Western cultures verbal communication is controlled more strongly than, for example, visual text or sound, these alternative modes are more susceptible to resistance and subversion by marginalized groups. Multimodality may be part of a larger shift in communication that potentially includes a systematic redistribution of power. With different modes and media of communication becoming available to a larger community of people, notions of hegemony and resistance may have to be adapted. As Kress (2010: 21) argues, 'in all domains of communication, these rearrangements in power can be conceptualized as a shift from "vertical" to "horizontal" structures of power, from *hierarchical* to (at least seemingly) more *open, participatory relations*, captured in many aspects of contemporary communications'. The full impact of these changes, being marked structurally by more potential for participation (e.g. through the openness of the internet), and in terms of modality (e.g. legitimation of a much broader spectrum of expressive forms than just verbal language), still remains open – but the necessity and timeliness of critical research dealing with such questions seems significant.

In the following section, we will discuss research concerned with power, interest, and voice that uses multimodal data in order to capture the more comprehensive picture. The first part engages with research reconstructing issues of power more thoroughly, by accepting that multimodal discourse adds another quality to communication by making particular interests seem 'natural', 'objective' and 'fact-like'. In the second part, we discuss how multimodal discourse provides opportunities to make otherwise marginalized voices more prominent in critical research.

Previous studies and exemplary research

Since it is simply impossible to discuss the entire scope of multimodality, we make the deliberate decision to focus on the interrelationship of two particular modes: the verbal and the visual. Despite other modes being relevant in practice (see, for instance, Pinch and Bijsterveld 2012, on sound), the area of visual research has, so far, received the most scholarly attention, and provides the richest pool of concrete examples. In their literature review, Meyer et al. (2013) argue that visual research comes in many forms and shapes, and that individual studies can be roughly classified according to the role that visual material plays in the research process. In more detail, they differentiate between: an *archaeological* approach that looks for traces of meaning in existing visual discourse; a *practice* approach that focuses on the actual use and manipulation of visual material in the field; a *strategic* approach that is more psychologically oriented and studies the cognitive impact of visual material on viewers; a *dialogical* approach, that uses visuals to initiate communication with actors in the field; and a *documenting* approach that sees visual material as an opportunity to create richer research documentation. Although all of these approaches have something to say about power and interest, we focus on two that are, from our point of view, highly promising points of departure for multimodal CDA: the archaeological and the dialogical approach.

'Unearthing' power and interest in multimodal discourse

Research in what we have called the archaeological tradition uses multimodal artefacts as a kind of 'window' to gain insight into the cultural system in which they are produced, thus enhancing our understanding of the meaning structures that are created, maintained and challenged. According to Preston et al. (1996), visuals can *reflect*, *mask/pervert*, and *constitute* social reality. While a naïve view only sees the reflection (i.e., the representation) of reality, a critical perspective acknowledges that visuals also hide aspects of reality that are not in the interest of the sign maker, and that the realities they constitute are always just one of several alternatives.

Exhibit 1: The archaeological approach to multimodal CDA

A common objective of critical archaeological approaches is to look into how particular people or groups are visually depicted, or made invisible, and what this may tell us about their status and power in society. Multimodality is important here, since the visual mode, for instance, may be purposefully used to transport messages that otherwise cannot be verbalized for legal or cultural reasons (McQuarrie and Phillips 2005).

Hardy and Phillips (1999), for example, apply such a critical approach to the study of editorial political cartoons (i.e., drawings and text) in the press, in

---

order to reconstruct the subject-positions that this discourse assigns to different actors in the Canadian immigration system. They first reconstruct the dominant objects of discussion (the refugee, the government, the immigration system, and the public), and then analyse the meanings assigned to these objects. They found, among other things, that refugees were commonly constituted as frauds, victims, or both, and also as privileged in comparison to other immigrants.

With a slightly different focus, Schroeder and Zwick (2004) analyse aspects of masculinity in corporate advertising. They use insights from art history, visual studies, and photography to reconstruct the 'mirror' as a root metaphor of consumer society, creating the person as an exhibited object for visual consumption.

Visual and multimodal analysis may also be utilized to reveal fundamental discursive structures and issues of presence and absence. Höllerer et al. (2013), for instance, focus on the underlying meaning structures of visual renditions of corporate social responsibility (CSR) in annual CSR reports in Austria. They identify a set of 21 'discourse carrying dimensions' that span polar opposites; these polar opposites are then clustered into a number of *topoi*. The study finds that images in the context of CSR discourse mediate spatial oppositions, bridge time, connect different institutional spheres, and help to overcome credibility gaps. Empirical results also indicate that some poles are dominant, while others are almost absent. The study is, therefore, a good example of research that reveals 'blind spots' in a particular discourse, and thus enables critical reflection.

The examples in Exhibit 1 illustrate how multimodality may considerably enrich traditional CDA. All of them include images in their analyses, but go beyond a discussion of visual content – the relationship between the individual visual and verbal parts is a central factor in understanding the performative power of text. It is the 'orchestration' (Kress 2010) of all of these elements that creates a particular version of social reality, and that serves some interests better than others.

Using multimodal discourse to give voice to marginalized subjects

Power is not only manifest in discursive presences. Often, it is constituted even more distinctly in *absences*. This might sound very abstract and ambiguous at first, but think of people who are not being heard on a particular topic for various reasons. Scholars of power and domination have long recognized that power is not only exerted in direct ways, but also indirectly, by creating non-issues and preventing some topics from even entering public discussions (e.g. Bachrach and Baratz 1962; Lukes 1974). One important concept in critical research is that of voice, concerning the question of who is legitimated to speak in a certain situation and on a particular topic – and who is not. By analysing only publicly available discursive traces, social science runs the risk of overemphasizing discourses of the powerful, therefore essentially reproducing their version of reality. We wish to draw attention to the enabling and empowering aspect of multimodality and, in particular, visuality, in this respect.

Exhibit 2: The dialogical approach to multimodal CDA

Critical research in a dialogical tradition is primarily concerned with voice of marginalized groups, and how research can be sure to capture 'silenced' discourses. This is achieved, on the one hand, by paying attention to narratives that are not represented in the (dominant) verbal mode, and, on the other, by systematically enabling actors in the field to share their experiences in a multimodal way.

An excellent example of how visuality may empower weaker groups in a particular context is provided by Bell (2012). Her study reveals how employees use visual discourse in order to resist the official, dominant verbal narrative of powerful actors within a corporation. By doing so, they create a subversive form of organizational memory that helps them to better deal with the 'death' of the organization: 'By producing images that represented Ford management as having murdered Jaguar, they presented an alternative view of the past in the present. This narrative is more tragic and sinister than could be conveyed through spoken and written words alone' (Bell 2012: 13).

A second example, the study of Slutskaya et al. (2012), systematically utilizes this empowering aspect of visuals in order to elicit richer and more adequate responses from interviewees. Their study on the 'dirty' work of butchers, and the associated threats to identity construction, met a severe challenge when established assumptions of masculinity and patriarchy, and the associated cultural and social positioning basically 'silenced' alternative voices in the profession. Purely verbal interviews failed, since interviewees did not feel comfortable in this situation, fearing that their answers would be 'insufficient'. Photo-elicitation (i.e., taking self-shot photographs as 'triggers' for conversations) proved much more useful, since photography was better suited to 'showing' the physicality of the occupation that was central to the butchers' professional identities.

Such multimodal forms of, for instance, interviewing are often more successful in surfacing discourse that otherwise would remain hidden; these novel methodological designs, therefore, provide ample potential for CDA.

The examples in Exhibit 2 show that marginalized voices that struggle to be heard in 'official' discourses use alternative routes, such as visualization, to create their version of 'how things are'. However, lack of voice is often related to a lack of rhetorical competence. As Warren (2005: 871) explains: 'Writing is a skill that is learned according to academic or literary conventions and depends, fundamentally, on the literacy of the writer, the extent of their vocabulary, knowledge of grammatical structure and, in creative writing, perhaps even prosaic construction and poetic tropes all of which are a function of education and by extension, of socio-economic circumstances'. The underprivileged are not only politically excluded from discourse, they are also often not able to put their reality into words, at least not in a way that is equally sophisticated. Genres such as photography (for instance, in the form of snapshots), however, do not require such skills. Images are often closer to people's life-worlds than sophisticated, wordy descriptions. Techniques such as photo-elicitation or photo-voice (e.g. Warren 2002, 2005) are, therefore, a suitable way for CDA to access discourses that are usually not available for scholarly study.

Summing up, the last pages have illustrated that multimodal discourse analysis is a rather comprehensive, broad, and 'fresh' endeavour. On the one hand, social reality is constructed, maintained and transformed in various multimodal ways: This entails that critical scholars need to acquire the necessary 'literacy' to deal with such rhetoric beyond that of the written and spoken word. On the other hand, multimodal discourse is a vehicle for subversive and alternative worldviews, while verbal discourse often favours the status quo as well as dominant interests and positions. This prompts critical researchers not to restrict their attention to verbal forms of communication in their studies. Power resides in the *access to*, in the *form*, as well as in the *content* of discursive modes – and, we should add, also in their *composition*.

A brief demonstration of analytical procedures

Some general remarks on methods of multimodal analysis

While there is a growing number of publications dealing with multimodal analysis (e.g. Jewitt 2009; Kress 2010; Kress and van Leeuwen 2001, 2006; Machin and Mayr 2012), there is, unfortunately, still a dearth of empirical applications that explicitly address the plurality of modes in discourse *and* systematically discuss their interrelationships as a central aspect of meaning making. The examples discussed earlier acknowledge that modes beyond the verbal are relevant; however, they do not explicitly elaborate on differences and links between them. We will, therefore, exemplify a useful analytical procedure by systematically discussing two multimodal texts in this section.

There is a number of disclaimers and caveats to be made before we present our methodological approach. First, *the* 'multimodal method' cannot exist, since the concrete form of analysis has to fit the particular research question, research context, and data. Second, 'multimodal' can mean very different things, and they all necessitate specific analytical tools. The analysis of sound (e.g. Pinch and Bijsterveld 2012), for instance, requires techniques that are very different from those of visual or verbal analysis. For these and other reasons, there are no standardized methods of analysis in multimodal research. Here, we present one specific method that is useful primarily for the analysis of multimodal material that encompasses verbal and visual text. But also in this area of application, different analytical approaches exist (and are required). A chapter on critical approaches to multimodal discourse analysis is, therefore, a rather difficult thing to write: multimodal discourse is significantly more complex than verbal discourse, and the volume at hand impressively demonstrates how many approaches – epistemological, method-ological, and analytical – exist even for verbal CDA. Moreover, in this chapter we are able to discuss only two exemplary 'texts'. These constitute discourse fragments, and we present them in isolation, which means that we cannot assess the extent to which they are typical and characteristic for a particular discourse strand or how they are located in a particular discourse thread. The following examples should, therefore, be understood as an illustration of the more detailed analysis of particular discourse fragments, not as a complete critical discourse analysis. We focus on a number of 'guiding questions' for analysis, and are selective in presenting particularly striking features of the material and our interpretations of those. At the end of the chapter, we pro-vide further readings that allow a deeper consideration of different topics and approaches in the field.

Introducing the method/methodology

The analytical procedure we present in this chapter is inspired by different strands of visual sociology and semiotics, especially Kress and van Leeuwen's (2006) social semiotics, Müller-Doohm's (1997) structural-hermeneutic sym-bolic analysis, and Bohnsack's (2007) documentary method. It was initially developed for a research project on the visual (re-)contextualization of corpo-rate social responsibility (CSR) in the Austrian context (Höllerer et al. 2013), and was further adapted specifically for multimodal discourse in a more recent study on the construction of the global financial crisis in business media (Höllerer et al. 2014). The major benefit of this analytical approach is that it enables us to work with larger quantities of visual and multimodal data with-out compromising the interpretive character of the overall analysis. It constitutes some sort of 'template' which may (and must) be adapted to the specific research question(s) and materials at hand. We suggest five ideal-typ-ical steps of analysis and illustrate them with two different multimodal texts. For each step, we suggest a number of 'guiding questions' that facilitate the analysis. Subsequently, we discuss how such analysis can be extended to larger samples, and which conceptual and methodological approaches might be uti-lized to do so. Our approach is flexible, in that some aspects and steps may be extended or scaled down, depending on the particular research objectives. Also, the guiding questions may vary accordingly, and different hermeneuti-cal techniques may be applied to answer the questions. Figure 8.1 provides a schematic overview.

In order to illustrate each step, we discuss two practical examples of multimodal texts (Figure 8.2 and Figure 8.3): a double page from a corporate annual financial report and a front page of a business newspaper.

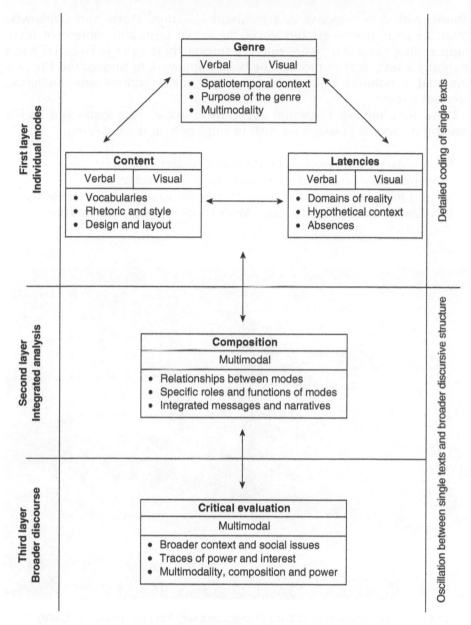

Figure 8.1 Overview of the methodological approach

Analysing two exemplary multimodal texts

Step 1: Characterizing the genre

A text genre is part of the institutional framework of a text (see also Reisigl and Wodak in this volume) and can be understood as 'typified communicative action invoked in response to a recurrent situation' (Yates and Orlikowski 1992). As such, it strongly influences the actual form and content of texts, commanding particular 'genre rules'. Knowing these rules is essential when analysing a text, as they provide the basic framework to understand the fundamental conditions under which authors make choices and audiences interpret a text.

There are a number of central questions to ask about a genre and its key dimensions, several of which we wish to emphasize in the following:

- *What is the spatiotemporal and sociocultural context of the text?*
- *Who is/are the producer/s of a text, and who is the audience?*
- *What is the purpose of the text genre? How institutionalized is the text genre?*
- *What are the particular genre characteristics with regard to multimodality?*

Figure 8.2 OMV Annual Report 2012 (reproduced with kind permission of OMV)

Example 1. Our first exemplary multimodal text is taken from the 2012 annual financial report of OMV, an integrated international oil and gas corporation with its headquarters in Vienna, Austria. Its main businesses are the exploration and production of oil and gas, natural gas distribution and power generation, and the refining and marketing of oil products. OMV is, in terms of revenue, by far the largest publicly traded corporation in Austria. As such, the text belongs to the domain of economy and business. A more detailed description of the spatiotemporal and sociocultural context of the text would emphasize, for instance, an era several years after the global financial crisis of 2008, the specificities of the oil and gas industry, the particular governance model in Austria, or the more global issues such as the multiple responsibilities of business (CSR, sustainability, shareholder value, etc.).

Annual reports of publicly traded corporations are available to the general public, and regularly provided for download on the focal corporation's website. In terms of their production, texts from the genre of annual reports are usually 'collectively crafted by executive management and communication experts on behalf of the corporation' (Höllerer 2013: 586). They are, unlike, for instance, print media, directed at more qualified audiences with nonetheless varying interests (e.g. financial analysts, shareholders, competitors, banks and creditors, regulators, journalists, or NGOs). The genre of annual reports is highly institutionalized (i.e., some content is required by legal regulation, and the structure is standardized, for instance, by guidelines such as the Global Reporting Initiative); at the same time, it offers considerable leeway for individualization and creativity, especially with regard to its non-verbal parts. Annual reports primarily serve the purpose of presenting the corporation (e.g. its history, mission, areas of operation, or current strategy) and accounting for practices and results (in terms of financial performance, but increasingly also with regard to the social and ecological dimension). In this way, they aim at shaping a qualified public's perception. While content and layout are driven by a subjective agenda, such texts inhere 'truth claims', meaning that the producers claim to present 'real' facts and figures.

Corporate annual reports instrumentalize multimodality to a high degree. Visual elements such as graphs, charts and figures, but also photographs and other images, are often used to enhance, amplify, or disguise verbal text. Some corporations go even further, adding material and haptic modes to their reports (for instance, different surfaces or three-dimensional elements), or feature video clips in the electronic version of the report. However, we also see trends that emphasize the symbolic over the fact-like character of visuals (our example goes in that direction), or, in an attempt to produce highly aesthetic reports, reduce visuals to ornaments of text layout.

Example 2. Our second example is a cover page of the *Australian Financial Review* from May 2012. It therefore belongs to the (business) media domain. The *Australian Financial Review* is the leading Australian voice within business, finance, economics, and policy with a high intermedia agenda-setting function. It is published by Fairfax Media in a compact format (six days a week), as well as online. Although offering a broad range of views and opinions, the newspaper has followed a consistent editorial line clearly favouring economic liberalism. An analysis of the text's spatiohistorical and sociocultural context would point to the recent financial crisis, the global financial markets, Australia's economic system and business landscape, and so on.

HOW THE RICH FIND WAYS TO SPEND MILLIONS ON RENOVATIONS • 5

PERSPECTIVE
Who's who in the China lobby
TONY WALKER 46

ARTS & REVIEW

Tina Arena's second coming
JANE ALBERT • 57

Mona Lisa's identical twin
JOHN McDONALD • 58

May 19–20, 2012 • $3.00 • afr.com

Weekend Edition

THE AUSTRALIAN FINANCIAL REVIEW

Knock-on effects on China increase risks for big projects

Euro fear drives share plunge

Philip Baker

Australian shares fell into negative territory for the first time this year, driven by fears that fallout from Europe will hit the Chinese economy.

Nearly $56.2 billion was wiped from the value of the S&P/ASX 200 index this week when it fell 5.6 per cent, in line with falls in other global sharemarkets, as fears spread that Spain is the latest flashpoint in the deepening European debt crisis that could trigger a sharp global economic slowdown. Officials in Europe are beginning to talk openly about Greece leaving the currency union.

The Australian index slumped 110.9 points, or 2.7 per cent on Friday to close at 4046.5, the lowest level since November, 2011. The index is down 0.25 per cent this year after being up as much as 9 per cent earlier this month.

"We've seen this sort of volatility before and it will remain choppy for the next few weeks," said Investors Mutual investment director Anton Tagliaferro. "I am surprised that Europe has caused such a reaction given it's been around for a while, but what is clear is that the best of the resources boom is over."

The dollar was hit too, dropping to as low as US97.95¢ on concerns of a fall in commodity prices. The dollar has fallen 10 per cent against the greenback since it hit $US1.0809 on March 1.

Fears of weaker demand from China pushed copper close to a four-month low, while oil slid to a six-month low of about $US92.56 a barrel. BHP Billiton slumped 9 per cent this week to its lowest level in a
Continued page 14

$9bn coal port plan scrapped

Mark Ludlow and **Dan Hall**

A $9 billion privately funded enlargement of Abbot Point coal terminal in North Queensland has been killed by the Newman state government, a project that would have created one of the largest coal ports in the world and helped expand the coal industry.

In another sign that Australia's resources boom is slowing, Queensland Deputy Premier and Infrastructure Minister Jeff Seeney said on Friday the new Liberal National Party government had decided to scrap the T4 to T9 expansion of the coal terminal and a $2.3 billion 12-berth cargo facility.

Other big resources projects also at risk from falling commodity prices include South Australia's giant Olympic Dam copper and uranium mine owned by BHP Billiton, which said this week it wouldn't spend $80 billion previously budgeted for new projects. Woodside Petroleum is slowing the pace of its troubled $35 billion Browse gas project in Western Australia.

Mr Seeney said the former Bligh Labor government tried to expand Abbot Point coal terminal too quickly. The port is designed to become the main export hub for the
Continued page 4
▷ Matthew Stevens, page 19

Disqualify dodgy MPs

Louise Dodson

Tony Windsor has foreshadowed moves to widen civil and criminal grounds for disqualifying MPs, indicating interest in a Greens plan to ask Parliament on Monday to set up a integrity commissioner to address principles raised by the Craig Thomson and Peter Slipper affairs.

Mr Windsor said there were civil and criminal convictions that could be added to the existing grounds for being excluded from Parliament.

Meanwhile, Mr Slipper has

accused former adviser James Ashby of waging an inappropriate publicity campaign against him.

Mr Thomson, suspended by the ALP, is preparing to defend himself in Parliament on Monday.

▷ Reports, 3 and 7

ATO blitz on trusts

Katie Walsh

The Australian Taxation Office is targeting baby boomers using trusts to avoid capital gains tax on wealth transfers, deputy commissioner of small and medium enterprises Michael Cranston has warned. The ATO will also use its expanded data-matching program to crack down on attempts to avoid tax. Mr Cranston said the Tax Office was seeing "some really aggressive behaviour" in this area.

▷ Report, page 8

Quigley ready to rumble

Exclusive
John McDuling

Mike Quigley says he will not be bullied. The NBN Co chief executive is in the political hot seat and faces rejection should the opposition, which opposes his $36 billion

broadband project, win the next federal election. Yet he is determined not to be silenced if his critics get their facts wrong and intends to speak out, even in an election campaign.

"Frankly, I think I have a responsibility, if statements are made about the company which I think are factually wrong," he said.

Mr Quigley's forceful advocacy of the NBN could make him a political asset for the Labor government.

▷ Perspective, page 45

CHANTICLEER ▶ WHAT HAPPENS IF GREECE GOES UNDER - BACK PAGE

FBA 001

Figure 8.3 Australian Financial Review (cover page, 19–20 May, 2012; reproduced with kind permission of Fairfax Media)

The media are a highly structured genre (e.g. van Dijk 1988). Business media reporting is a highly institutionalized 'story-telling' activity that conveys news in a way firmly governed by a '"logic of appropriateness" based on [...] professional and craft related roles' (Cook 1998: 61) – something that has also been described as a particular 'media logic' (e.g. Altheide and Snow 1979). The design and layout of cover pages is central within this logic, and often differs across cultural contexts of production as well as target audiences. For instance, in our example, the design broadly follows an Anglo-Saxon template (e.g. by starting several stories on the cover page to be continued later in the paper, by using rather catchy short titles, or by avoiding editorial commentary on the front page), and is a crucial decision made by the senior editorial team. The audience of the daily business news very much differs from consumers of mass media, as it primarily comprises the socioeconomic elite of business professionals and personal investors, among others.

Media news production has been expressively described by Tuchmann's (1973) now-classic phrase of 'routinizing the unexpected'. Business and financial news are often conceptualized as providing a 'global outlook on social reality' (Berglez 2008: 847). They provide, with a particular focus on the economic dimension, access to social reality for a broader audience. Most critically, they have a gate-keeping and agenda-setting function within public discourse (e.g. the choice to report on particular issues implies the silencing of others). Apart from claiming to report on 'true' facts and figures, they also take position with regard to the issues they deal with.

Media discourse has a strong tradition of using multimodality. Visual elements are frequently used to draw attention, and/or to frame, complement, or counter verbal text (for a systematization of 'multimodal techniques' in the media, see Höllerer et al. 2014; for previous studies on visual discourse in print and online newspapers, see for instance, de Cock et al. 2011; Fahmy 2010; Knox 2007, 2009).

Step 2: Capturing the manifest content

Analysing the manifest content of a text can take on a variety of forms, all of which are different approaches to content analysis. The primary function of this step is to sensitize the researchers to the 'language' of the text, as well as its most dominant features. As such, this step focuses on the conventional meaning of words and visual elements. We propose the following guiding questions:

- *What is the particular 'vocabulary' of the text?*
- *What kind of rhetorical and stylistic techniques and strategies are used?*
- *How can the 'design' and 'layout' of the overall text be described?*

In order to address these questions, researchers may rely on a variety of coding schemes taken from existing literature. For instance, in coding the visual vocabulary, a very basic start would be to look for different kinds of people (e.g. male/female, young/old), objects (e.g. mobile/immobile), actions (e.g. unidirectional/bidirectional), and settings (e.g. exterior/interior, private/commercial) in the visual text. For style, literature on photography and painting provides inspirations such as lighting, perspective, lines of sight, *mise-en-scène*, or interaction between viewer and image (and for a more detailed description of the analysis of verbal text, see for instance Reisigl and Wodak, and Mautner in this volume). Layout, finally, concerns the different ways of composing the overall text, including, among others, positioning, overlapping, or other 'references' between modes. We shall briefly illustrate this on the basis of our two examples.

Example 1. The verbal vocabulary of the text is characterized by a strong reliance on positive and technical language. Words such as 'divestment program', 'cost management', or 'working capital' necessitate a particular form of education. Apart from being very technical, the language is also distinctly positive, as shown by words such as 'stabilization', 'growth', 'strengthened', or 'progress'. The linguistic-rhetorical means are not very elaborate, except perhaps for the reliance on metaphors (primarily 'dead metaphors'; see, for instance, Lakoff and Johnson 1980); these will be discussed in more detail in Step 3 below.

By featuring the company's main refinery on the outskirts of Vienna, the visual vocabulary clearly emphasizes the corporation's industrial quality. It is, in its pure content, rather restricted, encompassing 'industrial architecture' in a minimalistic environment consisting almost entirely of the 'sky', but also comprising 'lights', 'green lines', and a form of 'checklist'. In terms of style, the image portrays the refinery at night, which stresses the effects of different forms of lighting. Light is, overall, a major factor in the impact of the image. Also, the viewer takes a 'worm's eye-view' in relationship to the object in the image. It is taken from a long shot, enabling a 'complete' view of the premises, but surroundings are systematically absent. The image also seems to be digitally enhanced.

The overall composition is arranged as a two-page spread. The image of the industrial complex is the background of the composition – but also its centre. The title of the page is on the upper left part, and there is a series of four small paragraphs that are arranged in a 'rising' pattern from the bottom left to the upper right. Each of these paragraphs is 'anchored' to the page with the pictogram of a 'checked box'.

Example 2. The verbal vocabulary of the newspaper page is much less restricted and also less technical. The charging is also decidedly negative. Several words point at the existence of immediate danger (e.g. 'flashpoint', 'crisis', 'fallout') and conflict (e.g. 'kill', 'criminal', 'silenced', 'opposition'). Also, completely contrary to our first example, the sense of direction is downward (e.g, 'slump', 'fall', 'drop', 'slide'). Given that it is an Australian newspaper, it is worth noting that 'Euro' and 'China' feature prominently. In addition, the vocabulary of the newspaper page also includes more numbers. Like the first example, the verbal text relies on metaphor to a certain degree. Numbers, as a form of rhetorical device, are used as for 'operationalization' and 'objectivation'.

The visual vocabulary is more restricted than in the first example, and focuses primarily on the human factor. The three photographs related to the main topic of the page are all centred on 'men' in 'formal dress'. In the central image, additional 'graphs' are added that show the dynamics of a number of measures related to stock performance and currency. Concerning visual rhetoric, gestures and countenance evoke moods and emotions. People are shown in close-up shots, making them more 'tangible' and 'personal' for the reader, but none of them looks into the camera directly.

The layout in this example is more complex than in the first one. On the one hand, there is a 'hierarchy' between parts of verbal text that is rather typical for the media (van Dijk 1988). The first title is by far the largest and most prominent, and it seems to create a 'frame' across the whole front page. The large image is in the very centre of the page, and it combines two visual elements as a collage. The two smaller portraits at the bottom of the page seem to 'grow into' the respective text that is aligned around the photograph. The complete article section is bounded at the top with the title of the newspaper, and at the bottom with a 'preview' of the next page.

Step 3: Reconstructing latent elements

The description of manifest content and rhetorical and stylistic strategies are supplemented by an analysis of broader structures of meaning that underlie the text. The central objective in this step is to transcend the manifest layer of meaning within the text and grasp its latent meanings. The overall questions are similar across perspectives:

- *What parts or 'domains' of social reality are featured within the text?*
- *How can the hypothetical social context be characterized in which the text 'makes sense'?*
- *What expected and unexpected 'absences' can be found in the text (e.g. in the sense of unrealized alternatives)?*

This means, primarily, that the analysis has to reconstruct the broader social and interdiscursive contexts that individual elements of the text refer to. Depending on text and genre, different coding strategies may be appropriate. Figures of speech, or tropes (e.g. metaphor, metonymy, irony) that were coded in the first step are a useful starting point for identifying such broader structures, as are various rhetorical (e.g. logos, pathos, ethos) and argumentative (e.g. enthymemes, topoi) structures. More generally, any form of hermeneutical analysis (e.g. Keller 2008; Hitzler and Honer 1997; Hitzler, Reichertz and Schröer 1999) may serve as inspiration and provide guidelines.

Example 1. The text shows a strong emphasis on professionalism and technology. Both visual and verbal vocabularies draw extensively from the domains of business and industry/technology. The organization, as depicted in the text, is agentic, capable, and 'energetic'. The vocabulary is active, and the focus on light, energy and movement in the visual part of the text amplifies this impression. Metaphors also draw from the domain of 'construction' (e.g. 'pillar', 'build up', 'set up') that is mirrored by the industrial building as the most central visual element on the spread. The vocabulary, therefore, creates an interesting tension between stability and movement that can be found both in the verbal as well as the visual parts of the text. The organization is constantly progressing at a substantial pace, implying that (constant) economic growth is not only possible, but a central objective. Expansion is necessary, but securing one's assets is equally important. Inertia, however, is undesirable. The colour code of the image (blue and green) mirrors the company logo, and green can also be interpreted as an allusion to the sphere of environmentalism. Despite being engaged in a 'dirty' industry (oil), the corporation provides essential and substantial services ('light'), values and implements 'green' procedures, and espouses environmental values.

The central absences in the text are 'people' and 'nature'. This is all the more striking, as it is consistent across the verbal and visual aspects of the text. The world constructed on the two-page spread is completely devoid of any human agents, be they employees, customers, or investors, or nature more generally. When the verbal text does not rely on passive constructions, it makes heavy use of 'abstract' actors, such as organizations or divisions. This reinforces the technological 'feel' of the text and creates an image of the organization as 'powerful machine'.

Example 2. In the newspaper article, domains are much more clearly cued in the verbal text. The language is largely one of disaster and conflict, sometimes reaching into the rather extreme vocabulary of armed conflict (e.g. 'kill', 'blitz'). It is completely focused on (negative) dynamics, with no substantial reference to stability. The hypothetical social context is strongly formal and serious. Money is quite literally the currency. There is nothing playful or creative about this world, especially now that it is in crisis. The sombre and dark (mostly black) colours reinforce the serious and dramatic impression of the overall text. Countenance and gestures of people support such interpretation. The three main personae exhibit desperation, helplessness and determination, respectively. This is also not a world for everybody. In the world of money and politics, male white elites dominate. Decisions are mainly taken by a chosen few, and the amounts of money at stake just baffle the average citizen.

The newspaper page has one striking absence – that of any form of diversity. The text creates an impression of the metaphorical 'old boys' club' that consists entirely of older white men in suits. This impression is even amplified when looking at the complete page. The only two women featuring on the page are both related to art rather than business – one as an artist, the other as a model. All depicted persons are Caucasian. While it might be argued that those images 'just represent reality', this is hardly ever the case. Images are always selections, particular 'framings' of social reality. Homogeneity in depiction is an editorial decision.

Step 4: Composition

A fourth step focuses on reconstructing the effects of 'composing' multimodal texts in particular ways. Kress (2010) has stressed such composition as one of the central aspects of multimodal meaning-making. While the previous steps have analysed the different modes largely in isolation from each other, we now turn to a more integrated approach.

- *How do verbal and visual elements relate to each other?*
- *What are the particular 'roles' and 'functions' of the verbal and the visual within the text?*
- *What integrated 'messages' or 'narratives' are created through this composition?*

In order to address these questions, researchers may focus on various aspects of the interrelationships between modes, such as hierarchical arrangements ('Is one mode on a higher or lower level of text structure than others?'), or issues of emphasis and dominance ('Which mode is at the focus of attention?'). In addition, similarities, differences, and references may also be grasped in terms of content and latent meaning ('How similar is their vocabulary?'; see steps above). It must be noted that multimodal texts rarely encompass only a single narrative. Rather, their multivocality is a central asset, connecting them to a multiplicity of divergent narratives at the level of the overall discourse. It is, therefore, impossible to present exhaustively the narratives that our examples evoke. We can offer only an indication of the most dominant stories they tell us.

Example 1. The verbal and visual parts of the text mutually reinforce and support each other distinctly. The verbal mode is used to 'inform'. It provides the context and the more detailed information. While the image is strongly stylized, the verbal text is supposed to tell the 'truth' and provide the 'facts'. The visual mode, on the other hand, 'personalizes' the message through the depiction of the concrete corporate building. It also adds those attributes that verbal text is not as easily able to communicate, like dynamics, and even a form of 'industrial romance'. Overall, it makes the message more 'tangible'. Layout, as a third mode, ties the other two modes together and adds emphasis and hierarchy. The composition as a whole creates an impression of potency, growth and movement, to the extent that even the way in which paragraphs are arranged imply an upward trend, and the checkboxes allude to objectives reached. This basically implies a bright future, since the corporation has chosen the right path. In addition, the corporation is presented as a 'well-oiled machine' that 'never sleeps' and provides essential services.

Example 2. In terms of mood and atmosphere, the verbal and visual aspects of the text strongly reinforce each other. The task of creating 'credibility' and 'facticity' is equally divided here between the verbal and the visual mode. While words provide the cast of actors, the sequence of events, and some numbers, the graphs show an 'objective' representation of developments. The visual mode adds 'emotion' in a slightly different way from in the first example since it is more closely tied to actual people. In the first article, which is focused on the fear of an economic downturn, such fear and worry is perfectly mirrored in the behaviour of the central actor in the image, and the diagrams make it rational and measurable. In the other articles, the faces of people depicted show aggravation and determination, accordingly. Overall, the page shows a 'triangle' structure of functions. The large image is the most symbolic and emotional one, connecting falling share prices to individual suffering and despair. The graphs 'rationalize' the message, and the two people on the bottom 'personalize' the issue. This creates an intricate equilibrium between metaphor and facticity in the story about the struggle and impotency of the societal (male) elite against the overwhelming forces of global (and possibly imported) recession and economic downturn.

Step 5: Conclusions and critical evaluation

All these previous steps build upon and inform each other in an effort to reconstruct the 'patterns' of social meaning within the text. In terms of critical analysis, the final set of questions we need to direct at the text are concerned with questions of interest and power. Of course, in the limited space provided here, it is by no means possible to present a fine-grained and exhaustive analysis. Rather, we simply point to some of the most striking elements and encourage readers to continue with their own analysis.

- *What does the analysis tell us about broader social issues and the particular institutional and cultural context in which the text is embedded?*
- *How can we describe the different traces of interest and power that we find within presences and absences?*
- *How do the different modes and their overall composition reinforce, challenge, or conceal such power?*

Example 1. We may reasonably infer that a composition like this points at a context where corporations are increasingly challenged to legitimize their own conduct towards differentiated audiences. The multimodal composition expresses power and speed, but also the potency to responsibly manage such dynamics. It perpetuates the 'meta-narrative' of unlimited growth and suggests that the corporation is able to sustain such growth. At the same time, such pursuit is presented as a not inherently self-interested behaviour – rather it serves the basic needs of society (energy; 'lighting up the dark'; 'being active while others sleep'), and does so in an environmentally responsible way (stressing the colour green, 'romantic' imagery). This is very much in line with recent findings that corporations use multimodal texts in an attempt to de-problematize seemingly contradictory expectations of their stakeholders (Höllerer et al. 2013).

Traces of interest and power in the composition vary in their visibility. The most obvious form of power is openly depicted: the power of the successful, expanding corporation that uses technology to provide essential services to its customers, but also assumes its broader responsibilities. Focusing on the particular 'absences' in the text, one can find more subtle aspects. By making the people that keep the machine running 'invisible', for instance, the composition ascribes power and agency not only to technology itself, but also to the corporation as an abstract, legal construct. The absence of people is especially striking since this particular corporation usually makes extensive use of people in their visualizations. A second aspect that is made invisible – usually a rather controversial aspect in the oil and gas industry – is the 'dirty' side of production.

The verbal part of the text is the actual 'report': it presents objectives met and challenges overcome, which is reinforced by the visual element of the 'ticked boxes'. The image provides these achievements with a 'face' – although an abstract one. Also, due to its immediate facticity, the image is able to portray a refinery as something actually 'beautiful' and aesthetic. By constant reinforcement and repetition (ticked boxes, upward alignment of paragraphs, speedy movement in the foreground, optimistic verbal text), the central message found in the heading ('Profitable Growth is well on track') is communicated through all modes simultaneously and, therefore, made much more persuasive.

Example 2. There are at least two related aspects to the context that seem striking. First, there is an – explicit as well as implicit – focus on measurability, precision and causality. Explicitly, this is shown, on the one hand, through the focus on precise numbers in the text, but also in the graphs and images. Even someone unable to understand the precise meaning of the graphs will 'get' this importance of precision. To a degree, such precision is also mirrored in the 'de-contextualized' depiction of people on the bottom of the page. The absence of any 'noise' in the image leaves no questions about who is central in these photographs. A second aspect that builds on such measurability, precision and causality, is constituted by the need to assign responsibility, accountability and blame. The big headline is very clear on what causes the 'share plunge', and in the other articles, it becomes equally clear who the culprits and the heroes are.

Interest and power are more subtle in our second example. It is primarily constituted by presences and absences. There is an implicit claim to 'truth' within the multimodal text that fits the context of 'serious' business media. Such a claim is represented, on the one hand, in 'realistic' photography, and, on the other hand, through the extensive use of numbers and charts. The visual part of the text also contains additional information on 'who is relevant'. We have noted before that 'business', in this text, is exclusively 'male' and perpetuates the discourse of 'male' leadership, especially in the situation of crises and the fight against 'the forces'. The placement of the females in the domain of the Arts even reinforces this impression. The images, in this sense, are much more than just illustrations of the verbal text. The combination of text and visuals specifies 'what kind of men' are the main characters (as leaders, heroes, or culprits): here, we are dealing with an elite group of white, older men wearing suits.

Extending the analysis to larger samples

So far, we have only illustrated the procedure for single multimodal texts. While some qualitative and hermeneutical approaches explicitly claim that single texts are sufficient for the study of particular questions, since every text contains the social and discursive structures in which it is embedded (see, for instance, the objective hermeneutics of Oevermann et al. 1979), often a larger sample is needed in order to reconstruct broader parts of the discourse thread, provide a comparative analysis of different threads, find patterns on the field level or across genres, or study developments over time.

Basically, such field-level analysis would use the same procedures as those of individual texts. Steps 1–3 would remain unchanged, they would be just applied to a larger set of texts. Starting with step 4, researchers would start a process of constant 'oscillation' between the single text and the broader discursive structure. The challenge here is to find useful concepts to work with in linking individual textual elements to discursive structure. The options are manifold. In our own research (e.g. Höllerer et al. 2013, 2014), we have, for instance, used framings (e.g. Gamson and Modigliani 1989; Meyer 2004; Meyer and Höllerer 2010), topoi (e.g. Jancsary 2013; Wengeler 2003), discourse-carrying dimensions (e.g. Bublitz 2011; Link 1997), and narratives (e.g. Czarniawska 2004; Rowlinson et al. 2014). Other analytical concepts include *Deutungsmuster* (e.g. Meuser and Sackmann 1991; Oevermann 2001), or legitimation strategies (e.g. Meyer and Lefsrud 2012; Vaara and Monin 2010; van Leeuwen and Wodak 1999). What all these approaches have in common is that they allow for a differentiated analysis of meaning structures in a particular field or on a specific topic. Social reality and meaning are seldom monolithic, but divided into particular 'zones' of meaning (Berger and Luckmann 1967). Multimodal research provides additional ways of understanding such zones and the ways in which they emerge, and are maintained or challenged.

Summary

In this chapter we have aimed at elaborating the main aspects, dimensions, and implications of multimodal CDA. We wish to emphasize that it is not so much a particular *variant* of CDA; rather, it encompasses a broad range of discourse-analytical approaches that deal with the multiple *ways and resources of (re-)constructing social reality*. Multimodal CDA engages with different forms of *data*, and therefore also employs a well-stocked conceptual and methodological toolbox. As a matter of fact, this chapter could not offer a comprehensive overview of all tools available. We provide, however, a selection of additional readings in the appendix that enable an in-depth engagement with more specific topics related to multimodal CDA.

We presented, in some detail, one specific methodological approach that is particularly suited for the analysis of large samples of multimodal material (i.e., visual and verbal elements) in order to detect the broader, underlying meaning structures that organize discourse and social reality. We are well aware that our methodological suggestions here do, by no means, provide a standardized 'schema' according to which multimodal CDA should proceed. It should therefore be understood as what it is: an illustration of how one could proceed in doing multimodal CDA. It is, nevertheless, our hope that in offering ideas in a more systematic way, we can inspire our readers as to how such analysis should be conducted. Also, we wish to stress that the strengths of our approach lie, particularly, in its flexibility, adaptability and its applicability to larger corpuses of multimodal data (as opposed to a methodology that excels in in-depth interpretation of single cases or small samples). While primarily developed for the analysis of verbal and visual text, our guiding questions can be adapted relatively easily for studies that aim at different modes of discourse.

Of course, multimodal analysis also has to face a number of important challenges. First, it entails a rather strong dependence on data and documentation. Some forms of data collection (e.g. interviews, surveys) are not tailored for modes beyond the verbal. Also, actors in the field might be reluctant to provide multimodal accounts of their experiences (e.g. photographs, videos, drawings). Second, multimodal research strains researchers' abilities to deal with a variety of modes at the same time, all of which require particular, and potentially very divergent, sets of analytical skills. Third, since different modes create meaning in rather specific ways, comparison is not trivial. Fourth, contemporary publication outlets are often ill equipped to deal with other modes than the verbal. Still, in order to capture contemporary social reality that is increasingly constructed, mediated, reproduced and challenged by a multitude of discursive modes that become ever more accessible, multimodal literacy becomes, in our view, a necessity for researchers of the social world.

Further reading

Kress, G. (2010) *Multimodality: A Social Semiotic Approach to Contemporary Communication.* Abingdon: Routledge.
In this book, Kress provides a rich and detailed introduction into multimodal discourse from a social semiotic perspective. The volume entails an elaborate theoretical discussion of meaning and communication, and makes ample use of examples and illustrations in order to make concepts and ideas more accessible.

Kress, G. and van Leeuwen, T. (2006) *Reading Images: The Grammar of Visual Design.* London: Routledge.
Focusing on the visual mode of communication, this book provides an in-depth engagement with the way visuals 'work' and how they can be more systematically understood. The authors engage with various aspects of the visual, from content to style to latent meaning. It is an invaluable resource for a better understanding of the visual elements in discourse.

Machin, D. and Mayr, A. (2012) *How to Do Critical Discourse Analysis: A Multimodal Introduction.* London: Sage.
Machin and Mayr make multimodality an explicit part of their version of CDA. Their book is an accessible and excellently structured overview of different aspects that such multimodal CDA encompasses. In a systematic way, it covers topics such as speech and speakers, representing people and action, absences, persuasion and 'truth'. Their book is rich with illustrations that exemplify their approach.

Meyer, R. E., Höllerer, M. A., Jancsary, D. and van Leeuwen, T. (2013) *The Visual Dimension in Organizing, Organization, and Organization Research: Core Ideas, Current Developments, and Promising Avenues.* Academy of Management Annals 7: 487–553.
This article provides a detailed and systematic overview of research on visuals and visuality in organization and management research; it also touches on related disciplines that have dealt with visuality extensively (such as, for instance, psychology, communication studies, or philosophy). Meyer and her colleagues suggest that visuals may play a multiplicity of different roles in (critical) research, and present a typology of approaches that also serves as inspiration for future research in this area.

Rose, G. (2007) *Visual Methodologies: An Introduction to the Interpretation of Visual Materials.* London: Sage.
Rose presents an elaborate overview of the most prominent and promising methodological approaches to visual analysis. The book covers content analysis, semiology, psychoanalysis, audience studies and anthropological approaches. It explicitly devotes two chapters to visual discourse analysis.

Tasks

(A) *Choose a cover page of any tabloid newspaper that seems of interest to you. Select one article on that page that encompasses some kind of visual element.*

1. Take a look at the 'vocabulary' of the verbal text. What are the most striking nouns, verbs and adjectives? Do they belong to a particular 'domain' (e.g. war, love, family, sports)?
2. In the same vein, take a look at the visual 'imagery'. What elements can you identify (e.g. people, objects, actions)?
3. Try to summarize the visual and the verbal text in a short narrative of no more than two or three sentences.

4. How do these stories relate to each other? Do they support or contradict each other, or do they seem to be unrelated? Is there an overall story that can be told across modes?
5. In whose interest is it to tell the story in this particular way? Can you identify winners and losers?

Some additional things to think about:

- Does it make any difference whether you perceive the verbal or visual part of the text first? If yes, what exactly changes?
- Is it important how the verbal and visual parts of the text are spatially positioned in relation to each other? If yes, what changes when you rearrange them?

(B) *Choose a scene from one of your favourite movies (preferably one where a dialogue between characters happens).*

1. What modes can you identify (e.g. spoken word, visual impressions, body language, composition of the shot)?
2. Try to define, for each of the modes you identified, what its role or function is in the overall composition. How does their impression on you differ from the others? One way to assess this could be to imagine how the scene would affect you if one mode was absent.
3. What information do you get through the particular interplay of modes that is not explicitly 'said' or 'shown' in the scene?

Some additional things to think about:

- Is there a particular 'sequence' to the use of modes in the scene (e.g. a strong visual impression first, spoken text comes later)? How does that influence your understanding of the scene?
- Could you completely change the meaning of the scene by changing individual modes? If you could, then how?

Acknowledgements

We gratefully acknowledge financial support from the Danish Research Council: DFF–1327-00030.

9

CRITICAL DISCOURSE STUDIES AND SOCIAL MEDIA: POWER, RESISTANCE AND CRITIQUE IN CHANGING MEDIA ECOLOGIES

MAJID KHOSRAVINIK AND JOHANN W. UNGER

CONTENTS

> ## Keywords
>
> critical discourse studies, CDS 2.0, digital discourse, affordances, critical digital discourse analysis, focus groups, participatory web, political resistance, power, prosumption, protest, social media

Introduction

The vast majority of adults and teenagers living in an affluent society use social media on a daily basis (see, e.g., Duggan and Smith 2013 for data about the USA). Increasingly, even more find that social media intersect with their lives in multiple ways (see also Thurlow 2012), e.g. the widespread use of hashtags and social media logos in promotional texts such as adverts and TripAdvisor reviews or new forms of protest mobilization, e.g. through Facebook. Less affluent societies have also been pervaded by social media use, both in similar ways to more affluent societies but also in different ways, for instance through the widespread use of text messaging for a variety of social and commercial practices (Aker and Mbiti 2010; Cole et al. 2013), or have afforded new spaces of citizenry power and collective identity construction (KhosraviNik and Zia 2014).

At the same time, traditional ways of interacting between individuals, groups and institutions have also been rapidly changing. Telephone calls are now much rarer than instant messages for some demographics, handwritten letters are becoming a curiosity, and even a relatively new and ubiquitous platform such as email is no longer taken for granted as the first choice for written communication (Lenhart 2012). Even though large media organizations still represent considerable concentrations of economic and political power, and thus continue to exercise influence on society, print newspapers are haemorrhaging readers and their circulation is on the decline (see Siles and Boczkowski 2012), at least for a large part of the (affluent) world. Newspaper websites are, meanwhile, flourishing, alongside the use of social media for news retrieval (for instance, Holcomb et al. (2013) report that roughly 30% of US adults retrieve their news via Facebook, though this may include following links to the websites of established media corporations).

The elephant in the room is that, with the increasing availability and growth of digitally mediated linguistic data and the impact of social media in various aspects of social, political and economic processes, a socially oriented critical approach such as CDS cannot remain oblivious to these changes, in terms of material communication concentration or the changes in norms of production and dissemination of social discourses. In the meantime, social media communication has given rise to a new dynamic of communication that breaks away from the traditional linear flow of content from certain (privileged) producers to (ordinary, powerless) consumers, as well as changing the distribution processes that were at the core of assumptions about power in the mass media. This communicative dynamic is at the heart of what has come to be labelled the participatory internet, or 'Web 2.0' (O'Reilly 2007). Seargeant and Tagg (2014) view the essence of social media as facilitating participation and interaction to allow users to produce content in a participatory manner. They are 'internet-based sites and platforms which facilitate the building and maintaining of networks or communities through the sharing of messages and other media' (2014: 3). Ritzer and Jurgenson (2010), on the other hand, view social media technologies as only a natural but subtler and less material continuation of what they label the process of 'prosumption' – putting consumers to work – whereby the distinction between producers and consumers in the material world erodes. Alongside wider prosumption practices, such as using self-service checkouts, web-based platforms such as Facebook and Twitter as well as Wikipedia, blogs, YouTube, Flickr and Instagram, all share the characteristic of facilitating the implosion of production and consumption (2010) as users create and upload content for other users to see and interact with. Fuchs and Sevignani (2013) and Fuchs (2014) take an explicitly Marxist perspective and view prosumers' activities on a wide variety of participatory platforms as *digital labour*. At the heart of this understanding is that the 'dominant capital accumulation model of contempo-rary corporate internet platforms is based on the exploitation of users' unpaid labour' (Fuchs and Sevignani 2013: 237), such that not only is 'value for profit generation' created through content production (including the sharing of personal information) but also labour for distribution processes is freely provided by users. Engagement in social networking sites (SNS) brings value for the platform owner, not only because immense volumes of data are generated (value as producer), but also because of the amount of time users spend on sites during which targeted ads are presented to them (value as consumer) (2013: 260). To draw an analogy to television, prosumers are not only viewers of creative content and advertisements, but also the co-creators and co-distributors of the very content themselves.

Ritzer and Jurgenson (2010) maintain that the application of a capitalist model to the participatory web entails new levels of complexity. For example, there is no absolute control over resources and the fact that a variety of social-communication affordances of the participatory web are taken advantage of by anti-capitalist and progressive movements, or primarily serve a purpose other than profit. Another complication is that it would be hard to argue for a Marxist notion of *exploitation* in the traditional sense because 'prosumers seem to enjoy, even love, what they are doing and are willing to devout long hours to it for no pay' (2010: 22), a phe-nomenon that has also been termed *playbour* (Fuchs 2014). In a traditional Marxist interpretation of the workforce, this exploitation is perceived as a coer-cive process, e.g. a physical threat or a threat to one's livelihood. There is also a considerable awareness of exploitation among those who are exploited. Although the apparent voluntary nature of work on social media does remove this under-standing of coercion, insofar as prosumers are the producers of online wealth that is appropriated by capital, it does share some characteristics of exploitative work relations (Fuchs 2014). It is also argued that the coercion exercised by Facebook on users is 'rather a social form of coercion that threatens the user with isolation and social disadvantages' (Fuchs and Sevignani 2013: 257). It is important to note that the corporate goal of SNS is to capture/broadcast con-tent and the nuanced life details of users (as content producers) and encourage them to spend time/activity on the platform (as audience) as much as possible, via various incentives – all of which serve a commercial purpose, one way or another. Hence, on the one hand, researchers can critique digitally mediated language and social actions that make use of social media as a mode of dissemination. But, on the other hand, we argue that it is also vital to consider and discuss the potential of newly created spaces for citizenry practices, while engaging in an overarching critique of media corporatization. This applies in the context of the general euphoria around technological solutions and the saturated consumerist market logic characteristic of late modern society. The generally abductive orientation of most critical discourse scholars suggests that we should be attentive to all of the above theoretical developments, while at the same time considering how specific forms and genres of data affect our analyses, and we should move between the two in establishing appropriate research questions and methods.

We begin by reviewing some of the past approaches to the web within CDS and consider the implications for social media research that they give rise to. The next sections will then discuss the challenges to theories from media and communication studies as well as other disciplines in light of the sweeping changes to media ecologies. Finally, we will examine some of the methodological challenges for CDS scholars who wish to engage with social media, before presenting two case studies that illustrate some of the issues raised in the previous discussion.

CDS principles and social media

CDS scholars have long argued for a 'socially committed analysis of language' and promoted a problem-oriented approach to what used to be a strictly descriptive academic endeavour (Blommaert 2005: 6). In fact, a commitment to the social contextualization of language is what distinguishes 'linguistic' analysis from 'discourse' analysis (see Cook (2001), who views discourse as text in context). But within scholarly traditions in linguistic studies, not all 'discourse analyses' are (or need to be) 'critical', and this allows a first point of contact between the tradition of research into computer-mediated communication and CDS. In response to a media-centric approach, which would foreground the impact of media technology on society at the expense of the significance of social (and individual) contexts that dominated early studies in computer-mediated communication, Androutsopoulos (2008) takes a more sociolinguistically and ethnographically oriented approach to social media to examine interactions, identity formation and language variation (among other linguistic phenomena). At the macro-level, anchoring the research in society rather than technology is the first step towards envisaging a CDS approach to social media. Interestingly, foregrounding society as the entry point of research is also a distinction between micro/descriptive approaches to discourse analysis and a broader CDS approach. In the meantime, it is important to acknowledge that traditions in linguistic discourse analysis have already made a useful break (from a CDS point of view) from isolated linguistic analysis, even though the degree to which sociopolitical contextualization should be foregrounded may be in dispute. Susan Herring's work (e.g. 2004) is of prime importance in this respect.

Herring (2004) takes the tradition of linguistic discourse analysis to digital media and tries to expand the scope of discourse analysis to include a new media ecology. Both Androutsopoulos's and Herring's work could be discussed from a CDS perspective by making a call for more focus on the contextualization of communication and user communities. For many CDS scholars, all linguistic features are to be described and then linked to various levels of context (see KhosraviNik 2010: 67). Criticality in CDS is thus associated with being reflexive, not only on the level of research methods but also with regard to the contextualization of the findings of (descriptive) discourse analysis (Wodak 2001: 9).

Writing in the mid-2000s, Mautner urged scholars to enter new communicative arenas and make use of the wealth of data sources available (Mautner 2005: 812). She highlights the 'lack of pre-ordering, and the indiscriminate mixing of voices and genres' (2005: 817) as a particular problem for classic CDS research at the time – though in some ways the participatory web may have become more organized since then, with its communities of practice, e.g. Facebook pages or Twitter hashtags. At the same time, it is the mix of genres itself which constitutes a main characteristic of the new communicative ecology. Instead of the specific genre forms and unidirectionality of textual practices in traditional (mass) media, users now deal with a wide variety of textual genres almost simultaneously. This includes relatively formal engagement with an institution, e.g. offering 'reactions' to a text by providing feedback on a site or reacting to a news article, and in peer-to-peer 'ordinary' communicative engagement, e.g. talking to friends using instant messaging protocols such as WhatsApp. Massively popular SNS, such as Facebook, accommodate both institutions and individuals (or powerful and ordinary texts) at the same time. These new combined spaces have helped to erode the genre differences and spillage of informal communication. There is also a sense of an unharnessed potential for textual power as the power of a text is now determined through pull communicative strategies to convince ordinary users to react (e.g. 'like' a post) rather than the push strategies of mass media. Despite the fact that there are many platforms that 'push' their content to users, especially with the increasing corporatization of web spaces, the participatory web is not a push or 'disruption' medium like [broadcast] television (Gretzel et al. 2000: 150). This is partly why communication on SNS can extend from the most mundane, local, private and personal forms of communication to communication that can have the most serious collective, political, financial and cultural significance.

There is also the problem of the a-historicity of the web, because sites and texts are subject to continuous change. This leads to a wider problem of replicability and transparency of data selection and analysis for CDS, i.e. concerning the systematicity of data selection and comparability of data sets. Nevertheless, we would argue that discussions over what constitute suitable data for research predate the web as CDS seeks to follow a systematic data selection procedure, which is *also* context-sensitive, along the lines of its problem-oriented research agenda.

Scollon and Scollon (2004) examined email, a form of digitally mediated interaction that preceded the web, never mind the participatory web, but which in its current status is considered to be a social medium by some scholars (Page et al. 2014: 6). One of Scollon and Scollon's key contributions to the study of social media from a CDS perspective is that they consider context not exclusively in terms of levels (see Unger 2013: 41ff), but rather as a network whereby each element (nexus) affects the others. Their work has also influenced (and links well with) more recent work on social media from the perspective of literacy studies (see for instance Barton and Lee 2013). A further compatible approach is that of Lemke (2002), who conducted multimodal analysis of institutional (pre-participatory) web pages. According to Lemke, in digitally mediated texts meanings are created not just via the interplay of different semiotic elements and the viewer's understanding of these, but also by the viewer's actions in reading and traversing between different parts of texts (i.e. through hyperlinks), which Lemke refers to as 'traversals'. A final contribution from a CDS perspective to the study of digitally mediated texts comes from Wodak and Wright (2006), who examined an online discussion forum set up by the EU to encourage participation in politics, and hence address the perceived 'democratic deficit'. They emphasize the importance of design and institutional (or individual) control over forms of topic development and argumentation – something that is also taken up by computer-mediated discourse analysis. Although his analysis is not specifically of social media texts, but rather of globalized, 'hypercapitalist' systems of semiosis and information flows, Graham (2006) discusses some of the social changes that accompany any change in media ecologies: 'Periods during which new media emerge, by definition, coincide with extensions and transformations in human relationships. They change the scale and character of human relationships, often irreversibly' (Graham 2006: 12).

Communicative power and social media

The essence of the communicative power assumed to reside in the textual analysis of CDA studies of *traditional* media (e.g. press and broadcast) hinges on the fact that there is a predominantly one-way flow of content from a few elite producers to masses of ordinary recipients. This assumes that, first, the flow of texts is linear and unidirectional from media (elites) to society, and second that there is a clear-cut separation between the processes of production and consumption of media texts.

The preferential control of symbolic elites over texts is assumed both in the macrostructural, i.e. industrial, political and economic sense, e.g. the owner concentration of media outlets, as well as in local communicative practices, e.g. textual nuances or recipients having little space to talk back. Even before the advent of new interactive and participatory affordances, approaches in media and communication studies had turned against what was perceived as an overemphasis on audience passivity and political oversimplification in effect models, sometimes at the expense of an oversimplified account of audience power. In light of recent technological changes, a number of scholars and media commentators have, somewhat breathlessly, announced sweeping social changes in the fields of politics, journalism, education and many others (see Morozov 2011 for a critical, albeit somewhat polemical, discussion; and Castells 2009 for a broader view of how digital media are changing communication). That does not mean, however, that these changes have brought about a utopia of equal and democratic access to media for all users (see for instance Wodak and Wright 2006), although it is evident that several multi-layered and multi-functional 'new spaces of (communicative) power' have opened up which may be adopted and used differently in various sociopolitical and technological contexts.

Social media are by their nature interactive, inherently and substantially multimodal and user-centred, as opposed to the unidirectional nature of message flows in traditional media. One consequence of this shift is the separating lines between 'official' and 'unofficial' texts; hence, the traditional dichotomy of powerful/powerless voices is eroding as more content is produced and consumed socially – even though market forces and macrostructures are systematically colonizing this new space and its infrastructures. While the institutional power *of* (or behind) discourse, i.e. mass media power, may appear to have been compromised, the power *in* discourse, i.e. bottom-up language-in-use, seems today to be the focus of interested domains of politics and the corporate world (see KhosraviNik 2014 for a full discussion of this aspect). Optimistically speaking, social media have now helped to decentralize the mass-mediated processes of pushing content onto audiences and offer some kind of participatory role to the individual communicator. By making access to the processes of production and distribution of texts possible, the locations of communicative power concentration 'are unfixed and shift according to the contextual environments' (Kelsey and Bennett 2014: 43), and such spaces for resistant discourses are not only afforded but taken up and used effectively (2014: 43 for an example). Despite the more recent wave of pessimism (e.g. Morozov 2011), the participatory web is still viewed by many as revolutionary and utopian. Cyber-libertarians are strong believers in both the internet and its links to postmodern radical individualism and the potential for democratization.

With regard to data, this new decentralization and the sudden unsolicited empowerment of media prosumers have yielded the interesting side-effect of creating large data sets that can be aptly used for social-science research. The kind of linguistic and multimodal data that would normally have been obtained via interviews, focus groups and physically co-present ethnographic observations can now be accessed via various web platforms (Koteyko 2010). There are, of course, several fundamental issues when considering this type of linguistic data, including the digital divide and accessibility, representativeness and confusion over the notion of communities of practice and diasporic identities, as well as ethical issues. Yet, it can be argued that social media have facilitated the construction and representation of a variety of non-mainstream identities which can be seen as the democratization of information and culture (Kahn and Kellner 2004). On the other hand, new data sources are interesting sites for critical language and communication studies, e.g. as one form of the consolidation of social attitudes and discourses (e.g. KhosraviNik and Zia 2014), especially because, sometimes, access to such bottom-up data may be well-nigh impossible for a variety of political, logistical and practical reasons. The two main forces of *traditional intrusive politics* (censorship and control) and the *capitalist colonization of the public sphere* have been the classic traditional barriers to democratization and the media's function as the fourth estate. The former of these may be more prevalent in less affluent areas of the world, while many communities in more affluent areas are hindered in the drive towards democratization by an acute surge of market forces and capitalist advancement. Therefore, the functions, characteristics and dynamic of the participatory web and what it may develop into in a given society could (radically) vary in different contexts. 'Social media can help to bring into being new practices of social inclusivity, group recognition and pluralized participation as well as different forms of political conversation and engagement' (Cottle 2011: 650, discussing the Arab Spring; drawing on Dahlgren 2009). Social networking sites such as Facebook have thus been argued as functioning to reconnect an apolitical public with political debate, and facilitating communication and debate between individual citizens and between citizens and politicians. However, the ideal of *re*-connection to politics arises from a largely non-political context of citizenry in developed/affluent contexts. In many parts of the world, as seen for example in the Egyptian uprising of 2011, it is not the social media that reconnect members of society with politics but rather a saturated politicized society which makes use of whatever affordances serve its purpose (cf. Tufekci and Wilson 2012). Thus it does not make sense to talk of a social media revolution, but rather of a revolution that makes use of social media and is visible on them. Hence, to go as far as labelling such movements a 'Twitter revolution' or 'Facebook revolution' would be a misreading and trivialization of the sociopolitical context of the country and do 'less than justice to both the political *and* media complexities involved' (Cottle 2011: 650). The point in these cases is not only to avoid making universalist assumptions about the nature of societies and the functions of digital (or even traditional) media, but to try to situate and view media performance in relation to the preceding 'structures of state power, the role(s) of the military and also the organization of political opposition in and across the different societies concerned' (p. 657). It remains true though that, in several undemocratic contexts, social-networking sites can function as platforms to make up for a lack of healthy deliberation spaces such as a relatively free journalistic field.

An emergent critical discursive approach to social media

We argue above that the research context of social media platforms raises a number of challenges to established theories in CDS, media studies and related fields. We now move on to ask what methodological challenges social media may offer, and below we suggest several ways to overcome them. In this section we will briefly outline two approaches mentioned above: Susan Herring's computer-mediated discourse analysis (CMDA) and Jannis Androutsopoulos's discourse-centred online ethnography (DCOE), after examining in more detail some of the methodological issues that social media give rise to for critical discourse scholars.

Research into social media, particularly within frameworks such as CDS – originally developed for very different media ecologies and mediation processes – does need to acknowledge the differences in data types and new affordances to account for the macro-qualities of texts before engaging in more micro-analysis.

However, the separation of the 'online world' as a strikingly different discursive arena, as advocated by early CMC studies, does not sit well theoretically with the socially critical aspirations of CDS research. Thus, just as CDS scholars would not endorse an analytical approach that strictly separates the data from their immediate or broader context, they should also not treat 'offline' and 'online' as separate and independent of one another, a worldview that Jurgenson (2012) terms 'digital dualism'. Until the advent of full artificial intelligence and machine consciousness, digitally mediated texts are always created by humans with physical bodies; even if they are generated by automated programs, these programs have in turn been created by humans. At the same time, as suggested in the introduction, the vast majority of human lives are affected or augmented in some way by digitally mediated practices, even if this is for some removed from their daily experience.

As a broad research programme, most critical studies of discourse are based on the analysis of a topic-related body of linguistic data positioned and explained in relation to a sociopolitical context with a critical angle. Within this broad framework, texts are analysed against genre-specific (institutional, media) backgrounds to address the processes of distribution. This includes providing some background to the nature of the data, the range and quality of the audience, the affordances and communicative options provided by the genre of communication, and the linguistic features of the language used. As illustrated in Figure 9.1, the two context levels of media practices and sociopolitical practices should always be considered in any analyses of communicative resources (i.e. data), be they texts from newspapers or online material. Although interactivity and the possibility of users changing roles, from text consumers to text producers, is an overall characteristic of the participatory web, this dynamic is not always present in various subgenres of the web. Participatory web communicative practices are a bundle of static organizational texts, e.g. adverts and blog posts as well as interactive users' communication as 'audiences' such as commentary sections in newspapers or Facebook. There is a strongly established tradition in CDS of dealing with certain powerful texts, e.g. of politicians, policy and the mass media. There have been numerous large-scale studies of such texts, especially newspaper articles and political speeches. It is tempting to see these textual resources as the most socially and politically relevant texts for research. But for a CDS study involving social media data, these institutional texts should be viewed and analysed within their new interactive context, while bearing in mind that the sociality of communication is the core quality of textual practice on the participatory web. While distinctions between user-generated content and official content are still discernible, there is a general ethos of 'crowdsourcing' in terms of what can become more important or attract attention, and in this sense user-generated content and formal texts compete with each other. As per Figure 9.1, the shape and quality of social media communication are influenced by the characteristics of the media institution itself, i.e. how it is organized and how it is linked to surveillance strategies. In other words, the first level of contextualization of the language (and other meaning-bearing resources) in use on social media involves seeing how this communication is afforded within media institutions. Within that framework, various discourses may be upheld, perpetuated, facilitated and constructed. The subgenre of the communication should also be considered carefully within established genre conventions, e.g. are we discussing blog posts, commentaries, a string or thread of instant messages etc. Finally, it must be noted that all these genre and media-specific considerations should be positioned within a wider sociopolitical context. This is where qualities of the public sphere, degrees and dominance of marketization and the dynamic of political communication in a particular context should be critically considered.

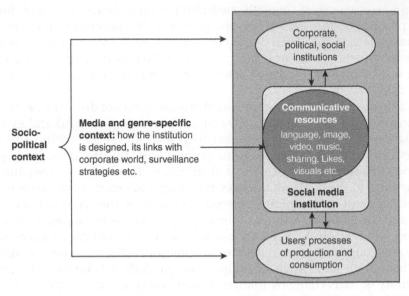

Figure 9.1   The dynamic of texts, society and social media institutions (adapted from KhosraviNik, **2015**, forthcoming)

In addition to positioning social media within broader sociopolitical and media contexts, as described above, we follow Herring in suggesting that paying attention to specific aspects of the medium and situation allows us to classify social media data more effectively, and thus conduct a more nuanced analysis. Table 9.1 shows some of the factors that can be considered in linguistic and semiotic analyses of social media data in general, and some of these are then taken up in the first case study to illustrate how they can be integrated into a CDS approach. Similarly, the genre categorization below combines textual features according to medium affordances on the one hand, and on the other specifies some of the social context of the participants.

Although many of the same methods of analysis that are typically applied to powerful texts can be applied to social media data, there are some confounding logistical issues regarding harnessing and defining analytical materials in social media, for instance:

1. How to collect and select data from the vast amounts available on some social media platforms.
2. How to deal with the inherent non-linearity of text-production and consumption processes.

Table 9.1 Medium and situation factors

Medium factors	Synchronicity	Asychronous–synchronous
	Message transmission	One-to-one; one-to-many; many-to-many
	Persistence of the transcript	Ephemeral – archived
	Size of message	Amount of text conveyed
	Channels of communication	Words, image, sound, video
	Privacy settings	Public, semi-public, semi-private, private contexts
	Anonymous	Extent to which the participants' identities are represented within a site
	Message format	Architectures for displaying interactions
Situation factors	Participation structure	Number of participants involved
	Participant characteristics	Stated or assumed demographic and ideological characteristics
	Purpose	Goals of interaction (either at Individual or group level)
	Topic	Subject matter
	Tone	Formal or informal
	Norms	Accepted practices established by the group
	Code	Language variety and choice of script

Source: Herring, 2007; quoted in Page et al., 2014

3. How to define context *vis-à-vis* social media.
4. How to deal with the fleeting nature of data and the constant changes in format and functions of platforms.
5. How to incorporate systematic observations to account for media and genre-specific contexts of communication.
6. How to decide on an ethical framework that respects individuals' rights and their understanding of how public their data should be.

The non-linear context of communication on the participatory web indicates the usefulness of more observational research approaches, i.e. attending to communicative events rather than communicative data themselves. Participant-observer methods (at least in the initial stages of a study) seem indispensable in seeking to account for the dynamics of users' communication, platform affordances, interconnectivity, genre features and media context. Hence, a case study approach to data and analysis seems to suit a CDS approach. We suggest three broad orientations:

1. As discourse analysts we consider the social context of the users and their communication.
2. As critical discourse analysts we are not satisfied with the mere description of genre, content and communication.

3. As social media scholars we view the participatory web as part of a media apparatus that is used by individuals in society, hence we do not treat digitally mediated texts as part of a 'virtual' world that is separate from the physical world and 'reality', despite acknowledging that digitally mediated contexts have specific features that may affect our analyses.

These and other issues around data are not only related to, but also directly determined by, choices of methodological framework. For instance, a more ethnographic approach will allow a narrower focus on smaller amounts of data, and this should mean it is possible to get informed consent from the participants, but perhaps at the expense of a broader view of different and varied practices on a given social media platform. By contrast, using corpus-assisted discourse studies (see Mautner in this volume) to examine social media data may allow the researcher to test assumptions about the broader sociopolitical context of data, but may make it harder to capture the nuances of individual interactions.

Starting from the traditions of sociolinguistics and discourse analysis, respectively, Jannis Androutsopoulos and Susan Herring have proposed influential approaches for the socially and contextually sensitive discourse analysis of computer-mediated communication. Both Androutsopoulos's (2008) discourse-centred online ethnography (DCOE) and Herring's (2004) Computer-Mediated Discourse Analysis (CMDA) call for a move from medium-oriented studies of CMC, i.e. how the new genres and platforms impact on the form and content of the language used, to user and context-sensitive approaches. Thurlow and Mroczek (2011) and Androutsopoulos and Beißwenger (2008) differentiate between the mainstream CMC analytical approaches and what they call computer-mediated discourse analysis as a problem-oriented, situationally focused approach to dealing with communication in new media. This shift in focus of CMC studies brings them closer to the CDS principles of being problem-oriented and socially relevant, though they do not necessarily espouse a very critical orientation.

Herring (2013) proposes that CMDA can be used as a theoretical lens, alongside critical discourse studies, to examine issues and specific linguistic (or semiotic) phenomena, such as 'linguistic expressions of status, conflict, negotiation, face-management, play; discourse styles/lects, etc.' (see Page et al. 2014: 40 for an overview). While Herring focuses on the examination of phenomena, Androutsopoulos (2008) provides practice-derived guidelines for observation and contact which suggest that social media researchers should not only be interested in the discursive and technological aspects of social media, but also in relationships and processes (i.e. in what users do and how they do it in relation to each other). This emphasis on repetition and confronting participants with material and observations, as well as on multiple methods and technologies, sits well with the CDS principles of retroductive/abductive reasoning, following in the tradition of C. S. Peirce, and triangulation following Cicourel (see Wodak and Meyer in this volume).

When it comes to which linguistic and semiotic phenomena to investigate, a CDS researcher who is interested in social media might consider whether many of the classic analytical categories still pertain, such as modality, presupposition, syntax, nominalization or metaphors (for instance, as used in the methods presented in some of the other chapters in this volume). It is important to note that the choice of phenomena is highly context- and genre-dependent. The web contains many genres that are directly comparable with their print or broadcast-based predecessors, such as news websites vs newspapers, or YouTube clips of political speeches vs televised broadcasts of speeches. Restricting ourselves only to digitally mediated texts, there are genres that existed in the pre-participatory web, such as email or text-based chat, those that have adapted to the participatory web, such as review websites, which now tend to include primarily user-generated rather than expert-generated content, and those that are or seem to be completely new, such as microblogs (e.g. Twitter). Herring (2013) categorises these as familiar, reconfigured and emergent, respectively. It is important to keep these genre differences in mind when establishing analytical categories, as phenomena that are highly salient in one genre (for instance, jokes and irony used in a formal speech by a politician) may be less so in social media contexts, or vice versa.

One frequent finding in relation to the distribution of and responses to texts in social media contexts is that things happen in much faster timescales than in traditional media ecologies (Tufekci and Wilson 2012). Different platforms may encourage either more synchronous interaction, where the interactions are ongoing with little pause (e.g. instant messaging), and asynchronous interaction, where there may be long interruptions before the conversation is resumed (e.g. emails). Note, however, that Darics (2014) among others points out that the boundaries between these categories are not fixed – email exchanges may be nearly instantaneous, while instant-messaging exchanges could be carried out over an extended period.

Having pointed out some of the potential issues involved in the critical analysis of social media data and some of the relevant linguistic and discursive features for analysis, we now move to two case studies. In the first one, we take a 'micro' view by briefly describing how to set up a social media 'focus group' and conduct analysis of some of the discussions that ensue. In the second, we focus more on the 'macro level' of media ecologies and processes by looking at recent global protests and images connected to them that are available on the web.

Case study 1: Conducting a Facebook 'focus group' on political resistance

Overview of case study

Overall research questions: What are Facebook users' attitudes to digitally mediated forms of political resistance and how do they discursively construct these? To what extent is Facebook a useful platform for focus-group-like data collection?

(Continued)

(Continued)

Source of data: A Facebook group set up specifically to collect data for this project.

Methods of data collection and analysis: A set of questions posted on the group generated a small number of responses from invited users based on the researcher's own peer networks. All responses were analysed with a particular emphasis on topic identification, identity construction and discursive strategies (see Reisigl and Wodak in this volume).

In this case study, we will focus more methodologically and consider some of the challenges and benefits involved in conducting something resembling a focus group using Facebook. The focus group in question was set up by one of the authors of this chapter as part of the Political Resistance Online Research Project (PRORP) and can be accessed at http://tinyurl.com/PRORP-FB, via Facebook. There is an extensive tradition of using face-to-face focus groups within the discourse-historical approach (e.g. Kovács and Wodak 2003; Unger 2013; Wodak et al. 1998; Wodak et al. 2009; see also Krzyzanowski 2008 for a guide to using focus groups in the qualitative social sciences), but this has not necessarily applied to critical discourse studies as a whole. As suggested above, critical discourse analysts have typically dealt with 'powerful' texts, but these do not necessarily allow a triangulated approach to a research problem (see Unger 2013). The aim of setting up this Facebook focus group, then, was partly to gain an overview of different political resistance practices for further investigation, and partly to gain insights into how political resistance was discussed by a group of Facebook users, starting with friends and colleagues of the researchers. It was also, however, partly an examination of the potential of a Facebook group as a site for data collection and a social media-based focus group of this kind as a research instrument. Among other benefits, this allows participants to take part across boundaries of time and space in ways that are not possible in traditional face-to-face focus groups. There are, of course, many other texts in the vast media ecology that could be used to investigate questions around political resistance. Some of these had already been considered by the researchers for inclusion in PRORP, including a corpus of emails from activist organizations, the tweets connected to particular events such as the London riots of 2011 and the Occupy Movement, and alternative and critical news curation in relation to the Ukraine/Russia crises on Reddit. Yet, one of the key constraints when using social media data is practicality. At the time of writing, Facebook explicitly allows research, unlike some other platforms, as long as the participants are given the opportunity to read a privacy statement. This means, however, that using data already generated (such as the content of a Facebook page about a specific movement or protest) could contravene Facebook's policies, quite apart from the difficulties of getting informed consent from the participants. Even once these difficulties have been negotiated, the next problem is how to generate sufficient responses to a particular form of data elicitation.

Without the resources to provide rewards for participation (which has its own set of ethical and methodological challenges), researchers are dependent on the goodwill of participants. So while on the one hand there is a vast and overwhelming amount of data available, the amount of data that can ethically and legally be used and is actually available for detailed qualitative research that involves verbatim reproductions of user content may be much smaller. Presenting a detailed and exhaustive analysis of the data is beyond the scope of this case study, but we will point out some of the salient linguistic and discursive features that could form part of a more 'micro' analysis of social media texts, alongside the methodological challenges this kind of data presents.

As suggested above, one of the first considerations in this kind of research is what ethical principles apply. This is both a practical problem, ensuring that all the standards required by the researcher's institution are met, but also something that should be linked to the problem-oriented and emancipatory stance adopted by most critical-discourse scholars: by exposing our participants to ethical risks, such as having their identity revealed due to the rather public data of many social media, we may be harming the very people we wish to help. There is of course also the question of whether we should use Facebook at all in critically oriented research, given the commercial and potentially exploitative nature of most of the 'free' social networking sites (where the users become the product for marketers and companies to exploit; see discussion above). However, by restricting the participants to people who are already on Facebook, rather than having joined specifically for the purposes of data collection, this risk is somewhat mitigated. As already mentioned, Facebook has its own rules for research. At the time of writing, these require researchers to identify any research taking place via the platform and to have a privacy policy. This was displayed prominently on the group page and all new users were asked to read it before taking part. A further decision related to anonymity: it is virtually impossible to fully anonymize publicly available texts. Therefore, participants are warned that they will remain identifiable (at least to group members) as long as their posts remain on the group page; but as a compromise, only their first names are used in any other reproductions of their data. Indeed, there may not be much point in omitting the name of an institution named by one of the participants as long as the data are still easily available and searchable on the web. However, a participant could choose at any point to delete their data, whereas once they are committed to a publication, that can no longer be done. And should participants choose to delete their data, they would not necessarily be immediately identifiable so the ethical risk is somewhat mitigated.

The next consideration was what questions to pose to elicit the desired responses. Unlike face-to-face and physically co-present focus groups, where questions are usually spoken and require participants to formulate a response with minimal preparation, in a digitally mediated group of this kind there is time for participants to think about their responses before posting them. For this reason, questions could include relatively complex components or followups, which in a face-to-face focus-group situation might only be gradually introduced by the moderator, or allowed to come out through discussion and the negotiation of meanings between participants.

The questions chosen for the Facebook focus group were as follows:

Tell us a little about yourself (e.g. why you joined the group, what you typically use the internet for etc.)

What, to you, is 'political resistance'?

What kinds of activities do you take part in online that might be called 'political resistance'?

How effective do you find online political resistance compared to offline? Can you give some examples?

Have social media like Facebook or Twitter changed political resistance? In what way? Can you give some examples?

What about political resistance on the internet before social media became widespread (e.g. via websites, bulletin boards, e-mail etc.)?

How do you think (online) political resistance will develop in the future?

These were posted both in a single block, allowing participants to answer all of them in one post, and in separate posts, which they could answer individually, and also engage with each other's answers (which some participants did).

The third stage was recruiting participants. This involved starting with the researcher's own friends, colleagues, students and contacts who were also asked to tell their Facebook friends about it. This snowballing method of participant recruitment is common in qualitative and ethnographic social-science research. While not in any way aiming for a representative sample of users, it does eventually broaden out the participant group from the researcher's own contacts. There is a risk that the 'filter bubble' effect (Pariser 2011) could mean that all participants share the researcher's general worldview. However, by the time the recruitment 'snowball' has reached a second or third wave of friends of friends (of friends), this effect should be somewhat diluted. Previous focus-group-based studies have usually sought to confront 'ordinary' participants with specific and often complex concepts that are important in the research, such as national identity, neutrality, discrimination, linguistic identity. However, the opposite is also often an aim, so that concepts are confronted with the negotiation of meaning by participants, so as to establish how robust they are as concepts that can be empirically investigated. In this Facebook focus group, the initial set of questions was designed to establish the range and nature of political resistance practices, as well as to begin to think about how these practices were constructed in talk – or perhaps in type – given the written medium. In the end, each question was answered by between two and five people in the initial data-collection phase from mid-2011 to early 2012, which was rather disappointing in some ways. However, the responses from the participants (some quite extensive, ranging from 1 to 200 words) raised a number of interesting issues. We will briefly reflect on these below. The analysis involved topic identification, followed by a close textual analysis of the linguistic features used to construct the participants' identities and the concept of political resistance.

A typical phase in face-to-face focus groups is the identification of primary and secondary discourse topics (Krzyzanowski 2008; Unger 2013). This is also possible for a Facebook focus group. For example, in response to question 2, all the participants except one explicitly mentioned digitally mediated resistance practices in some form in their response to the question, although they were not specifically asked about these, for example:

Jonathon: *For me, political resistance is the act of going against the momentum of (usually governmental) decisions which you strongly disapprove of. Unfortunately, human inertia tends to limit resistance to more polar issues. I think political resistance is active, and is carried through web-based channels such as breaking national censorship laws (twitter to uncover super injunctions in the UK and social media in Iran (today's Guardian news site) as two examples).*

This is not surprising, however, as the first (introductory question) asked what participants typically use the internet for, and they could also, if they wished, look at all the questions before answering any of them. Furthermore, the context in which the focus group took place, Facebook, is likely to have made digitally mediated resistance practices relevant. Most of the contributions made use of explicit hedges, mitigation strategies or stance markers ('For me', 'In my opinion', 'I think'). This may reflect the participants' shifts in footing (drawing on the concept from Goffman 1979) to construct identities as 'non-experts', which later shift again when they more confidently introduce narratives from their own experience or talk about specific digitally mediated resistance practices they are familiar with. This is illustrated in the responses to question 4, given below, 'How effective do you find online political resistance compared to offline? Can you give some examples?' It should be noted that while these responses clearly differ from spoken focus-group responses (see Page et al. 2014: ch. 2 for an overview of different linguistic studies of social media), they are similar in terms of topic development and the negotiation of identities. They are also similar to other forms of digitally mediated discussion (e.g. forum posts, comments on online news articles). Since one aim of the study was to identify different forms of digitally mediated political resistance and attitudes towards these, the content of the contributions was important, but as is common with discourse analyses of focus-group data, paying attention to the form allowed a deeper understanding of attitudes and the relation of participants to the wider context.

Lisa-Maria: *As shortly mentioned above, I am of the opinion that online political resistance can only be a (crucial) part of offline protests. I think it is inevitable in order to get people together and to get one's opinion and ideas 'out there', but I do not think that it can entirely replace offline events. If looking at the occupation of the University of [omitted] in 2009, for example, I am practically convinced that a merely online movement would have not brought the same results and definitely not the same attention from other media, such as TV and newspapers. By occupying a building, students did not only force specific politicians to*

> deal with the problem of tuition fees and insupportable conditions at the university but also other parties. Unfortunately, a piece of paper can easily be shoved into a drawer or thrown away, even if it documents the support of many people for a matter of concern. This is also true for online political resistance; I think if they are not combined with offline events, they can only too easily be overlooked.

Jonathon: *Online resistance can be very powerful. The modality of online media makes a big difference: watching online videos tagged, liked and reposted thousands of times is easier to access as media and easier to 'read'. Online media can be distributed, re-modeled (in the spirit of web 2.0/3.0) and accessed by a broad demographic with little need for organization or division of labour. One recent example which does not target the 'axis of evil' countries (which obviously has another deeper agenda when promoted by different nations) is the New York bicycle incident. A cyclist got a ticket for riding on the road to avoid roadworks. He then posted a video 'obeying the law' by crashing into various things while staying in the cycle lane.*

Annamária: *Again, I agree: online resistance is *one* tool for political movements but not the *only* one. I would like to add the example of the Arab spring again, where people got organised with the help of online tools. Idem for what was happening in the UK this summer. So, yes, online political resistance is possible, it can be effective, but I do not think, or at least I haven't heard of a movement that was 100% online.*

Sylva: *I think that people are already used to communicate virtually, so online resistance is more effective. I signed an environmental petition addressed to the local government for cleaner neighbourhood (in [omitted], London, where I lived) – this was done on paper in a local park. I did not believe this petition could have any effect – very few people knew that it was happening, those who signed it were just random passers-by and the names, contact details and signatures written by hand must have been illegible.*

The question presupposes that online and offline political resistance are different and can exist independently of each other; in other words, it espouses a digital dualistic worldview (these questions were drafted before Jurgenson's work in this area challenged this concept, see above). The participants, however, challenged this in various ways, mainly by arguing for the importance of 'offline' action to accompany 'online' resistance, whereas Sylva uses her example to suggest that 'offline only' actions are not effective. The participants adopt the categories (online vs offline) proposed in the question, and use them to frame their answers, but introduce (as requested) their own examples as well. While they make some use of the affordances of this written medium for pragmatic effect (asterisks for emphasis, scare quotes to distance themselves), the responses seem to be carefully formulated. They are almost entirely free of non-standard language use or typos, and some use technical or academic registers ('modality', 'communicate virtually'). This may not be surprising given the background of the participants – all were university students or staff at the time of data collection.

The interactive features in the responses, such as 'I agree with X ...' are also noteworthy. While some of the responses contain explicit cohesive links to previous responses (either by the participant herself in Lisa-Maria's case, or to the responses of others, in Annámaria's case in the examples above), each response was posted at least three weeks apart, with over three months between the last two responses. The possibility of dialogue and interaction is thus not necessarily time-bound; as a number of researchers have pointed out (see, e.g., Darics 2014), synchronicity and asynchronicity are not straightforward in social media data. This opens up considerable potential for critical analysis employing digitally mediated focus groups, as one of the main challenges of organizing focus groups is the practicalities of getting a group of people into the same physical location at the same time. One thing that may affect interaction, however, is the fluidity of identity performance on social networking sites such as Facebook. This is illustrated by a response from one participant to an earlier post by another. The response uses the first poster's name, which has, however, since been changed. Thus, anyone looking at the site at the time of writing may not realize who is being responded to, thus breaking a cohesive link. Furthermore, this also presents a further ethical challenge: if a participant has changed their name on Facebook, it may be that uses of their previous name 'out' them in some way, potentially putting them at risk.

The participants who responded during this initial data-collection period gave very thoughtful and relevant responses, even for example reflecting (without being prompted) on the process of taking part in a Facebook focus group in response to question 7:

Annámaria: ... *five or ten years ago, who would have thought that a researcher will use facebook to start a qualitative survey on political resistance online?*

This is not to say that all participants would necessarily provide data that are as rich. With different (perhaps more contentious) questions, heated debates could develop and potentially escalate into 'flaming'. Alternatively, without any motivation or incentives for participants, it is feasible that no-one would respond at all. The responses do show, however, that there is considerable potential in this data-collection method. Some of the features that make focus groups valuable to critical discourse researchers, particularly positioning relative to a topic, the introduction of secondary discourse topics, and the negotiation of meanings via interaction between participants (albeit limited in this focus group), are all present. These ways of writing about digitally mediated political resistance practices, together with scholarly literature and theories, provided an abductive basis for further research into digitally mediated protests in the second case study, where we focus more on the 'macro' issues of media production and consumption, via social media, around political protests.

Case study 2: The role of technologies and multilingualism in digitally mediated protest

Overview of case study

Overall research question: In what ways do digitally mediated technologies cause or facilitate, complicate or frustrate communication by, to and between protestors?

Source of data: Images taken by protestors and journalists of signs and placards at physical locations associated with particular protest movements.

Methods of data collection and analysis: Images retrieved from Google image search using specific search terms. Systematic content analysis of images and particularly of text within images. Abductive relation of data to theories related to protests, social movements, globalization.

As a first phase, we begin by considering what it is we are actually interested in studying. Since the protests and uprisings in the Middle East and North Africa region, the so-called 'Arab Spring', the various manifestations of the 'Occupy' movement and the protests again austerity measures in London and various other affluent cities, scholars in politics, media studies and various other socially engaged disciplines have been trying to unpick the role that social media have played in these contexts. We have been particularly interested in those global movements and revolutions that have not only brought about change to some political systems, but which also seem to have fundamentally changed the way we can debate and analyse changes to political systems. In this second analysis, we examine these changes in relation to political resistance practices, particularly those involving digital media. We thus consider mediated technologies of protest, and the ways in which these cause or facilitate, complicate or frustrate communication by, to and between protestors.

Much of the media coverage of the Arab Spring and other protest movements such as Occupy has involved photographs and videos of events happening in public spaces in large cities, many of them provided by protestors using their own cameras or smartphones. But even for people not holding a device in their hands while on Tahrir Square or on the steps of the London Stock Exchange, their physical realities will have been mediated in some way by social media. Tufekci and Wilson (2012: 3) state that 'Social media alter the key tenets of collective action [...] and, in doing so, create new vulnerabilities for even the most durable of authoritarian regimes.' Their overall finding is that social media accelerated, but were of course not wholly responsible for, those vulnerabilities (as some mainstream Western media would have had us believe at the time). The image in Figure 9.2 is of signs laid out in Tahrir Square protesting against the Egyptian President, Hosni Mubarak, who was ousted in 2011 after massive protests across Egypt, and particularly in Tahrir Square, in one of the key events of the Arab Spring.

Figure 9.2 Anti-Mubarak signs in Tahrir Square (Source: Al Jazeera English under a CC:BY:SA licence)

These signs will have been seen by thousands of people in their physical location (perhaps as laid out there, or separately before and after the photo was taken). But they may also have been seen by thousands if not hundreds of thousands more people as images circulated on the web, via social media and on websites associated with more traditional news media. While the analysis of the image itself (the various texts, languages and linguistic varieties used, the arrangement of semiotic elements, for instance drawing on Kress and van Leeuwen (2006) and their grammar of visual semiosis) is an important stage, in this case study we are focusing on the bigger picture: the relation of images such as these to broader media ecologies and global sociopolitical changes. There is also some medium-related contextual information that can be retrieved with a little detective work. The image appears on the first results page of a Google image search for 'Tahrir Square signs' (see Figure 9.3), suggesting Google's algorithms rate it highly. This may be because it is widely linked to, because it is frequently clicked on, or for various other reasons that Google algorithms have decided indicate an image is worthy of attention. The metadata available with the image also give some clues. At the time of writing, it has been viewed approximately 2,500 times on its source page, Al Jazeera's English Flickr page, which is not a huge number, but in addition to being on Flickr, it is also visible on the Wikimedia Foundation page from which it was retrieved for this chapter. While there are currently no Wikipedia pages linking to it, a Google image-match search shows that this version of the photo has been used on a number of online news sites. The Flickr page also gives a considerable amount of information about the image, for instance that it was taken on a particular type of camera (an entry-level single-lens reflex camera) that might be used by a keen hobby photographer or perhaps a freelance journalist, rather than a mobile device or a professional-level camera.

However, the fact that the image is found on Al Jazeera's official Flickr page suggests that it was taken either by a journalist associated with the media corporation, or that they bought the image from someone who was not previously affiliated. All this is valuable information for an analysis of the media/institutional context, and it gives us some clues as to the production and consumption of this digitally mediated image, though it does not of course give all the information that we might wish for as CDS analysts, or that might be revealed through further ethnographic work or contact with the image producer(s) (as advocated by Androutsopoulos, see above).

There is of course value in doing ethnographic work in the physical spaces where events related to a protest are taking place. Indeed, to learn more about linguistic and political behaviours, and depending on the scholarly traditions we draw on, this kind of work may be essential. Through 'on-the-ground' ethnographic work we can get access to local (or glocal?) representations (or sometimes misrepresentations?) of global movements, but to grasp fully how global media (mis)represent local voices, we of course need to include texts drawn from these media in our analysis. A good example of this kind of work is Gaby and Caren's (2012) analysis of recruitment to Occupy's Facebook pages. Interestingly, they found that although images and videos were highly effective in recruiting new members to Facebook groups, these did not necessarily depict events in the physical place where the protest was taking place. Many of them were memes of a humorous or historically or culturally salient nature.

Moreover, many of these movements are not about global problems but about local (or at least national) ones, or local manifestations of global problems. Many of the most powerful actions and images from various protests since 2011 have been oriented towards achieving local objectives – though they have then been photographed, videoed, described in blogs, put on Twitter and then reproduced and recontextualized globally. What many activists have been successful in doing is using intertextual references to highlight the links and similarities between different movements – where these exist – and in using previous successes (e.g. Tunisia) to present visual and verbal arguments pertaining to their present plight. Thus, we would argue that many of these movements are at best quasi-global because they do not necessarily address truly global issues, such as world trade or climate change, so we might ask why these local protests with their quasi-global orientations happen in particular places and at particular times. We draw on the notion of political opportunity structures that Kitschelt (1986: 58) finds are 'comprised of specific configurations of resources, institutional arrangements and historical precedents for social mobilization, which facilitate the development of protest movements in some instances and constrain them in others'. This notion seems highly compatible with the context-sensitive analysis of institutions as well as accounting for sociopolitical contexts of communication supported by most critical discourse scholars (see Figure 9.1). In the present case study, the conditions that led to the Arab Spring long preceded the advent of social media: repressive political or military regimes, restrictions on free communication, poverty and violence, heavy-handed policing and many other factors contributed. However, as Tufekci and Wilson (2012) argue, the advent of social media helped to facilitate and accelerate different kinds of communication and we argue that SNS should thus be regarded as one element of the political opportunity structures.

As aforementioned, in this example, we are particularly interested in specific 'technologies of protest'. These are not just technologies in the sense of gadgets running on electricity. Rather, any deliberate act of semiosis makes use of a technology, even if it is the human voice. The argument is that protestors in any context will make use of the technologies that are available to them, and they will utilize these to the maximum extent possible within their affordances. One technology we were particularly struck by was the use of banners, posters or placards – often handwritten or hand-painted – and the subsequent appearance of these signs in images shared via social media. The use of signs of this kind is of course not new, and their appearance in mainstream press photographs has a similarly long pedigree. What is relatively new, however, is the speed at which images of these signs can be spread to viewers not physically co-present and shared and recontextualized on various social media platforms. This thus provides us with a compelling reason for studying digitally mediated texts in this context: the strategic (and perhaps sometimes accidental) distribution of specific images from a physical protest location via social and traditional media has become a vital link within and between social movements. However, at the same time that protesters are trying to get their message out, garner more support, seek help from abroad etc., they are working unpaid for social media corporations and generating advertising revenue.

The strong intertextual and interdiscursive links between signs in various contexts also warranted further examination. For instance, one image of a handheld sign in Tahrir Square, photographed in February 2011, bears the slogan 'Egypt Supports Wisconsin Workers; One World, One Pain', thus expressing support for workers in the US State of Wisconsin, who were at the time protesting against proposed laws attacking their employment rights and pensions (see http://crooksandliars.com/scarce/sign-tahrir-square). The full extent of this intertextuality becomes apparent when digitally mediated texts are brought into the physical environment of a protest, e.g. a poster showing a Facebook 'Like' icon or Twitter hashtag, which is then remediated by being photographed and posted and shared via social media. Furthermore, various ways of challenging dominant ideologies, for example drawing on anti-capitalism or calls for political freedom, as well as connections between events, such as references to the Tunisian revolution in the Egyptian uprising, are intertextual bridges between different, but related, more-or-less mediated contexts.

We might ask whether it is the emergence of digital and social media that has made these sorts of strong intertextual links between different protest movements possible in the first place. This is not to suggest that the technologies literally cause the protests, but it is evident that they form part of the political opportunity structures. However, new structures around protests, such as flat hierarchies, shared decision-making and the absence of leaders that have characterized movements such as Occupy, may have been made possible by changes in communication structures; in other words, they may have fundamentally changed the relationships between affected individuals and groups, as predicted by Graham (2006, see above). This is supported by González-Bailón et al.'s (2011: 5–6) analysis of the use of Twitter in the Spanish May protests. They found that communication via Twitter involves a:

trade-off between global bridges (controlled by well connected users) and local networks: the former are efficient at transmitting information, the latter at transmitting behavior. This is one reason why Twitter has played a prominent role in so many recent protests and mobilizations: it combines the global reach of broadcasters with local, personalized relations.

Our key finding, however, is that the relationships between protest movements across the globe are not unlike those between linguistic communities, whereby global languages (particularly English) often dominate. Furthermore, the hegemonic power structures found in the global economic system are partially reproduced in the way technologies and texts flow between protests, much as in the case of academic publishing, where 'Western' publications in the English language are seen as more prestigious and desirable in many disciplines (see, for instance, Meriläinen et al. 2008). We make these claims for two reasons: First, while some research points to the many multilingual and intertextual signs found in Tahrir Square (e.g. Aboelezz 2014), we have found very little evidence that the protests around Occupy Wall Street or in London were similarly multilingual. They were strongly intertextual – but what was notably absent from these contexts was much engagement with other global-resistance movements. This is easily supported by systematic content and structural analysis of the most popular image search results for 'Tahrir square signs' vs 'Occupy Wall Street signs', just a few of which are depicted in Figures 9.3 and 9.4, and image blogs such as 'wearethe99percent' on tumblr. Again, the details of the analysis go beyond the scope of this case study, but these involved categorizing each image according to which language(s) and language variety(ies) were used in the signs, and specific categories that arose from the data themselves related to the messages on the signs (e.g. regime-critical, ironic, intertextual references).

Figure 9.3 Google Image search results for 'Tahrir square signs' on 8 October 2014, limited in this chapter to images labelled for reuse with modification

Figure 9.4 Google Image search results for 'Occupy Wall Street signs' on 8 October 2014, limited in this chapter to images labelled for reuse with modification

The disparity in languages used and between references to and from each protest location may of course be just because the pictures and descriptions of the protests that we saw during our period of data collection were already mediated by news organizations, bloggers and tweeters, which/who will naturally focus on data that are globally accessible, i.e. in English, if we are talking about 'Western' reporting. But as suggested earlier on, it is mainly these globally accessible images and reports that have the potential to forge links between protest movements. Iconic images emerge, and by being shared and linked to repeatedly, they become more prominent in search results, which then makes them more likely to be reused. It is the most popular images – the ones linked to, reproduced, recontextualized – that constitute the global discourse on the protest movements. Thus, we argue that these are an appropriate site for research in themselves and carry the same, if not higher, levels of 'authenticity' as data sources when considering global flows of media production, consumption and 'prosumption'. There are of course references to the Arab Spring by the protestors in Occupy protests and even in interviews conducted with UK rioters. In fact, Tahrir was central to the formation of Occupy, if we take the *Adbusters'* call to occupy Wall Street as the starting point: 'Are you ready for a Tahrir moment? On 17 September, flood into lower Manhattan, set up tents, kitchens, peaceful barricades and occupy Wall Street'. We found, however, that in the signs and texts produced by the occupiers, these references were mainly instrumentalized in two ways: first, in arguments about the right to protest, and in attempts to highlight the hypocrisy of governments that support protests abroad while suppressing them at home; and second, as a symbolic claim of the global nature of the movement. However, they did not necessarily indicate any direct engagement with or links between these protestors and those in other global resistance movements.

The second reason for our claims about global hegemonic flows is that it is significant that much of the infrastructure for the social media platforms and digital devices used to augment the physical protests is based in the United States or other 'Western' countries, and most of this infrastructure is run by companies that are owned by shareholders who are expecting a return on their investment. This becomes relevant when we consider, as suggested above, that social media can be used as effectively by governments to survey protestors as they can by protestors to organize (a point ably illustrated by Morozov 2011). Furthermore, this was an important part of the narratives of the protests presented in the 'Western' media, particularly with the labels 'Twitter revolution' or 'Facebook revolution'. While the mainstream English-language media have often presented a compelling narrative of 'liberation, democratization and social change caused by "Western" technology', the reality is of course often much more complex.

With regard to linguistic practices, we see particularly notable changes in the channels and modes of communication, rather than in the linguistic forms being used. These are not, however, restricted to social struggles but are common to many forms of digital communication in the public sphere. Social and digital media have undoubtedly played a role in organizing these protests, in making the views of protestors public and in holding public figures to account (as suggested by Tufekci and Wilson 2012). Their particular value to protesters has been in drawing global attention to local issues and in circumventing traditional media outlets that are restricted by state control or commercial interests. Nevertheless, they are themselves also susceptible to state or commercial control, and thus we should not be too utopian about their role. With regard to multilingualism, the picture is complex: much as in international business and politics, English occupies a hegemonic position in the global communication of issues being protested about. Multilingualism appears at times to be symbolic – and to be heavily instrumentalized, or even commodified, as part of local protest goals.

Summary

We hope we have demonstrated above that the broad research programme of CDS *can* (and should) incorporate social media with theoretical and methodological rigour. The core theoretical principles of CDS, such as problem orientation and a focus on linguistic/discursive features, abduction etc., are still relevant to new spaces for discursive practices. There is a substantial amount of discursive practice and communicative concentration on social media that turns the participatory web into new spaces of power and influence for society. Consequently, a dynamic critique of power still applies to communication in these digitally mediated spaces. There is also a need for the contextualization of language-in-use on these sites by drawing on the sociopolitical context of the audience and networks of discourse in place, both in the immediate online context and in the sociopolitical context of society. CDS scholars are interested in real language-in-use in society; and as such, even though the mainstream mass media may still be a powerful domain for sociopolitical discourses, a large proportion of day-to-day verbal and visual communication has migrated to various participatory web platforms, and there is increasing evidence that this paradigm shift is ongoing.

As a socially committed approach, CDA needs to engage and account for this form of communication, as its effects on society and dominant discourses are indispensable. Furthermore, the central questions of CDS such as 'who is communicating with whom, under what conditions, how and to what end' should be the focus of a CDS approach to social media, which should allow researchers to account for both the 'macro' issues of institutional context and media ecologies, and the 'micro' dynamics of communicative affordances. Approaches developed specifically for computer-mediated discourse, such computer-mediated discourse analysis or discourse-centred online ethnography, can contribute a lot at the micro-level. Furthermore, the shift towards multi-modal analysis more generally allows the different affordances of social media to be more thoroughly and systematically explored by analysts. Theoretical frame-works from media and communication, cultural studies, politics and sociology, while themselves undergoing a transformation in response to changing media ecologies, are also vital for a thorough understanding of social media and, more broadly, digitally mediated communication. In effect, the CDS approach to social media we outline in this chapter (re-)emphasizes the core of interdisciplinarity in CDS with an added focus on the distribution processes of texts and discursive practices. In other words, previous calls for interdisciplinarity in CDS sought to enrich the explanatory level of discourse analysis, i.e. providing a sociological, political, psychological, historical etc. explanation of why given discourses are the way they are and how the findings can be explained in a wider macro-struc-tural sense. When considering social media contexts, however, we foreground an interdisciplinary focus that incorporates insights from a media-technology approach, including insights from information science, computing and other kinds of internet research in the broadest sense. The methodological anchor for CDS, however, continues to be a focus on discourse, not the technology *per se*.

Existing CDS approaches claim to welcome and incorporate observational research but, with some exceptions, particularly in the discourse-historical approach, they have generally focused on the analysis of elite texts. Texts are analysed after they are produced and then related back to their contexts, whereas the fluid and dynamic nature of social media texts makes this more difficult. Thus, observational approaches such as those advocated by Androutsopoulos and ethnomethodologically inspired categories such as those suggested by Herring (see above) must become more central to CDS if we are to take account of the participatory web. Digital media data do not lend them-selves to being frozen in time and are often recontextualized (by linking, sharing etc.) very rapidly in evolving situations. Thus engagement with the practices of production, distribution and consumption of texts and communi-cation in more central ways than in the past is inevitable. This focus on practices is also inspired by work from literacy studies, which has been at the periphery of CDS for some considerable time but should now become more central, alongside other more ethnographic and anthropological approaches from media research (surveys, interviews, observation). The multimodal nature of many social media texts gives rise to a need for new frameworks of multimodal analysis, which again have been part of CDS for a considerable time but which are often left aside because they are difficult to integrate into text-based studies. Finally, the eclecticism of traditional CDS approaches is an important part of the new framework needed to deal with social media data, but these must go beyond just accessing new sources and genres of data (which is of course useful and important) and should be used to keep developing an interdisciplinary abductive approach that draws on relevant media and technology (and other) theories. Thus, we hope that the various approaches outlined in other chapters in this volume may be adapted, using some of the additional concepts and methods we describe above, to ensure that CDS remains a relevant approach in today's highly digitally mediated world.

Further reading

Fuchs, Christian (2014) *Social Media: A Critical Introduction*. London: Sage.
In this introductory textbook on social media, Fuchs considers different aspects of digital and participatory culture through the lens of Critical Theory. He makes very clear that social media use is always political, even when not related to 'politics' in the narrow sense. This will be a useful book for researchers who are broadly familiar with linguistic analysis of social media texts, but have not thus far considered wider sociopolitical contexts in their analyses.

KhosraviNik, M. (2016 forthcoming) Social Media Critical Discourse Studies (SM-CDS). In: J. Flowerdew and J. E. Richardson (eds), *Handbook of Critical Discourse Analysis*. London: Routledge.
This chapter provides an overview of potentials and challenges of CDA in the context of social media. It attends to theoretical and methodological developments which could be incorporated into an emerging Social Media Critical Discourse Studies (SM-CDS) and argues for a number of considerations towards developing a viable, relevant and necessary application of CDS to participatory web.

KhosraviNik, M. and Zia, M. (2014) Persian nationalism, identity and anti-Arab sentiments in Iranian Facebook discourses: Critical Discourse Analysis and social media communication. *Journal of Language and Politics*, 13(4): 755–80.
This research paper examines the functions of social media communication in a Middle Eastern public sphere. It speaks to the surge of socially generated texts/linguistic data, made available via social communication – specifically in this case, Facebook. It critically analyses a nationalist discourse among ordinary Iranians who may have limited access to official communication platforms, i.e. mass media.

Page, R., Barton, D., Unger, J. W. and Zappavigna, M. (2014) *Researching Language in Social Media*. London: Routledge.
In this textbook, Page et al. outline some of the key issues in researching language in social media contexts. There are chapters on ethics, research design, qualitative and ethnographic research, alongside more quantitative approaches. This is a good starting point for researchers who have never engaged with social media contexts or data before.

Thurlow, C. and Mroczek, K. R. (2011) *Digital Discourse: Language in the New Media*. Oxford: Oxford University Press.
This edited collection outlines some of the key issues in the sociolinguistics (in the broader sense) of digital media. Various chapters in sections on metadiscourse of digital media language, genre and stance, as well as a more methodologically oriented section, will provide numerous examples of specific linguistic and discursive features that researchers can analyse, as well as some suggestions for appropriate methods.

Tasks

(N.B. Please consider any issues around ethics, as well as legal issues in your current location, that may affect your completion of these tasks.)

1. Identify a particular social problem or wrong you are interested in. Use a range of digital tools (e.g. search engines, journal databases) to get an overview of the issues around this social problem and consider whether there are any particular social media texts that are either used to talk about the problem or could be used to perpetuate it or challenge the conditions that led to it.
2. Explore a given collective cultural, social or political identity representation on a social media platform. Describe what this identity is, how it is represented through textual, visual and other modalities and why (i.e. why people do what they do, what kinds of social and political impact it may have, and what kind of critique there may be for it).
3. Explore how participatory discussion forums or groups may be contributing to deliberations on local issues by focusing on a problem or issue familiar to you. Explore any new or different affordances of the platform, analyse the content and discuss how the digital mediation may be influencing the social issue.
4. If you use Facebook, visit the Political Resistance Online Research Project Facebook group (http://tinyurl.com/PRORP-FB) and contribute to the discussion about political resistance.

GLOSSARY

Affordances. What is made possible through technologies (see Ryder and Wilson 1996). This can include non-digital technologies such as paper or the voice, but in this context it refers mainly to what social media platforms allow users to do (or prevent them from doing).

Argumentation. Argumentation is a linguistic and cognitive pattern of problem-solving that manifests itself sequentially in a more or less coherent network of speech acts. It serves the justification or challenging of validity claims such as truth and normative rightness. Its purpose is to persuade. The validity claim of truth relates to questions of knowledge, certainty and theoretical insight. The validity claim of normative rightness relates to questions of what should or should not be done or what must not be done.

Collocation. Lexical items are said to *collocate* with one another if they habitually co-occur. The phenomenon is referred to as *collocation*, and items that are typically found near the so-called node word (i.e., the word you have searched for) are its *collocates*. One also speaks of the *collocational behaviour* of words.

Concordancer. A concordancing program, or concordancer, is a computer program that displays textual data in such a way that the search word is shown within its textual environment, usually in the middle of a line (also referred to as the *Keyword-in-context* format, or *KWIC*). Concordancers also compute frequencies and calculate various other statistical measures. Among the best known currently on the market are Wordsmith, AntConc and MonoConc Pro.

Context. The term derives from Latin *contextere*, meaning 'interweave', 'tie together'. 'Context' refers to the fact that language/discourse and society are always interwoven and that a specific utterance relates to other utterances, texts and discourse fragments. The concept of 'context' includes dimensions such as (1) the language or text internal co-text and co-discourse; (2) the intertextual and interdiscursive relationship between utterances, texts, genres and discourses; (3) the social variables and institutional frames of a specific 'context of situation'; (4) the broader sociopolitical and historical context (including fields of action), which discursive practices are embedded in and related to.

Digital media, digitally mediated texts, computer-mediated communication. Texts and other semiotic resources that are shared between people (or within groups) using digital technologies such as computers and mobile devices, e.g. tablets and smartphones.

Dispositive. A constantly evolving synthesis of knowledge that is built into linguistically performed practices (i.e. thinking, speaking, writing), non-linguistically performed practices (*vulgo* 'doing things'), and materializations (i.e., natural and produced things).

Intensification or mitigation. The modification (increasing or weakening) of the illocutionary force and thus the epistemic or deontic status of an utterance.

Keyword. In a given corpus, a word is considered a *keyword* if its frequency in that corpus differs significantly from its frequency in another.

Knowledge. From a socio-cognitive point of view, knowledge is defined as the shared beliefs of the members of epistemic communities, represented in long term memory, and meeting the epistemic criteria of the community, such as reliable observation, reliable discourse and reliable inference, typically presupposed in the public discourses of the community, and applied in the construction of mental models of discourse and interaction.

Mental models. The subjective representation of human experience in episodic memory, the autobiographical part of long term memory. *Semantic* mental models may represent specific situations, events and actions we participate in, observe, think about or communicate *about*. *Pragmatic* mental models or *Context Models* define the appropriateness of discourse and represent the relevant properties of the communicative situation, such as the spatiotemporal setting, participants (and their identities, roles, and relations), social action, goals and shared knowledge.

Methodological triangulation. Methodological triangulation refers to the use of more than one method and more than one data set to examine the same phenomenon.

Mode. A mode can be defined as a culturally available resource for constructing meaning. This entails a mode being something to be employed in communication. There is no comprehensive list of modes: the most common, however, are verbal text, visuals, gesture, spatial layout/design and sound. Whether a specific mode is available in a social situation, and what kind of meaning may be expressed in a particular mode, is largely influenced by the specific institutional and cultural context in which communication happens to occur.

Multimodality. The term multimodality describes the fact that most of our communication does not just include a single mode – but utilizes a multiplicity of them. Multimodal discourse analysis, therefore, has to acknowledge that people use different materials and meaning resources simultaneously and/or for different objectives. It therefore focuses on the various functions of each of these modes, their composition and orchestration, and their specific contribution to meaning (re-)construction.

Nomination. The discursive construction of social actors, objects, events, processes and actions by semiotic means of naming such as names, nouns, verbs, deictics, tropes etc.

Participatory web. Social media platforms that encourage content creation and participation by a large number of users, and in turn are shaped by these users. Examples include encyclopaedias such as Wikipedia, review sites such as TripAdvisor, navigation apps such as Waze (where users can correct map errors), auction sites such as eBay, or photo-sharing sites such as Flickr. This is often called 'Web 2.0'. By contrast, in the pre-participatory web, content is largely created and curated by 'experts' and institutions, and the potential for interaction with 'ordinary' users is limited.

Perspectivization. The positioning of the speaker's or writer's point of view and the expression of involvement or distance.

Predication. The discursive qualification of social actors, objects, events, processes and actions by semiotic means of ascription and attribution such as adjectives, prepositional phrases, relative clauses, conjunctional clauses, infinitive clauses and participial clauses or groups.

Recontextualization. This is a term for the way particular social practices (including communicative practices) are represented in the context of other social practices. This involves selective representation, the addition of motives (including evaluations of, and purposes and legitimations or de-legitimations) for the practices or parts thereof which are motivated by the needs and interests of the practices into which the particular social practices are recontextualized.

Deactivation recontextualizes social actions through objectivation, e.g. by means of nominalizations, process nouns or metonyms, or through descriptivization, that is, through supposedly more or less permanent characteristics of social actors (e.g. 'he is honest' instead of 'he tells the truth').

De-agentialization recontextualizes social actions as brought about by factors impermeable to human agency, such as natural forces or unconscious processes.

Generalization recontextualizes social actions by abstracting away from the specific actions that make up a social practice or some episode of it and replacing them by labels for the practice or episode as a whole' (e.g. 'performance review' or 'annual meeting').

Abstraction recontextualizes social actions by means of a quality distilled from them which has particular relevance in the given context, usually for purposes of legitimation (e.g. 'building rapport' or 'eliminating roadblocks').

Reference corpus. A reference corpus is a large corpus that is used as a standard of comparison.

Representativeness. A corpus is considered representative if the texts it contains have been selected so that they adequately reflect the totality of texts in the genre or social domain concerned.

Semantic preference. A word is said to have a particular semantic preference if there is a pattern of co-occurrence between the word and a category of words with a common semantic feature.

Semantic prosody. Semantic prosody is the positive or negative evaluative load carried by a linguistic item.

Social cognition. The mental representations shared by members of social groups or communities, such as their knowledge, attitudes and ideologies, presupposed by all discourse and human communication and interaction in general.

Social media (platforms). Any site or service that enables communication between individuals or groups, be it one-to-one (e.g. instant messaging, Skype), one-to-many (e.g. Twitter, Weibo) or many-to-one (e.g. petition sites, fan pages). Some platforms may combine different elements (e.g. Facebook allows status messages, private messages, photo-sharing, fan pages, etc.). We include services that are not necessarily restricted to operation via the web or even the internet – for instance, short message service (SMS), WhatsApp and email could all be considered social media platforms.

Social networking sites. Specific social media platforms (e.g. Facebook, Weibo, Google+) that are specifically designed for communication between users, often within networks of 'friends' or 'followers'.

Strategy. A strategy is a plan of practices (including discursive practices) adopted to achieve a social, political, psychological or linguistic goal. Discursive strategies are located at different levels of linguistic organization and complexity. The DHA distinguishes among discursive strategies of nomination, predication, argumentation, perspectivization and intensification or mitigation.

Subjects. Social constructions of individuals or collectives (e.g. organizations, nations) that feel, think and act in certain ways. An overlapping concept is that of 'actors'.

Topos. A topos is a formal or content-related conclusion rule that connects the argument(s) with the conclusion. It is a premise that enables us to move on from the argument(s) to the claim. Topoi are socially conventionalized and habitualized. They are not always expressed explicitly, but can always be made explicit as conditional or causal paraphrases such as 'if x, then y' or 'y, because x'.

Visual. The visual mode basically refers to meaning resources that we primarily experience with our sense of sight. In contrast to verbal language that works according to principles of sequence and linearity, visual structures create meaning primarily through immediacy and spatial arrangements. Vision, however, is also socially constructed/regulated (i.e., social rules and conventions influence what we are able and allowed to 'see'). The visual encompasses a large variety of different expressive forms and artefacts. This includes more 'physical' genres such as photographs, pictures, paintings, drawings and sketches as well as 'non-physical' ones, such as charts, diagrams, models and typography. The visual comprises still images as well as motion pictures.

REFERENCES

Aboelezz, M. (2014) The geosemiotics of Tahrir Square: A study of the relationship between discourse and space. *Journal of Language and Politics*, 13: 599–622.

Agar, M. (2002) *The Professional Stranger*. San Diego, CA: Academic Press.

Aker, J. C. and Mbiti, I. M. (2010) Mobile phones and economic development in Africa. *The Journal of Economic Perspectives*, 24 (3): 207–32.

Altheide, D. L. and Snow, R. P. (1979) *Media Logic*. Beverly Hills, CA: Sage.

Althusser, L. (2006) Ideology and ideological state apparatuses (notes towards an investigation). In: M. G. Durham and D. M. Kellner (eds), *Media and Cultural Studies*. Malden, MA: Blackwell Publishing. pp. 79–87.

Androutsopoulos, J. (2008) Potentials and limitations of discourse-centred online ethnography. *Language@Internet* 5.

Androutsopoulos, J. and Beißwenger, M. (2008) Introduction: Data and methods in computer-mediated discourse analysis. *Language@Internet* 5.

Angermueller, J., Maingueneau, D. and Wodak, R. (2014) The Discourse Studies Reader: An Introduction. In: J. Angermueller, D. Maingueneau and R. Wodak (eds), *The Discourse Studies Reader: Main Currents in Theory and Analysis*. Amsterdam/Philadelphia: John Benjamins. pp. 1–14.

Angouri, J. and Wodak, R. (2014) They became big in the shadow of the crisis: The Greek success story and the rise of the far right. *Discourse & Society*, 25: 540–65.

Anthonissen, C. (2001) On the effectivity of media censorship: An analysis of linguistic, para-linguistic and other communicative devices used to defy media restrictions. PhD thesis, University of Vienna.

Aries, P. (1962) *Centuries of Childhood: A Social History of Family Life*. New York: Vintage Books.

Bachrach, P. and Baratz, M. S. (1962) Two faces of power. *American Political Science Review*, 56: 947–52.

Baker, P. (2006) *Using Corpora in Discourse Analysis*. London, New York: Continuum.

Baker, P. and McEnery, T. (2005) A corpus-based approach to discourses of refugees and asylum seekers in UN and newspaper texts. *Journal of Language and Politics*, 4: 197–226.

Baker, P., Gabrielatos, C., Khosravinik, M., Krzyanowski, M., McEnery, T. and Wodak, R. (2008) A useful methodological synergy? Combining critical discourse analysis and corpus linguistics to examine discourses of refugees and asylum seekers in the UK press. *Discourse & Society*, 19: 273–305.

Baker, P., McEnery, T. and Gabrielatos, C. (2007) Using collocation analysis to reveal the construction of minority groups. The case of refugees, asylum seekers and immigrants in the UK press. Paper presented at Corpus Linguistics 2007.

Balke, F. (1998) Was zu denken zwingt. Gilles Deleuze, Felxi Guattari und das Außen der Philosophie. In: J. Jurt (ed.), *Zeitgenössische Französische Denker: Eine Bilanz*. Freiburg im Bresgau: Rombach Litterae. pp. 187–210.

Barton, D. and Lee, C. (2013) *Language Online: Investigating Digital Texts and Practices*. Abingdon: Routledge.

Bauer, M. W. and Aarts, B. (2000) Corpus construction: A principle for qualitative data collection. In: M. W. Bauer and G. Gaskell (eds), *Qualitative Researching with Text, Image and Sound*. London: Sage. pp. 19–37.

Bednarek, M. and Caple, H. (2014) Why do news values matter? Towards a new methodological framework for analysing news discourse in Critical Discourse Analysis and beyond. *Discourse & Society*, 25: 135–58.

Bell, A. (1994) Climate of opinion: public and media discourse on the global environment. *Discourse & Society*, 5: 33–64.

Bell, E. (2012) Ways of seeing organisational death: A critical semiotic analysis of organisational memorialisation. *Visual Studies*, 27: 4–17.

Berger, P. L. and Luckmann, T. (1966/1967) *The Social Construction of Reality*. Harmondsworth: Penguin.

Berglez, P. (2008) What is global journalism? Theoretical and empirical conceptualizations. *Journalism Studies*, 9: 845–58.

Bernstein, B. B. (1981) Codes, modalities, and the process of cultural reproduction: A model. *Language in Society*, 10: 327–63.

Bernstein, B. B. (1986) On pedagogic discourse. In: J. G. Richardson (ed.), *Handbook for Theory and Research in the Sociology of Education*. Westport, CT: Greenwood Press. pp. 205–40.

Bhaskar, R. (1986) *Scientific Realism and Human Emancipation*. London: Verso.

Billig, M. (2008) Nominalizing and de-nominalizing: a reply. *Discourse & Society*, 19: 829–841.

Blau, P. M. (1964) *Exchange and Power in Social Life*. New York: Wiley.

Blommaert, J. (2005) *Discourse: A Critical Introduction*. Cambridge: Cambridge University Press.

Bohnsack, R. (2007) Die dokumentarische Methode in der Bild- und Fotointerpretation. In: R. Bohnsack, I. Nentwig-Gesemann and A-M. Nohl (eds), *Die dokumentarische Methode und ihre Forschungspraxis*. Wiesbaden: VS Verlag. pp. 69–91.

Boukala, S. (2013) The Greek media discourse and the construction of European identity: Supranational identity, Fortress Europe and Islam as radical otherness. PhD thesis, Lancaster University.

Bourdieu, P. (1977) *Outline of a Theory of Practice*. Cambridge, MA: Cambridge University Press.

Bourdieu, P. (1980) *The Logic of Practice*. Cambridge: Polity Press.

Bourdieu, P. (1982) *Ce que parler veut dire: L'economie des échanges linguistiques*. Paris: Librairie Arthème Fayard.

Bourdieu, P. (1984) *Homo academicus*. Paris: Les Éditions de Minuit.

Bourdieu, P. (1986) The forms of capital. In: J. G. Richardson (ed.), *Handbook of Theory and Research for the Sociology of Education*. New York: Greenwood. pp. 241–58.

Bourdieu, P. (1987) What makes a social class? On the theoretical and practical existence of groups. *Berkeley Journal of Sociology*, 32: 1–18.

Bourdieu, P. (1989) *La Noblesse d'etat. Grands écoles et esprit de corps*. Paris: Edition de Minuit.

Bourdieu, P. (1990) *In Other Words: Essays Towards a Reflexive Sociology*. Cambridge: Polity Press.

Bourdieu, P. (1991) *Language and Symbolic Power*. Cambridge: Polity Press.

Bourdieu, P. and Passeron, J.-C. (1977) *Reproduction in Education, Society, and Culture*. London: Sage.

Bourdieu, P. and Wacquant, L. J. D. (1992) *An Invitation to Reflexive Sociology*. Chicago, IL: University of Chicago Press.

Boykoff, M. T. (2011) *Who Speaks for the Climate? Making Sense of Media Reporting on Climate Change*. Cambridge: Cambridge University Press.

Boykoff, M. T. and Boykoff, J. M. (2004) Balance as bias: global warming and the US prestige press. *Global Environmental Change*, 14: 125–36.

Brown, G. and Yule, G. (1983) *Discourse Analysis*. Cambridge: Cambridge University Press.

Brown, M. B. and Coates, K. (1996) *The Blair Revelation: Deliverance for Whom?* Nottingham: Spokesman.

Bublitz, H. (1999) *Foucaults Archäologie des kulturellen Unbewußten: Zum Wissensarchiv und Wissensbegehren moderner Gesellschaften*. Frankfurt am Main: Campus.

Bublitz, H. (2011) Differenz und Integration. Zur diskursanalytischen Rekonstruktion der Regelstrukturen sozialer Wirklichkeit. In: R. Keller, A. Hirseland, W. Schneider and W. Viehöver (eds), *Handbuch Sozialwissenschaftliche Diskursanalyse. Band 1: Theorien und Methoden*. Wiesbaden: VS Verlag. pp. 245–82.

Burr, V. (2003) *Social Constructionism*. Hove: Routledge.

Caborn, J. (1999) Die Presse und die, Hauptstadtdebatte': Konstrukte der deutschen Einheit. In: U. Kreft, H. Uske and S. Jäger (eds), *Kassensturz: Politische Hypotheken der Berliner Republik*. Duisurg: DISS. pp. 61–84.

Caborn, J. (2006) *Schleichende Wende: Diskurse von Nation und Erinnerung bei der Konstituierung der Berliner Republik*. Münster: Unrast-Verlag.

Carter, S. and Little, M. (2007) Justifying knowledge, justifying method, taking action: epistemologies, methodologies, and methods in qualitative research. *Qualitative Health Research*, 17: 1316–28.

Carvalho, A. (2005) Representing the politics of the greenhouse effect: discursive strategies in the British media. *Critical Discourse Studies*, 2: 1–29.

Carvalho, A. (2008) Media(ted) discourse and society: rethinking the framework of critical discourse analysis. *Journalism Studies*, 9: 161–77.

Carvalho, A. and Burgess, J. (2005) Cultural circuits of climate change in UK broadsheet newspapers, 1985–2003. *Risk Analysis*, 25: 1457–69.

Castells, M. (1996) *The Rise of the Network Society*. Oxford: Blackwell.

Castells, M. (2009) *Communication Power*. Oxford: Oxford University Press.

Chilton, P. (2004) *Analysing Political Discourse: Theory and Practice*. London: Routledge.

Chilton, P. (2005) Missing links in mainstream CDA: modules, blends and the critical instinct. In: R. Wodak and P. Chilton (eds), *A New Research Agenda in Critical Discourse Analysis: Theory and Interdisciplinarity*. Lancaster: John Benjamins. pp. 19–52.

Chilton, P. (2008) *Critical Discourse Analysis*. In: *Cambridge Encyclopedia of the Language Sciences*. Cambridge: Cambridge University Press.

Chilton, P., Tian, H. and Wodak. R. (2010) Reflections on discourse and critique in China and the West. *Journal of Language and Politics*, 9: 489–507.

Chouliaraki, L. (1995) Regulation and heteroglossia in one institutional context: The case of a 'progressivist' English classroom. PhD thesis, University of Lancaster.

Chouliaraki, L. and Fairclough, N. (1999) *Discourse in Late Modernity*. Edinburgh: Edinburgh University Press.

Chouliaraki, L. and Fairclough, N. (2010) Critical discourse analysis in organizational studies: Towards an integrationist methodology. *Journal of Management Studies*, 47: 1213–18.

Church, K. and Hanks, P. (1990) Word association norms: mutual information, and lexicography. *Computational Linguistics*, 16: 22–9.

Clarke, J. and Newman, J. (1998) *A Modern British People? New Labour and the Reconstruction of Social Welfare*. Copenhagen: Department of Intercultural Communication and Management, Copenhagen Business School.

Clear, J. (1993) From Firth principles: Computational tools for the study of collocation. In: M. Baker, G. Francis and E. Tognini-Bonelli (eds), *Text and Technology: In Honour of John Sinclair*. Amsterdam/Philadelphia: John Benjamins. pp. 271–92.

Cole, J. I., Suman, M., Schramm, P., Zhou, L., Reyes-Sepulveda E. and Lebo, H. (2013) *The World Internet Project*. www.worldinternetproject.net/_files/_//307_2013worldinternetreport.pdf, accessed 24 August 2015.

Connolly, W. E. (1991) *Identity/Difference*. Ithaca. NY: Cornell University Press.

Cook, G. (2001) *The Discourse of Advertising*. London: Routledge.

Cook, T. E. (1998) *Governing with the News. The News Media as Political Institution*. Chicago, IL: University of Chicago Press.

Cotterill, J. (2001) Domestic discord, rocky relationships: semantic prosodies in representations of marital violence in the O.J. Simpson trial. *Discourse & Society*, 12: 291–312.

Cottle, S. (2011) Media and the Arab uprisings of 201: Research notes. *Journalism*, 12: 647–59.

Creswell, J. W. and Miller, D. L. (2010) Determining validity in qualitative inquiry. *Theory Into Practice*, 39: 124–30.

Czarniawska, B. (2004) *Narratives in Social Science Research*. London: Sage.

Dahlgren, P. (2009) *Media and Political Engagement: Citizens, Communication, and Democracy*. Cambridge: Cambridge University Press.

Darics, E. (2014) The blurring boundaries between synchronicity and asynchronicity: New communicative situations in work-related instant messaging. *International Journal of Business Communication*, 51: 337–58.

de Beaugrande, R. (1997) The story of discourse analysis. In: T. A. van Dijk (ed.), *Discourse as Structure and Process*. London: Sage. pp. 35–62.

de Cock, C., Baker, M. and Volkmann, C. (2011) Financial phantasmagoria: Corporate image-work in times of crisis. *Organization*, 18: 153–72.

Deleuze, G. (1988) *Foucault*. Minneapolis, MN: University of Minnesota Press.

Döring, H. and Hirschauer, S. (1997) Die Biographie der Dinge: Eine Ethnographie musealer Representation. In: S. Hirschauer and K. Amann (eds), *Die Befremdung der eigenen Kultur*. Frankfurt am Main: Suhrkamp. pp. 267–97.

Dorostkar, N. and Preisinger, A. (2012) CDA 2.0 – Leserkommentarforen aus kritisch-diskursan-alytischer Perspektive: Eine explorative Studie am Beispiel der Online-Zeitung der Standard. at. *Wiener Linguistische Gazette*, 7: 1–47.

Dorostkar, N. and Preisinger, A. (2013) Kritische Online-Diskursanalyse: Medienlinguistische und diskurshistorische Ansätze zur Untersuchung von Leserkommentarforen. In: C. Fraas, S. Meier and C. Pentzold (eds), *Online-Diskurse. Theorien und Methoden transmedialer Online-Diskursforschung*. Cologne: Halem. pp. 313–45.

Drews, A., Gerhard, U. and Link, J. (1985) Moderne Kollektivsymbolik: Eine diskurstheoretisch orientierte Einführung mit Auswahlbiographie. *Internationales Archiv für Sozialgeschichte der deutschen Literatur (IASL)*, 1. Sonderheft Forschungsreferate, Tübingen. pp. 256–375.

Dreyfus, H. L. and Rabinow, P. (1982) *Michel Foucault: Beyond Structuralism and Hermeneutics*. Sussex: The Harvester Press.

Drori, G. S., Meyer, J. W. and Hwang, H. (eds) (2006) *Globalization and Organization: World Society and Organizational Change*. Oxford: Oxford University Press.

Duggan, M. and Smith, A. (2013) Pew Internet and American Life Project. In: *Social Media Update 2013*. http://www.pewinternet.org/2013/12/30/social-media-update-2013, accessed 24 August 2015.

Durkheim, E. (1933) *The Division of Labor in Society*. New York: The Free Press.

Durkheim, E. (1976) *The Elementary Forms of Religious Life*. London: Allen and Unwin.

Durkheim, E. and Mauss, M. (1963) *Primitive Classification*. London: Cohen and West.

Ehlich, K. (1983) *Text und sprachliches Handeln. Die Entstehung von Texten aus dem Bedürfnis nach Überlieferung*. Munich: Fink.

Emerson, R. M. (1962) Power-dependence relations. *American Sociological Review*, 27: 31–41.

Emerson, R. M. (1975) Social exchange theory. *Annual Review of Sociology*, 2: 335–62.

Emerson, R. M., Fretz, R. I. and Shaw, L. L. (1995) *Writing Ethnographic Fieldnotes*. Chicago, IL: University of Chicago Press.

Evison, J. (2010) What are the basics of analysing a corpus? In: A. O'Keefe and M. McCarthy (eds), *The Routledge Handbook of Corpus Linguistics*. Abingdon, New York: Routledge. pp. 122–35.

Fahmy, S. (2010) Contrasting visual frames of our times: A framing analysis of English- and Arabic-language press coverage of war and terrorism. *International Communication Gazette*, 72: 695–717.

Fairclough, N. (1991) *Language and Power*. London: Longman.

Fairclough, N. (1992a) *Critical Language Awareness*. London: Longman.

Fairclough, N. (1992b) *Discourse and Social Change*. Cambridge: Polity Press.

Fairclough, N. (1993) Critical discourse analysis and the marketization of public discourse: The universities. *Discourse & Society*, 4: 133–68.

Fairclough, N. (1995a) *Critical Discourse Analysis*. London: Longman.

Fairclough, N. (1995b) *Media Discourse*. London: Edward Arnold.

Fairclough, N. (1996) A reply to Henry Widdowson's 'Discourse analysis: a critical view'. *Language and Literature*, 5: 49–56.

Fairclough, N. (2000a) *New Labour, New Language?* London: Routledge.

Fairclough, N. (2000b) Represenciones del cambio en discurso neoliberal. *Cuadernos de Relaciones Laborales*, 16: 13–36.

Fairclough, N. (2003) *Analysing Discourse: Text Analysis for Social Research*. London: Routledge.

Fairclough, N. (2005) Critical discourse analysis in transdisciplinary research. In: R. Wodak and P. Chilton (eds), *A New Agenda in (Critical) Discourse Analysis*. Amsterdam/Philadelphia: John Benjamins. pp. 53–70.

Fairclough, N. (2006) *Language and Globalization*. London: Routledge.

Fairclough, N. (2010) *Critical Discourse Analysis: The Critical Study of Language*. London: Routledge.

Fairclough, N., Jessop, B. and Sayer, A. (2004) Critical realism and semiosis. In: J. Joseph and J. M. Roberts (eds), *Realism, Discourse and Deconstruction*. London: Routledge. pp. 23–42.

Fairclough, N. and Wodak, R. (1997) Critical discourse analysis. In: T. van Dijk (ed.), *Discourse as Social Interaction*. London: Sage. pp. 258–84.

Fay, B. (1987) *Critical Social Science*. Cambridge: Polity Press.

Firth, J. R. (1935 [1957]) The technique of semantics. In: *Papers in Linguistics*. London: Oxford University Press. pp. 7–33.

Flick, U. (2004) *Triangulation. Eine Einführung*. Wiesbaden: VS Verlag für Sozialwissenschaften.

Flowerdew, J. (ed.) (2014) *Discourse in Context*. London: Bloomsbury.

Forchtner, B. and Tominc, A. (2012) Critique and argumentation: On the relation between the discourse-historical approach and pragma-dialectics. *Journal of Language and Politics*, 11: 31–50.

Foucault, M. (1963) *Naissance de la clinique. Une archéologie du retard medical*. Paris: P.U.F.

Foucault, M. (1972) *The Archaeology of Knowledge*. New York: Pantheon Books.

Foucault, M. (1975) *Surveiller et punir: Naissance de la prison*. Paris: Gallimard.

Foucault, M. (1977) *Language, Counter-Memory, Practice: Selected Essays and Interviews*. Ithaca, NY: Cornell University Press.

Foucault, M. (1979) *Discipline and Punish: The Birth of the Prison*. Harmondsworth: Penguin Books.

Foucault, M. (1980a) The Confession of the Flesh. In: C. Gordon (ed.), *Power/Knowledge: Selected Interviews and Other Writings 1972–1977 by Michel Foucault*. New York: Pantheon Books. pp. 194–228.

Foucault, M. (1980b) Truth and power. In: C. Gordon (ed.), *Power/Knowledge: Selected Interviews and Other Writings 1972–1977 by Michel Foucault*. New York: Pantheon Books. 107–33.

Foucault, M. (1982) The subject and power. *Critical Inquiry*: 777–95.

Foucault, M. (1983) *Der Wille zum Wissen: Sexualität und Wahrheit 1*. Frankfurt am Main: Suhrkamp.

Foucault, M. (1990) *Was ist Kritik?* Berlin: Merve.

Foucault, M. (1991) *Remarks on Marx: Conversations with Duccio Trombadori*. New York: Semiotext(e).

Foucault, M. (1996) What is critique? In: J. Schmidt (ed.), *What Is Enlightenment? Eighteenth-Century Answers and Twentieth-Century Questions*. Berkeley, CA: University of California Press. pp. 382–98.

Foucault, M. (2001) *Fearless Speech*. Los Angeles, CA: Semiotext(e).

Foucault, M. (2002) *The Archaeology of Knowledge*. London: Routledge.

Foucault, M. (2004) *Sécurité, Territoire et Population*. Paris: Éditions Gallimard/Édition du Seuil.

Fowler, R., Hodge, R., Kress, G. and Trew, T. (eds) (1979) *Language and Control*. London: Routledge.

French, J. R. P. and Raven, B. (1959) The bases of social power. In: D. Cartwright (ed.), *Studies in Social Power*. Ann Arbor, MI: Institute for Social Research, University of Michigan. pp. 150–67.

Froschauer, U. (2002) Artefaktanalyse. In: S. Kühl and P. Strodtholz (eds), *Methoden der Organisationsforschung*. Reinbek: rororo. pp. 361–95.

Fuchs, C. (2014) *Social Media: A Critical Introduction*. London: Sage.

Fuchs, C. and Sevignani, S. (2013) What is digital labour? What is digital work? What's their difference? And why do these questions matter for understanding social media? *tripleC*, 11: 237–93.

Gaby, S. and Caren, N. (2012) Occupy online: How cute old men and Malcolm X recruited 400,000 US users to OWS on Facebook. *Social Movement Studies*, 11: 367–74.

Gamson, W. A. and Modigliani, A. (1989) Media discourse and public opinion on nuclear power: A constructionist approach. *American Journal of Sociology*, 95: 1–37.

Gee, J. (2004) *Discourse Analysis: Theory and Method*. London: Routledge.

Giddens, A. (1984) *The Constitution of Society. Outline of the Theory of Structuration*. Cambridge: Polity Press.

Gilbert, N. G. (2008) Research, theory and method. In: N. G. Gilbert (ed.), *Researching Social Life*. London: Sage. pp. 21–40.

Girnth, H. (1996) Texte im politischen Diskurs. Ein Vorschlag zur diskursorientierten Beschreibung von Textsorten. *Muttersprache*, 106: 66–80.

Glaser, B. and Strauss, A. L. (1967) *The Discovery of Grounded Theory: Strategies for Qualitative Research*. Chicago, IL: Chicago University Press.

Gleason, H. A., Jr. (1973) Contrastive analysis in discourse structure. In: Á. Makkai and D. G. Lockwood (eds), *Readings in Stratificational Linguistics*. Tuscaloosa, AL: University of Alabama Press.

Goffman, E. (1979) Footing. *Semiotica*, 25: 1–30.

González-Bailón, S., Borge-Holthoefer, J., Rivero, A., Moreno, Y. (2011) The dynamics of protest recruitment through an online network. *Scientific Reports*, 1: 1–7.

Gore, A. (2007) *Wege zum Gleichgewicht: Ein Marshallplan für die Erde* (trans. F. Hörmann and W. Brumm). Hamburg: Fischer-Rowohlt.

Graham, P. (2006) *Hypercapitalism: New Media, Language, and Social Perceptions of Value*. New York: Peter Lang.

Graham, P. W. and Paulsen, N. (2002) Third-sector discourses and the future of (un)employment: Skilled labor, new technologies, and the meaning of work. *Text*, 22: 443–67.

Graves, O. F., Flesher, D. L. and Jordan, R. E. (1996) Pictures and the bottom line: The television epistemology of U.S. annual reports. *Accounting, Organizations and Society*, 21: 57–88.

Gray, B. and Biber, D. (2011) Corpus approaches to the study of discourse. In: K. Hyland and B. Paltridge (eds), *Continuum Companion to Discourse Analysis*. London, New York: Continuum. pp. 138–52.

Gretzel, U., Yuan, Y.-L. and Fesenmaier, D. R. (2000) Preparing for the new economy: Advertising strategies and change in destination marketing organizations. *Journal of Travel Research*, 39: 146–56.

Grimes, J. E. (1975) *The Thread of Discourse*. The Hague: Mouton.

Habermas, J. (1967) *Erkenntnis und Interesse*. Frankfurt am Main: Suhrkamp.

Habermas, J. (1972) *Knowledge and Human Interests*. London: Heinemann.

Habermas, J. (1996) *Die Einbeziehung des Anderen: Studien zur politischen Theorie*. Frankfurt am Main: Suhrkamp.

Hall, S. (1992) The West and the rest: Discourse and power. In: S. Hall and B. Gieben (eds), *Formations of Modernity*. Oxford: Polity in Association with Open University. pp. 275–332.

Halliday, M. A. K. (1978) *Language as Social Semiotic*. London: Arnold.

Halliday, M. A. K. (1985) *Introduction to Functional Grammar*. London: Arnold.

Halliday, M. A. K. (1994) *An Introduction to Functional Grammar*. London: Arnold.

Hammersley, M. and Atkinson, P. (2007) *Ethnography: Principles in Practice*. London: Routledge.

Hardt-Mautner, G. (1995) Only connect: Critical discourse analysis and corpus linguistics. *UCREL Technical Paper 6*.

Hardy, C. and Phillips, N. (1999) No joking matter: Discursive struggle in the Canadian refugee system. *Organization Studies*, 20: 1–24.

Hart, C. and Cap, P. (eds) (2014) *Contemporary Critical Discourse Studies*. London: Bloomsbury.

Harvey, D. (1996) *Justice, Nature and the Geography of Difference*. Oxford: Blackwell.

Harvey, D. (2003) *The New Imperialism*. Oxford: Oxford University Press.

Hassan, R. and Purser, R. E. (eds) (2007) *24/7: Time and Temporality in the Network Society*. Stanford, CA: Stanford University Press.

Hay, C. (2007) *Why We Hate Politics*. Cambridge: Polity.

Heer, H., Manoschek, W. Pollak, A. and Wodak, R. (eds) (2008) *The Discursive Construction of History: Remembering the Wehrmacht's War of Annihilation*. London: Palgrave.

Herring, S. C. (2004) Computer-mediated discourse analysis: An approach to researching online behavior. In: S. Barab, R. Kling and J. Gray (eds), *Designing for Virtual Communities in the Service of Learning*. Cambridge: Cambridge University Press. pp. 338–76.

Herring, S. C. (2007) A faceted classification scheme for computer-mediated discourse. *Language@Internet*, 4.

Herring, S. C. (2013) Discourse in Web 2.0: Familiar, reconfigured, and emergent. In: D. Tannen and A. M. Trester (eds), *Discourse 2.0: Language and New Media*. Washington, DC: Georgetown University Press. pp. 1–25.

Hitzler, R. and A. Honer (eds) (1997) *Sozialwissenschaftliche Hermeneutik. Eine Einführung*. Opladen: UTB.

Hitzler, R., Reichertz, J. and Schröer, N. (eds) (1999) *Hermeneutische Wissenssoziologie. Standpunkte zur Theorie der Interpretation*. Konstanz: UVK Universitäts-Verlag.

Holcomb, J., Gottfried, J. and Mitchell, A. (2013) *Pew Research Journalism Project*. In: *News use across social media platforms*. www.journalism.org/2013/11/14/news-use-across-social-media-platforms, accessed 24 August 2015.

Höllerer, M. A. (2013) From taken-for-granted to explicit commitment: The rise of CSR in a corporatist country. *Journal of Management Studies*, 50: 573–606.

Höllerer, M. A., Jancsary, D. and Grafström, M. (2014) 'A picture is worth a thousand words': Visually assigned meaning and meta-narratives of the global financial crisis. Working Paper, WU Vienna.

Höllerer, M. A., Jancsary, D., Meyer, R. E. and Vettori, O. (2013) Imageries of corporate social responsibility: Visual re-contextualization and field-level meaning. In: M. Lounsbury and E. Boxenbaum (eds), *Institutional Logics in Action, Part B (Research in the Sociology of Organizations, Vol. 39B)*. Bingley: Emerald. pp. 139–74.

Holzscheiter, A. (2005) Discourse as capability. *Millenium: Journal of International Studies*, 33: 723–46.

Holzscheiter, A. (2012) *Children's Rights in International Politics. The Transformative Power of Discourse*. Basingstoke: Palgrave Macmillan.

Horkheimer, M. (1937) Traditionelle und kritische Theorie. *Zeitschrift für Sozialforschung* 6 / 2, 245–92.

Horkheimer, M. and Adorno, T. W. (1991 [1969, 1974]) *Dialektik der Aufklärung*. Frankfurt am Main: Fischer.

Hundt, M., Nesselhauf, N. and Biewer, C. (2007) *Corpus Linguistics and the Web*. Cambridge: Cambridge University Press.

Hunston, S. (2002) *Corpora in Applied Linguistics*. Cambridge: Cambridge University Press.

Hunston, S. (2004) Counting the uncountable: Problems of identifying evaluation in a text and in a corpus. In: A. Partington, J. Morley and L. Haarman (eds), *Corpora and Discourse*. Berne: Peter Lang. pp. 157–88.

Iedema, R. (1997) Interactional dynamics and social change: Planning as morphogenesis. PhD thesis, University of Sydney.

Iedema, R. and Wodak, R. (1999) Introduction: Organizational discourse and practices. *Discourse & Society* 10: 5–19.

Ieţcu, I. (2006) *Discourse Analysis and Argumentation Theory*. Bucharest: Editura Universităţii din Bucureşti.

IPCC (2013) Intergovernmental Panel on Climate Change Report 2013. www.ipcc.ch/report. ar5/wg1, accessed 5 November 2014.

Jäger, M. (1996) *Fatale Effekte: Die Kritik am Patriarchat im Einwanderungsdiskurs*. Duisburg: Unrast-Verlag.

Jäger, M. and Jäger, S. (2007) *Deutungskämpfe: Theorie und Praxis Kritischer Diskursanalyse*. Wiesbaden: VS Verlag.

Jäger, S. (2004) *Kritische Diskursanalse. Eine Einführung*. Münster: Unrast-Verlag.

Jäger, S. (2012) *Kritische Diskursanalse. Eine Einführung*. Münster: Unrast-Verlag.

Jäger, S. and Maier, F. (2009) Theoretical and methodological aspects of Foucauldian critical discourse analysis and dispositive analysis. In: R. Wodak and M. Meyer (eds), *Methods of Critical Discourse Analysis*. London: Sage. pp. 34–61.

Jancsary, D. (2013) *Die rhetorische Konstruktion von Führung und Steuerung: Eine argumentationstheoretische Untersuchung deutschsprachiger Führungsgrundsätze*. Frankfurt am Main: Peter Lang.

Jessop, B. (2002) *The Future of the Capitalist State*. Cambridge: Polity Press.

Jessop, B. (2004) Critical semiotic analysis and cultural political economy. *Critical Discourse Studies*, 1: 159–74.

Jessop, B. (2008) The cultural political economy of the knowledge-based economy and its implications for higher education. In: N. Fairclough, B. Jessop and R. Wodak (eds), *Education and the Knowledge-Based Economy in Europe*. Amsterdam: Sense Publishers.

Jewitt, C. (ed.) (2009) *The Routledge Handbook of Multimodal Analysis*. Abingdon: Routledge.

Jurgenson, N. (2012) When atoms meet bits: Social media, the mobile web and augmented revolution. *Future Internet*, 4: 83–91.

Kahn, R. and Kellner, D. (2004) New media and internet activism: From the 'Battle of Seattle' to blogging. *New Media & Society*, 6: 87–95.

Katz, E. and Lazarsfeld, P. F. (1955) *Personal Influence*. Glencoe, IL: Free Press.

Keller, R. (2008) *Wissenssoziologische Diskursanalyse. Grundlegung eines Forschungsprogramms*. Wiesbaden: VS Verlag.

Kelsey, D. and Bennett, L. (2014) Discipline and resistance on social media: Discourse, power and context in the Paul Chambers Twitter Joke Trial. *Discourse, Context & Media*, 3: 37–45.

KhosraviNik, M. (2010) Actor descriptions, action attributions, and argumentation: towards a systematization of CDA analytical categories in the representation of social groups. *Critical Discourse Studies*, 7 (1): 55–72.

KhosraviNik, M. (2014) Critical discourse analysis, power and new media discourse: issues and debates. In: Y. Kalyango and M. W. Kopytowska (eds), *Why Discourse Matters: Negotiating Identity in the Mediatized World*. New York: Peter Lang. pp. 287–305.

KhosraviNik, M. (2015 forthcoming) *Discourse, Identity and Legitimacy: Self and Other in Representations of Iran's Nuclear Programme*. Amsterdam/Philadelphia: John Benjamins.

KhosraviNik, M. and Zia, M. (2014) Persian identity and anti-Arab sentiments in Iranian Facebook discourses: critical discourse analysis and social media communication. *Journal of Language and Politics*, 13: 755–780.

KhosraviNik, M. (2016 forthcoming) Social Media Critical Discourse Studies (SM-CDS): towards a CDS understanding of discourse analysis on participatory web. In: J. Flowerdew and J. E. Richardson (eds), *Handbook of Critical Discourse Analysis*. London: Routledge.

Kienpointner, M. (1992) *Alltagslogik. Struktur und Funktion von Argumentationsmustern*. Stuttgart-Bad Cannstatt: Frommann-holzboog.

Kienpointner, M. (1996) *Vernünftig argumentieren*. Hamburg: Rowohlt.

Kienpointner, M. and Kindt, W. (1997) On the problem of bias in political argumentation: An investigation into discussions about political asylum in Germany and Austria. *Journal of Pragmatics*, 27: 555–85.

Kindt, W. (1992) Argumentation und Konfliktaustragung in Äußerungen über den Golfkrieg. *Zeitschrift für Sprachwissenschaft*, 11: 189–215.

Kitschelt, H. P. (1986) Political opportunity structures and political protest: Anti-nuclear movements in four democracies. *British Journal of Political Science*, 16: 57–85.

Klaus, V. (2007) *Blauer Planet in günen Fesseln! Was ist bedroht: Klima oder Freiheit?* Vienna: Carl Gerold's Sohn Verlagsbuchhandlung.

Klemperer, V. (2000) *Language of the Third Reich*. London: Continuum.

Klemperer, V. (2001) *I Will Bear Witness: A Diary of the Nazi Years*. New York: Modern Library.

Klemperer, V. (2006) *The Language of the Third Reich: LTI – Lingua Tertii Imperii: A Philologist's Notebook*. London: Continuum.

Knight, K. (2006) Transformations of the concept of ideology in the twentieth century. *American Political Science Review*, 100: 619–26.

Knox, J. (2007) Visual-verbal communication on online newspaper home pages. *Visual Communication*, 6: 19–53.

Knox, J. (2009) Punctuating the home page: Image as language in an online newspaper. *Discourse & Communication*, 3: 145–72.

Koester, A. (2010) Building small specialised corpora. In: A. O'Keefe and M. McCarthy (eds), *The Routledge Handbook of Corpus Linguistics*. Abingdon: Routledge. pp. 66–79.

Koller, V. and Mautner, G. (2004) Computer applications in Critical Discourse Analysis. In: A. Hewings, C. Coffin and K. O'Halloran (eds), *Applying English Grammar*. London: Arnold. pp. 216–28.

Kopperschmidt, J. (2000) *Argumentationstheorie zur Einführung*. Hamburg: Junius.

Koteyko, N. (2010) Mining the Internet for linguistic and social data: an analysis of carbon compounds in web feeds. *Discourse & Society*, 21: 655–74.

Kovács, A. and Wodak, R. (eds) (2003) *Nato, Neutrality and National Identity: The Case of Austria and Hungary*. Vienna: Böhlau.

Kress, G. (2010) *Multimodality. A Social Semiotic Approach to Contemporary Communication*. Abingdon: Routledge.

Kress, G. and Hodge, R. (1979) *Language as Ideology*. London: Routledge.

Kress, G. and van Leeuwen, T. (2001) *Multimodal Discourse: The Modes and Media of Contemporary Communication*. London: Hodder Education.

Kress, G. and van Leeuwen, T. (2006) *Reading Images: The Grammar of Visual Design*. London: Routledge.

Krishnamurthy, R. (1996) Ethnic, racial, tribal: The language of racism? In: C. R. Caldas-Coulthard and M. Coulthard (eds), *Texts and Practices: Readings in Critical Discourse Analysis*. London: Routledge. pp. 129–49.

Krzyzanowski, M. (2008) Analyzing focus group discussions. In: *Qualitative Discourse Analysis in the Social Sciences*. Basingstoke: Palgrave Macmillan. pp. 162–81.

Laclau, E. (1980) Populist rupture and discourse. *Screen Education* 34: 87–93.

Lakoff, G. (1987) *Women, Fire and Dangerous Things*. Chicago, IL: University of Chicago Press.

Lakoff, G. and Johnson, M. (1980) *Metaphors We Live By*. Chicago, IL: University of Chicago Press.

Lakoff, G. and Johnson, M. (1999) *Philosophy in the Flesh*. New York: Basic Books.

Latif, M. (2012) *Globale Erwärmung*. Stuttgart: Ulmer.

Latour, B. (2005) *Reassembling the Social: An Introduction to Actor-Network-Theory*. Oxford: Oxford University Press.

Leitch, S. and Palmer, I. (2010) Analysing texts in context: Current practices and new protocols for critical discourse analysis in organization studies. *Journal of Management Studies*, 47: 1194–212.

Lemke, J. L. (1995) *Textual Politics*. London: Taylor & Francis.

Lemke, J. L. (2002) Travels in hypermodality. *Visual Communication* 1: 299–325.

Lenhart, A. (2012) Teens, smartphones and texting. *Pew Internet and American Life Project*. www.away.gr/wp-content/uploads/2012/03/PIP_Teens_Smartphones_and_Texting.pdf, accessed 24 August 2015.

Lévi-Strauss, C. (1964) *Totemism*. Harmondsworth: Penguin.

LeVine, P. and Scollon. R. (eds) (2004) *Discourse and Technology. Multimodal Discourse Analysis*. Washington, DC: Georgetown University Press.

Levinson, S. C. (1983) *Pragmatics*. Cambridge Cambridge University Press.

Link, J. (1982) Kollektivsymbolik und Mediendiskurse. *kulturRRevolution*, 1: 6–21.

Link, J. (1983) Was ist und was bringt Diskurstaktik. *kulturRRevolution*, 2: 60–6.

Link, J. (1988) Literaturanalyse als Interdiskursanalyse. In: J. Fohrmann and H. Müller (eds), *Diskurstheorien und Literaturwissenschaft*. Frankfurt am Main: Suhrkamp.

Link, J. (1992) Die Analyse der symbolischen Komponente realer Ereignisse: Ein Beitrag der Diskurstheorie zur Analyse neorassistischer Äußerungen. In: S. Jäger and F. Januschek (eds), *Der Diskurs des Rassismus*. Oldenburg: Osnabrücker Beiträge zur Sprachtheorie 46. pp. 37–52.

Link, J. (1997) *Versuch über den Normalismus. Wie Normalität produziert wird*. Opladen: Westdeutscher Verlag.

Link, J. and Link-Heer, U. (1990) Diskurs/Interdiskurs und Literaturanalyse. *Zeitschrift für Linguistik und Literaturwissenschaft (LiLi)*, 77: 88–99.

Louw, B. (1993) Irony in the text or insincerity in the writer? The diagnostic potential of semantic prosodies. In: M. Baker, G. Francis and E. Tognini-Bonelli (eds), *Text and Technology: In Honour of John Sinclair*. Amsterdam/Philadelphia: John Benjamins. pp. 157–76.

Luckmann, T. (1983) *Life-world and Social Realities*. London: Heinemann.

Lueger, M. (2004) *Grundlagen qualitativer Feldforschung*. Vienna: WU.

Luhmann, N. (1975) *Macht*. Stuttgart: Enke.

Lukes, S. M. (1974) *Power: A Radical View*. London: Macmillan.

Lukes, S. M. (2005) *Power – A Radical View: The Original Text with two major new chapters*. London: Palgrave Macmillan.

Machin, D. and Mayr, A. (2012) *How to Do Critical Discourse Analysis: A Multimodal Introduction*. London: Sage.

Machin, D. and van Leeuwen, T. (2007) *Global Media Discourse: A Critical Introduction*. London: Routledge.

Maier, F. (2009) Doing hair – doing age: Perspectives of emancipated ageing. In: M. Beisheim et al. (eds), *Perspectives of Women's Age at the Work Place*. Berne: Peter Lang Europäischer Verlag der Wissenschaften. pp. 119–36.

Malinowski, B. (1923) The problem of meaning in primitive languages. In: C. K. Ogden and I. Armstrong Richards (eds), *The Meaning of Meaning*. London: Routledge and Kegan Paul. pp. 296–336.

Malinowski, B. (1935) *Coral Gardens and Their Magic*. London: Allen & Unwin.

Martin, J. R. (1984) Lexical cohesion, field and genre: parceling experience and discourse goals. In: J. E. Copeland (ed.), *Linguistics and Semiotics: Text Semantics and Discourse Semantics*. Houston, TX: Rice University Press.

Martin, J. R. (1992) *English Text: System and Structure*. Amsterdam/Philadelphia: John Benjamins.

Matouschek, B., Wodak, R. and Januschek, F. (1995) *Notwendige Maßnahmen gegen Fremde? Genese und Formen von rassistischen Diskursen der Differenz*. Vienna: Passagen Verlag.

Matsumoto, Y. (2003) Lexical knowledge acquisition. In: R. Mitkov (ed.), *The Oxford Handbook of Computational Linguistics*. Oxford: Oxford University Press. pp. 395–413.

Mautner, G. (2005) Time to get wired: Using web-based corpora in critical discourse analysis. *Discourse & Society*, 16: 809–28.

Mautner, G. (2007) Mining large corpora for social information: The case of 'elderly'. *Language in Society*, 36: 51–72.

Mautner, G. (2008) Analysing newspapers, magazines and other print media. In: R. Wodak and M. Krzyzanowski (eds), *Qualitative Discourse Analysis in the Social Sciences*. Basingstoke: Palgrave Macmillan. pp. 30–53.

Mautner, G. (2010) *Language and the Market Society: Critical Reflections on Discourse and Dominance*. London: Routledge.

McEnery, T. and Hardie, A. (2012) *Corpus Linguistics: Method, Theory and Practice*. Cambridge: Cambridge University Press.

McEnery, T. and Wilson, A. (2001) *Corpus Linguistics: An Introduction*. Edinburgh: Edinburgh University Press.

McEnery, T., Xiao, R. and Tono, Y. (2006) *Corpus-Based Language Studies. An Advanced Resource Book*. London: Routledge.

McQuarrie, E. F. and Phillips, B. J. (2005) Indirect persuasion in advertising: How consumers process metaphors presented in pictures and words. *Journal of Advertising*, 34: 7–20.

Meriläinen, S., Tienari, J., Thomas, R. and Davies, A. (2008) Hegemonic academic practices: Experiences of publishing from the periphery. *Organization*, 15: 584–97.

Merton, R. K. (1967) *On Theoretical Sociology*. New York: Free Press.

Meuser, M. and Sackmann, R. (eds) (1991) *Analyse sozialer Deutungsmuster. Beiträge zur empirischen Wissenssoziologie*. Pfaffenweiler: Centaurus.

Meyer, J. W. (2009) *World Society: The Writings of John W. Meyer*. Oxford: Oxford University Press.

Meyer, J. W. and Jepperson, R. L. (2000) The 'actors' of modern society: The cultural construction of social agency. *Sociological Theory*, 18: 100–20.

Meyer, M., Buber, R. and Aghamanoukjan, A. (2013) In search of legitimacy: managerialism and legitimation in civil society organizations. *Voluntas: International Journal of Voluntary and Nonprofit Organizations*, 24: 167–93.

Meyer, R. E. (2004) *Globale Managementkonzepte und lokaler Kontext. Organisationale Wertorientierung im österreichischen öffentlichen Diskurs*. Vienna: WU.

Meyer, R. E. and Lefsrud, L. M. (2012) Science or science fiction? Professionals' discursive construction of climate change. *Organization Studies*, 33: 1477–506.

Meyer, R. E. and Höllerer, M. A. (2010) Meaning structures in a contested issue field: A topographic map of shareholder value in Austria. *Academy of Management Journal*, 53: 1241–62.

Meyer, R. E.,. Höllerer, M. A., Jancsary, D. and van Leeuwen, T. (2013) The visual dimension in organizing, organization, and organization research: Core ideas, current developments, and promising avenues. *Academy of Management Annals*, 7: 487–553.

Mitchell, W. J. T. (1994) *Picture Theory. Essays on Verbal and Visual Representation*. Chicago, IL: University of Chicago Press.

Morozov, E. (2011) *The Net Delusion: How Not to Liberate the World*. London: Allen Lane.

Moscovici, S. (2000) *Social Representations*. Cambridge: Polity Press.

Mouffe, C. (2005) *On the Political*. London: Routledge.

Mulderrig, J. (2006) The governance of education: A corpus-based critical discourse analysis of UK education policy texts 1972 to 2005. PhD thesis, Lancaster University.

Müller-Doohm, S. (1997) Bildinterpretation als struktural-hermeneutische Symbolanalyse. In: R. Hitzler and A. Honer (eds), *Sozialwissenschaftliche Hermeneutik: Eine Einführung*. Opladen: Leske + Budrich. pp. 81–108.

Mullins, W. E. (1972) On the concept of ideology in political science. *American Political Science Review*, 66: 498–510.

Muntigl, P. (2002a) Policy, politics, and social control: A systemic-functional linguistic analysis of EU employment policy. *Text*, 22: 393–441.

Muntigl, P. (2002b) Politicization and depoliticization: Employment policy in the European Union. In: P. Chilton and C. Schäffner (eds), *Politics as Text and Talk*. Amsterdam/Philadelphia: John Benjamins. pp. 45–79.

Muntigl, P., Weiss, G. and Wodak, R. (2000) *European Union Discourses on Unemployment: An Interdisciplinary Approach to Employment Policy-Making and Organizational Change*. Amsterdam/Philadelphia: John Benjamins.

Nelson, M. (2005) Semantic associations in Business English: A corpus-based analysis. *English for Specific Purposes*, 25: 217–34.

NN (2013) Climate Change 2013: The Physical Science Basis. Contribution of Working Group I to the Fifth Assessment Report of the Intergovernmental Panel on Climate Change. Paper presented at IPCC (Intergovernmental Panel on Climate Change). Cambridge: Cambridge University Press.

O'Halloran, K. L. (ed.) (2004) *Multimodal Discourse Analysis*. London: Continuum.

O'Halloran, K. (2012) Electronic deconstruction: Revealing tensions in the cohesive structure of persuasion texts. *International Journal of Corpus Linguistics*, 17: 91–124.

O'Halloran, K. (2014) Digital argument deconstruction: A practical and ethical software-assisted critical discourse analysis for highlighting where arguments fall apart. In: C. Hart and P. Cap (eds), *Contemporary Critical Discourse Studies*. London: Bloomsbury Continuum. pp. 237–280.

O'Halloran, K. and Coffin, C. (2004) Checking overinterpretation and underinterpretation: Help from corpora in critical linguistics. In: A. Hewings, C. Coffin and K. O'Halloran (eds), *Applying English Grammar*. London: Arnold. pp. 275–97.

O'Reilly, T. (2007) What is Web 2.0: Design patterns and business models for the next generation of software. *Communications and Strategies*, 65: 17–37.

Oevermann, U. (2001) Die Struktur sozialer Deutungsmuster – Versuch einer Aktualisierung. *Sozialer Sinn* Heft, 1: 35–81.

Oevermann, U., Allert, T., Konau, E. and Krambeck, J. (1979) Die Methodologie einer 'objektiven Hermeneutik' und ihre allgemeine forschungslogische Bedeutung in den Sozialwissenschaften. In: H-G. Soeffner (ed.), *Interpretative Verfahren in den Sozial- und Textwissenschaften*. Stuttgart: Metzler. pp. 352–434.

Oreskes, N. (2004) Beyond the ivory tower: The scientific consensus on climate change. *Science*, 306.

Oreskes, N. and Conway, Erik M. (2010) *Merchants of Doubt. How a Handful of Scientists Obscured the Truth on Issues from Tobacco Smoke to Global Warming*. New York: Bloomsbury Press.

Orpin, D. (2005) Corpus linguistics and critical discourse analysis: Examining the ideology of sleaze. *International Journal of Corpus Linguistics*, 10: 37–61.

Page, R., Barton, D., Unger, J. W. and Zappavigna, M. (2014) *Researching Language and Social Media*. London: Routledge.

Palonen, K. (1993) Introduction: From policy and polity to politicking and politicization. In: K. Paolonen and T. Parvikko (eds), *Reading the Political: Exploring the Margins of Politics*. Helsinki: FPSA. pp. 6–16.

Pariser, E. (2011) *The Filter Bubble: What the Internet Is Hiding from You*. New York: Penguin Press.

Parsons, T. (1977) *The Structure of Social Action*. Chicago, IL: Free Press.

Parsons, T. and Shils, E. A. (eds) (1951) *Towards a General Theory of Action*. Cambridge, MA: Harvard University Press.

Partington, A. (2004) Utterly content in each other's company: Semantic prosody and semantic preference. *International Journal of Corpus Linguistics*, 9: 131–56.

Partington, A. (2014) Mind the gaps: The role of corpus linguistics in researching absences. *International Journal of Corpus Linguistics*, 19: 118–46.

Philipps, A. (2012) Visual protest material as empirical data. *Visual Communication*, 11: 3–21.

Pieterse, J. N. (2004) *Globalization or Empire?* London: Routledge.

Pinch, T. and Bijsterveld, K. (eds) (2012) *The Oxford Handbook of Sound Studies*. New York: Oxford University Press.

Popitz, H. (1992) *Phänomene der Macht*. Tübingen: Mohr.

Potts, A. (2013) *At Arm's Length: Methods of Investigating Constructions of the 'Other' in American Disaster and Disease Reporting*. Lancaster: Lancaster University.

Preston, A. M., Wright, C. and Young, J. J. (1996) Imag[in]ing annual reports. *Accounting, Organizations and Society*, 21: 113–37.

Purvis, T. and Hunt, A. (1993) Discourse, ideology, ideology, discourse, ideology ... *British Journal of Sociology*, 44: 473–99.

Rahmstorf, S. and Schellnhuber, H.-J. (2012) *Der Klimawandel – Diagnose, Prognose, Therapie*. Munich: Beck.

Rancière, J. (1995) *On the Shores of Politics*. London: Verso.

Rancière, J. (2006) *Hatred of Democracy*. London: Verso.

Reeves, F. (1983) *British Racial Discourse: A Study of British Political Discourse about Race and Related Matters*. Cambridge: Cambridge University Press.

Reisigl, M. (2003) *Wie man eine Nation herbeiredet: Eine diskursanalytische Untersuchung zur sprachlichen Konstruktion der östereichischen Identität in politischen Gedenkreden*. Vienna: WU.

Reisigl, M. (2007) *Nationale Rhetorik in Gedenk – und Festreden*. Tubingen: Stauffenberg.

Reisigl, M. (2011) Grundzüge der Wiener Kritischen Diskursanalyse. In: R. Keller, A. Hirseland, W. Schneider and W. Viehöver et al. (eds), *Handbuch Sozialwissenschaftliche Diskursanalyse. Band 1: Theorien und Methoden*. Wiesbaden: VS Verlag für Sozialwissenschaften. pp. 459–97.

Reisigl, M. (2014) Argumentation analysis and the Discourse-Historical Approach: A methodological framework. In: C. Hart and P. Cap (eds), *Contemporary Critical Discourse Studies*. London: Bloomsbury. pp. 69–98.

Reisigl, M. and Wodak, R. (2001) *Discourse and Discrimination. Rhetorics of Racism and Antisemitism*. London: Routledge.

Renkema, J. (ed.) (2004) *Introduction to Discourse Studies*. Amsterdam/Philadelphia: John Benjamins.

Richardson, J. E., Krzyzanowski, M., Machin, D. and Wodak, R. (eds) (2013) *Advances in Critical Discourse Studies*. London: Routledge.

Ritzer, G. and Jurgenson, N. (2010) Production, consumption, prosumption: The nature of capitalism in the age of the digital prosumer. *Journal of Consumer Culture*, 10: 13–36.

Rowlinson, M., Casey, A., Hansen, P. H. and Mills, A. J. (2014) Narratives and memory in organizations. *Organization*, 21: 441–6.

Royce, T. D. and Bowcher, W. L. (eds) (2007) *New Directions in the Analysis of Multimodal Discourse*. Mahwah, NJ: Lawrence Erlbaum.

Rubinelli, S. (2009) *Ars Topica: The Classical Technique of Constructing Arguments from Aristotle to Cicero*. Dordrecht/Cambridge: Springer.

Ryder, M. and Wilson, B. (1996) Affordances and constraints of the internet for learning and instruction. Paper presented to a joint session of the Association for Educational Communications Technology, Indianapolis.

Sauvêtre, P. (2009) Michel Foucault: problématisation et transformation des institutions. *Tracés: Revue de Sciences humaines*, 17: 165–77.

Sayer, A. (2009) Who's afraid of critical social science? *Current Sociology*, 57: 767–86.

Schank, R. C. and Abelson, R. B. (1977) *Scripts, Plans, Goals and Understanding*. Hillsdale, NJ: Lawrence Erlbaum.

Schiffrin, D. (1994) *Approaches to Discourse* Oxford: Basil Blackwell.

Schroeder, J. E. and Zwick, D. (2004) Mirrors of masculinity: Representation and identity in advertising images. *Consumption Markets & Culture*, 7: 21–52.

Scollon, R. and Scollon, S. W. (2004) *Nexus Analysis: Discourse and the Emerging Internet*. London: Routledge.

Scott, M. (2010) What can corpus software do? In: A. O'Keefe and M. McCarthy (eds), *The Routledge Handbook of Corpus Linguistics*. Abingdon: Routledge. pp. 122–35.

Seargeant, P. and Tagg, C. (2014) *The Language of Social Media: Identity and Community on the Internet*. London: Palgrave Macmillan.

Sedlaczek, A. (2012) Die visuelle repräsentation des klimawandels in dokumentarfilmen: Eine multimodale kritische diskursanalyse. MA dissertation, University of Vienna.

Sedlaczek, A. (2014) Multimodale Repräsentation von Klimawandel und Klimaschutz. *Wiener Linguistische Gazette*, 78a: 14–33.

Siles, I. and Boczkowski, P. J. (2012) Making sense of the newspaper crisis: A critical assessment of existing research and an agenda for future work. *New Media & Society*, 14: 1375–94.

Slutskaya, N., Simpson, A. and Hughes, J. (2012) Lessons from photoelicitation: Encouraging working men to speak. *Qualitative Research in Organizations and Management: An International Journal*, 7: 16–33.

Snelling, D. (2014) *END OF THE WORLD Top scientist reveals "We're f*****!"*. In: *Daily Star (digital version), 8 August 2014*. www.dailystar.co.uk/tech/393400/END-OF-THE-WORLD-Top-global-warming-scientist-reveals-We-re-f-ked, accessed 24 August 2015.

Sondermann, K. (1997) Reading politically: national anthems as textual Icons. In: T. Carver and M. Hyvärinen (eds), *Interpreting the Political: New Methodologies*. London: Routledge. pp. 128–42.

Spradley, J. P. (1979) *The Ethnographic Interview*. New York: Holt, Rinehart and Winston.

Spradley, J. P. (1980) *Participant Observation*. Fort Worth. TX: Harcourt Brace Jovanovich College Publishers.

Strauss, A. (1987) *Qualitative Analysis for Social Scientists*. Cambridge: Cambridge University Press.

Strauss, A. and Corbin, J. (1990) *Basics of Qualitative Research*. Newbury Park, CA: Sage.

Street, J. (2001) *Mass Media, Politics, and Democracy*. Basingstoke: Palgrave.

Stubbs, M. (1997) Whorf's children: Critical comments on critical discourse analysis. In: A. Ryan and A. Wray (eds), *Evolving Models of Language*. Clevedon: Multilingual Matters. pp. 100–16.

Stubbs, M. (2001) *Words and Phrases: Corpus Studies of Lexical Semantics*. Oxford/Cambridge, MA: Blackwell.

Styhre, A. (2010) *Visual Culture in Organizations: Theory and Cases*. London: Routledge.

Talbot, M. R. (2003) *Language and Power in the Modern World*. Edinburgh: Edinburgh University Press.

Teubert, W. (1999) Zum Verlust von Pluralität im politisch-gesellschaftlichen Diskurs: Das Beispiel Besitzstände. In: U. Kreft, H. Uske and S. Jäger (eds), *Kassensturz: Politische Hypotheken der Berliner Republik*. Duisburg: DISS. pp. 29–48.

Teubert, W. and Cermakova, A. (2004) *Corpus Linguistics. A Short Introduction*. London/New York: Continuum.

Thompson, J. B. (1988) *Critical Hermeneutics*. Cambridge: Cambridge University Press.

Thompson, J. B. (1990) *Ideology and Modern Culture*. Cambridge: Cambridge University Press.

Thurlow, C. (2012) Fakebook: synthetic media, pseudo-sociality and the rhetorics of Web 2.0. In: D. Tannen and A. M. Trester (eds), *Discourse 2.0: Language and New Media*. Washington, DC: Georgetown University Press. pp. 225–49.

Thurlow, C. and Mroczek, K. R. (2011) *Digital Discourse: Language in the New Media*. Oxford: Oxford University Press.

Titscher, S., Meyer, M. and Mayrhofer, W. (2008) *Organisationsanalyse: Konzepte und Methoden*. UTB Facultas.

Titscher, S., Meyer, M., Wodak, R. and Vetter, E. (2000) *Methods of Text and Discourse Analysis*. London: Sage.

Tognini-Bonelli, E. (2001) *Corpus Linguistics at Work*. Amsterdam/Philadelphia: John Benjamins.

Toolan, M. J. (ed.) (2002) *Critical Discourse Analysis: Critical Concepts in Linguistics*. London: Routledge.

Tuchmann, G. (1973) Making news by doing work: Routinizing the unexpected. *American Journal of Sociology*, 79: 110–31.

Tufekci, Z. and Wilson, C. (2012) Social media and the decision to participate in political protest: Observations from Tahrir Square. *Journal of Communication*, 62: 363–79.

Unger, J. W. (2013) *The Discursive Construction of the Scots Language: Education, Politics and Everyday Life*. Amsterdam/Philadelphia: John Benjamins.

Unsworth, L. and Cléirigh, C. (2009) Multimodality and reading: The construction of meaning through image-text interaction. In: C. Jewitt (ed.), *The Routledge Handbook of Multimodal Analysis*. Abingdon: Routledge. pp. 151–63.

Vaara, E. and Monin, P. (2010) A recursive perspective on discursive legitimation and organizational action in mergers and acquisitions. *Organization Science*, 21: 3–22.

van Dijk, T. A. (1980) *Macrostructures: An Interdisciplinary Study of Global Structures in Discourse, Interaction, and Cognition*. Hillsdale, NJ: Lawrence Erlbaum.

van Dijk, T. A. (1984) *Prejudice in Discourse*. Amsterdam/Philadelphia: John Benjamins.

van Dijk, T. A. (1988) *News as Discourse*. Hillsdale, NJ: Lawrence Erlbaum.

van Dijk, T. A. (1993) Principles of critical discourse analysis. *Discourse & Society*, 4: 249–83.

van Dijk, T. A. (ed.) (1997) *Discourse as Structure and Process*. London: Sage.

van Dijk, T. A. (1998) *Ideology: A Multidisciplinary Approach*. London: Sage.

van Dijk, T. A. (ed.) (2007) *Discourse Studies*. London: Sage.

van Dijk, T. A. (2008) *Discourse and Context: A Sociocognitive Approach*. Cambridge: Cambridge University Press.

van Dijk, T. (2013) *CDA is NOT a method of critical discourse analysis*. In: *EDISO Debate – Asociacion de Estudios Sobre Discurso y Sociedad*. www.edisoportal.org/debate/115–cda-not-method-critical-discourse-analysis, accessed 24 August 2015.

van Eemeren, F. H. and Grootendorst, R. (1992) *Argumentation, Communication and Fallacies. A Pragma-Dialectical Perspective.* Hillsdale, NJ: Lawrence Erlbaum.

van Eemeren, F. H., Garssen, B. and Meuffels, B. (2009) *Fallacies and Judgments of Reasonableness: Empirical Research Concerning the Pragma-Dialectical Discussion Rules.* Dordrecht: Springer.

van Leeuwen, T. (2005) *Introducing Social Semiotics.* London: Routledge.

van Leeuwen, T. (2006) *Critical Discourse Analysis.* In: K. Brown (ed.), *Encyclopedia of Language and Linguistics.* Oxford: Elsevier. pp. 290–4.

van Leeuwen, T. (2007) Legitimation in discourse and communication. *Discourse & Communication,* 1: 91–112.

van Leeuwen, T. (2008) *Discourse and Practice: New Tools for Critical Discourse Analysis.* New York: Oxford University Press.

van Leeuwen, T. and Wodak, R. (1999) Legitimizing immigration control: a discourse-historical analysis. *Discourse Studies,* 1: 83–118.

Viehöver, W. (2003/2010) Die Wissenschaft und die Wiederverzauberung des sublunaren Raumes: Der Klimadiskurs im Licht der narrativen Diskursanalyse. In: R. Keller, A. Hirseland, W. Schneider and W. Viehöver (eds), *Handbuch Sozialwissenschaftliche Diskursanalyse.* Wiesbaden: VS. pp. 233–70.

Wacquant, L. (2004) *Body & Soul: Notebooks of an Apprentice Boxer.* Oxford: Oxford University Press.

Waldenfels, B. (1991) Ordnung in Diskursen. In: F. Ewald and B. Waldenfels (eds), *Spiele der Wahrheit: Michel Foucaults Denken.* Frankfurt am Main: Suhrkamp. pp. 277–97.

Warren, S. (2002) 'Show me how it feels to work here': Using photography to research organizational aesthetics. *ephemera,* 2: 224–45.

Warren, S. (2005) Photography and voice in critical qualitative management research. *Accounting, Auditing & Accountability Journal,* 18: 861–82.

Webb, E. J, Campbell, D. T., Schwartz, R. D. and Sechrest, L. (1966) *Unobtrusive Measures. Nonreactive Research in the Social Sciences.* Chicago, IL: Rand–McNally.

Weber, M. (1980) *Wirtschaft und Gesellschaft.* Tübingen: Mohr.

Weick, K. E. (1974) Middle range theories of social systems. *Behavioral Science,* 357–67.

Weingart, P., Engels, A. and Pansegrau, P. (2008) *Von der Hypothese zur Katastrophe: Der anthropogene Klimawandel im Diskurs zwischen Wissenschaft, Politik und Massenmedien.* Opladen: Leske and Budrich.

Wengeler, M. (2003) *Topos und Diskurs. Begründung einer argumentationsanalytischen Methode und ihre Anwendung auf den Migrationsdiskurs (1960-1985).* Tübingen: Niemeyer.

Wetherell, M., Taylor, S. and Simeon, Y. (eds) (2001) *Discourse as Data.* London: Sage.

Whorf, B. L. (1956) *Language, Thought and Reality.* Cambridge, MA: MIT Press.

Widdowson, H. G. (1995) Discourse analysis: A critical view. *Language and Literature,* 4: 157–72.

Widdowson, H. G. (2004a) Text, context, pretext. *International Journal of Applied Linguistics,* 15: 421–4.

Widdowson, H. G. (2004b) *Text, Context, Pretext: Critical Issues in Critical Discourse Analysis.* Oxford: Blackwell.

Wittgenstein, L. (1989 [1952]) Philosophischen Untersuchungen. In: L. Wittgenstein (ed.), *Werkausgabe Band 1: Tractatus logico-philosophicus – Tagebücher 1914–1916 – Philosophische Untersuchungen.* Frankfurt am Main: Suhrkamp. pp. 224–580.

Wodak, R. (ed.) (1989) *Language, Power and Ideology.* Amsterdam/Philadelphia: John Benjamins.

Wodak, R. (1996) *Disorders in Discourse.* London: Longman.

Wodak, R. (2001) What CDA is about – a summary of its history, important concepts and its developments. In: R. Wodak and M. Meyer (eds), *Methods of Critical Discourse Analysis.* London: Sage. pp. 1–13.

Wodak, R. (2004) Critical discourse analysis. In: C. Seale, G. Gobo, J. F. Gubrium and D. Silverman (eds), *Qualitative Research Practice.* London: Sage. pp. 197–213.

Wodak, R. (2006a) Dilemmas of discourse (analysis). *Language in Society,* 35: 595–611.

Wodak, R. (2006b) Critical linguistics and critical discourse analysis. In: J.-O. Östman and J. Verschueren (eds), *Handbook of Pragmatics.* Amsterdam/Philadelphia: John Benjamins. pp. 1–24.

Wodak, R. (2007) Pragmatics and Critical Discourse Analysis. *Pragmatics and Cognition,* 15: 203–25.

Wodak, R. (2011a) Critical discourse analysis. In: K. Hyland and B. Paltridge (eds), *The Continuum Companion to Discourse Analysis.* London: Continuum. pp. 38–53.

Wodak, R. (2011b) *The Discourse of Politics in Action: Politics as Usual*, 2nd rev. edn. Basingstoke: Palgrave Macmillan.

Wodak, R. (ed.) (2012a) *Critical Discourse Analysis* (Sage Major Works, 4 volumes). London: Sage.

Wodak, R. (2012b) Critical Discourse Analysis: overview, challenges, and perspectives. In: G. Ajimer and K. Andersen (eds), *Pragmatics of Society*. Berlin: De Gruyter.

Wodak, R. (2012c) Editor's Introduction: Critical Discourse Analysis – challenges and perspectives. In: R. Wodak (ed.), *Critical Discourse Analysis*. London: Sage. pp. xix–xliii.

Wodak, R. (2014) Political discourse analysis – Distinguishing frontstage and backstage contexts. A discourse-historical approach. In: J. Flowerdew (ed.) *Discourse in Context*. London: Bloomsbury. pp. 522–49.

Wodak, R. (2015a) *The Politics of Fear: Understanding the Meanings of Right-wing Populist Discourses* London: Sage.

Wodak, R. (2015b, in press) Argumentation, political. In: *International Encyclopedia of Political Communication*. Oxford: Elsevier.

Wodak, R. and Chilton, P. (eds) (2005) *A New Agenda in (Critical) Discourse Analysis*. Amsterdam: John Benjamins.

Wodak, R. and Krzyzanowski, M. (2008) *Qualitative Discourse Analysis in the Social Sciences*. Basingstoke: Palgrave Macmillan.

Wodak, R. and van Leeuwen, T. (2002) Discourse of un/employment in Europe: The Austrian case. *Text*, 22: 345–67.

Wodak, R. and Wright, S. (2006) The European Union in cyberspace: multilingual democratic participation in a virtual public sphere? *Journal of Language and Politics*, 5: 251–75.

Wodak, R., De Cillia, R., Reisigl, M. and Liebhart, K. (1998) *Zur diskursiven Konstruktion nationaler Identität*. Berlin: Suhrkamp.

Wodak, R., De Cillia, R., Reisigl, M. and Liebhart, K. (1999) *The Discursive Construction of National Identity*. Edinburgh: Edinburgh University Press.

Wodak, R., De Cillia, R., Reisigl, M. and Liebhart, K. (2009) *The Discursive Construction of National Identity*, 2nd rev. edn. Edinburgh: Edinburgh University Press.

Wodak, R., Nowak, P., Pelikan, J., Gruber, H., de Cillia, R. and Mitten, R. (1990) *'Wir sind alle unschuldige Täter'. Diskurshistorische Studien zum Nachkriegsantisemitismus*. Frankfurt: Suhrkamp.

Wright, W. (1975) *Sixguns and Society – A Structural Study of the Western*. Berkeley and Los Angeles, CA: University of California Press.

Yates, J. and Orlikowski, W. J. (1992) Genres of organizational communication: A structurational approach to studying communication and media. *Academy of Management Review*, 17: 299–326.

Young, L. and Fitzgerald, B. (2006) *The Power of Language: How Discourse Influences Society*. London: Equinox.

INDEX

abstraction, 150
affordances, 207, 210–216, 222–223,
    227, 231
Althusser, L., 112
Androutsopoulos, J., 208, 212, 216
anti-racism, 75–84
Arab Spring, 224–227, *225*, 228–230, *228*
argument from ignorance, 53–54
argument from nature, 53
argumentation, 33, 34–36, **43**, 45–56
argumentum ad consequentiam, 50
argumentum ad verecundiam, 46–47, 50
Aristotle, 96
artefact analysis, 133
attitudes, 67, 69

Baker, P., 156, 161, 176
Beißwenger, M., 216
Bell, A., 39
Bell, E., 188
Berger, P. L., 147–148
Bernstein, B. B., 87–88, 140
Bhaskar, R., 91
Bijsterveld, K., 186
Blair, T., 95, 98–105
Bohnsack, R., 190
Bourdieu, P., 7, 11, 140
Box, J., 30, 44, 46–49
bricolage, 134
British National Corpus (BNC), 164

Caborn, J., 133
Cap, P., 19
Caren, N., 226
catachreses (image fractures), 123
Chilton, P., 106
Chinaglia, A., 78
Chouliaraki, L., 90, 175
Clarke, J., 103
climate change, 13, 34–56
cognitive sciences, 13
cognitive structures, 66–70
collective symbols, 122–123

computer-mediated discourse analysis
    (CMDA), 212, 216
concordance programs, 155, 158–162, **158**,
    160, **162**, 175–176
context, 30–31
context models, 67
conversation analysis, 2, 20
corpus linguistics (CL)
    critique of, 171–176
    examples of, 156, 158–162, **158**, **160**, **162**,
        165–171, **167–169**
    key concepts in, 158–165, **158**, **160**, **162**,
        163, **165**
    role in critical discourse studies, 155–157
Corpus of Contemporary American English
    (COCA), 164
Cottle, S., 212
critical discourse analysis (CDA), use of
    term, 4, 63
critical discourse studies (CDS)
    aims and goals of, 2–3
    critical impetus in, 6–8
    data collection in, 21
    discourse in, 5–6
    history of, 4–5
    ideology and power in, 8–12
    major approaches to, 17–21, *18*, *20*. *See
        also specific approaches*
    research agenda and challenges in,
        12–13
    research process in, 15–16, *15*
    theoretical grounding and objectives of,
        13–14, *14*, 16–17
    use of term, 3, 63
Critical Linguistics, 7
critical theory, 6–7, 24–25
critique
    definition of, 6–8
    in dialectical-relational approach, 88
    in discourse-historical approach,
        24–25, 56
    in Foucauldian approach, 119–120
    in multimodal CDA, 183–184